D1384723

ADOLESCENCE
Contemporary Studies

ADOLESCENCE
Contemporary Studies

ALVIN E. WINDER
University of Massachusetts

DAVID L. ANGUS
University of Michigan

VAN NOSTRAND REINHOLD COMPANY
New York   Cincinnati   Toronto   London   Melbourne

Cover photo: S. Szasz, Photo Researchers Inc.

VAN NOSTRAND REINHOLD COMPANY REGIONAL OFFICES:
Cincinnati   New York   Chicago   Millbrae   Dallas

VAN NOSTRAND REINHOLD COMPANY FOREIGN OFFICES:
London   Toronto   Melbourne

Copyright © 1968 by LITTON EDUCATIONAL PUBLISHING, INC.

Manufactured in the United States of America

Published by VAN NOSTRAND REINHOLD COMPANY
450 West 33rd Street, New York, N. Y. 10001

15 14 13 12 11 10 9 8 7 6 5 4

American Book Company   NEW YORK

Acknowledgments

Grateful acknowledgment is made to the following publishers and individuals for permission to reprint material which is in copyright or of which they are the authorized publishers:

The American Academy of Arts and Sciences: for selected passages by Lee Rainwater from *Daedalus, The Journal of the American Academy of Arts and Sciences,* Winter 1966, Vol. 95, No. 1.

The American Academy of Political and Social Science: for passages by H. Kirk Dansereau from *The Annals of the American Academy of Political and Social Science,* November 1961, Vol. 338. Reprinted by permission of the American Academy of Political and Social Science.

The American Orthopsychiatric Association: for passages by Dana L. Farnsworth, Howard E. Freeman, and Kermit T. Wiltse from *The American Journal of Orthopsychiatry,* July 1965, Vol. 35, No. 4, and October 1963, Vol. 33, No. 5. By permission of the authors and *The American Journal of Orthopsychiatry.* Copyright, the American Orthopsychiatric Association, Inc. Reproduced by permission.

The American Sociological Association: for passages by Kingsley Davis and Edgar Z. Friedenberg from *The American Sociological Review,* August 1940, Vol. 5, and October 1964, Vol. 29, No. 5. Reprinted by permission of the authors and the American Sociological Association.

Basic Books, Inc., and **the American Academy of Arts and Sciences:** for passages by Erik H. Erikson and S. N. Eisenstadt from *Youth: Change and Challenge,* edited by Erik H. Erikson, © 1961 by the American Academy of Arts and Sciences in *Daedalus, The Journal of the American Academy of Arts and Sciences,* Winter 1962, Vol. 91; and 1963 by Basic Books, Inc., Publishers, New York.

The Beacon Press: for passages by Howard Zinn from *SNCC: The New Abolitionists.* Reprinted by permission of The Beacon Press, copyright © 1964, 1965 by Howard Zinn.

The College Entrance Examination Board: for passages by Edgar Z. Friedenberg from *College Admissions 10: The Behavorial Sciences and Education,* New York, 1963.

Columbia University Press: for passages by Harold E. Jones from *The Family in a Democratic Society, Anniversary Papers of the Community Service Society of New York.* Reprinted by permission of Columbia University Press.

Harper & Row, Publishers: for passages by Sandor Lorand from *Adolescents: Psychoanalytic Approach to Problems and Therapy,* edited by Sandor Lorand and Henry I. Schneer, copyright © 1961 by Hoeber Medical Division, Harper & Row, Publishers.

Horizon Press: for passages reprinted by permission of the publisher, Horizon Press, from *Compulsory Mis-Education* by Paul Goodman, copyright 1964.

Indiana University Press: for passages by Frank Musgrove from *Youth and the Social Order.* Reprinted by permission of Indiana University Press.

International Universities Press, Inc.: for passages by Anna Freud from *Psychoanalytic Study of the Child,* Vol. 13, 1958. Used with permission of International Universities Press, Inc.

The Journal of Social Issues: for passages by Walter B. Miller from *The Journal of Social Issues,* 1958, Vol. 14, No. 3. Reprinted by permission of the publishers.

Liberation: for "The Triple Revolution" from the April 1964 number and "Poverty and the Federal Government" from the March 1966 number.

McGraw-Hill, Inc.: for passages from *Negro Self-Concept* by William C. Kvaraceus et al. Copyright © by McGraw-Hill, Inc. Used by permission of McGraw-Hill Book Company. And for passages from *Understanding Media: The Extensions of Man* by Marshall McLuhan. Copyright © 1964 by Marshall McLuhan. McGraw-Hill Book Company. Used by permission.

Monthly Labor Review: for passages by Vera Perrella, Forrest A. Bogan, and Thomas E. Swanstrom from the November 1964 and December 1964 numbers.

The National Association of Social Workers: for passages by Yitzhak Bakal, William Madaus, and Alvin E. Winder reprinted with permission of the National Association of Social Workers, from *Social Work,* April 1968 (in press).

Random House, Inc.: for passages by Paul Goodman from *Growing Up Absurd.* Reprinted by permission of the author and Random House, Inc.

Saturday Review: for passages by Rochelle Gatlin and Ivor Kraft from *Saturday Review,* October 16, 1965, and December 18, 1965. Reprinted by permission of the authors and *Saturday Review.*

The University of Chicago Magazine: for passages by Bruno Bettelheim and Sidney E. Mead from *The University of Chicago Magazine,* February 1966, Vol. 58, and May 1966, Vol. 58. Reprinted by permission of the authors and the University of Chicago.

Preface

Young people in America today are a focus of interest from several academic directions. Teachers, counselors and others in the educational community who work with youth are asking new questions about the present generation of students. What do they want? What is education's responsibility to them? How can they best be reached? From another vantage point, sociologists and others who watch the American cultural scene are devoting increasing attention to the role of youth in contemporary society—as both innovators and reactors. And as adolescence comes to be viewed less as a time of apprenticeship for adulthood than as a lifestage in its own right, it has become a subject of renewed interest to many contemporary psychologists as well.

Each of these disciplines is producing a growing body of articles and commentaries on adolescents and the so-called "youth culture." But to date little of this literature has been easily accessible for assigned reading on a class basis. Courses in teacher preparation and counseling, sociology, and adolescent psychology have not been materially assisted by the fact that college and university libraries offer single-copy availability of virtually all that is being written in this expanding area. Culling significant articles from the burgeoning mass of work in the field has been time-consuming and providing multiple copies difficult.

This collection, the outgrowth of classes in adolescent psychology, educational sociology, foundations of education, and principles of guidance, attempts to bring together in one volume the best contemporary work on the dynamics of adolescence in this society. It has been designed to be interesting and provocative to students of contemporary problems as well as to those who will work directly with adolescents in a variety of professional contexts.

Following an overall rationale that we have called "Adolescence as a Subject for Study," we present thirty-one contemporary studies of adolescence. Heading the collection in Part I, which treats this age as "A Period of Definition," five essays explore fundamental physical, psychological, and anthropological factors at play during this critical stage of life.

Parts II and III present essays discussing ways in which family, school, peer-group, work and sociopolitical institutions are experienced, first, by adolescents from dominant social strata and, second, by young people whose socialization has occurred largely outside the American mainstream—those often referred to as "disadvantaged" youth.

Part IV, in conclusion, suggests some of the probable ways in which this generation of young people may differ, as adults, from their parents. Significant changes underway in the areas of mental health care, employment, income patterns, and religion are treated in this section.

An attempt has been made to include pieces representative of the many forms in which contemporary studies of adolescence are being written today. Some clinical discussions have been included, as have several speculative articles by recognized spokesmen. The volume also contains psychoanalytically oriented treatments of personality, several sociologically oriented views of youth within the society as a whole, and a few firsthand documents from youth themselves. Many articles appeared originally in scholarly journals. Some come from the popular press, which has been concerning itself increasingly with the phenomenon of youth in modern America. Governmental reports are also represented.

Selections have been chosen for readability as well as relevance. Each has been included for the unique contribution it makes to the total collection, which is structured so that it can readily form the basis of any exploration into the conditions of adolescence. It can also be used selectively in a supplementary capacity in courses stressing, for example, disadvantaged youth or, perhaps, feelings of alienation among young people.

Short introductory essays preceding each of the four parts are designed to present the student with key themes he will encounter in each section. Brief headnotes to each article further delineate issues involved, and a small number of broad discussion topics have been provided at the conclusion of each part. Care has been taken to insure that technical concepts are on a level that will be accessible to the general student reader. A glossary has been devised to assist with specialized vocabulary.

The editors hope that students will discover through contact with the authors represented here something of the excitement of the current inquiry into youth and its place in our society.

Contents

Preface   *vii*
Adolescence as a Subject for Study   *xiii*

I. A PERIOD OF DEFINITION   *1*

1. The Growth Process

Harold E. Jones—Adolescence in Our Society   *4*

2. Personality Development

Anna Freud—Adolescence   *13*
Sandor Lorand—Treatment of Adolescents   *24*
Erik H. Erikson—Youth: Fidelity and Diversity   *33*

3. A Cultural Phenomenon

S. N. Eisenstadt—Archetypal Patterns of Youth   *53*

Discussion Topics   *64*

II. ADOLESCENCE IN THE MAINSTREAM   *65*

1. The Family

Kingsley Davis—The Sociology of Parent-Youth Conflict   *69*

2. The Peer Group

Dana L. Farnsworth—Sexual Morality and
the Dilemma of the Colleges   *80*
Alvin E. Winder—Bob Dylan and J. R. R. Tolkien:
Two World Views to Which Adolescents Respond   *86*

CONTENTS

3. The School

Edgar Z. Friedenberg—The School as a Social Environment 90
Paul Goodman—The Universe of Discourse in Which They Grow Up 102
Edgar Z. Friedenberg—The Dignity of Youth and Other Atavisms 111
Bruno Bettelheim—Notes on the Future of Education 114

4. Work

H. Kirk Dansereau—Work and the Teen-Ager 118
Paul Goodman—Jobs 127

5. Sociopolitical Action

Frank Musgrove—Youth and Social Change 138
Rochelle Gatlin—A Radical Frame of Mind 156
Alvin E. Winder—The Restless Undergraduates 158

Discussion Topics 161

III. THE DISADVANTAGED ADOLESCENT 163

1. The Family

Lee Rainwater—Crucible of Identity:
The Negro Lower-Class Family 166
Kermit T. Wiltse—Orthopsychiatric Programs
for Socially Deprived Groups 181

2. The Peer Group

Walter B. Miller—Lower Class Culture
as a Generating Milieu of Gang Delinquency 189
Yitzhak Bakal, William Madaus, and *Alvin E. Winder*—
A Motivational Approach to Compensatory Education 204

3. The School

William C. Kvaraceus—Negro Youth and Social Adaptation: The
Role of the School as an Agent of Change 216
Ivor Kraft—Are We Overselling the Pre-School Idea? 240

4. Work

Vera C. Perrella and Forrest A. Bogan—Out-of-School Youth—Part I 243
Thomas E. Swanstrom—Out-of-School Youth—Part 2 255

5. Sociopolitical Action

Howard Zinn—The New Abolitionists 264

Five Documents from Greenville, Mississippi—
  Poverty and the Federal Government   274

Discussion Topics   281

IV. PROJECTION FOR ADULTHOOD   283

1. Emotional Issues

Howard E. Freeman—Social Change and
                  the Organization of Mental Health Care   286
Sidney E. Mead—The Lost Dimension and the Age of Longing   292

2. Technological Change

Marshall McLuhan—Automation: Learning a Living   299
The Ad Hoc Committee on the Triple Revolution, W. H. Ferry et al—
  The Triple Revolution   308

Discussion Topics   321

The Contributors   322
The Editors   325

Glossary   327
Index   333

To the Student

Adolescence
as a Subject for Study

Youth are probably the center of more attention today than at any other period in western culture. Advertising designed to capture the affluent youth market has created an image of slim, carefree, uninhibited youth that appeals not only to adolescents but to most adults as well. An "accent on youth" in fashion, entertainment, and general demeanor has provided an entire nation with a new model that says it is better to be young and beautiful than mature and responsible.

At the same time, modern communications media have zeroed in on adolescents' quarrels with the adult world and, in the process, may even have sharpened the differences between established society and its reluctant heirs. Adolescents and adults coexist uneasily today in a maelstrom of confusion about one another. Accusations and counter-accusations are traded in news media. Youth's outspoken pronouncements on social, moral and political issues often shock their elders, many of whom feel that today's young people are "further out" than they ought to be. In spite of a popular worship of youth, today's amplified dialogue between the generations is producing a good deal of static.

Interpreters have come forward from all corners to explain youth to the adult community and to itself. Adolescents are said to doubt the capacity of the adult world to offer them an appropriate way of life. Adults are represented as defensive: pricked by guilt over the compromises they have made, for which idealistic youth now indicts them. It appears that the static is, after all, an indicator of disturbances. Indeed, the very nature of adolescence as a life stage in our society appears to be shifting.

At one time, it was enough to say that adolescence was a "difficult" period in which young people no longer quite understood the nature or limits of their physical makeup. They were said to kick over lamps, lose control of their voices, and experience all manner of physical sensations that were new and strange. We now know that much more than physical maturation takes place at this stage of life. It is also a period of psychological transformation, often called the discovery of self. As the education critic Edgar Friedenberg states:

Adolescence is the period during which a young person learns who he is, and what he really feels. It is the time during which he differentiates himself from his culture, though on the culture's terms. It is the age at which, by becoming a person in his own right, he becomes capable of deeply felt relationships to other individuals perceived clearly as such [1]

Viewed in this light, adolescence is a time of transition between childhood and adulthood. If, as has been suggested, there is a reluctance on the adolescent's part to enter the adult society, then the nature of this life stage must be altered. It will no longer be a transition. It will become a stage that the individual will be reluctant to leave. It will become not a preparation for adult life but a way of life in itself. Under such conditions, adolescence as we know it could even become extinct.

Let us explore this idea further. Anthropologists have often noted that non-literate societies have nothing that quite corresponds to adolescence as we understand it. There is instead the *rite de passage:* a ceremony of widely varying duration that symbolizes the end of one life stage, childhood, and the entree into a second, adulthood, with its commensurate privileges and responsibilities. The end of childhood may be determined by chronological age or by an event signaling the attainment of a certain capacity, such as the killing of one's first buck. In neither case is the attainment of what we call maturity requisite to the assumption of adult roles.

But growing up in a modern industrial democracy is a very different affair. The privileges of childhood begin to fade around ten or eleven years of age, although full acceptance into adult society is still ten or more years away. What is expected to occur during the transition period is the attainment of a highly differentiated and closely secured individual identity. Unlike non-literate tribal societies, the conditions of life in a modern urbanized nation-state demand flexibility, mobility, and, above all, the capacity to engage in a lifetime of consistent choice-making. Whereas nonliterate tribesmen are assured their position in the total social scheme virtually by birth, our society demands, increasingly, that its members carve out their places through their own efforts. Their ability to do so is contingent upon their having evolved a highly differentiated personal identity.

We have seen that this kind of identity is not a human universal. It is rather an adjunct to, perhaps a requirement of, a certain mode of social life. But modes of human behavior have a way of becoming valued over and above their relation to the conditions which gave rise to them. Thus, individuality, which emerged as a by-product of our social system, has become a value in itself. The historian Herbert Muller has asserted that civilization's only gain, in comparison with the values and virtues of tribal and peasant cultures, has been the growth of individual self-consciousness. It seems clear that, through most of America's history at least, the ideal of the strongly motivated, autonomous

[1] Edgar Z. Friedenberg, *The Vanishing Adolescent* (New York: Dell, 1959), p. 29.

individual has played a decisive role in shaping our society. Are we now about to discard that ideal? Have we created a social system in which individual identity—and hence the traditional function of the adolescent period—is no longer relevant?

It is Marshal McLuhan's thesis, in *Understanding Media,* that modern society is undergoing a "retribalization" or return to older modes of social organization. He has said that new technologies have reversed the centuries-old trend toward rationalization and fragmentation which gave rise to the ideal of individual self-consciousness and the private point of view. No less a partisan of individualism than Edgar Friedenberg has been pushed to a reexamination of his position by the strength of McLuhan's analysis. If the developments which McLuhan envisions do occur, the extinction of adolescence as we know it would seem assured.

It seems important today, therefore, that we understand more about the nature of the adolescent experience and how it is being affected by changes in American society as a whole. This collection is an attempt to foster such an understanding through selected pieces from the growing body of professional literature on adolescence. Although psychologists have long been interested in the dynamics of the transition from childhood to a fully formed adult personality, attention to the cultural and institutional setting in which the process occurs has come about only in the last two or three decades. We are now evolving what might be called a sociology of adolescence, to complement an older psychology of adolescence.

This in turn has led some psychologists to reexamine the adolescent period in the light of new insights concerning the influence of social institutions on adolescent personality formation. What has emerged is a dual view of the adolescent as at once an individual and a member of society. The articles in this collection have been selected to underscore both the individual psychological nature of adolescence and its cultural and institutional components.

Part I presents some physical and psychological foundations basic to an understanding of the adolescent experience. Parts II and III provide a review of the social conditions of adolescence. We have found it desirable to distinguish here between ways in which institutions function in relation to middle- and working-class youth and ways they function in relation to disadvantaged youth. Part IV suggests some major dimensions of the future adult society in which today's adolescents will live.

We hope that the student will find this choice and organization of material helpful in understanding the adolescent experience in contemporary society.

A PERIOD
OF DEFINITION

I

In this collection we are especially interested in the sociocultural conditions of contemporary adolescence. Accordingly, much of our focus will fall on adolescence in the context of American society during the present decade. But adolescence is, first and foremost, a period when the individual defines himself as an emergent personality. His first task at this time is to revise his view of himself to reflect the fact that he is no longer a child. Only after differentiating his newly maturing self from an earlier, less defined personality can he look about him and begin with some assurance to carve out a role in the ongoing adult society.

An initial approach to the study of adolescence, therefore, is to examine the relationship of physical maturation to the development of the adolescent's self concept. In our keynote article, Jones summarizes findings in this area which contribute to an overview of the normative ages for the growth spurt at this stage of life, the onset of puberty, and the fact of physiological instability during adolescence. Because growth studies have often confined themselves to the adolescent who comes to physical maturation either earlier or later than average, however, such studies have not always shed sufficient light on the more important relationships between physical growth and psychological identity formation. Undoubtedly, researchers in adolescent behavior have felt on safer ground when restricting themselves to the exploration of anatomic and physiological variables than when venturing into the complex and little-understood relationships between physical and emotional development.

Examination of the dramatic emotional upheavals of adolescence prompts Anna Freud, in the second article, to suggest that the adolescent upset is inevitable. "We all know individual children," she points out, "who as late as the ages of 14, 15, or 16 show no outer evidence of inner unrest. They remain, as they have been during the latency period, good children." But, convenient as this may be for the parent who fears the onset of friction, it signifies a delay in normative development and constitutes, as such, a signal to be heeded. Anna Freud believes the upset—easily recognized behaviorally by the inconsistency and unpredictability of the adolescent's actions—is necessary if the emerging adult is to free himself from dependence on his parents and defend himself against an upsurge of unconscious infantile impulses.

Pathologies that can occur when normal adolescence is blocked or delayed are outlined by a psychoanalyst in the third article. Lorand explains that what happens in these cases is that—unable to manage their moody, passive attitudes at one time and their impulsiveness and acting-out behavior at other times—disturbed adolescents regard themselves as at the mercy of powerful forces they do not understand. The author suggests that a therapist can enhance such adolescents' ability to master themselves by presenting them, through identification with the therapist, with a more functional ego ideal.

Whether normal fluctuations in adolescent behavior will disappear on schedule or will develop into pathologies is highly dependent on the presence of such a viable ego ideal, for without it the individual will be unable to achieve that integration of personality which Erikson has called "ego identity." Such integration occurs only if the adolescent's perception of who he is, was, and will become appears to be matched by others' perceptions of him. The tangible promise of a career is considered by many to be a necessary condition for such matching.

Current psychological and sociological theories of adolescence employ the twin concepts *alienation* and *commitment* to symbolize the failure or success that an adolescent experiences in his attempt to carve out a new identity. In this regard Erikson speaks of fidelity—a sense of disciplined devotion—as the strongest need, and greatest virtue, of the adolescent years. At this time youth asks two questions: first, "Is there a place for me in the future?" and, second, "Do I have the capacities to fit myself into this place?" The first question can be answered affirmatively only as the adolescent relates himself to the adults in his world who have found "their place." Poorly adjusted adults who attempt to convey an image of adjustment while actually unhappy and unsure of their capabilities are quickly unmasked as "finks" by today's adolescents. Indeed, the pursuit of "truth" is a distinguishing feature of this period of life when the young person is carefully assessing reality.

Eisenstadt views the acquisition of personal identity as the major task of youth. However, his historical and cross-cultural studies reveal wide differences in the conditions and processes by which this occurs. Thus the final article in this part adds a sociological and anthropological dimension to our view of adolescence, a dimension which has yielded a growing body of professional literature of a category usually designated culture and personality studies.

Regarding youth's second question, the tangible promise of an appropriate career, it is instrumental to consider a popular maxim sported by youthful button-wearers of the 'Sixties: "Reality is a crutch." Adults may respond by shaking their heads, but Eisenstadt interprets the slogan as proof that youth in the post-industrial society has been robbed of its opportunity to entertain romantic dreams of the future. If the adult world does little to elicit tangible commitment, the process of definition becomes subject to vicissitudes of the unconscious. Should youth be unable to find a person and a cause which merit his fidelity, he will diffuse his energies, withdrawing from parents, schoolwork, and all plans for the future. Thus unable to control either his aggressive or his devotional, loving impulses, he may become prey to unconscious fantasies of negative identity in which he sees himself either as a potential killer or as too vulnerable to give or receive love.

Eisenstadt suggests that both the tangible promise of an acceptable career and the possibilities for necessary identification with adult models have been greatly weakened in modern society. He cites the fact that age is no longer a significant factor in the awarding of political, economic and social roles. This is particularly a problem for youth because they are weak in the experience, wealth, education, and technical competence that society rewards. In addition, occupations are no longer transmitted through the family, which has ceased to serve as a basic unit of political or ritual activities.

How has youth attempted to maintain itself when faced with the loss of traditionally protective institutions? By the creation of a new institution, the peer group. The peer group—or, as it is often called, the youth culture—that begins to emerge in these first articles is a force of still uncertain potential in American society. A symptomatic reaction to the dynamics of social change now shaping western culture, it seems to hold a key to future directions those forces may yet assume.

1 THE GROWTH PROCESS

How does the adolescent's physical development affect his view of himself? What effect does it have on the way his peers view him? These and other questions stemming from the physiological changes that mark adolescence are explored in the following article. The author's conclusions are drawn from over twenty-five years' study of the physical growth and social behavior of one group of young people.

Harold E. Jones

Adolescence in Our Society

The period of adolescence is sometimes referred to as a flowering and fulfillment, sometimes as a calamity. Taken literally, adolescence is the process of becoming adult, growing into maturity. But the term has gained other, less favorable meanings. These are implied when we speak of adolescent "stress and strain," "growing pains," "teen-age troubles," "the silly phase," and other phenomena to which we attach the adjective "adolescent," sometimes in a resigned mood and sometimes in exasperation.

Many persons have raised the question of whether this process of growing up is naturally and inevitably a difficult one, or whether its painfulness is in some sense a disease of society, and therefore remediable through appropriate social changes The answer to this question has varied widely according to the preoccupations of the person answering it. The biological answer stresses changes in hormone secretions, changes in the rate of skeletal growth, and temporary imbalances in body structure and function. It is these imbalances, we are told, which are the immediate source of adolescent maladjustment. The sociological and anthropological answer, on the other hand, stresses the conditions and demands of the culture in which the child is growing up. It is

4

pointed out that the same processes of biological maturing that place a child in jeopardy in one culture may offer no special problems in another culture. Each of these answers is a partial one. Adolescence is not necessarily a period of acute disturbance. When disturbance occurs, the determining agencies lie in multiple form both in the organism and in society; we cannot hope to achieve understanding or control if we look at merely one of these two groups of factors.

It may be appropriate to begin this discussion with some account of the physical aspects of adolescence and of the developmental processes which set off this period so clearly from earlier childhood.

First, we know that at about eight or nine years of age on an average, in girls, and some two years later in boys, a change occurs in the rate of physical growth.[1] In the preceding years, ever since early childhood, growth has occurred at a fairly even and steady pace; growth in height, for example, involves gains of about 4 percent per year during these childhood years. But now, near the end of childhood, growth becomes slower; there is often a pause which marks the transition point between the slow, gradual development of childhood and the accelerated, more irregular growth changes of adolescence. It is as though the organism needed a little time in which to consolidate childhood gains, to muster resources, and to get ready for the abrupt transformations that are now to take place. This is a figurative way of putting it, but it does appear that we have during this period an interval in which the growth controls of childhood are fading and the adolescent growth factors are not yet fully ready to function.

In some respects, the problems of adolescence bear a resemblance to the problems of infancy, so that adolescence is sometimes called a second infancy. Physiologically, this may in a way be justified, in view of the fact that infants show an instability in many physiological processes, and gradually win a greater degree of equilibrium. With the beginning of the puberal cycle we have a renewal of unstable conditions. Basal metabolism, for example, may show marked fluctuations at this time.[2]

In an adult such metabolic changes could readily be a matter of some concern; in an adolescent they are physiological in the sense that they are very commonly and perhaps normally shown in the process of adjusting to the new phase of more rapid growth and to new conditions in the internal environment. At the same time, changes are also occurring in other basal functions. Among girls, for example, in the three years just preceding the menarche the average pulse rate increases and then decreases; the systolic blood pressure increases and then levels off.[3]

[1] F. K. Shuttleworth, "The Physical and Mental Growth of Girls and Boys Age Six to Nineteen, in Relation to Age at Maximum Growth," *Monographs of the Society for Research in Child Development*, 1939, Vol. 4, No. 3.

[2] N. W. Shock, "The Effect of Menarche on Basal Physiological Functions in Girls," *American Journal of Physiology*, 1943, 139, pp. 288–292.

[3] N. W. Shock, "Basal Blood Pressure and Pulse Rate in Adolescents," *American Journal of Diseases of Children*, 1944, 68, pp. 16–22.

It is not surprising that the adjustments in bodily processes should not always be smooth and orderly. The adolescent awkwardness, which we sometimes observe at the level of motor skills, may have its parallel in a kind of physiological awkwardness. The transition to a changed body economy may be difficult, and there may be further difficulties because of an interacting relationship with social and psychological transitions.

In a standard work on pediatrics the author observes that "the age of puberty is attended with many dangers to health. The changes in the organs are sudden. The heart grows larger, the blood vessels narrower. . . . At this time particularly mental disorders may develop and hereditary defects appear. Anemic conditions arise and may be followed by constitutional diseases. . . ." [4] Such statements may cause unnecessary alarm and over-emphasize the health hazards of adolescence, and yet it is true that the morbidity rate increases during the 'teens, and you have only to enter any classroom of adolescent youngsters to observe in posture, skin color, and, particularly, in skin conditions such as acne, abundant evidence of defects in the smooth course of adolescent maturing. Growth discrepancies also occur in the proportionate development of legs, arms, and trunk and in the deposition of fat. The timing of growth for different parts of the body may vary in different individuals, resulting in cases of poorly synchronized and markedly disproportionate development. [5]

Psychoanalysts have emphasized another way in which adolescence is like a second infancy, in that it involves a recurrence, in their terms, of infantile sexual impulses. The increased sexual drives of adolescence are countered by inhibitions; the adolescent may be afraid of these drives in the genital form in which they now appear, and may regress to more familiar infantile forms of sexuality. Fenichel [6] points out that adolescence is often marked by contradictory psychological expressions: "Egoism and altruism, pettiness and generosity, sociability and loneliness, cheerfulness and sadness, silly jocularity and over-seriousness, intense loves and sudden abandonment of these loves, submission and rebellion, materialism and idealism, rudeness and tender consideration— all are typical." These contradictions as cited by Fenichel are related to the fact that in adolescence there appear side by side or following one another "genital heterosexual impulses, all kinds of infantile sexual behavior, and attitudes of extreme asceticism, which not only try to repress all sexuality but everything pleasant as well." [7] The intensification of the sexual impulses at puberty, and the resulting conflicts, mark the end of the relatively peaceful latency period. Fenichel expresses the view that all the mental phenomena characteristic of puberty may be regarded as reactions to these disturbances, and as attempts to re-establish the equilibrium of the latency period, and he adds that "in a society

---

[4] J. Divan, "Peculiarities of Disease in Childhood," in I. A. Abt (ed.), *Pediatrics*, Saunders, 1923, Vol. II, p. 192.

[5] H. R. Stolz and L. M. Stolz, "Adolescent Problems Related to Somatic Variations," Chicago: University of Chicago Press, *43rd Yearbook of the National Society for the Study of Education*, 1944, Pt. 1, pp. 81–99.

[6] O. Fenichel, *The Psychoanalytic Theory of Neurosis*, Norton, 1945, p. 111.

[7] O. Fenichel, *The Psychoanalytic Theory of Neurosis*, Norton, 1945, pp. 110–111.

that treated infantile sexuality differently puberty, too, would assume a different course." [8]

In commenting upon this interpretation we may return again to our earlier statement that the difficulties of adolescence have a multiple origin and cannot be interpreted solely in terms of psychological, or cultural, or biological agencies. The student of child development is aware of many factors, by no means evidently related to sexual dilemmas or the Oedipus complex, which emerge at puberty to bedevil and perplex the child, his parents, and his teachers. Some of these factors have already been mentioned in connection with disturbances in physiological functions and in physical growth. Since adolescence is a period of increased susceptibility to psychosomatic disorders, no doubt a certain proportion of these cases of physiological disturbance trace more or less directly to the child's psychosexual development. A psychosomatic origin may also be found for some instances of disturbed physical growth. But we should not be too confident that all or even a majority of the physiological and physical anomalies which occur in adolescence have a primarily psychological source. The child's reaction to these apparent anomalies, the extent to which he tolerates them or is deeply worried by them, is a psychological matter, but their source and incidence seem quite as likely to depend upon intrinsic factors in the biological growth pattern as upon factors in the family situation or in the child's personality structure.

It is difficult to discuss the physical aspects of adolescence without reference to the factor of timing, and to differences in the age at which the puberal growth cycle begins. Let us consider first the facts as to the timing of puberty, and then the bearing of these facts upon adolescent problems. We shall see that it is of the first importance to know not merely what bodily changes are brought about by puberal growth, but also when these changes are induced.

In the case of girls, the most commonly used landmark for recording individual differences in puberal maturing is the menarche or the time of first menstruation. This occurs, of course, relatively late in the puberal growth cycle: a little more than a year after the adolescent growth spurt has reached its peak, and a little more than three years after the beginning of the growth spurt.[9]

In our California sample the menarche coincides, on the average, with the beginning of the teen age, falling at thirteen years and one month. In some Eastern studies a somewhat later age has been indicated, nearer thirteen and a half or even fourteen The question has been asked whether this difference is due to the stimulation of being near Hollywood, or whether it is an example of earlier maturing in a milder climate. The latter may be a factor, but we should point out the error in the popular idea that adolescence comes earliest in the Tropics. Adolescence is probably earliest in the Temperate Zone, and arrives somewhat later as we go north into the colder regions or south into

[8] O. Fenichel, *The Psychoanalytic Theory of Neurosis*, Norton, 1945, p. 111.
[9] F. K. Shuttleworth, "Sexual Maturation and the Physical Growth of Girls Age Six to Nineteen," *Monographs of the Society for Research in Child Development*, 1937, Vol. 2, No. 5.

tropical countries. For example, in a recent study in South America,[10] the average age of menarche directly under the equator, both in the mountains and in coastal areas, and for different ethnic groups, was found to be retarded almost a full year as compared with our California records.

We cannot be sure, however, that this is related to climate in any direct way rather than to general socio-economic conditions and conditions of health. Unfavorable living standards apparently tend to retard the beginning of adolescence; recent observers of child development in war-stricken areas of Europe have been impressed by this fact. A related finding may be the tendency for American children in the same social groups to mature earlier in this generation than was true fifty or a hundred years ago.[11] This is probably an illustration of the complex, biosocial nature of adolescence; for while earlier maturing may be attributable to gains in health and nutrition, these, in turn rest upon social trends.

There is an implication here which may be worth noting. One effect of civilized living has been to extend the term of social adolescence, by delaying the time at which young people can begin to earn their own living. As society becomes more complex, educational demands increase, and more years must be devoted to preparation for adult life. One effect of this has been, of course, to delay the age of marriage and to lengthen the period of sexual postponements or compromises. But social adolescence is also being lengthened at the other end, by pushing the time of maturing down to an earlier age. It is probably safe to say that the period of social adolescence is now from two to three times as long as was the case in America several generations ago. Thus the improved conditions for healthy physical growth, which our society has gradually achieved, tend to make more difficult some of the adolescent problems of mental hygiene, because of the much greater length of time during which these problems must be faced.

Our chief purpose, however, is not to discuss the average age of maturing of various groups, but the great diversity within any group. In any normal sampling of schoolgirls we may expect to find some who reach the menarche at eleven years of age or even a little earlier; and some who are delayed until sixteen or even a little later. In terms of physical growth changes, some girls in a normal sample show the beginning of rapid puberal growth as early as nine years of age and others not until after twelve or thirteen. These extreme differences are not without important after effects. The early-maturing girl who reaches her peak of growth at eleven or even earlier also reaches an early limit of growth. By thirteen she has attained nearly her adult stature, and this adult stature is short.[12] The adolescent growth period is more or less abruptly brought to an end, epiphyses at the growing ends of the bones are closed, and no further

---

[10] U. D. Arrieta, "Menstrual Biology of the Peruvian Woman," *La Cronica Medica*, 1932, 49, pp. 277–287.

[11] C. A. Mills, *Medical Climatology*, Thomas, 1939.

[12] N. Bayley, "Size and Body Build of Adolescents in Relation to Rate of Skeletal Maturing," *Child Development*, 1943, 14, pp. 47–90.

increase in height is possible. If you plot the growth curves of early- and of late-maturing girls, you will find that the former are taller in childhood, even at six or seven years of age; they gain in relative height until the age of twelve, when they may be as much as four inches taller than the late-maturing, but by fifteen they are definitely in a shorter-than-average classification.

At the University of California we conducted a series of studies to determine the relationship of these early changes to problems of adjustment. In general, it appears that the very early-maturing girl, at least in an urban culture, is in many respects in a disadvantageous position. In one of our studies, ... we selected two groups of early- and late-maturing girls, on the basis of skeletal maturity as read from X rays. These were not clinical deviates nor cases of endocrine pathology, but merely the physically more precocious 20 percent and the physically most retarded 20 percent in a normal sample of girls from a public school. The two groups were similar in intelligence, in socio-economic status, in racial background, and in their childhood health records. When we compared them, however, with regard to various social traits, as noted by careful observers in a long series of records, we found that the early-maturing were below the average in prestige, sociability, and leadership; below the average in popularity; below the average in cheerfulness, poise, and expressiveness. In the opinion of their classmates, as judged from a reputation test, they were considered to be rather submissive, withdrawn, and lacking in assurance.

These deficiencies in social attitudes and behavior may indeed be interpretable in terms of deeper layers of personality, but before seeking a more recondite explanation we may point out certain obvious and external ways in which the early-maturing girl is handicapped. The first thing to note is that she has become physically very conspicuous, at a time when conspicuousness is not valued. She finds herself embarrassingly tall and heavy; she is embarrassed by a greater breast development than seems to her to be normal; she is handicapped when she attempts to participate in the active playground games which are still within the interests of her classmates—for in the case of girls, sexual maturing, although it brings greater strength, often leads to a decreased skill in physical activities involving running and jumping.

The early-maturing girl quite naturally has interests in boys and in social usages and activities more mature than those of her chronological age group. But the males of her own age are unreceptive, for while she is physiologically a year or two out of step with the girls in her class, she is three or four years out of step with the boys—a vast and terrifying degree of developmental distance.

Sometimes the early-maturing girl manages to escape into an older age group, and to associate with other adolescents in her neighborhood who are nearer her own physiological level. In doing this, however, she may encounter other problems that are even more serious. Some of these may be involved in the attitudes of her parents, who are scarcely prepared for this sudden jump into young womanhood. They may feel that she is not yet old enough to go to parties or to have "dates"; they may demand that she continue to dress and act like other eleven- or twelve-year-olds. In this they may have some slight justification; for, unfortunately, a physical growth spurt does not carry with it any corresponding spurt in mental growth, and the physiologically mature youngster may not have the judgment nor mental level which go with longer living. So she is caught in this dilemma: if she remains in her own age group she is frustrated and ill at ease; if she moves into an older group she may fall under parental restrictions and, in any event, may lack the social maturity necessary to make a good adjustment among others of greater experience. To a considerable extent these difficulties are due to the age-grade system of our public schools, which make a physiologically deviate child conspicuous among her classmates. This would be less likely to occur in a small modern school which can make flexible provisions for individuals or, indeed, in the old-time district school, in which the grades are mixed in a single room. A completely heterogeneous grouping, as in the latter instance, may have disadvantages from a teaching standpoint, but for both early- and late-maturing children it may carry great advantages from a social standpoint.

In the case of girls, however, the late-maturing appear to need no special aids or compensations, unless their growth lag is so great as to imply a pathological condition. In the study mentioned above, the girls who were late-maturing were not only superior to the early-maturing but also superior to the average in a great number of the characteristics included in our social observation schedules. They were significantly higher than the early-maturing in traits related to personal appearance and attractiveness, in expressiveness and activity, in buoyance, poise, and cheerfulness, and also in sociability, leadership, and prestige. We are here, of course, speaking of each group taken as a whole; individual cases can be found which do not by any means conform to these generalizations.

Several points may be noted in explaining the apparently better status of so many of the late-maturing girls. The first is a physical advantage. Because of lateness in sexual maturing and in the closing of the epiphyses at the growing points of the bones, she has a long time in which to grow. Her growth is less sudden, less abrupt, than in the early-maturing, seldom reaches as great a velocity at the peak of growth, and involves fewer hazards of physiological imbalance and physical disproportion. The longer period of growth affects particularly the legs, and the late-maturing girl is therefore long-legged, and tends to conform closely to our American standards of beauty of figure, which in the present code of commercial advertising must always be long-legged and usually a bit hypofeminine.

Moreover, in this slower process of adolescence, the parents and the girl herself have a longer time in which to get used to the new interests, new impulses, and new requirements as to behavior. One further point is probably rather important. The late-maturing girl is more nearly in step with the boys in her age group than is the case with the early- or average-maturing girl. The two-year lag in the average maturity patterns of boys as compared with girls is reduced or eliminated among those girls who mature late, and their interests in mixed social activities, when they emerge, are more immediately satisfied.

If now we consider what adolescence may mean to the early- or the late-maturing boy, we find results quite the reverse of those reported for girls. The early-maturing boy enters adolescence at a time when girls in his age group are appreciative of male acquaintance who no longer insist upon being children. He also acquires traits of strength and athletic ability which give him prestige with his own sex. He is likely to be nearer the Apollonian build than the boys who mature later. He wins friends and influences people through the mere fact of physiological precocity, and through the physical dominance which follows.[13]

This is, of course, not without its hazards. The hazard lies partly in discrepancies in different aspects of growth, and discrepancies between what a boy is prepared to do and what his parents and other adults expect and demand of him. The boy who at thirteen is as tall as an adult may be assigned tasks beyond his years. His teacher chooses him for positions of responsibility. The athletic coach grooms him for the first team. His parents expect him to carry a larger share of the family burdens. A thirteen-year-old may not be ready for all this. Muscular development tends to lag somewhat behind skeletal development, and although he is strong, the early-maturing boy is not so strong as he looks. These new demands fall upon him at a time when he is already carrying a heavy load of adjustment to a changed physical structure, a new body image, and new interests and impulses. Nevertheless, in spite of these handicaps, and his very rapid rate of physical change, the early-maturing boy may readily find more advantages than disadvantages in his position. Moreover, unlike the physically precocious girl, his growth is not arrested at an early age; he reaches an average height as an adult, and somewhat better than average strength and general physical ability.

On the other hand, the boy who matures late, like the girl who matures early, is out of step with all the others in his age group. At fifteen or even sixteen he may still be a little boy, ignored by other boys and girls alike, and unable to compete effectively in playground games. In my book *Development in Adolescence*,[14] I have presented an example of such a case, a boy who developed many subjective inferiorities in connection with his retarded maturing, and whose compensation took the form of an ineffective social striving. Many of our late-maturing boys adjust by withdrawing from competition, becoming submissive and self-effacing. Others may take a more positive line of action; these are the active small boys, noisy, aggressive, and attention-getting. When at long last the late-maturing boy attains his growth spurt he is likely to reach normal height, but he may be slow to recover from the psychological

[13] H. E. Jones, *Motor Performance and Growth*, University of California Press, 1949.
[14] H. E. Jones, *Development in Adolescence: Approaches to the Study of the Individual*, Appleton-Century-Crofts, 1943.

scars of the period when he was a deviate. Such boys can be helped by giving them a prediction of their adult height and of the time when they may expect to enter the puberal phase of rapid growth. On the basis of Bayley's [15] work, we can now make this prediction, from skeletal X rays, with a fair degree of accuracy. The boy's pressing but often unasked question, "Am I normal?" can usually be answered in the affirmative. He can be more patient in waiting for nature to take its course, if he understands that his difficulty is merely one of timing and not of basic deficiency.

We have mentioned the sex difference in puberal maturing, which inducts girls into adolescence a year or two earlier, on the average, than boys. Another sex difference has been pointed out from one of our other studies by Dr. Caroline Tryon.[16] Achieving manhood or womanhood in our society

> is a long, complex, and often confusing learning task. . . . For the most part boys and girls work at these tasks in a stumbling, groping fashion, blindly reaching for the next step without much or any adult assistance. Many lose their way. It seems probable that our adult failure to give assistance derives as much from ignorance about this developmental process as it does from the extensive taboos on sex which characterize our culture.

One of the aspects of this developmental process is that, at least in an urban American culture, girls appear to have a greater problem than boys in adjusting to changing social requirements. In the adolescent culture itself girls encounter many changes in the conception as to what constitutes desirable behavior, changes and even reversals in the value system and in the relative ranking of traits which are important for popularity and prestige. Perhaps the principal single change which we have found in our California group is that at the beginning of adolescence the group standards for conduct among girls emphasize a quiet, demure, rather lady-like demeanor. By the age of fifteen this has altered, and we find that the girls who are now most popular in their set are active, talkative, and marked by a kind of "aggressive good fellowship." These traits, which may in part be adaptations to the hesitant and immature social approaches of boys, must again undergo considerable change in the later years of adolescence, if a girl is to maintain her status in the group. Dr. Tryon points out that boys, by comparison, seem to have a somewhat more consistent set of criteria to meet in developing their sex roles during this growth period.

[15] N. Bayley, "Tables for Predicting Adult Height from Skeletal Age and Present Height," *Journal of Pediatrics,* 1946, 28, pp. 49–64.
[16] Caroline Tryon, "The Adolescent Peer Culture," Chicago: University of Chicago Press, 43rd *Yearbook of the National Society for the Study of Education,* 1944, Pt. 1, pp. 217–239.

2 PERSONALITY DEVELOPMENT

First in this group of articles on the personality which develops during adolescence is the psychoanalytic view of Anna Freud. Writing ten years after Jones and twenty years after her own early work in the field, yet preceding the current wave of interest in adolescence, the author attempts to apply established principles of psychoanalysis to adolescent behavior. Specifically, she asks whether the typical adolescent crisis is inevitable, and she answers in the affirmative.

Anna Freud

Adolescence[1]

I. ADOLESCENCE IN THE PSYCHOANALYTIC THEORY

Introduction

I return to the subject of adolescence after an interval of twenty years. During this time much has happened in analytic work to throw added light on the problems concerned and to influence the conditions of life for young people, whether normal or abnormal. Nevertheless, in spite of partial advances, the position with regard to the analytic study of adolescence is not a happy one, and especially unsatisfactory when compared with that of early childhood. With the latter period, we feel sure of our ground, and in possession of a wealth of material and information which enables us to assume authority and apply analytic findings to the practical problems of upbringing. When it comes to adolescence,

[1] The content of this paper is based on material collected in the Hampstead Child-Therapy Clinic with the aid of grants by The Field Foundation, Inc., New York, The Foundations' Fund for Research in Psychiatry, New Haven, Connecticut, The Ford Foundation, New York, The Psychoanalytic Foundation, Inc., New York, and The Grant Foundation, Inc., New York.

we feel hesitant and, accordingly, cannot satisfy the parents or educational workers who apply for help to us and to our knowledge. One can hear it said frequently that adolescence is a neglected period, a stepchild where analytic thinking is concerned.

These complaints, which come from two sides, from the parents as well as from the analytic workers themselves, seem to me to warrant closer study and investigation than they have received so far. . . .

II. CLINICAL APPLICATIONS

What follows is an attempt to apply at least some of our hard-won insights to three of the most pressing problems concerning adolescence.

Is the adolescent upset inevitable?

There is, first, the ever recurrent question whether the adolescent upheaval is welcome and beneficial as such, whether it is necessary and, more than that, inevitable. On this point, psychoanalytic opinion is decisive and unanimous. The people in the child's family and school, who assess his state on the basis of behavior, may deplore the adolescent upset which, to them, spells the loss of valuable qualities, of character stability, and of social adaptation. As analysts, who assess personalities from the structural point of view, we think otherwise. We know that the character structure of a child at the end of the latency period represents the outcome of long drawn-out conflicts between id and ego forces. The inner balance achieved, although characteristic for each individual and precious to him, is preliminary only and precarious. It does not allow for the quantitative increase in drive activity, nor for the changes of drive quality which are both inseparable from puberty. Consequently, it has to be abandoned to allow adult sexuality to be integrated into the individual's personality. The so-called adolescent upheavals are no more than the external indications that such internal adjustments are in progress.

On the other hand, we all know individual children who as late as the ages of fourteen, fifteen, or sixteen show no such outer evidence of inner unrest. They remain, as they have been during the latency period, "good" children, wrapped up in their family relationships, considerate sons of their mothers, submissive to their fathers, in accord with the atmosphere, ideas, and ideals of their childhood background. Convenient as this may be, it signifies a delay of normal development and is, as such, a sign to be taken seriously. The first impression conveyed by these cases may be that of a quantitative deficiency of drive endowment, a suspicion which will usually prove unfounded. Analytic exploration reveals that this reluctance to "grow up" is derived not from the id but from the ego and superego aspects of the personality. These are children who have built up excessive defenses against their drive activities and are now crippled by the results, which act as barriers against the normal maturational processes of phase development. They are, perhaps more than any others, in need of therapeutic help to remove the inner restrictions and clear the path for normal development, however "upsetting" the latter may prove to be.

Is the adolescent upset predictable?

A second question which we are asked to answer frequently concerns the problem whether the manner in which a given child will react in adolescence can be predicted from the characteristics of his early infantile or latency behavior. Apart from the more general affirmative answer given by Ernest Jones (1922),[2] only one among the authors named above has made clear the positive assertions in this respect. Siegfried Bernfeld (1923),[3] when discussing his protracted type of male adolescence and its characteristics, established the links between this form of puberty and a specific type of infantile development based on the following three conditions: (a) that the frustration of infantile sex wishes has been shattering for the child's narcissism; (b) that the incestuous fixations to the parents have been of exceptional strength and have been maintained throughout the latency period; (c) that the superego has been established early, has been delineated sharply from the ego, and that the ideals contained in it are invested with narcissistic as well as with object libido.

Other and less precise answers to the same question are scattered through the literature. We find the opinion that, in the majority of cases, the manifestations of the adolescent process are not predictable since they depend almost wholly on quantitative relations, i.e., on the strength and suddenness of drive increase, the corresponding increase in anxiety causing all the rest of the upheaval.

I suggested in another place (1936)[4] that adolescence brings about occasionally something in the nature of a spontaneous cure. This happens in children whose pregenital activities and characteristics remained dominant throughout latency until the increase in genital libido produces a welcome decrease in pregenitality. This latter occurrence, on the other hand, can be matched by a corresponding one which produces the opposite effect: where phallic characteristics have remained dominant during latency, the increase in genital libido produces the effect of an exaggerated and threatening aggressive masculinity.

It seems to be generally accepted that a strong fixation to the mother, dating not only from the oedipal but from the preoedipal attachment to her, renders adolescence especially difficult. This latter assertion, on the other hand, has to

[2] Jones, E. (1922), *Some Problems of Adolescence. Papers on Psycho-Analysis.* London: Bailliere, Tindall & Cox, fifth edition, 1948.
[3] Bernfeld, S. (1923), "Uber eine typosche Form der mannlichen Pubertat," *Imago,* IX.
[4] Freud, A. (1936), *The Ego and the Mechanisms of Defense.* New York: International Universities Press, 1946. See Chapters X and XI.

be correlated with two recent findings of a different nature which we owe to work done in our Hampstead Child-Therapy Clinic. One of these findings is derived from the study of orphaned children who were deprived of the relationship to a stable mother figure in their first years. This lack of a mother fixation, far from making adolescence easier, constitutes a real danger to the whole inner coherence of the personality during that period. In these cases adolescence is preceded frequently by a frantic search for a mother image; the internal possession and cathexis of such an image seems to be essential for the ensuing normal process of detaching libido from it for transfer to new objects, i.e., to sexual partners.

The second finding mentioned above is derived from the analyses of adolescent twins, in one case children whose twin relationship in infancy had been observed and recorded in minute detail.[5] In their treatments it transpired that the "adolescent revolt" against the love objects of infancy demands the breaking of the tie to the twin in no lesser degree than the breaking of the tie to the mother. Since this libidinal (narcissistic as well as object-directed) cathexis of the twin is rooted in the same deep layer of the personality as the early attachment to the mothers, its withdrawal is accompanied by an equal amount of structural upheaval, emotional upset, and the resulting symptom formation. Where, on the other hand, the twin relationship survives the adolescent phase, we may expect to see a delay in the onset of maturity or a restrictive hardening of the character of the latency period similar to the instances mentioned above in which the childhood love for the parents withstands the onslaught of the adolescent phase.

To return to the initial question: it seems that we are able to foretell the adolescent reactions in certain specific and typical constellations but certainly not for all the individual variations of infantile personality structure. Our insight into typical developments will increase with the number of adolescents who undergo analysis.

Pathology in Adolescence

This leaves us with a third problem which, to my mind, outweighs the preceding ones so far as clinical and theoretical significance are concerned. I refer to the difficulty in adolescent cases to draw the line between normality and pathology. As described above, adolescence constitutes by definition an interruption of peaceful growth which resembles in appearance a variety of other emotional upsets and structural upheavals.[6] The adolescent manifestations come close to symptom formation of the neurotic, psychotic or dissocial order and merge almost imperceptibly into borderline states, initial, frustrated or fully

---

[5] Burlingham, D. (1952), *Twins*. New York: International Universities Press.
[6] Adolescence, of course, is not the only time in life when alterations of a physiological nature cause disturbances of mental equilibrium. The same happens in later years in the climacterium; and recently, Grete L. Bibring has given a convincing description of similar damage to the equilibrium of mental forces during pregnancy.

fledged forms of almost all the mental illnesses. Consequently, the differential diagnosis between the adolescent upsets and true pathology becomes a difficult task.

For the discussion of this diagnostic problem I leave most other authors in the field to speak for themselves and summarize my own impressions based on past and present clinical experience.

In 1936, when I approached the same subject from the aspect of the defenses, I was concerned with the similarity between the adolescent and other emotional disturbances rather than with the differences between them. I described that adolescent upsets take on the appearance of a neurosis if the initial, pathogenic danger situation is located in the superego with the resulting anxiety being felt as guilt; that they resemble psychotic disturbances if the danger lies in the increased power of the id itself, which threatens the ego in its existence or integrity. Whether such an adolescent individual impresses us, then, as obsessional, phobic, hysterical, ascetic, schizoid, paranoid, suicidal, etc., will depend on the one hand on the quality and quantity of the id contents which beset the ego, on the other hand on the selection of defense mechanisms which the latter employs. Since, in adolescence, impulses from all pregenital phases rise to the surface and defense mechanisms from all levels of crudity or complexity come into use, the pathological results—although identical in structure—are more varied and less stabilized than at other times of life.

Today it seems to me that this structural description needs to be amplified, not in the direction of the similarity of the adolescent to other disorders but in that of their specific nature. There is in their etiology at least one additional element which may be regarded as exclusive to this period and characteristic for it: namely that the danger is felt to be located not only in the id impulses and fantasies but in the very existence of the love objects of the individual's oedipal and pre-oedipal past. The libidinal cathexis to them has been carried forward from the infantile phases, merely toned down or inhibited in aim during latency. Therefore the reawakened pregenital urges, or—worse still—the newly acquired genital ones, are in danger of making contact with them, lending a new and threatening reality to fantasies which had seemed extinct but are, in fact, merely under repression.[7] The anxieties which arise on these grounds are directed toward eliminating the infantile objects, i.e., toward breaking the tie with them. Anny Katan [8] has discussed this type of defense, which aims above all at changing the persons and the scene of conflict, under the term of "removal." Such an attempt may succeed or fail, partially or totally. In any case, I agree with Anny Katan that its outcome will be decisive for the success or failure of the other, more familiar line of defensive measures which are directed against the impulses themselves.

---

[7] An important clinical instance of this can be found in adolescent girls with anorexia nervosa. Here the infantile fantasies of oral impregnation receive added impetus from the new real possibilities of motherhood opened up by genital development. Consequently, the phobic measures adopted against the intake of food on the one hand and identification with the mother on the other hand are overemphasized to a degree which may lead to starvation.

[8] Katan-Angel, A. (1937), "The Role of Displacement in Agoraphobia." *Int. J. Psa.*, XXXII, 1951.

A number of illustrations will serve to clarify the meaning of this assumption.

(I) Defense Against the Infantile Object Ties

Defense by Displacement of Libido

There are many adolescents who deal with the anxiety aroused by the attachment to their infantile objects by the simple means of flight. Instead of permitting a process of gradual detachment from the parents to take place, they withdraw their libido from them suddenly and altogether. This leaves them with a passionate longing for partnership which they succeed in transferring to the environment outside the family. Here they adopt varying solutions. Libido may be transferred, more or less unchanged in form, to parent substitutes, provided that these new figures are diametrically opposed in every aspect (personal, social, cultural) to the original ones. Or the attachment may be made to so-called "leaders," usually persons in age between the adolescent's and the parent's generation, who represent ideals. Equally frequent are the passionate new ties to contemporaries, either of the same or of the opposite sex (i.e., homosexual friendships) and the attachments to adolescent groups (or "gangs"). Whichever of these typical solutions is chosen, the result makes the adolescent feel "free," and revel in a new precious sense of independence from the parents who are treated, then, with indifference bordering on callousness.

Although the direction taken by the libido in these instances is, in itself, on lines of normality, the suddenness of the change, the carefully observed contrast in object selection, and the overemphasis on the new allegiances mark it as defensive. It represents an all too hasty anticipation of normal growth rather than a normal developmental process.

It makes little further difference to the emotional situation whether the libidinal flight is followed by actual flight, i.e., whether the adolescent also "removes" himself bodily from his family. If not, he remains in the home in the attitude of a boarder, usually a very inconsiderate one so far as the older and younger family members are concerned.

On the other hand, the withdrawal of cathexis from the parents has most decisive consequences for the rest of the defensive processes. Once the infantile objects are stripped of their importance, the pregenital and genital impulses cease to be threatening to the same degree. Consequently, guilt and anxiety decrease and the ego becomes more tolerant. Formerly repressed sexual and aggressive wishes rise to the surface and are acted on, the actions being taken outside the family in the wider environment. Whether this acting out will be on harmless, or idealistic, or dissocial, or even criminal lines will depend essentially on the new objects to which the adolescent has attached himself. Usually, the ideals of the leader, of the adolescent group, or of the gang, are taken over wholeheartedly and without criticism.

Adolescents of this type may be sent for treatment after their actions have brought them into conflict with their schools, their employers, or the law. As far as psychoanalytic therapy is concerned, they seem to offer little chance for the therapeutic alliance between analyst and patient without which the analytic technique cannot proceed. Any relationship to the analyst and, above all, the transference to him would revive the infantile attachments which have been discarded; therefore the adolescent remains unresponsive. Also, the escape from these attachments has suspended the feeling of internal conflict, at least temporarily; consequently, the adolescent does not feel in need of psychological help. A. Aichhorn [9] had these points in mind when he maintained that adolescents of the dissocial and criminal type needed a long period of preparation and inner rearrangement before they could become amenable to analytic treatment. He maintained that the latter would be successful only if, during this preparation in a residential setting, the adolescent made a new transference of object love, reawakened his infantile attachments, internalized his conflicts once more, in short became neurotic. To try and analyze an adolescent in his phase of successful detachment from the past seems to be a venture doomed to failure.

Defense by Reversal of Affect

A second typical reaction to the same danger situation is, although less conspicuous outwardly, more ominous in nature inwardly.

Instead of displacing libido from the parents—or, more likely, after failing to do so—the adolescent ego may defend itself by turning the emotions felt toward them into their opposites. This changes love into hate, dependence into revolt, respect and admiration into contempt and derision. On the basis of such reversal of affect the adolescent imagines himself to be "free" but, unluckily for his peace of mind and sense of conflict, this conviction does not reach further than the conscious surface layer of his mind. For all deeper intents and purposes he remains as securely tied to the parental figures as he has been before; acting out remains within the family; and any alterations achieved by the defense turn out to his disadvantage. There are no positive pleasures to be derived from the reversed relationships, only suffering, felt as well as inflicted. There is no room for independence of action, or of growth; compulsive opposition to the parents proves as crippling in this respect as compulsive obedience to them can prove to be.[10] Since anxiety and guilt remain undiminished, constant reinforcement of defense is necessary. This is provided in the first place by two methods: denial (of positive feeling) and reaction formations (churlish, unsympathetic, contemptuous attitudes). The behavioral picture that emerges at this stage is that of an uncooperative and hostile adolescent.

Further pathological developments of this state of affairs are worth watching. The hostility and aggressiveness, which serve as a defense against object love in the beginning, soon become intolerable to the ego, are felt as threats, and are warded off in their own right. This may happen by means of projection; in that

[9] Aichhorn, A. (1925), *Wayward Youth*. New York: Viking Press, 1948.
[10] S. Ferenczi has pointed to this effect of "compulsive disobedience" many years ago.

case the aggression is ascribed to the parents who, consequently, become the adolescent's main oppressors and persecutors. In the clinical picture this appears first as the adolescent's suspiciousness and, when the projections increase, as paranoid behavior.

Conversely, the full hostility and aggression may be turned away from the objects and employed inwardly against the self. In these cases, the adolescents display intense depression, tendencies of self-abasement and self-injury, and develop, or even carry out, suicidal wishes.

During all stages of this process, personal suffering is great and the desire to be helped intense. This, in itself, is no guarantee that the adolescent in question will submit to analytic therapy. He will certainly not do so if treatment is urged and initiated by the parents. Whenever this happens, he will consider analysis as their tool, extend his hostility or his suspicions to include the person of the analyst, and refuse cooperation. The chances are better if the adolescent himself decides to seek help and turns to analysis, as it were, in opposition to the parents' wishes. Even so, the alliance with the analyst may not be of long duration. As soon as a true transference develops and the positive infantile fantasies come into consciousness, the same reversal of affect tends to be repeated in the analytic setting. Rather than relive the whole turmoil of feelings with the analyst, many adolescent patients run away. They escape from their positive feelings, although it appears to the analyst that they break off treatment in an overwhelmingly strong negative transference.

Defense by Withdrawal of Libido to the Self

To proceed in the direction of increasing pathology:

Withdrawal of libido from the parents, as it has been described above, does not, in itself, decide about its further use, or fate. If anxieties and inhibitions block the way toward new objects outside the family, the libido remains within the self. There, it may be employed to cathect the ego and superego, thereby inflating them. Clinically this means that ideas of grandeur will appear, fantasies of unlimited power over other human beings, or of major achievement and championship in one or more fields. Or, the suffering and persecuted ego of the adolescent may assume Christ-like proportions with corresponding fantasies of saving the world.

On the other hand, the cathexis may become attached to the adolescent's body only and give rise there to the hypochondriacal sensations and feelings of body changes that are well known clinically from initial stages of psychotic illness.

In either case analytic therapy is indicated as well as urgent. Treatment will dispel the appearance of severe abnormality if it reopens a path for the libido, either to flow backwards and recathect the original infantile objects, or to flow forward, in the direction described above, to cathect less frightening substitutes in the environment.

What taxes the analyst's technical skill in these cases is the withdrawn state of the patient, i.e., the problem of establishing an initial relationship and transference. Once this is accomplished, the return from narcissistic withdrawal to object cathexis will relieve the patient, at least temporarily.

I believe, there are many cases where the analyst would be wise to be content with this partial success without urging further treatment. A further, and deeper, involvement in the transference may well arouse all the anxieties described above and, again, lead to abrupt termination of the analysis due to the adolescent's flight reaction.

Defense by Regression

The greater the anxiety aroused by the object ties, the more elementary and primitive is the defense activity employed by the adolescent ego to escape them. Thus, at the extreme height of anxiety, the relations with the object world may be reduced to the emotional state known as "primary identification" with the objects. This solution with which we are familiar from psychotic illnesses implies regressive changes in all parts of the personality, i.e., in the ego organization as well as in the libido. The ego boundaries [11] are widened to embrace parts of the object together with the self. This creates in the adolescent surprising changes of qualities, attitudes and even outward appearance. His allegiance to persons outside himself betrays itself in these alterations of his own personality (i.e., his identifications) rather than in an outflow of libido. Projections, together with these identifications, dominate the scene and create a give-and-take between the self and object which has repercussions on important ego functions. For example, the distinction between the external and internal world (i.e., reality testing) becomes temporarily negligible, a lapse in ego functioning which manifests itself in the clinical picture as a state of confusion.

Regression of this kind may bring transitory relief to the ego by emptying the oedipal (and many of the preoedipal) fantasies of their libidinal cathexis.[12] But this lessening anxiety will not be long-lived. Another and deeper anxiety will soon take its place which I have characterized on a former occasion [13] as the fear of emotional surrender, with the accompanying fear of loss of identity.

(II) Defense Against Impulses

Where the defenses against the oedipal and preoedipal object ties fail to achieve their aim, clinical pictures emerge which come nearest to the borderline toward psychotic illness.

[11] Federn, P. (1952), *Ego Psychology and the Psychoses.* New York: Basic Books. Freeman, T., Cameron, L. J. and McGhie, A. (1958), *Chronic Schizophrenia.* New York: International Universities Press.

[12] Katan, M. (1950), "Structural Aspects of a Case of Schizophrenia." *This Annual*, V.

[13] Freud, A. (1951), "A Connection between the States of Negativism and of Emotional Surrender (Horigkeit)." Paper read at the International Psycho-Analytical Congress, Amsterdam, August 1951. Summary in *Int. J. Psa.*, XXXIII, 1952, p. 265.

The "Ascetic" Adolescent

One of these, the "ascetic" adolescent, I have described before as fighting all his impulses, preoedipal and oedipal, sexual and aggressive, extending the defense even to the fulfillment of the physiological needs for food, sleep, and body comfort. This, to me, seems the characteristic reaction of an ego, driven by the blind fear of overwhelming id quantities, an anxiety which leaves no room for the finer distinctions between vital or merely pleasant satisfactions, the healthy or the morbid, the morally permitted or forbidden pleasures. Total war is waged against the pursuit of pleasure as such. Accordingly, most of the normal processes of instinct and need satisfaction are interfered with and become paralyzed. According to clinical observation, adolescent asceticism is, with luck, a transitory phenomenon. For the analytic observer it provides precious proof of the power of defense, i.e., of the extent to which the normal, healthy drive derivatives are open to crippling inferences by the ego.

On the whole, analytic treatment of the ascetic type does not present as many technical difficulties as one would expect. Perhaps, in these individuals, defense against the impulses is so massive, that they can permit themselves some object relationship to the analyst and, thus, enter into transference.

The "Uncompromising" Adolescent

Another, equally abnormal adolescent, is described best as the "uncompromising" type. The term, in this instance, does refer to more than the well-known conscious, unrelenting position adopted by many young people who stand up for their ideas, refuse to make concessions to the more practical and reality-adapted attitudes of their elders, and take pride in their moral or ascetic principles. "Compromise," with these adolescents, includes processes which are as essential for life as, for example, the cooperation between impulses, the blending of opposite strivings, the mitigation of id strivings by interference from the side of the ego. One adolescent whom I observed in analysis did his utmost, in pursuit of this impossible aim, to prevent any interference of his mind with his body, of his activity with his passivity, his loves with his hates, his realities with his fantasies, the external demands with his internal ones, in short, of his ego with his id.

In treatment this defense was represented as a strong resistance against any "cure," the idea of which he despised in spite of intense suffering. He understood correctly that mental health is based in the last resort on harmony, i.e., on the very compromise formations which he was trying to avoid.

III. THE CONCEPT OF NORMALITY IN ADOLESCENCE

Where adolescence is concerned, it seems easier to describe its pathological manifestations than the normal processes. Nevertheless, there are in the above exposition at least two pronouncements which may prove useful for the concept: (1) that adolescence is by its nature an interruption of peaceful growth, and (2) that the upholding of a steady equilibrium during the adolescent process is in itself abnormal. Once we accept for adolescence disharmony within the psychic structure as our basic fact, understanding becomes easier. We begin to see the upsetting battles which are raging between id and ego as beneficient attempts to restore peace and harmony. The defensive methods which are employed either against the impulses, or against the object cathexis, begin to appear legitimate and normal. If they produce pathological results, this happens not because of any malignancy in their nature, but because they are overused, overstressed, or used in isolation. Actually, each of the abnormal types of adolescent development, as it is described above, represents also a potentially useful way of regaining mental stability, normal if combined with other defenses, and if used in moderation.

To explain this last statement in greater detail: I take it that it is normal for an adolescent to behave for a considerable length of time in an inconsistent and unpredictable manner; to fight his impulses and to accept them; to ward them off successfully and to be overrun by them; to love his parents and to hate them; to revolt against them and to be dependent on them; to be deeply ashamed to acknowledge his mother before others and, unexpectedly, to desire heart-to-heart talks with her; to thrive on imitation of and identification with others while searching unceasingly for his own identity; to be more idealistic, artistic, generous, and unselfish than he will ever be again, but also the opposite: self-centered, egoistic, calculating. Such fluctuations between extreme opposites would be deemed highly abnormal at any other time of life. At this time they may signify no more than that an adult structure of personality takes a long time to emerge, that the ego of the individual in question does not cease to experiment and is in no hurry to close down on possibilities. If the temporary solutions seem abnormal to the onlooker, they are less so, nevertheless, than the hasty decisions made in other cases for one-sided suppression, or revolt, or flight, or withdrawal, or regression, or asceticism, which are responsible for the truly pathological developments described above.

While an adolescent remains inconsistent and unpredictable in his behavior, he may suffer, but he does not seem to me to be in need of treatment. I think that he should be given time and scope to work out his own solution. Rather, it may be his parents who need help and guidance so as to be able to bear with him. There are few situations in life which are more difficult to cope with than an adolescent son or daughter during the attempt to liberate themselves.

IV. SUMMARY

In the foregoing papers the author has reviewed and summarized some of the basic literature on adolescence, as well as her own views on the subject. Her former description of the defensive processes in adolescence has been amplified to include specific defense activities directed against the oedipal and preoedipal object ties.

In contrast to Anna Freud, who attempted a psychoanalytic definition of normal adolescence, Dr. Lorand discusses those cases in which normal development has not occurred for one reason or another. As co-editor of one of the earlier collections of essays on the psychoanalytic treatment of disturbed adolescents, Dr. Lorand here addresses his colleagues. He sets forth guidelines for the relationship between analyst and patient, illustrated with two case studies of severe adolescent conflict.

Sandor Lorand

Treatment of Adolescents

In *Three Essays on the Theory of Sexuality* Freud [1] described, as the most significant and most painful psychic achievement of the adolescent, his detachment from parental authority. Indeed, in our observation of the adolescent, whether normal or maladjusted, we see a continual struggle with this problem. The strong conscious drives for independence, and at the same time the unconscious need to maintain dependence on the parents, result in various degrees of confusion, exaggerated by the fact that the adolescent is at this time going through biological as well as psychological changes. The continuous, strong tensions which the adolescent experiences during bodily changes and this phase of emotional development bring many new hardships in adjustment, particularly in the sexual sphere. All of these problems set difficulties in the way of ego growth and expansion, which starts to take place on a larger scale, in adolescence, and which may therefore be seriously affected.

In 1922 Ernest Jones,[2] in an important paper, drew attention to the manifold problems which confront the adolescent, but, with the exception of Bernfeld [3] and Aichhorn,[4] neither psychoanalysts nor psychiatrists followed up these early studies to contribute further material until about a decade ago. At that time a

[1] Freud, *Three Essays on the Theory of Sexuality*, in *Standard Edition*, London: Hogarth Press, Ltd., 1953, vol. 7.
[2] E. Jones, "Some Problems of Adolescence," in *Papers on Psycho-Analysis*, Baltimore: The Williams & Wilkins Co., 1948.
[3] S. Bernfield, "Types of Adolescence," *Psychoanalytic Quarterly*, 7:243, 1938
[4] A. Aichhorn, *Wayward Youth*, New York: The Viking Press, Inc., 1935.

number of essays began to appear containing clinical reports on the therapy of the adolescent, as well as theoretical conclusions. Until then, however, examination and clarification of the depth psychology of adolescent behavior had been neglected.

The chapters in this volume deal with these topics and are intended to help clarify the dynamic and theoretical formulations of adolescent problems as well as to illustrate the concepts with clinical case studies. They give valuable insights into the many complex problems of the adolescent.

Before entering into a discussion of the various therapeutic approaches used with the adolescent, let me summarize again the problems with which we have to deal in treating the adolescent. Many of the problems described are present in normal adolescent development as well as in the troubled and neurotic. What makes the difference is the degree of emotional tension, which results in overt behavior deviating from what we look upon as normal. In addition to psychological difficulties, the adolescent also has the important problem of body consciousness, which is by no means a less important source of disturbance. Some boys and girls feel awkward in their growth; they feel unattractive; they try to hide or are ashamed of their developing physiques, the sign of maturation. Their attitude and the behavior they exhibit show clearly the conflict between being partly children who are having difficulties growing up, and partly young adults trying to be independent and to imitate father, mother, or older siblings.

The problem of the adolescent is intimately connected with problems of ego functioning. The expanding young ego is pressured from many different sides. The adolescent is not ready to adapt to the overwhelming pressures and demands of reality adjustment. Confused by demands of reality for adaptation, they become impatient and impulsive; they attempt to regress and run away, frightened of the problems and of the consequences which taking the responsibility for growing up involves. Their confusion and anxiety caused by these tensions lead to various defenses. When attempts at grasping the situation and satisfying reality demands meet with failure, various defenses are developed against progress and growth.

Corrective attempts on the part of parents or authority figures in school will fail because the young adolescent has no insight into his difficulties and no comprehension of what causes his impulsive behavior; he cannot cope with his moody, passive attitude at one time and with his impulsiveness and his acting-out behavior at other times. He is confused about his schoolwork, which he frequently cannot master. He is self-centered, shy, and absorbed in his daydreams; he is easily hurt and feels as if he does not belong, as if he were an outsider.

THERAPEUTIC APPROACHES

The therapeutic approach is always a difficult one in the early phases of adolescence because of the adolescents' lack of insight into their problems, and the difficulty in communicating with them and making clear what it is that disturbs them. They feel troubled by fear and guilt, which they resent discussing; this is true also of their sexual problems and their preoccupation with masturbation fantasies. If they are willing to come for therapy, they are characteristically impatient, demanding quick results. They are intolerant and refuse to cooperate in the therapeutic setting, all of which makes it appear, at times, that the adolescent cannot be treated at all. Difficulties in this initial contact with the adolescent may discourage the therapist from trying to improve the relationship or creating a therapeutic atmosphere

In the various essays written about adolescent problems and therapy, there are many contradictory suggestions as to the types of approaches appropriate to the treatment of adolescents. Adolescence is a phase of development which extends from about the age of 12 up to and including 18; therefore, when talking about adolescent development, it is important to think of it as consisting of many age levels. Hence, when talking about the therapy of adolescents, we must keep in mind the fact that different therapeutic approaches will be called for at the different stages of development. Therapy must be adjusted to the age level of the patient. Papers written on the subject of therapy in general and of psychoanalytic therapy with adolescents, by Anna Freud,[5] Leo Spiegel,[6] Maxwell Gitelson,[7] and others, all emphasize the difficulties involved in using the various kinds of therapy. In a detailed paper, Elizabeth R. Geleerd [8] discusses the various stages of development and the type of psychoanalytic therapy useful at each stage.

Therapy must try to create a dependency relationship on the part of the adolescent patient to the therapist. In creating this relationship, an atmosphere is provided in which the patient *can* be more dependent, more trusting, and more reliant on his therapist than he can be in his outside environment where he feels criticized, misunderstood, and unsupported. This may open the way for the young patient to start communicating more easily. What can also be done at the beginning is to enlarge upon and to explain in understandable language what his problems with his environment and with his reality situation may be.

The therapist cannot expect that his young patient will often acquire even partial insight at the beginning of treatment. The gaining of insight usually comes later, as therapy progresses. The patient then can understand more about himself and will be ready to verbalize and communicate more readily. Transference will develop, and manipulations of the transference relationship will be possible. Creating a positive transference is difficult, and the therapist will have to be versatile if he is to make the patient trusting and to an extent dependent, which also includes the beginning of identification with the therapist. To control the

[5] A. Freud, *Psychoanalytic Treatment of Children*, London: Imago Publishing Company, 1927.

[6] L. A Spiegel, "Comments on the Psychoanalytic Psychology of Adolescence," in *The Psychoanalytic Study of the Child*, New York: International Universities Press, Inc , 1957, vol. 13.

[7] M. Gitelson, "Character Synthesis: The Psychotherapeutic Problems in Adolescence," *American Journal of Orthopsychiatry*, 18:3, 1948.

[8] E. R Geleerd, "Some Aspects of Psychoanalytic Technique in Adolescence," in *The Psychoanalytic Study of the Child*, New York: International Universities Press, Inc., 1957, vol. 13.

acting-out, impulsive behavior, the therapist will have to exercise a great deal of tolerance; he must have skill and elasticity in addition to empathy and sympathy with the patient's difficulties. At the same time, the therapist will have to be objective, avoid taking over the patient's parents' attitude, and, instead, be a different type of parent substitute—understanding, but also firm when needed. Success in establishing a therapeutic relationship with the patient depends to a large extent on the therapist's personality, ease, self-assurance, and patience, and especially on flexibility in using all types of psychotherapy.

Psychoanalysts hold widely divergent opinions about the possibility of a more or less classical analysis of adolescents. It is generally agreed, by those who are treating adolescents psychoanalytically, that analysis cannot be carried out along strictly classical lines and that one should not attempt to conduct it that way. Variations in the technical approach and modifications must be employed in order to achieve therapeutic success. Moreover, analytic treatment of any sort in some cases is impossible. In the later phases of adolescence, when a boy or girl already has some insight into his or her difficulties and wants to be helped, psychoanalysis can be applied, but even then with modifications. Some psychoanalysts advocate analytical therapy in specific phases of the therapeutic process. But the distrustful, rebellious attitude, the noncooperation of the adolescent who is usually brought to therapy, makes the degree of success of the therapy uncertain.

Therapeutic goals in treatment of adolescents are not very clearly defined in present-day literature. It appears that the center of the therapeutic goal is ego expansion, thus strengthening the ego to cope with the various ramifications of and vicissitudes in the adolescent's adjustment. The continual pressure of new kinds of experiences arising out of the adolescent's changing relationship to the external world, his aggressive strivings, ambitions, and his sexual experiences and feelings—all have to be directed into a unifying channel in order to provide the basis for permanent character structure in later adulthood. In trying to enable the adolescent to control his behavior, one has to make him realize what his actions mean, and the reasons for his acting as he does. Under the guidance of the therapist, the adolescent has to acquire a stronger ego in order to master his current problems and to control his strong tendencies toward acting out, which are connected with tendencies to regress to an earlier phase of development when he was not expected to behave in the controlled manner now required of him.

Therapy is frequently adjusted to the patient's needs. The various therapies may all have their value and bring practical results if used with caution, and if the therapist knows well what his aim is—namely to make the patient able to bear anxiety and discomfort, which will then open the way to improved emotional stability. The therapist has to keep in mind that, however difficult it is for the adolescent to express himself, however rebellious he may be in expressing himself, however difficult it is for him to be able to see his problems in the proper light, his main difficulty psychologically is that he is really helpless and wants to be dependent, while at the same time trying to prove himself independent. His rebellious and acting-out behavior may by itself indicate his inner feelings of the need to be helped, to depend, and to be advised. That these feelings should be present is quite natural, for adolescence is, to a great extent, a revival of earlier phases of emotional experience transposed, which interfere with the adolescent's attempts to adjust to new experiences.

The therapist has an important role in the strengthening of the adolescent's weak ego by giving him a better ego ideal with which to identify. One type of approach will work with one patient or with one therapist, and another type of technique will work with another patient and another therapist. This is why, at times, we see cases where better results are obtained after a patient changes therapists.

Should adolescents be analyzed at all? Some authors speak about a first, second, and final phase of adolescence and suggest that in only one or another of these phases is analysis possible. We can say definitely that certain types of adolescents can be treated with psychoanalytic therapy, but that this therapy will never be the so-called orthodox analysis. As a number of authors have pointed out, various psychotherapeutic approaches may have to be used; much re-education and a more positive, directive attitude will be involved at certain stages than is possible in classical analysis. The therapeutic approach selected will depend, to a great extent, on the maturity or weakness of the patient's ego, especially from the standpoint of ego control. Treatment of adolescents really begins when the young patient has some insight into his problems, when he feels he has difficulties and wants to be helped.

To illustrate some of the theoretical formulations, clinical problems, and therapeutic approaches to the general problems of adolescence, I am presenting two cases of "delayed" adolescence which I had the opportunity of analyzing for a number of years. In both cases the early adolescent problems, in all their intensity, were re-enacted by the patient, revealing the struggle which these young people had to go through not only in the various phases of adolescence but from infancy up to adolescence. In the course of therapy there was opportunity to investigate and understand the earlier phases of development which were instrumented in creating the neurosis and which resulted in the patients seeking treatment.

In the transference relationship they re-experienced all the emotional upheavals to which their home environment and early schooling exposed them. Especially important were their dreams. Nearly all dealt with home, parents, siblings, early schooling, abandonment, anxieties, and sadomasochistic sexual tendencies. The dreams were of great assistance in reconstructing the forgotten earlier phases of childhood and thus helped to recall the repressed past where the pathology originated. The analysis of these patients differed a great deal from the analysis of adults. There was constant acting out and impulsive behavior which not only had to be interpreted but, at times, actively blocked. Thus modifications of classical analytic techniques had to be used at times.

CASE REPORTS

A young man of 18, who had just left college in the middle of the term because of inability to concentrate, came with great reluctance for a consultation because he had been told by psychiatrists that he was urgently in need of therapy. He resented the diagnosis; it made him feel pushed into therapy. Nevertheless he came, and his initial symptom was to talk not about his school difficulties but about how well he was getting along with his professors and his classmates and how much they liked him. He conceded, however, that he was backward in his studies, that he could not concentrate, and hence would not get along at college.

His friends had originally all been in the city where he lived, and it would have been possible to go to college there. He felt that he had been forced by his parents to go out of town to college. He admitted that, at times, his behavior at home was not the best, but he insisted that it wasn't so bad as to deserve being sent away from home. One of the reasons his parents wanted him to go away from home was that they hoped he would go for treatment. He had refused to go for therapy in his home town. When home, he was constantly arguing with his father and trying to correct his father's attitude toward him in all kinds of matters—the amount of his allowance, whether or not his father should buy him a car, etc. (He was a sports-car enthusiast and talked for hours about cars and drivers.)

The young man also had a bad relationship with his mother. At times, days would pass without his speaking to her. Later in therapy it was revealed that this behavior was a defense against expression of his sexual fantasies about his mother, with which he was still struggling at the age of 17, just before he left for college. Talking to his mother would have meant contact, and from that would have sprung a desire to establish a closer contact. Therefore he avoided his mother as much as he could. Even when sitting at the table with her, he did not speak to her or greet her.

Very soon in the analytical therapy, it turned out that he was really not in great favor with his friends. He talked well and could make people interested in him, since he was clever and well informed, but he was incapable himself of really liking anybody. On the surface he seemed well adjusted to people, but there was no real warmth in his relationships with his friends or parents. This maladjustment showed itself particularly in his sexual life.

Two important problems presented themselves quite early in analysis; they were the problems which had actually motivated him to come for treatment. One was his sexual problem; he was a chronic masturbator, with masochistic fantasies which amused him to the point of laughing about them. Another important symptom was his "wanderlust" which drove him to compulsive walking for long hours at night.

In his fantasies he was preoccupied with homosexuality but, although attracted to boys, he never had homosexual experiences. He went out with girls and, on many occasions, was on the verge of having a sexual relationship at the girl's instigation, but he always managed to avoid it. Attracted to boyish girls, he was very defensive against becoming strongly interested in any of them. Parallel to his masochism, was the counterpart: a strongly sadistic attitude toward girls, with his masochistic behavior serving as a defense against his sadistic tendencies. He fought people off by not becoming concerned, or looking through them as if they weren't there, giving them the "silent treatment," as he frequently did with the analyst. He was afraid of getting into fights with men or with friends of his, but he enjoyed the company of girls. The achievement of making them fall in love with him, and then abandoning them, was a source of gratification.

He fought his parents in a calm, composed way, insisting that his will be carried out, contradicting them, and attempting to prove them wrong at every step. He forced them to keep him at home by accepting psychiatric treatment. At the same time, he refused to go to college here, because he had left college in the middle of the term and was waiting until the next term started. He insisted that he wanted a job and that, in order to go to work, he needed a car, which he demanded that his parents give him. He spent his days sleeping late. He did nothing around the house except telephone friends and make dates; evenings he spent out.

In analysis he complained a great deal about the situation with his parents, and cited memories from childhood and early adolescence, when his father and mother were often away. This was especially true in early childhood. At that time he had a continually changing succession of nursemaids, some of whom punished him severely. Thus, his contrary, defiant attitude toward his parents developed early.

He related many dreams, all of which dealt with childhood memories and experiences. Among them were frankly incestuous dreams referring to his mother and his desire to be nursed and to be taken care of by her. He consciously denied, however, all need to depend on anyone or be taken care of. All thoughts of becoming attached or involved emotionally with a girl, or, for that matter, of forming close friendships or confidential relationships with any of his male friends, he avoided. His external, adultlike behavior was purely imitation and acting. His dreams showed confusion between heterosexual and homosexual drives. The following short dream will illustrate the nature of his conflict and confusions concerning sexual involvement, or any deep emotional involvement with either young men or young women: "I had two visitors, a husband and wife, and the husband grabs one of my legs, pulls it out, and runs away with it, and I have quite a time running after him on crutches to get my leg back. I screw the leg back on and then the woman grabs my leg and runs away with it, and I again have to make difficult efforts to retrieve my leg. Then I wake up."

His associations to and discussions of the dream are too lengthy to reproduce here. They expressed his fear of forming deep attachments to either men or women because he might be damaged (castrated) or they might take advantage of him. On an earlier level the dream naturally referred to his father and mother competing as to who would be able to alter his behavior, and his distrust of them and fear of becoming attached to either one because of the fear of a repetition of the disappointments of childhood, when he felt abandoned by them. The dream illustrates the concept of the adolescent as being at a crossroad and not knowing what direction to take; whether to go ahead and take an adult attitude, adjusting to adult life in all respects (adult object relationships and independence of parents), or whether to remain a youngster, an adolescent, so that the threats and responsibilities of adult life and the dangers of frustration and sexual involvements can be avoided.

In another case, a girl of 19 felt ready for treatment because it involved getting away from her home city and her environment. From the age of 9 she had been under the care of physicians and psychiatrists because she was always in trouble. Her home situation had become unbearable because of antagonistic relationships with parents and siblings. The oldest of a large family, she had felt rejected from an early age, with added emphasis each time a new sibling arrived. Her behavior toward her parents and governesses, and later at school, was antagonistic, defiant, and spiteful in every respect. With regard to eating, she did the opposite of whatever she felt was expected of her. In elementary school, when urged to be temperate, she became very fat from overeating. When away at boarding school, she threw the food down the toilet and became emaciated. She had to spend a great deal of time in the infirmary and could not attend classes. Eventually, she had to be taken home, which was her conscious aim. She suffered from a mild form of anorexia nervosa which, with occasional remissions, was still present to a mild degree during her analysis. In her early adolescence, 12 to 14, she was a tomboy, excelling the boys in diving, swimming, and other sports. Socially, at this period, she did not get along well with either boys or girls. She had few friends and was rather aggressive toward everyone. Her pleasure was to make fun of others and to torture them. When the other girls began to date, she was not asked. At this time she began to be troubled by feelings of inferiority, especially with regard to her body. She felt she was too strong and muscular, too much like a boy and not like a girl.

The patient had trouble establishing a menstrual cycle. Her menstruation started late, and for months at a time she did not menstruate at all, which made her feel that there was definitely something wrong with her. She developed all kinds of fears concerning feminine functioning. When she menstruated, she feared that she might bleed to death. If she did not menstruate, she felt she was abnormal. Her ideas about sex were very much distorted and were connected with notions of illness. Pregnancy, she thought, was dangerous and·might kill the woman. She thought that by kissing anyone, including her parents, she would get germs in her mouth, so she had to keep away from affectionate embraces or contacts with everyone. She was angry at boys and men, and was aggressive toward them, being consciously envious of their masculinity and the greater liberties they enjoyed. These attitudes, forms of behavior, and thoughts (they were not mere fantasies) she retained even to the time she came to analysis, where she expressed her wish to be a man.

These deep disturbances, including states of panic and sleepwalking, started in childhood. At the period of adolescence when she had to sleep with other girls in one room at the boarding school, there were times when she could not fall asleep for at least half the night. The slightest noise in the room disturbed her sleep. A fear that there would be some noise, or anticipation that some of the girls might make noises, made her furious. Then the fury and the aggression kept her awake. At times she had fantasies that she would die in her sleep or that she might kill somebody while sleepwalking. These were the main reasons for her insomnia and fear of falling asleep.

When this young girl came to analysis at 19 she was considered by some of the members of her family to be promiscuous, and unable to discriminate between the young men with whom she was going out. Actually, she had so great a fear of sex and so much disgust, that promiscuity was impossible. She made it appear so, however, in order to be criticized and talked about. Despite her parents' and friends' opinions, she formed a friendship with a male Negro college student. She wanted to challenge people, that is, to challenge the members of her family, in particular her mother and father.

Therapy in this case was very arduous. In the beginning there was much reluctance to relate her thoughts and feelings. She acted out in the analytical hour, being spiteful, defiant, and abusive. In the later phase this changed to greater compliance, but then, failing to get all the reassurance and protection which she expected, particularly at those times when her parents visited and interfered with her life, she again acted out continuously in the analytical hour. The hour was divided; the first half was spent in screaming, crying, and temper tantrums, and the other half in the analyst's relating that behavior to the behavior of early childhood and adolescence. Gradually, a very strong positive transference developed, making the analyst a father and mother ideal who was better and kinder to her, who would magically help her to adjust, and who cared for her more than her parents and siblings did. Naturally, this strong positive attachment and dependence carried with it the consequence that she was very easily hurt, and felt rejected because the analyst did not take her in as one of his family or even give her positive, definite instructions as to what to do in certain situations. On such occasions she felt a strong desire to torture the analyst, to shoot him, to kill him, all of which corresponded to her early desires and to her attempts at torturing her playmates, siblings, pets, animals of all sorts, etc. Only gradually did she begin to grow up in analysis, and to take a more adult, feminine attitude. While she still did not easily identify with the mother figure, she began at least to make a number of good friends of girls her own age.

The important problem in the therapy of this patient was for the therapist to gauge the patient's acting out and regression to childish ways of behaving in the analytical situation, and to know when to step in to curtail it.

DISCUSSION

The problems of the patients cited here are characteristic of all adolescents in varying degrees. The degree of acting out, which is a form of aggressive behavior, is of primary importance in determining therapeutic handling in analysis and in psychotherapy, because it indicates the strength of the influence of earlier conflicts on the adolescent. When the ego does not have the strength to meet the demands of reality, the tendency is to regress to a less disturbing period when the superego was not so harsh, or the young child could avoid the harshness by various forms of behavior which a child naturally does use at certain periods in his development.

Naturally, not all late adolescent cases are as amenable to analysis as the two cited above. Sometimes, even at this age, one starts analysis, and then the therapy must change to a different type. At times, the most that can be accomplished is to reconstruct, from the actual types of behavior, earlier forms of behavior, and induce the patient to give up and change this early behavior pattern.

In this final article on adolescent personality, the noted student of human development, Erik Erikson, writes that the adolescent's search for identity is at bottom a search for something to which he can fully commit himself. Through analyses of the youthful tragic hero, Hamlet, and one of Sigmund Freud's case studies, Erikson develops the concept that adolescents need to explore a diversity of alternatives as preparation for the critical act of fixing their fidelity on a realistic goal.

Erik H. Erikson

Youth:
Fidelity and Diversity

The subject of this paper is a certain strength inherent in the age of youth. I call it the sense of and the capacity for Fidelity. To do justice to this theme, I would have to account for the strengths (I call them basic virtues, in the older sense of the world) arising in the stages of life which precede and follow youth. Only in this way could I hope to indicate the place of youth in the evolutionary scheme of the human life cycle, only in this way make plausible the fact that the virtue Fidelity could not develop earlier in life and must not, in the crises of youth, fail its time of ascendance. Obviously, however, such an accounting would demand more than space allows. I must refer the reader to a footnote,[1] which can do no more than list the virtues of which Fidelity is one, and point to publications offering a rationale of the evolutionary scheme from which they all emerge. We can take only a brief look at the stage of life which immediately precedes youth, the school age, and then turn to youth itself.

The school age, which intervenes between childhood and youth, finds the child, previously dominated by the experience of play, ready, willing, and able to apply himself to the rudimentary skills required, eventually wielding the tools and weapons, the symbols and concepts, of his culture. Also, it finds him eager to realize actual roles (previously play-acted) which promise him an eventual identity within the specializations of his culture's technology. However, the stage by stage acquisition during individual childhood of each of man's evolutionary gains leaves the mark of infantile experience on his proudest achievements. The play age bequeaths to all methodical pursuits a quality of grandiose delusion; and the school age leaves man with a naive acceptance of "what works."

As the child makes methods his own, he also permits accepted methods to make him their own. To consider as good only what works, and to feel accepted only if things work, to manage and to be managed, can become his dominant delight and value. And since technological specialization is an intrinsic part of the human horde's or tribe's or culture's system and world image, man's pride in the tools that work with materials and animals extends to the weapons which work against other humans as well as against other species. That this can awaken a cold cunning as well as an unmeasured ferocity rare in the animal world is, of course, due to a combination of developments. Among these we will be most concerned (because it comes to the fore during youth) with man's need to combine technological pride with a sense of identity: a double sense of personal self-sameness slowly accrued from infantile experiences and of shared sameness experienced in encounters with a widening part of the community.

This need too is an evolutionary necessity as yet to be understood and influenced by planning: for men—not being a natural species any more, and not a mankind as yet—need to feel that they are of some special kind (tribe or nation, class or caste, family, occupation, or type), whose insignia they will wear with vanity and conviction, and defend (along with the economic claims they have staked out for their kind) against the foreign, the inimical, the not-so-

---

[1] Virtue once connoted "inherent strength" and "active quality." In this sense, I consider the following basic virtues (essential to, if not identical with, ego strength) to be anchored in the successive stages of life: Hope, in infancy; Will and Purpose, in the play age; Skill, in the school age; Fidelity, in youth; Love, in young adulthood; Care, in adulthood; Wisdom, in old age. For an evolutionary and genetic rationale of this concept of the life cycle, see the writer's "The Roots of Virtue," in *The Humanist Frame*, Sir Julius Huxley, ed. London: Allen and Unwin, 1961; Harper and Brothers, 1961. For a more detailed exposition, see the writer's forthcoming book, *Life Cycle and Community*, in which the other stages of development are treated in chapters analogous to the one presented here.

human kinds. Thus it comes about that they can use all their proud skills and methods most systematically against other men, even in the most advanced state of rationality and civilization, with the conviction that they could not morally afford not to do so.

It is not our purpose, however, to dwell on the easy perversion and corruptibility of man's morality, but to determine what those core virtues are which —at this stage of psychosocial evolution—need our concerted attention and ethical support; for antimoralists as well as moralists easily overlook the bases in human nature for a strong ethics. As indicated, Fidelity is that virtue and quality of adolescent ego strength which belongs to man's evolutionary heritage, but which—like all the basic virtues—can arise only in the interplay of a life stage with the individuals and the social forces of a true community.

The evidence in young lives of the search for something and somebody to be true to is seen in a variety of pursuits more or less sanctioned by society. It is often hidden in a bewildering combination of shifting devotion and sudden perversity, sometimes more devotedly perverse, sometimes more perversely devoted. Yet, in all youth's seeming shiftiness, a seeking after some durability in change can be detected, whether in the accuracy of scientific and technical method or in the sincerity of conviction; in the veracity of historical and fictional accounts or the fairness of the rules of the game; in the authenticity of artistic production (and the high fidelity of reproduction) or in the genuineness of personalities and the reliability of commitments. This search is easily misunderstood, and often it is only dimly perceived by the individual himself, because youth, always set to grasp both diversity in principle and principle in diversity, must often test extremes before settling on a considered course. These extremes, particularly in times of ideological confusion and widespread marginality of identity, may include not only rebellious but also deviant, delinquent, and self-destructive tendencies. However, all this can be in the nature of a moratorium, a period of delay, in which to test the rock-bottom of some truth before committing the powers of body and mind to a segment of the existing (or a coming) order. "Loyal" and "legal" have the same root, linguistically and psychologically; for legal commitment is an unsafe burden unless shouldered with a sense of sovereign choice and experienced as loyalty. To develop that sense is a joint task of the consistency of individual life history and the ethical potency of the historical process.

Let a great tragic play tell us something of the elemental nature of the crisis man encounters here. If it is a prince's crisis, let us not forget that the "leading families" of heaven and history at one time personified man's pride and tragic failure. Prince Hamlet is in his twenties, some say early, some late. We will say he is in the middle of his third decade, a youth no longer young and about to forfeit his moratorium. We find him in a tragic conflict in which he cannot make the one step demanded simultaneously by his age and his sex, his education, and his historical responsibility.

If we want to make Shakespeare's insight into one of "the ages of man" explicit, we know that such an endeavor seems reprehensible to the students of drama, if undertaken by a trained psychologist. Everybody else (how could he do otherwise?) interprets Shakespeare in the light of some prevailing if naive psychology. I will not try to solve the riddle of Hamlet's inscrutable nature, because his inscrutability is his nature. I feel sufficiently warned by Shakespeare himself, who lets Polonius speak like the caricature of a psychiatrist:

> And I do think—or else this brain of mine
> Hunts not the trail of policy so sure
> As it has us'd to do—that I have found
> The very cause of Hamlet's lunacy.

Hamlet's decision to play insane is a secret which the audience shares with him from the start, without their ever getting rid of the feeling that he is on the verge of slipping into the state he pretends. "His madness," says T. S. Eliot, "is less than madness, and more than feigned."

If Hamlet's madness is more than feigned, it appears to be aggravated at least fivefold: by habitual melancholy, an introverted personality, Danishness, an acute state of mourning, and love. All this makes a regression to the Oedipus complex, postulated by Ernest Jones as the main theme of this as of other great tragedies, entirely plausible.[2] This would mean that Hamlet cannot forgive his mother's recent illegitimate betrayal, because he had not been able as a child to forgive her for having betrayed him quite legitimately with his father; but, at the same time, he is unable to avenge his father's recent murder, because as a child he had himself betrayed him in phantasy and wished him out of the way. Thus he forever postpones—until he ruins the innocent with the guilty—his uncle's execution, which alone would free the ghost of his beloved father from the fate of being,

> doomed for a certain term to walk the night
> and for the day confined to fast in fires.

No audience, however, can escape the feeling that he is a man of superior conscience, advanced beyond the legal concepts of his time, consumed by his own past and by that of his society.

One further suggestion is inescapable, that Hamlet displays some of the playwright's and the actor's personality: for where others lead men and change the course of history, he reflectively moves characters about on the stage (the play within the play); in brief, where others act, he play-acts. And indeed, Hamlet may well stand, historically speaking, for an abortive leader, a still-born rebel.

We shall return to this in another context. In the meantime, all that has been stated can only support a biographic view which concentrates on Hamlet's age and status as a young intellectual of his time: for did he not recently return

---

[2] Ernest Jones, *Hamlet and Oedipus*. New York: Doubleday, Anchor, 1949.

from studies at Wittenberg, the hotbed of humanist corruption, his time's counterpart to Sophist Athens (and today's existentialist centers of learning)?

There are five young men in the play, all Hamlet's age mates, and all sure (or even overdefined) in their identities as dutiful sons, courtiers, and future leaders. But they are all drawn into the moral swamp of infidelity, which seeps into the fiber of all those who owe allegiance to "rotten" Denmark, drawn by the multiple intrigue which Hamlet hopes to defeat with his own intrigue: the play within the play.

Hamlet's world, then is one of diffuse realities and fidelities. Only through the play within the play and through the madness within the insanity, does Hamlet, the actor within the play-actor, reveal the identity within the pretended identities —and the superior fidelity in the fatal pretense.

His estrangement is one of identity diffusion. His estrangement from existence itself is expressed in the famous soliloquy. He is estranged from being human and from being a man: "Man delights me not; no, nor woman either"; and estranged from love and procreation: "I say we will have no more marriage." He is estranged from the ways of his country, "though I am native here and to the manner born"; and much like our "alienated" youth, he is estranged from and describes as "alienated" the overstandardized man of his day, who "only got the tune of time and outward habit of encounter."

Yet Hamlet's single-minded and tragically doomed search for Fidelity breaks through all this. Here is the essence of the historical Hamlet, that ancient model who was a hero on the folk stage for centuries before Shakespeare modernized and eternalized him: [3]

> He was loth to be thought prone to lying about any matter, and wished to be held a stranger to any falsehood; and accordingly he mingled craft and candor in such a wise that, though his words did not lack truth, yet there was nothing to betoken the truth and to betray how far his keenness went.

It accords with the general diffusion of truth in Hamlet that this central theme is announced in the old fool's message to his son:

> Polonius: This above all: to thine own self be true
> And it must follow, as the night the day,
> Thou canst not then be false to any man.

Yet it is also the central theme of Hamlet's most passionate pronouncements, which make his madness but an adjunct to his greatness. He abhors conventional sham, and advocates genuineness of feeling:

> Seems, madam! Nay, it is; I know not "seems."
> 'Tis not alone my inky cloak, good mother,

[3] Saxo Grammaticus, *Danish History*, translated by Elton, 1894 (quoted in Jones, *Hamlet and Oedipus*. New York: Doubleday, Anchor, 1949, pp. 163–164).

> Nor customary suits of solemn black,
> Nor windy suspiration of forc'd breath,
> No, nor the fruitful river in the eye,
> Nor the dejected havior of the visage,
> Together with all forms, moods, shapes of grief
> That can denote me truly. These indeed seem,
> For they are actions that a man might play:
> But I have that within which passes show;
> These but the trappings and the suits of woe.

He searches for what only an elite will really understand—"honest method":

> I heard thee speak me a speech once but it was never
> acted; or, if it was, not above once; for the play I
> remember, pleased not the million ... ! it was (as I
> received it, and others, whose judgments cried in
> the top of mine) an excellent play, well digested
> and in the scenes, set down with as much modesty **and**
> cunning. I remember one said there were no sallets
> in the lines to make the matter savoury, nor no matter
> in the phrase that might indict the author of affection;
> but called it an honest method.

He fanatically insists on purity of form and fidelity of reproduction:

> ... let your discretion be your tutor. Suit the
> action to the word, the word to the action, with this
> special observance, that you o'erstep not the modesty
> of nature; for anything so overdone is from the purpose
> of playing whose end, both at the first and now, was,
> and is to hold, as 'twere, the mirror up to nature,
> to show virtue her own image and the very age and
> body of time his own form and pressure.

And finally, the eager (and overeager) acknowledgment of genuine character in his friend:

> Since my dear soul was mistress of her choice
> And could men distinguish, her election
> Hath sealed thee for herself; for thou hast been
> As one in suffering all, that suffers nothing,
> A man that fortune buffets and rewards
> Hast ta'en with equal thanks; and bless'd are those
> Whose blood and judgement are so co-mingled
> That they are not a pipe for fortune's finger
> To sound what stop she please. Give me that man
> That is nor passion's slave, and I will wear him
> in my heart's core, ay in my heart of heart,
> As I do thee. Something too much of this.

This, then, is the Hamlet within Hamlet. It fits the combined play-actor, the intellectual, the youth, and the neurotic that his words are his better deeds, that he can say clearly what he cannot live, and that his fidelity must bring doom to those he loves: for what he accomplishes at the end is what he tried to avoid, even as he realizes what we would call his negative identity in becoming exactly what his own ethical sense could not tolerate: a mad revenger. Thus do inner reality and historical actuality conspire to deny tragic man the positive identity for which he seems exquisitely chosen. Of course, the audience all along has sensed in Hamlet's very sincerity an element of deadliness. At the end he gives his "dying voice" to his counterplayer on the historical stage, victorious young Fortinbras, who in turn insists on having him,

> ... born like a soldier to the stage
> For he was likely, had he been put on,
> To have prov'd most royal.

The ceremonial fanfares, blaring and hollow, announce the end of this singular youth. He is confirmed by his chosen peers, with the royal insignia of his birth. A special person, intensely human, is buried—a member of his special kind.

To be a special kind, we have said, is an important element in the human need for personal and collective identities—all, in a sense, pseudospecies. They have found a transitory fulfillment in man's greatest moments of cultural identity and civilized perfection, and each such tradition of identity and perfection has high-lighted what man could be, could he be all these at one time. The utopia of our own era predicts that man will be one species in one world, with a universal identity to replace the illusory superidentities which have divided him, and with an international ethics replacing all moral systems of superstition, repression, and suppression. Whatever the political arrangement that will further this utopia, we can only point to the schedule of human strengths which potentially emerge with the stages of life and indicate their interdependence on the structure of com-munal life. In youth, ego strength emerges from the mutual confirmation of in-dividual and community, in the sense that society recognizes the young individual as a bearer of fresh energy and that the individual so confirmed recognizes society as a living process which inspires loyalty as it receives it, maintains allegiance as it attracts it, honors confidence as it demands it.

Let us go back, then, to the origins of that combination of drivenness and dis-ciplined energy, of irrationality and courageous capability which belong to the best discussed and the most puzzling phenomena of the life cycle. The puzzle, we must grant throughout, is in the essence of the phenomenon. For the unity of the personality must be unique to be united, and the functioning of each new generation unpredictable to fulfill its function.

Of the three sources of new energy, physical growth is the most easily measured and systematically exercised, although its contribution to the aggressive drives is little understood. The youthful powers of comprehension and cognition can be experimentally studied and with planning applied to apprenticeship and study, but their relation to ideological imagination is less well known. Finally, the long delayed genital maturation is a source of untold energy, but also of a drivenness accompanied by intrinsic frustration.

When maturing in his physical capacity for procreation, the human youth is as yet unable to love in that binding manner which only two identities can offer each other; nor to care consistently enough to sustain parenthood. The two sexes, of course, differ greatly in these respects, and so do individuals, while societies provide different opportunities and sanctions within which individuals must fend for their potentials—and for their potency. But what I have called a psychosocial moratorium, of some form and duration between the advent of genital maturity and the onset of responsible adulthood, seems to be built into the schedule of human development. Like all the moratoria in man's developmental schedules, the delay of adulthood can be prolonged and intensified to a forceful and a fateful degree; thus it accounts for very special human achievements and also for the very special weaknesses in such achievements. For, whatever the partial satisfactions and partial abstinences that characterize premarital sex life in various cultures—whether the pleasure and pride of forceful genital activity without commitment, or of erotic states without genital consummation, or of disciplined and devoted delay—ego development uses the psychosexual powers of adolescence for enhancing a sense of style and identity. Here, too, man is never an animal: even where a society furthers the genital closeness of the sexes, it does so in a stylized manner. On the other hand, the sex act, biologically speaking, is the procreative act, and there is an element of psychobiological dissatisfaction in any sexual situation not favorable in the long run to procreative consummation and care—a dissatisfaction which can be tolerated by otherwise healthy people, as all partial abstinences can be borne: for a certain period, under conditions otherwise favorable to the aims of identity formation. In the woman, no doubt, this dissatisfaction plays a much greater role, owing to her deeper engagement, physiologically and emotionally, in the sex act as the first step in a procreative commitment of which her monthly cycle is a regular bodily and emotive reminder.

The various hindrances to a full consummation of adolescent genital maturation have many deep consequences for man which pose an important problem for future planning. Best known is the regressive revival of that earlier stage of psychosexuality which preceded even the emotionally quiet first school years, that is, the infantile genital and locomotor stage, with its tendency toward auto-erotic manipulation, grandiose phantasy, and vigorous play.[4] But in youth, auto-

---

[4] The classical psychoanalytic works concerned with psychosexuality and the ego defenses of youth are: Sigmund Freud, *Three Essays on the Theory of Sexuality,* standard edition (London, The Hogarth Press, 1953), vol. 7; and Anna Freud, *The Ego and the Mechanisms of Defence,* New York, International Universities Press, 1946. For the writer's views, see his *Childhood and Society.* New York: W. W. Norton, 1950.

erotism, grandiosity, and playfulness are all immensely amplified by genital potency and locomotor maturation, and are vastly complicated by what we will presently describe as the youthful mind's new historical perspective.

The most widespread expression of the discontented search of youth is the craving for locomotion, whether expressed in a general "being on the go," "tearing after something," or "running around"; or in locomotion proper, as in vigorous work, in absorbing sports, in rapt dancing, in shiftless *Wanderschaft*, and in the employment and misuse of speedy animals and machines. But it also finds expression through participation in the movements of the day (whether the riots of a local commotion or the parades and campaigns of major ideological forces), if they only appeal to the need for feeling "moved" and for feeling essential in moving something along toward an open future. It is clear that societies offer any number of ritual combinations of ideological perspective and vigorous movement (dance, sports, parades, demonstrations, riots) to harness youth in the service of their historical aims; and that where societies fail to do so, these patterns will seek their own combinations, in small groups occupied with serious games, good-natured foolishness, cruel prankishness, and delinquent warfare. In no other stage of the life cycle, then, are the promise of finding oneself and the threat of losing oneself so closely allied.

In connection with locomotion, we must mention two great industrial developments: the motor engine and the motion picture. The motor engine, of course, is the very heart and symbol of our technology and its mastery, the aim and aspiration of much of modern youth. In connection with immature youth, however, it must be understood that both motor car and motion pictures offer to those so inclined passive locomotion with an intoxicating delusion of being intensely active. The prevalence of car thefts and motor accidents among juveniles is much decried (although it is taking the public a long time to understand that a theft is an appropriation for the sake of gainful possession), while automobiles more often than not are stolen by the young in search of a kind of automotive intoxication, which may literally run away with car and youngster. Yet, while vastly inflating a sense of motor omnipotence, the need for active locomotion often remains unfulfilled. Motion pictures especially offer the onlooker, who sits, as it were, with the engine of his emotions racing, fast and furious motion in an artificially widened visual field, interspersed with close-ups of violence and sexual possession—and all this without making the slightest demand on intelligence, imagination, or effort. I am pointing here to a widespread imbalance in adolescent experience, because I think it explains new kinds of adolescent outbursts and points to new necessities of mastery. The danger involved is greatly balanced in that part of youth which can take active charge of technical development, manages to learn, and to identify with the ingeniousness of invention, the improvement of production and the care of machinery, and is thus offered a new and unlimited application of youthful capacities. Where youth is underprivileged in such technical experience, it must explode in riotous motion; where it is ungifted, it will feel estranged from the modern world, until technology and nontechnical intelligence have come to a certain convergence.

The cognitive gifts developing during the first half of the second decade add a powerful tool to the tasks of youth. J. Piaget calls the gains in cognition made toward the middle teens, the achievement of "formal operations." [5] This means that the youth can now operate on hypothetical propositions, can think of possible variable and potential relations, and think of them in thought alone, independent of certain concrete checks previously necessary. As Jerome S. Bruner puts it, the child now can "conjure up systematically the full range of alternative possibilities that could exist at any given time." [6] Such cognitive orientation forms not a contrast but a complement to the need of the young person to develop a sense of identity, for, from among all possible and imaginable relations, he must make a series of ever narrowing selections of personal, occupational, sexual, and ideological commitments.

Here again diversity and fidelity are polarized: they make each other significant and keep each other alive. Fidelity without a sense of diversity can become an obsession and a bore; diversity without a sense of fidelity, an empty relativism.

The sense of ego identity, then, becomes more necessary (and more problematical) wherever a wide range of possible identities is envisaged. Identity is a term used in our day with faddish ease; at this point, I can only indicate how very complicated the real article is.[7] For ego identity is partially conscious and largely unconscious. It is a psychological process reflecting social processes; but with sociological means it can be seen as a social process reflecting psychological processes; it meets its crisis in adolescence, but has grown throughout childhood and continued to re-emerge in the crises of later years. The overriding meaning of it all, then, is the creation of a sense of sameness, a unity of personality now felt by the individual and recognized by others as having consistency in time— of being, as it were, an irreversible historical fact.

The prime danger of this age, therefore, is identity confusion, which can express itself in excessively prolonged moratoria (Hamlet offers an exalted example); in repeated impulsive attempts to end the moratorium with sudden choices, that is, to play with historical possibilities, and then to deny that some irreversible commitment has already taken place; and sometimes also in severe regressive pathology, which we will illustrate presently. The dominant issue of this, as of any other stage, therefore, is that of the active, the selective, ego being in charge and being enabled to be in charge by a social structure which grants a given age group the place it needs—and in which it is needed.

In a letter to Oliver Wendell Holmes, William James speaks of wanting to "rebaptize himself" in their friendship—and this one word says much of what is involved in the radical direction of the social awareness and the social needs of youth. From the middle of the second decade, the capacity to think and the

---

[5] B. Inhelder and J. Piaget, *The Growth of Logical Thinking from Childhood to Adolescence*. New York: Basic Books, 1958.

[6] Jerome S. Bruner, *The Process of Education*. Cambridge: Harvard University Press, 1960.

[7] See the writer's "The Problem of Ego-Identity" in *Identity and the Life Cycle: Psychological Issues* (New York: International Universities Press, 1959), vol. I, no. 1.

power to imagine reach beyond the persons and personalities in which youth can immerse itself so deeply. Youth loves and hates in people what they "stand for" and chooses them for a significant encounter involving issues that often, indeed, are bigger than you and I. We have heard Hamlet's declaration of love to his friend Horatio, a declaration quickly broken off—"something too much here." It is a new reality, then, for which the individual wishes to be reborn, with and by those whom he chooses as his new ancestors and his genuine contemporaries.

This mutual selection, while frequently associated with, and therefore, interpreted as a rebellion against or withdrawal from, the childhood environment, is an expression of a truly new perspective which I have already called "historical"—in one of those loose uses of an ancient overspecialized word which sometimes become necessary in making new meanings specific. I mean by "historical perspective" something which every human being newly develops during adolescence. It is a sense of the irreversibility of significant events and an often urgent need to understand fully and quickly what kind of happenings in reality and in thought determine others, and why. As we have seen, psychologists such as Piaget recognize in youth the capacity to appreciate that any process can be understood when it is retraced in its steps and thus reversed in thought. Yet it is no contradiction to say that he who comes to understand such a reversal also realizes that in reality, among all the events that can be thought of, a few will determine and narrow one another with historical fatality, whether (in the human instance) deservedly or undeservedly, intentionally or unintentionally.

Youth, therefore, is sensitive to any suggestion that it may be hopelessly determined by what went before in life histories or in history. Psychosocially speaking, this would mean that irreversible childhood identifications would deprive an individual of an identity of his own; historically, that invested powers should prevent a group from realizing its composite historical identity. For these reasons, youth often rejects parents and authorities and wishes to belittle them as inconsequential; it is in search of individuals and movements who claim, or seem to claim, that they can predict what is irreversible, thus getting ahead of the future—which means, reversing it. This in turn accounts for the acceptance by youth of mythologies and ideologies predicting the course of the universe or the historical trend; for even intelligent and practical youth can be glad to have the larger framework settled, so that it can devote itself to the details which it can manage, once it knows (or is convincingly told) what they stand for and where it stands. Thus, "true" ideologies are verified by history—for a time; for if they can inspire youth, youth will make the predicted history come more than true.

By pointing to what, in the mind of youth, people "stand for," I did not mean to overemphasize the ideological explicitness in the meaning of individuals to youth. The selection of meaningful individuals can take place in the framework of pointed practicalities such as schooling or job selection, as well as in religious and ideological fellowship; while the methods of selection can range from banal amenity and enmity to dangerous play with the borderlines of sanity and legality. But the occasions have in common a mutual sizing up and a mutual plea for being recognized as individuals who can be more than they seem to be, and whose potentials are needed by the order that is or will be. The representatives of the adult world thus involved may be advocates and practitioners of technical accuracy, of a method of scientific inquiry, of a convincing rendition of truth, of a code of fairness, of a standard of artistic veracity, or of a way of personal genuineness. They become representatives of an elite in the eyes of the young, quite independently of whether or not they are also viewed thus in the eyes of the family, the public, or the police. The choice can be dangerous, but to some youths the danger is a necessary ingredient of the experiment. Elemental things are dangerous; and if youth could not overcommit itself to danger, it could not commit itself to the survival of genuine values—one of the primary steering mechanism of psychosocial evolution. The elemental fact is that only when fidelity has found its field of manifestation is the human as good as, say, the nestling in nature, which is ready to rely on its own wings and to take its adult place in the ecological order.

If in human adolescence this field of manifestation is alternately one of devoted conformism and of extreme deviancy, of rededication and of rebellion, we must remember the necessity for man to react (and to react most intensively in his youth) to the diversity of conditions. In the setting of psychosocial evolution, we can ascribe a long-range meaning to the idiosyncratic individualist and to the rebel as well as to the conformist, albeit under different historical conditions. For healthy individualism and devoted deviancy contain an indignation in the service of a wholeness that is to be restored, without which psychosocial evolution would be doomed. Thus, human adaptation has its loyal deviants, its rebels, who refuse to adjust to what so often is called, with an apologetic and fatalistic misuse of a once good phrase, "the human condition."

Loyal deviancy and identity formation in extraordinary individuals are often associated with neurotic and psychotic symptoms, or at least with a prolonged moratorium of relative isolation, in which all the estrangements of adolescence are suffered. In *Young Man Luther* I have attempted to put the suffering of a great young man into the context of his greatness and his historic position.[8]

It is not our purpose, however, to discuss what to many youths is the most urgent question, and yet to us the most difficult to answer, namely, the relation of special giftedness and neurosis; rather, we must characterize the specific nature of adolescent psychopathology, or, even more narrowly, indicate the relevance of the issue of fidelity to the psychopathology of youth.

In the classical case of this age group, Freud's first published encounter with an eighteen-year-old girl suffering from *"petite hysterie* with the commonest of all ... symptoms,"* it is interesting to recall that at the end of treatment Freud

---

[8] *Young Man Luther.* New York: W. W. Norton, 1958; London: Faber and Faber, 1959.

was puzzled as to "what kind of help" the girl wanted from him. He had communicated to her his interpretation of the structure of her neurotic disorder, an interpretation which became the central theme of his classical publication on the psychosexual factors in the development of hysteria.[9] Freud's clinical reports, however, remain astonishingly fresh over the decades, and today his case history clearly reveals the psychosocial centering of the girl's story in matters of fidelity. In fact, one might say, without seriously overdoing it, that three words characterize her social history: sexual infidelity on the part of some of the most important adults in her life; the perfidy of her father's denial of his friend's sexual acts, which were in fact the precipitating cause of the girl's illness; and a strange tendency on the part of all the adults around the girl to make her a confidante in any number of matters, without having enough confidence in her to acknowledge the truths relevant to her illness.

Freud, of course, focused on other matters, opening up, with the concentration of a psychosurgeon, the symbolic meaning of her symptoms and their history; but, as always, he reported relevant data on the periphery of his interests. Thus, among the matters which somewhat puzzled him, he reports that the patient was "almost beside herself at the idea of it being supposed that she had merely fancied" the conditions which had made her sick; and that she was kept "anxiously trying to make sure whether I was being quite straightforward with her—or perfidious like her father. When at the end she left analyst and analysis "in order to confront the adults around her with the secrets she knew," Freud considered this an act of revenge on them, and on him; and within the outlines of his interpretation, this partial interpretation stands. Nevertheless, as we can now see, there was more to this insistence on the historical truth than the denial of an inner truth—and this especially in an adolescent. For, the question as to what confirms them irreversibly as a truthful or a cheating, a sick or a rebellious type is paramount in the minds of adolescents; and the further question, whether or not they were right in not accepting the conditions which made them sick, is as important to them as the insight into the structure of their sickness can ever be. In other words, they insist that the meaning of their sickness find recognition within a reformulation of the historical truth as revealed in their own insights and distortions, and not according to the terms of the environment which wishes them to be "brought to reason" (as Dora's father had put it, when he brought her to Freud).

No doubt, Dora by then was a hysteric, and the meaning of her symptoms was psychosexual; but the sexual nature of her disturbance and of the precipitating events should not blind us to the fact that other perfidies, familial and communal, cause adolescents to regress in a variety of ways to a variety of earlier stages.

Only when adolescence is reached does the capacity for such clear regression and symptom formation occur: only when the historical function of the mind is

[9] Sigmund Freud, *Fragment of an Analysis of a Case of Hysteria,* standard edition (London: The Hogarth Press, 1953), vol. 7.

consolidated can significant repressions become marked enough to cause consistent symptom formation and deformation of character. The depth of regression determines the nature of the pathology and points to the therapy to be employed. However, there is a pathognomic picture which all sick youth have in common and which is clearly discernible in Freud's description of Dora's total state. This picture is characterized first of all by a denial of the historical flux of time, and by an attempt to challenge retrospectively, while retesting in the present all parental premises before new trust is invested in the (emancipated) future.

The sick adolescent thus gradually stops extending experimental feelers toward the future; his moratorium of illness becomes an end in itself and thus ceases to be a moratorium (Dora suffered from a "taedium vitae which was probably not entirely genuine," Freud wrote). It is for this reason that death and suicide can be at this time such a spurious preoccupation—one leading unpredictably to suicide (and to murder)—for death would conclude the life history before it joins others in inexorable commitment. (Dora's parents found "a letter in which she took leave of them because she could no longer endure life. Her father . . . guessed that the girl had no serious suicidal intentions.") There is also a social isolation which excludes all sense of solidarity and can lead to a snobbish isolation which finds companions but no friends (Dora "tried to avoid social intercourse," was "distant" and "unfriendly"). The energy of repudiation which accompanies the first steps of an identity formation (and in some youngsters can lead to the sudden impulse to annihilate) is in neurotics turned against the self ("Dora was satisfied neither with herself nor with her family").

A repudiated self in turn cannot offer loyalty, and, of course, fears the fusion of love or of sexual encounters. The work inhibition often connected with this picture (Dora suffered from "fatigue and lack of concentration") is really a career inhibition, in the sense that every exertion of skill or method is suspected of binding the individual to the role and the status suggested by the activity; thus, again, any moratorium is spoiled. Where fragmentary identities are formed, they are highly self-conscious and are immediately put to a test (thus Dora obviously defeated her wish to be a woman intellectual). This identity consciousness is a strange mixture of superiority, almost a megalomania ("I am a majority of one," one of my patients said), with which the patient tries to convince himself that he is really too good for his community or his period of history, while he is equally convinced of being nobody.

We have sketched the most obvious social symptoms of adolescent psychopathology, in part to indicate that, besides the complicated structure of specific symptoms, there is in the picture presented of each stage an expression of the dominant psychosocial issue, so open that one sometimes wonders whether the patient lies by telling the simple truth or tells the truth when he seems most obviously to lie.

The sketch presented, however, also serves as a comparison of the isolated adolescent sufferer with those youths who try to solve their doubt in their elders by joining deviant cliques and gangs. Freud found that "psychoneuroses are, so to speak, the negative of perversions,"[10] which means that neurotics suffer under the repression of tendencies which perverts try to "live out." This has a counterpart in the fact that isolated sufferers try to solve by withdrawal what the joiners of deviant cliques and gangs attempt to solve by conspiracy.

If we now turn to this form of adolescent pathology, the denial of the irreversibility of historical time appears to be expressed in a clique's or a gang's delusion of being an organization with a tradition and an ethics all its own. The pseudo-historical character of such societies is expressed in such names as "The Navahos," "The Saints," or "The Edwardians"; while their provocation is countered by society (remember the Pachucos of the war years) with a mixture of impotent rage wherever murderous excess does actually occur, and with a phobic overconcern followed by vicious suppression wherever these "secret societies" are really no more than fads lacking any organized purpose. Their pseudo-societal character reveals itself in their social parasitism, and their pseudo-rebellion in the conformism actually governing their habits. Yet the seemingly unassailable inner sense of callous rightness is no doubt due to an inner realignment of motivations, which can best be understood by briefly comparing the torment of the isolated youngster with the temporary gains derived by the joiner from the mere fact that he has been taken into a pseudo-society. The time diffusion attending the isolate's inability to envisage a career is "cured" by his attention to "jobs"—theft, destruction, fights, murder, or acts of perversion or addiction, conceived on the spur of the moment and executed forthwith. This "job" orientation also takes care of the work inhibition, because the clique and the gang are always "busy," even if they just "hang around." Their lack of any readiness to wince under shaming or accusation is often considered the mark of a total personal perdition, while in fact it is a trademark, an insignia of the "species" to which the youngster (mostly marginal in economic and ethnic respects) would rather belong than to a society which is eager to confirm him as a criminal and then promises to rehabilitate him as an ex-criminal.

As to the isolate's tortured feelings of bisexuality or of an immature need for love, the young joiner in social pathology, by joining, has made a clear decision: he is male with a vengeance, she, a female without sentimentality; or they are both perverts. In either case, they can eliminate the procreative function of genitality together and can make a pseudo-culture of what is left. By the same token, they will acknowledge authority only in the form chosen in the act of joining, repudiating the rest of the social world, where the isolate repudiates existence as such and, with it, himself.

The importance of these comparative considerations, which have been stated in greater detail elsewhere, lies in the impotent craving of the isolated sufferer to be true to himself, and in that of the joiner, to be true to a group and to its insignia and codes. By this I do not mean to deny that the one is sick (as his physical and mental symptoms attest), nor that the other can be on the way

---

[10] Sigmund Freud, *Fragment of an Analysis of a Case of Hysteria*, standard edition (London: The Hogarth Press, 1953), vol. 7.

to becoming a criminal, as his more and more irreversible acts and choices attest. Both theory and therapy, however, lack the poper leverage, if the need for (receiving and giving) fidelity is not understood, and especially if instead the young deviant is confirmed by every act of the correctional or therapeutic authorities as a future criminal or a life-long patient.

In Dora's case, I have tried to indicate the phenomenology of this need. As to young delinquents, I can only quote again one of those rare newspaper reports which convey enough of a story to show the elements involved. Kai T. Erikson and I have used this example as an introduction to our article, "The Confirmation of the Delinquent." [11]

JUDGE IMPOSES ROAD GANG TERM FOR BACK TALK

Wilmington, N.D. (UP)—A "smart alecky" youth who wore pegged trousers and a flattop haircut began six months on a road gang today for talking back to the wrong judge.

Michael A. Jones, 20, of Wilmington, was fined $25 and costs in Judge Edwin Jay Roberts Jr.'s superior court for reckless operation of an automobile. But he just didn't leave well enough alone.

"I understand how it was, with your pegged trousers and flattop haircut," Roberts said in assessing the fine. "You go on like this and I predict in five years you'll be in prison."

When Jones walked over to pay his fine, he overheard Probation Officer Gideon Smith tell the judge how much trouble the "smart alecky" young offender had been.

"I just want you to know I'm not a thief," interrupted Jones to the judge.

The judge's voice boomed to the court clerk: "Change that judgment to six months on the roads."

I quote the story here to add the interpretation that the judge in this case (neither judge nor case differs from a host of others) took as an affront to the dignity of authority what may have also been a desperate "historical" denial, an attempt to claim that a truly antisocial identity had not yet been formed, and that there was enough discrimination and potential fidelity left to be made something of by somebody who cared to do so. But instead, what the young man and the judge made of it was likely, of course, to seal the irreversibility and confirm the doom. I say "was likely to," because I do not know what happened in this case; we do know, however, the high recidivity of criminality in the young who, during the years of identity formation, are forced by society into intimate contact with criminals.

Finally, it cannot be overlooked that at times political undergrounds of all kinds can and do make use of the need for fidelity as well as the store of wrath in those deprived in their need by their families or their societies. Here social rejuvenation can make use of and redeem social pathology, even as in individuals special giftedness can be related to and redeem neurosis. These are

[11] Erik H. Erikson and Kai T. Erikson, "The Confirmation of the Delinquent," *The Chicago Review*, Winter 1957, 10:15–23.

matters too weighty to be discussed briefly and, at any rate, our concern has been with the fact that the psychopathology of youth suggests a consideration of the same issues which we found operative in the evolutionary and developmental aspects of this stage of life.

To summarize: Fidelity, when fully matured, is the strength of disciplined devotion. It is gained in the involvement of youth in such experiences as reveal the essence of the era they are to join—as the beneficiaries of its tradition, as the practitioners and innovators of its technology, as renewers of its ethical strength, as rebels bent on the destruction of the outlived, and as deviants with deviant commitments. This, at least, is the potential of youth in psychosocial evolution; and while this may sound like a rationalization endorsing any high-sounding self-delusion in youth, any self-indulgence masquerading as devotion, or any righteous excuse for blind destruction, it makes intelligible the tremendous waste attending this as any other mechanism of human adaptation, especially if its excesses meet with more moral condemnation than ethical guidance. On the other hand, our understanding of these processes is not furthered by the "clinical" reduction of adolescent phenomena to their infantile antecedents and to an underlying dichotomy of drive and conscience. Adolescent development comprises a new set of identification processes, both with significant persons and with ideological forces, which give importance to individual life by relating it to a living community and to ongoing history, and by counterpointing the newly won individual identity with some communal solidarity.

In youth, then, the life history intersects with history: here individuals are confirmed in their identities, societies regenerated in their life style. This process also implies a fateful survival of adolescent modes of thinking in man's historical and ideological perspectives.

Historical processes, of course, have already entered the individual's core in childhood. Both ideal and evil images and the moral prototypes guiding parental administrations originate in the past struggles of contending cultural and national "species," which also color fairytale and family lore, superstition and gossip, and the simple lessons of early verbal training. Historians on the whole make little of this; they describe the visible emergence and the contest of autonomous historical ideas, unconcerned with the fact that these ideas reach down into the lives of generations and re-emerge through the daily awakening and training of historical consciousness in young individuals.

It is youth, then, which begins to develop that sense of historical irreversibility which can lead to what we may call acute historical estrangement. This lies behind the fervent quest for a sure meaning in individual life history and in collective history, and behind the questioning of the laws of relevancy which bind datum and principle, event and movement. But it is also, alas, behind the bland carelessness of that youth which denies its own vital need to develop and cultivate a historical consciousness—and conscience.

To enter history, each generation of youth must find an identity consonant with its own childhood and consonant with an ideological promise in the perceptible historical process. But in youth the tables of childhood dependence begin slowly to turn: no longer is it merely for the old to teach the young the meaning of life, whether individual or collective. It is the young who, by their responses and actions, tell the old whether life as represented by the old and as presented to the young has meaning; and it is the young who carry in them the power to confirm those who confirm them and, joining the issues, to renew and to regenerate, or to reform and to rebel.

I will not at this point review the institutions which participate in creating the retrospective and the prospective mythology offering historical orientation to youth: obviously, the mythmakers of religion and politics, the arts and the sciences, the stage and fiction—all contribute to the historical logic preached to youth more or less consciously, more or less responsibly. And today we must add, at least in the United States, psychiatry; and all over the world, the press, which forces leaders to make history in the open and to accept reportorial distortion as a major historical factor.

I have spoken of Hamlet as an abortive ideological leader. His drama combines all the elements of which successful ideological leaders are made: they are the postadolescents who make out of the very contradictions of adolescence the polarities of their charisma. Individuals with an uncommon depth of conflict, they also have uncanny gifts, and often uncanny luck with which they offer to the crisis of a generation the solution of their own crisis—always, as Woodrow Wilson put it, being "in love with activity on a large scale," always feeling that their one life must be made to count in the lives of all, always convinced that what they felt as adolescents was a curse, a fall, an earthquake, a thunderbolt, in short, a revelation to be shared with their generation and with many to come. Their humble claim to being chosen does not preclude a wish to universal power. "Fifty years from now," wrote Kierkegaard in the journal of his spiritual soliloquy, "the whole world will read my diary." He sensed, no doubt, that the impending dominance of mass ideologies would bring to the fore his cure for the individual soul, existentialism. We must study the question (I have approached it in my study of young Luther) of what ideological leaders do to history—whether they first aspire to power and then face spiritual qualms, or first face spiritual perdition and then seek universal influence. Their answers often manage to subsume under the heading of a more embracing identity all that ails man, especially young man, at critical times: danger from new weapons and from natural forces aggravated by man's misuse of nature; anxiety from sources within the life-history typical for the time; and existential dread of the ego's limitations, magnified in times of disintegrating superidentities and intensified in adolescence.

But does it not take a special and, come to think of it, a strange sense of calling, to dare and to care to give such inclusive answers? Is it not probable and in fact demonstrable that among the most passionate ideologists there are unreconstructed adolescents, transmitting to their ideas the proud moment of their transient ego recovery, of their temporary victory over the forces of existence and history, but also the pathology of their deepest isolation, the defensiveness of their forever adolescing egos—and their fear of the calm of adulthood? "To live beyond forty," says Dostoevsky's underground diarist, "is bad taste." It warrants study, both historical and psychological, to see how some of the most influential leaders have turned away from parenthood, only to despair in middle age of the issue of their leadership as well.

It is clear that today the ideological needs of all but intellectual youth of the humanist tradition are beginning to be taken care of by a subordination of ideology to technology: what works, on the grandest scale, is good. It is to be hoped that the worst implications of this trend have outlived themselves already in fascism. Yet, in the technological superidentity, the American dream and the Marxist revolution also meet. If their competition can be halted before mutual annihilation, it is just possible that a new mankind, seeing that it can now build and destroy anything it wishes, will focus its intelligence (feminine as well as masculine) on the ethical question concerning the workings of human generations—beyond products, powers, and ideas. Ideologies in the past have contained an ethical corrective, but ethics must eventually transcend ideology as well as technology: the great question will be and already is, what man, on ethical grounds and without moralistic self-destruction, must decide *not* to do, even though he could make it work—for a while.

Moralities sooner or later outlive themselves, ethics never: this is what the need for identity and for fidelity, reborn with each generation, seems to point to. Morality in the moralistic sense can be shown by modern means of inquiry to be predicated on superstitions and irrational inner mechanisms which ever again undermine the ethical fiber of generations; but morality is expendable only where ethics prevail. This is the wisdom that the words of many languages have tried to tell man. He has tenaciously clung to the words, even though he has understood them only vaguely, and in his actions has disregarded or perverted them completely. But there is much in ancient wisdom which can now become knowledge.

As in the near future peoples of different tribal and national pasts join what must become the identity of one mankind, they can find an initial common language only in workings of science and technology. This in turn may well help them to make transparent the superstitions of their traditional moralities and may even permit them to advance rapidly through a historical period during which they must put a vain superidentity of neonationalism in the place of their much exploited historical identity weakness. But they must also look beyond the major ideologies of the now "established" world, offered them as ceremonial masks to frighten and to attract them. The overriding issue is the creation not of a new ideology but of a universal ethics growing out of a universal technological civilization. This can be advanced only by men and women who are neither ideological youths nor moralistic old men, but who know that from generation to generation the test of what you produce is in the *care* it inspires. If there is any chance at all, it is in a world more challenging, more workable, and more venerable than all myths, retrospective or prospective: it is in historical reality, at last ethically cared for.

3 A CULTURAL PHENOMENON

In addition to its meaning for the individual, adolescence carries a social significance. Here, a sociologist examines characteristics of a culture that encourage a lessening of traditional kinship ties and a corresponding increase in new cultural subgroupings along age lines. Drawing from what is known of youth in other cultures, the author characterizes contemporary American adolescents as a strong and potentially influential subgroup in the modern technological welfare state.

S. N. Eisenstadt

Archetypal Patterns of Youth

. . . .

The transition from childhood and adolescence to adulthood, the development of personal identity, psychological autonomy and self-regulation, the attempt to link personal temporal transition to general cultural images and to cosmic rhythms, and to link psychological maturity to the emulation of definite role models—these constitute the basic elements of any archetypal image of youth. However, the ways in which these various elements become crystallized in concrete configurations differ greatly from society to society and within sectors of the same society. The full dramatic articulation of these elements in the *rites de passage* of primitive societies constitutes only one—perhaps the most extreme and articulate but certainly not the only—configuration of these archetypal elements of youth.

In order to understand other types of such configurations, it is necessary to analyze some conditions that influence their development. Perhaps the best starting point is the nature of the social organization of the period of adolescence: the process of transition from childhood to adulthood, the social context in which the process of growing up is shaped and structured. There are two major criteria that shape the social organization of the period of youth. One is the extent to which age in general and youth in particular form a criterion for the allocation of roles in a society, whether in politics, in economic or cultural activity—aside from the family, of course, in which they always serve as such a criterion. The second is the extent to which any society develops specific age groups, specific corporate organizations, composed of members of the same "age," such as youth movements or old men's clubs. If roles are allocated in a society according to age, this greatly influences the extent to which age constitutes a component of a person's identity. In such cases, youth becomes a definite and meaningful phase of transition in an individual's progress through life, and his budding self-identity acquires content and a relation to role models and cultural values. No less important to the concrete development of identity is the extent to which it is influenced, either by the common participation of different generations in the same group as in the family, or conversely by the organization of members of the same age groups into specific, distinct groups.

The importance of age as a criterion for allocating roles in a society is closely related to several major aspects of social organization and cultural orientation. The first aspect is the relative complexity of the division of labor. In general, the simpler the organization of the society, the more influential age will be as a criterion for allocating roles. Therefore, in primitive or traditional societies (or in the more primitive and traditional sectors of developed societies) age and seniority constitute basic criteria for allocating social, economic, and political roles.

The second aspect consists of the major value orientations and symbols of a society, especially the extent to which they emphasize certain general orientations, qualities, or types of activity (such as physical vigor, the maintenance of cultural tradition, the achievement and maintenance of supernatural prowess) which can be defined in terms of broad human qualities and which become expressed and symbolized in specific ages.

The emphasis on any particular age as a criterion for the allocation of roles is largely related to the concrete application of the major value orientations in a society. For instance, we find that those primitive societies in which military values and orientations prevail emphasize young adulthood as the most important age, while those in which sedentary activities prevail emphasize older age. Similarly, within some traditional societies, a particular period such as old age may be emphasized if it is seen as the most appropriate one for expressing major cultural values and symbols—for instance, the upholding of a given cultural tradition.

The social and cultural conditions that determine the extent to which specific age groups and youth groups develop differ from the conditions that determine the extent to which age serves as a criterion for the allocation of roles. At the same time, the two kinds of conditions may be closely related, as we shall see.

Age groups in general and youth groups in particular tend to arise in those societies in which the family or kinship unit cannot ensure (it may even impede) the attainment of full social status on the part of its members. These conditions appear especially (although not uniquely[1]) in societies in which family or kinship groups do not constitute the basic unit of the social division of labor. Several features characterize such societies. First, the membership in the total society (citizenship) is not defined in terms of belonging to any such family, kinship group, or estate, nor is it mediated by such a group.

Second, in these societies the major political, economic, social, and religious functions are performed not by family or kinship unit but rather by various specialized groups (political parties, occupational associations, etc.), which individuals may join irrespective of their family, kinship, or caste. In these societies, therefore, the major roles that adults are expected to perform in the wider society differ in orientation from those of the family or kinship group. The children's identification and close interaction with family members of other ages does not assure the attainment of full self-identity and social maturity on the part of the children. In these cases, there arises a tendency for peer groups to form, especially youth groups; these can serve as a transitory phase between the world of childhood and the adult world.

This type of social division of labor is found in varying degrees in different societies, primitive, historical, or modern. In several primitive tribes such a division of labor has existed,[2] for example, in Africa, among the chiefless (segmentary) tribes of Nandi, Masai, or Kipigis, in the village communities of Yako and Ibo, or in more centralized kingdoms of the Zulu and Swazi, and among some of the Indian tribes of the Plains, as well as among some South American and Indian tribes.

Such a division of labor likewise existed to some extent in several historical societies (especially in city states such as Athens or Rome), although most great historical civilizations were characterized mainly by a more hierarchical and ascriptive system of the division of labor, in which there were greater continuity and harmony between the family and kinship groups and the broader institutional contexts. The fullest development of this type of the social division of labor, however, is to be found in modern industrial societies. Their inclusive membership is usually based on the universal criterion of citizenship and is not conditioned by membership in any kinship group. In these societies, the family does not constitute a basic unit of the division of labor, especially not in production and distribution, and even in the sphere of consumption its functions become more limited. Occupations are not transmitted through heredity. Similarly, the family or kinship group does not constitute a basic unit of political or ritual activities. Moreover, the general scope of the activities of the family has been

---

[1] A special type of age groups may also develop in familistic societies. See S. N. Eisenstadt, *From Generation to Generation*, Chicago: The Free Press of Glencoe, Illinois, 1956 (ref. 1) chapter 5.

[2] For fuller details, see S. N. Eisenstadt, *From Generation to Generation*, especially chapters 3 and 4.

continuously diminishing, while various specialized agencies tend to take over its functions in the fields of education and recreation.

To be sure, the extent to which the family is diminishing in modern societies is often exaggerated. In many social spheres (neighborhood, friendship, informal association, some class relations, community relations), family, kinship, and status are still very influential. But the scope of these relations is more limited in modern societies than in many others, even if the prevalent myth of the disappearance of the family has long since been exploded. The major social developments of the nineteenth century (the establishment of national states, the progress of the industrial revolution, the great waves of intercontinental migrations) have greatly contributed to this diminution of scope, and especially in the first phase of modernization there has been a growing discontinuity between the life of the children, whether in the family or the traditional school and in the social world with its new and enlarged perspectives.

Youth groups tend to develop in all societies in which such a division of labor exists. Youth's tendency to coalesce in such groups is rooted in the fact that participation in the family became insufficient for developing full identity or full social maturity, and that the roles learned in the family did not constitute an adequate basis for developing such identity and participation. In the youth groups the adolescent seeks some framework for the development and crystallization of his identity, for the attainment of personal autonomy, and for his effective transition into the adult world.

Various types of youth organizations always tend to appear with the transition from traditional or feudal societies to modern societies, along with the intensified processes of change, especially in periods of rapid mobility, migration, urbanization, and industrialization. This is true of all European societies, and also of non-Western societies. The impact of Western civilization on primitive and historical-traditional peoples is usually connected with the disruption of family life, but beyond this it also involves a change in the mutual evaluation of the different generations. The younger generation usually begin to seek a new self-identification, and in one phase or another this search is expressed in ideological conflict with the older.

Most of the nationalistic movements in the Middle East, Asia, and Africa have consisted of young people, students, or officers who rebelled against their elders and the traditional familistic setting with its stress on the latters' authority. At the same time there usually has developed a specific youth consciousness and ideology that intensifies the nationalistic movement to "rejuvenate" the country.

The emergence of the peer group among immigrant children is a well-known phenomenon that usually appears in the second generation. It occurs mainly because of the relative breakdown of immigrant family life in the new country. The more highly industrialized and urbanized that country (or the sector absorbing the immigrants) is, the sharper the breakdown. Hence, the family of the immigrant or second-generation child has often been an inadequate guide to the new society. The immigrant child's attainment of full identity in the new land is usually related to how much he has been able to detach himself from his older, family setting. Some of these children, therefore, have developed a strong predisposition to join various peer groups. Such an affiliation has sometimes facilitated their transition to the absorbing society by stressing the values and patterns of behavior in that society—or, on the contrary, it may express their rebellion against this society, or against their older setting.

All these modern social developments and movements have given rise to a great variety of youth groups, peer groups, youth movements, and what has been called youth culture. The types and concrete forms of such groups varies widely: spontaneous youth groups, student movements, ideological and semi-political movements, and youth rebellions connected with the Romantic movement in Europe, and, later, with the German youth movements. The various social and national trends of the nineteenth and twentieth centuries have also given impetus to such organizations. At the same time there have appeared many adult-sponsored youth organizations and other agencies springing out of the great extension of educational institutions. In addition to providing recreative facilities, these agencies have also aimed at character molding and the instilling of civic virtues, so as to deepen social consciousness and widen the social and cultural horizon. The chief examples are the YMCA, the Youth Brigades organized in England by William Smith, the Boy Scouts, the Jousters in France, and the many kinds of community organizations, hostels, summer camps, or vocational guidance centers.

Thus we see that there are many parallels between primitive and historical societies and modern societies with regard to the conditions under which the various constellations of youth groups, youth activities, and youth images have developed. But these parallels are only partial. Despite certain similarities, the specific configurations of the basic archetypal elements of the youth image in modern societies differ greatly from those of primitive and traditional societies. The most important differences are rooted in the fact that in the modern, the development of specific youth organizations is paradoxically connected with the weakening of the importance of age in general and youth in particular as definite criteria for the allocation of roles in society.

As we have already said, the extent to which major occupational, cultural, or political roles are allocated today according to the explicit criterion of age is very small. Most such roles are achieved according to wealth, acquired skills, specialization, and knowledge. Family background may be of great importance for the acquisition of these attributes, but very few positions are directly given people by virtue of their family standing. Yet this very weakening of the importance of age is always connected with intensive developments of youth groups and movements. This fact has several interesting repercussions on the organization and structure of such groups. In primitive and traditional societies, youth groups are usually part of a wider organization of age groups that covers a very long period of life, from childhood to late adulthood and even old age. To be sure, it is during youth that most of the dramatic elements of the transition from one age to another are manifest, but this stage constitutes only part of a longer series of continuous, well-defined stages.

From this point of view, primitive or traditional societies do not differ greatly from those in which the transition from youth to adulthood is not organized in specific age groups but is largely effected within the fold of the family and kinship groups. In both primitive and traditional societies we observe a close and comprehensive linkage between personal temporal transition and societal or cosmic time, a linkage most fully expressed in the *rites de passage*. Consequently, the transition from childhood to adulthood in all such societies is given full meaning in terms of ultimate cultural values and symbols borne or symbolized by various adult role models.

In modern societies the above picture greatly changes. The youth group, whatever its composition or organization, usually stands alone. It does not constitute a part of a fully institutionalized and organized series of age groups. It is true that in many of the more traditional sectors of modern societies the more primitive or traditional archetypes of youth still prevail. Moreover, in many modern societies elements of the primitive archetypes of youth still exist. But the full articulation of these elements is lacking, and the social organization and self-expression of youth are not given full legitimation or meaning in terms of cultural values and rituals.

The close linkage between the growth of personality, psychological maturation, and definite role models derived from the adult world has become greatly weakened. Hence the very coalescence of youth into special groups only tends to emphasize their problematic, uncertain standing from the point of view of cultural values and symbols. This has created a new constellation of the basic archetypal elements of youth. This new constellation can most clearly be seen in what has been called the emergence of the problems and stresses of adolescence in modern societies. While some of these stresses are necessarily common to adolescence in all societies, they become especially acute in modern societies.

Among these stresses the most important are the following: first, the bodily development of the adolescent constitutes a constant problem to him (or her). Since social maturity usually lags behind biological maturity, the bodily changes of puberty are not usually given a full cultural, normative meaning, and their evaluation is one of the adolescent's main concerns. The difficulty inherent in attaining legitimate sexual outlets and relations at this period of growth makes these problems even more acute. Second, the adolescent's orientation toward the main values of his society is also beset with difficulties. Owing to the long period of preparation and the relative segregation of the children's world from that of the adults, the main values of the society are necessarily presented to the child and adolescent in a highly selective way, with a strong idealistic emphasis. The relative unreality of these values as presented to the children—which at the same time are not given full ritual and symbolic expression—creates among the adolescents a great potential uncertainty and ambivalence toward the adult world.

This ambivalence is manifest, on the one hand, in a striving to communicate with the adult world and receive its recognition; on the other hand, it appears in certain dispositions to accentuate the differences between them and the adults and to oppose the various roles allocated to them by the adults. While they orient themselves to full participation in the adult world and its values, they usually attempt also to communicate with this world in a distinct, special way.

Parallel developments are to be found in the ideologies of modern youth groups. Most of these tend to create an ideology that emphasizes the discontinuity between youth and adulthood and the uniqueness of the youth period as the purest embodiment of ultimate social and cultural values. Although the explicitness of this ideology varies in extent from one sector of modern society to another, its basic elements are prevalent in almost all modern youth groups.

These processes have been necessarily accentuated in modern societies by the specific developments in cultural orientations in general and in the conception of time that has evolved in particular. The major social developments in modern societies have weakened the importance of broad cultural qualities as criteria for the allocation of roles. Similarly, important changes in the conception of time that is prevalent in modern societies have occurred. Primordial (cosmic-mythical, cyclical, or apocalyptical) conceptions of time have become greatly weakened, especially in their bearing on daily activities. The mechanical conception of time of modern technology has become much more prevalent. Of necessity this has greatly weakened the possibility of the direct ritual links between personal temporal changes and cosmic or societal progression. Therefore, the exploration of the actual meaning of major cultural values in their relation to the reality of the social world becomes one of the adolescent's main problems. This exploration may lead in many directions—cynicism, idealistic youth rebellion, deviant ideology and behavior, or a gradual development of a balanced identity.

Thus we see how all these developments in modern societies have created a new constellation of the basic archetypal elements of youth and the youth image. The two main characteristics of this constellation are the weakened possibility of directly linking the development of personality and the personal temporal transition with cosmic and societal time, on the one hand, and with the clear role models derived from the adult world, on the other.

In terms of personality development, this situation has created a great potential insecurity and the possible lack of a clear definition of personal identity. Yet it has also created the possibility of greater personal autonomy and flexibility in the choice of roles and the commitment to different values and symbols. In general, the individual, in his search for the meaning of his personal transition, has been thrown much more on his own powers.

These processes have provided the framework within which the various attempts to forge youth's identity and activities—both on the part of youth itself and on the part of various educational agencies—have developed. These attempts may take several directions. Youth's own activities and attempts at self-expression may first develop in the direction of considerable autonomy in the choice of roles and in commitment to various values. Conversely, they may develop in the direction of a more complete, fully organized and closed ideology connected with a small extent of personal autonomy. Second, these attempts may differ greatly in their emphasis on the direct linkage of cultural values to a specific social group and their view of these groups as the main bearers of such values.

In a parallel sense, attempts have been made on the part of various educational agencies to create new types of youth organizations within which youth can forge its identity and become linked to adult society. The purpose of such attempts has been two-fold: to provide youth with opportunities to develop a reasonably autonomous personality and a differentiated field of activity; and to encompass youth fully within well-organized groups set up by adult society and to provide them with full, unequivocal role models and symbols of identification. The interaction between these different tendencies of youth and the attempts of adult society to provide various frameworks for youth activities has given rise to the major types of youth organizations, movements, and ideologies manifested in modern societies.

These various trends and tendencies have created a situation in which, so far as we can ascertain, the number of casualties among youth has become very great—probably relatively much greater than in other types of societies. Youth's search for identity, for finding some place of its own in society, and its potential difficulties in coping with the attainment of such identity have given rise to the magnified extent of the casualties observed in the numerous youth delinquents of varying types. These failures, however, are not the only major youth developments in modern societies, although their relatively greater number is endemic in modern conditions. Much more extensive are the more positive attempts of youth to forge its own identity, to find some meaningful way of defining its place in the social and cultural context and of connecting social and political values with personal development in a coherent and significant manner.

The best example in our times of the extreme upsurge of specific youth consciousness is seen in the various revolutionary youth movements. They range from the autonomous free German youth movements to the less spectacular youth movements in Central Europe and also to some extent to the specific youth culture of various more flexible youth groups. Here the attempt has been made to overcome the dislocation between personal transition and societal and cultural time. It is in these movements that the social dynamics of modern youth has found its fullest expression. It is in them that dreams of a new life, a new society, freedom and spontaneity, a new humanity and aspirations to social and cultural change have found utterance. It is in these youth movements that the forging of youth's new social identity has become closely connected with the development of new symbols of collective identity or new social-cultural symbols and meanings.

. These movements have aimed at changing many aspects of the social and cultural life of their respective societies. They have depicted the present in a rather shabby form; they have dubbed it with adjectives of materialism, restriction, exploitation, lack of opportunity for self-fulfillment and creativity. At the same time they have held out hope for the future—seemingly, the not very far off future—when both self-fulfillment and collective fulfillment can be achieved and the materialistic civilization of the adult world can be shaken off. They have tried to appeal to youth to forge its own self-identity in terms of these new collective symbols, and this is why they have been so attractive to youth, for whom they have provided a set of symbols, hopes, and aims to which to direct its activities.

Within these movements the emphasis has been on a given social group or collectivity—nation, class, or the youth group itself—as the main, almost exclusive bearer of the "good" cultural value and symbols. Indeed, youth has at times been upheld as the sole and pure bearer of cultural values and social creativity. Through its association with these movements, youth has also been able to connect its aspiration for a different personal future, its anxiety to escape the present through plans and hopes for a different future within its cultural or social setting.

These various manifestations have played a crucial part in the emergence of social movements and parties in modern societies. Student groups have been the nuclei of the most important nationalistic and revolutionary movements in Central and Eastern Europe, in Italy, Germany, Hungary, and Russia. They have also played a significant role in Zionism and in the various waves of immigration to Israel. Their influence has become enormous in various fields, not only political and educational but cultural in general. In a way, education itself has tended to become a social movement. Many schools and universities, many teachers, have been among the most important bearers of collective values. The very spread of education is often seen as a means by which a new epoch might be ushered in.

The search for some connection between the personal situation of youth and social-cultural values has also stimulated the looser youth groups in modern societies, especially in the United States, and to some extent in Europe as well—though here the psychological meaning of the search is somewhat different. The looser youth groups have often shared some of the characteristics of the more defined youth movements, and they too have developed an emphasis on the attainment of social and cultural change. The yearning for a different personal future has likewise become connected with aspirations for changing the cultural setting, but not necessarily through a direct political or organized expression. They are principally important as a strong link with various collective, artistic, and literary aspirations aimed at changing social and cultural life. As such they are affiliated with various cultural values and symbols, not with any exclusive social groups. Thus they have necessarily developed a much greater freedom in choice of roles and commitment to values.

Specific social conditions surround the emergence of all these youth groups. In general, they are associated with a breakdown of traditional settings, the onset of modernization, urbanization, secularization, and industrialization. The less organized, more spontaneous types of youth organization and the more flexible kind of youth consciousness arise when the transition has been relatively smooth and gradual, especially in societies whose basic collective identity and political framework evince a large degree of continuity and a slow process of modernization. On the other hand, the more intensive types of youth movements tend to develop in those societies and periods in which the onset of modernization is connected with great upheavals and sharp cleavages in the social structure and the structure of authority and with the breakdown of symbols of collective identity.

In the latter situation the adult society has made many efforts to organize youth in what may be called totalistic organizations, in which clear role models and values might be set before youth and in which the extent of choice allowed youth is very limited and the manifestations of personal spontaneity and autonomy are restricted. Both types of conditions appeared in various European societies and in the United States in the nineteenth and early twentieth centuries, and in Asian and African societies in the second half of the twentieth century. The relative predominance of each of these conditions varies in different periods in these societies. However, with the progress of modernization and the growing absorption of broad masses within the framework of society, the whole basic setting of youth in modern society has changed—and it is this new framework that is predominant today and in which contemporary youth problems are shaped and played out.

The change this new framework represents is to some extent common both to the fully organized totalistic youth movements and to the looser youth groups. It is connected mainly with the institutionalizing of the aims and values toward the realization of which these movements were oriented, with the acceptance of such youth organizations as part of the structure of the general educational and cultural structure of their societies.

In Russia youth movements became fully institutionalized through the organization of the Komsomol. In many European countries the institutionalizing of youth groups, agencies, and ideologies came through association with political parties, or through acceptance as part of the educational system—an acceptance that sometimes entailed supervision by the official authorities. In the United States, many (such as the Boy Scouts) have become an accepted part of community life and to some extent a symbol of differential social status. In many Asian and African countries, organized youth movements have become part of the nationalistic movements and, independence won, have become part of the official education organizations.

This institutionalizing of the values of youth movements in education and community life has been part of a wider process of institutionalizing various collective values. In some countries this has come about through revolution; in others, as a result of a long process of political and social evolution.

From the point of view of our analysis, these processes have had several important results. They have introduced a new element into the configuration of the basic archetypal elements of youth. The possibility of linking personal transition both to social groups and to cultural values—so strongly emphasized in the youth movements and noticeable to some extent even in the looser youth culture —has become greatly weakened. The social and sometimes even the cultural dimension of the future may thus become flattened and emptied. The various collective values become transformed. Instead of being remote goals resplendent with romantic dreams, they have become mundane objectives of the present, with its shabby details of daily politics and administration. More often than not they are intimately connected with the processes of bureaucratization.

All these mutations are associated with a notable decline in ideology and in preoccupation with ideology among many of the groups and strata in modern societies, with a general flattening of political-ideological motives and a growing apathy to them. This decline in turn is connected with what has been called the spiritual or cultural shallowness of the new social and economic benefits accruing from the welfare state—an emptiness illustrated by the fact that all these benefits are in the nature of things administered not by spiritual or social leaders but, as Stephen Toulmin has wittily pointed out, "the assistant postmaster." As a consequence, we observe the emptiness and meaninglessness of social relations, so often described by critics of the age of consumption and mass society.

In general, these developments have brought about the flattening of the image of the societal future and have deprived it of its allure. Between present and future there is no ideological discontinuity. The present has become the more important, if not the more meaningful, because the future has lost its characteristics as a dimension different from the present. Out of these conditions has grown what Riesman has called the cult of immediacy. Youth has been robbed, therefore, of the full experience of the dramatic transition from adolescence to adulthood and of the dramatization of the difference between present and future. Their own changing personal future has become dissociated from any changes in the shape of their societies or in cultural activities and values.

Paradoxically enough, these developments have often been connected with a strong adulation of youth—an adulation, however, which was in a way purely instrumental. The necessity of a continuous adjustment to new changing conditions has emphasized the potential value of youth as the bearers of continuous innovation, of noncommitment to any specific condition and values. But such an emphasis is often couched in terms of a purely instrumental adaptability, beyond which there is only the relative emptiness of the meaningless passage of time— of aging.[3]

[3] For an exposition of this view, see Paul Goodman, "Youth in Organized Society," *Commentary*, February 1960, pp. 95–107; and M. R. Stein, *The Eclipse of Community* (Princeton University Press, 1960), especially pp. 215 ff.; also, the review of this book by H. Rosenberg, "Community, Values, Comedy," *Commentary*, August 1960, pp. 150–157.

Yet the impact on youth of what has been called postindustrial society need not result in such an emptiness and shallowness, although in recent literature these effects appear large indeed. It is as yet too early to make a full and adequate analysis of all these impacts. But it should be emphasized that the changes we have described, together with growing abundance and continuous technological change, have necessarily heightened the possibility of greater personal autonomy and cultural creativity and of the formation of the bases of such autonomy and of a flexible yet stable identity during the period of youth.

These new conditions have enhanced the possibility of flexibility in linking cultural values to social reality; they have enhanced the scope of personal and cultural creativity and the development of different personal culture. They have created the possibility of youth's developing what may be called a nonideological, direct identification with moral values, an awareness of the predicaments of moral choice that exist in any given situation, and individual responsibility for such choices—a responsibility that cannot be shed by relying on overarching ideological solutions oriented to the future.

These new social conditions exist in most industrial and postindustrial societies, sometimes together with the older conditions that gave rise to the more intensive types of youth movements. They constitute the framework within which the new configuration of the archetypal elements of youth and the new possibilities and problems facing youth in contemporary society develop. It is as yet too early to specify all these new possibilities and trends: here we have attempted to indicate some of their general contours.

DISCUSSION TOPICS

1. Erikson points out that Hamlet rebels against his allegiance to "rotten Denmark." Give examples from the music, the customs, and the activities of modern youth which suggest that they feel today as Hamlet felt. How close is the parallel between symptoms of estrangement shown by youth today and those displayed by Hamlet?

2. What is the effect of the timing of physical changes during puberty on an adolescent's adjustment to self and to peers?

3. Using as a point of reference the adolescent who remains a "good child," how can we define the concepts of normality and abnormality in adolescence?

4. Enumerate some major sources of adult models in contemporary society. What are the characteristics of the modern-day hero as presented in the mass media? Is the astronaut a suitable adolescent model, given Erikson's criteria?

5. What youth organizations serve the function in our society that Eisenstadt attributes to age groups in other societies? To what extent is the American school an agency that provides a smooth transition from the warmth and support of family life to the highly competitive existence of adults in America today?

II ADOLESCENCE IN THE MAINSTREAM

It is in the nature of all established societies to devise intricate ways and means of passing on to each new generation the keys to the kingdom. The dozen articles in this part of our collection represent an attempt systematically to explore the world of the American adolescent not only as he experiences it subjectively but as it is presented to him through several highly structured agencies: the family unit, the group formed by his peers, the school system, the world of work, and the social conventions that sanction or discourage his attempts to modify "the system."

We remind the student that these articles are relevant primarily for youth who have grown up within the dominant social strata in America—those who have gone through the common system for enculturation in this society and have been socialized according to widely accepted middle-class American values and life-styles.

Kingsley Davis' introductory article is helpful in suggesting the nature of the antagonism that arises as the adolescent dissociates himself from his family unit and commits himself to a new group composed of fellow youth. It appears to be within this peer-oriented sub-society that what we have called the youth culture derives its momentum. The precise reasons why current youth may be clinging to their separateness rather than moving on into the adult society are still in dispute. However, discussions of contemporary adolescent morality and tastes can help to illuminate some of the contours of the current youth culture

Apparently, it serves the function of protecting young people from the stress created by the highly selective and unrealistic view of the world which adults in this culture present to children and adolescents. Not infrequently, youth seems to serve as a convenient scapegoat for adults who are dissatisfied with their own adaptations. Adults' fears and guilt may lend strength to the edifices they erect as training hurdles for the next generation. Fears that America is weak, for example, spawn programs for increased physical fitness in the schools. Concern over the harmful effects of cigarette smoking, drinking, and driving fast automobiles leads to repressive measures to inhibit the use of these commodities by adolescents. Guilt over their own sexual practices leads adults to impose heavy restrictions on the sexual activities of high school and college youth.

In reaction, the youth culture turns to media that oppose the message of the mass culture: *Mad Magazine*, for example, and the message songs of Bob Dylan, as examined in the third article in this part. It turns also to moralities better adapted to the individual who is biologically mature but still denied the possibility of "leading his own life" through the assumption of an adult social role. Hence the new morality, as described by Dana Farnsworth, with its criterion of mutual consent as the basis for premarital sexual relations—a denial of the traditional ethic which restricts sex to those who have already assumed adult roles. In these and other ways, the peer culture tends to protect itself against the discontinuities between itself and the adult culture. One of its best defenses is its encapsulation.

We have already observed that one of the more curious aspects of American culture is the way in which a love, if not a worship, of youth is conjoined with fear and distrust of the young. This value confusion is evident when we look at the school system as well. On the one hand, the pressure on young people to accept adult "responsibility" earlier and more fully in certain circumscribed areas is increasing today, especially in an academic rat race that begins in the junior high school and continues, for many, through the Ph.D. Yet the basis on which success most depends is, paradoxically, the willingness to defer gratification. But what is the "payoff" for submitting to the academic pressure? The answer is well known: occupational success. What, in turn, are Americans encouraged to expect from occupational success? Two things: hardware and fun. Thus we come full circle. Young people are pressured to become responsible miniature adults so that they can afford to be children when they are older. Kenneth Keniston, speaking of the little alienations of the well-adjusted adult, has defined him sharply in relation to his children. "Perhaps," he says, "we sacrifice so readily for children because by living on in them we hope we can spare them, our new selves, the adulthood we ourselves must live."

Submission to the academic rat race involves participation in a schooling process which can be called the development of "competence"—the acquisition of both technical and personal skills. Friedenberg has defined competence, in the lingo of middle-class youth, as: smile, don't get hung up, and, above all, win. It follows that the most visible pathologies should arise in those who reject, defer, cannot attain, or exceed the prescribed levels of competence. Youth from the dominant social strata appear to view their school experience as training not in understanding but in techniques for survival in the upcoming professional rat race. Eager to learn those behaviors that will bring greatest tangible success, they use the school to learn standard approved responses. The indigenous jokes of the poor, the immigrant and the rich, for example, are all reduced to the guarded good humor of the executive. This apparent lack of meaningful values in education is examined in Bruno Bettelheim's essay.

For those thoroughly alienated by their failure to acquire a meaningful identity in adolescence, there are other avenues of behavior. Some opt for various forms of bohemianism and head for a subculture like that described by Paul Goodman, in which disc jockeys, liquor or drugs become central interests and hip-talk is the semi-articulate speech. Some accept conventional careers while continuing to hold alienated ideas, viewing the careers as merely a form of adult role-playing. But many others decide that the world of work offers them no more meaning than the world of school. They come to feel, with Paul Goodman, that America's system of production for profit rather than for use has succeeded in making its jobs and products profitable but useless. And soon, if Professor Dansereau is correct, even the meaningless jobs will begin to disappear. With the onset of automation and the resultant reduction of the work week, he believes, adult society will organize around leisure rather than work. As this occurs, teen-age culture with its emphasis on fun may become the functional prototype of future adult culture.

When we turn to the question of youth's ability to actually transform the adult world with which it is in conflict, it is useful to recall sociologist Karl Mannheim's theory that youth *must* play a central role if progress and change are to be achieved in any society. Frank Musgrove has explored relationships which seem necessary between youth and adult groups in any society in which youth are likely to exert influence. He reminds us that the low status of youth in our own society is similar to that of other societies undergoing rapid social change and that America's youth, divorced as they seem to be from the adult society, may well be in a pivotal position to bring about social change.

If we examine the actions and speeches of alienated youth in the 'Sixties for clues as to their future behavior, we find adolescents in two distinct camps: the hippie movement, with its ideology of "turn on, tune in, and drop out," and the student activist movement. The latter seems to appeal to action-oriented mainstream youth whose attempts to function in adult society have been frustrated in one way or another. Turning from the standard future possibilities open to them, they have sought to build a bridge between themselves and the underprivileged.

Speaking for this group, Rochelle Gatlin indicates that they reject overarching ideological commitments like those of what they call the Old Left, because such can too easily be made to serve institutionalized adult purposes. Instead, these youth choose to call themselves the New Left and to follow the injunction, "Don't trust anybody over 30." Thus they extend the adolescent moratorium for nearly an extra decade and commit themselves to a non-ideological movement characterized specifically by its lack of program.

Some of these youth have marched with S.N.C.C. in Mississippi, others with the peace movement in Boston, Washington, and New York. Many have participated in student demonstrations for greater individual autonomy on mass university campuses such as that of the University of California at Berkeley, which is discussed in the concluding article in this part. Their new commitment, articu-- lated in "free speech movement" newsletters issued during the demonstrations, lies in the refusal of these mainstream youth to "play the game" with the old rules. They see their rebellion not as destructive but as an act of fidelity to mankind and the future. Unlike the Hippies, who shun responsibility or external involvement, these alienated youths appear eager to assume greater adult responsibility in the parliament of the University—suggesting the possibility of direct, albeit disorderly, succession of the next generation. In effect, they embody the adolescent's recurrent need to challenge the present and to create new institutions which will once more open the culture to its youth.

1 THE FAMILY

Students of social processes have long attempted to explain common adolescent-parent conflicts as the inevitable problem of communication between generations. Kingsley Davis, in the following selection, distinguishes between universals that appear to underlie all such conflicts and specific conditions in modern American society which aggravate the basic possibilities for conflict and determine their form and substance.

Kingsley Davis

The Sociology
of Parent-Youth Conflict

Why does contemporary western civilization manifest an extraordinary amount of parent-adolescent conflict? In other cultures the outstanding fact is generally not the rebelliousness of youth, but its docility. . . . What, then, are the peculiar features of our society which give us one of the extremest examples of endemic filial friction in human history?

Our answer to this question makes use of constants and variables, the constants being the universal factors in the parent-youth relations, the variables being the factors which differ from one society to another. Though one's attention, in explaining the parent-youth relations of a given milieu, is focused on the variables, one cannot comprehend the action of the variables without also understanding the constants, for the latter constitute the structural and functional basis of the family as a part of society.

THE RATE OF SOCIAL CHANGE

The first important variable is the rate of social change. Extremely rapid change in modern civilization, in contrast to most societies, tends to increase parent-youth conflict, for within a fast-changing social order the time-interval between generations, ordinarily but a mere moment in the life of a social system, becomes historically significant, thereby creating a hiatus between one generation and the next. Inevitably, under such a condition, youth is reared in a milieu different from that of the parents; hence the parents become old-fashioned, youth rebellious, and clashes occur which, in the closely confined circle of the immediate family, generate sharp emotion.

THE BIRTH-CYCLE AND DECELERATING SOCIALIZATION

Note, however, that rapid social change would have no power to produce conflict were it not for two universal factors: first, the family's duration; and second, the decelerating rate of socialization in the development of personality. "A family" is not a static entity but a process in time, a process ordinarily so brief compared with historical time that it is unimportant, but which, when history is "full" (i.e., marked by rapid social change), strongly influences the mutual adjustment of the generations. This "span" is basically the birth-cycle—the length of time between the birth of one person and his procreation of another. It is biological and inescapable. It would, however, have no effect in producing parent-youth conflict, even with social change, if it were not for the additional fact, intimately related and equally universal, that the sequential development of personality involves a constantly decelerating rate of socialization. This deceleration is due both to organic factors (age—which ties it to the birth-cycle) and to social factors (the cumulative character of social experience). Its effect is to make the birth-cycle interval, which is the period of youth, the time of major socialization, subsequent periods of socialization being subsidiary.

Given these constant features, rapid social change creates conflict because to the intrinsic (universal, inescapable) differences between parents and children it adds an extrinsic (variable) difference derived from the acquisition, at the same stage of life, of differential cultural content by each successive generation. Not only are parent and child, at any given moment, in different stages of development, but the content which the parent acquired at the stage where the child now is, was a different content from that which the child is now acquiring. Since the parent is supposed to socialize the child, he tends to apply the erstwhile but now inappropriate content. He makes this mistake, and cannot remedy it, because, due to the logic of personality growth, his basic orientation was formed by the experiences of his own childhood. He cannot "modernize" his point of view, because *he* is the product of those experiences. He can change in superficial ways, such as learning a new tune, but he cannot change (or *want to* change) the initial modes of thinking upon which his subsequent social experience has been built. To change the basic conceptions by which he has learned to judge the rightness and reality of all specific situations would be to render subsequent experience meaningless, to make an empty caricature of what had been his life.

PHYSIOLOGICAL DIFFERENCES

Though the disparity in chronological age remains constant through life, the precise physiological differences between parent and offspring vary radically from one period to another. The organic contrasts between parent and *infant*, for example, are far different from those between parent and adolescent. Yet whatever the period, the organic differences produce contrasts (as between young and old) in those desires which, at least in part, are organically determined. Thus, at the time of adolescence the contrast is between an organism which is just reaching its full powers and one which is just losing them. The physiological need of the latter is for security and conservation, because as the superabundance of energy diminishes, the organism seems to hoard what remains.

Such differences, often alleged (under the heading of "disturbing physiological changes accompanying adolescence") as the primary cause of parent-adolescent strife, are undoubtedly a factor in such conflict, but, like other universal differences to be discussed, they form a constant factor present in every community, and therefore cannot in themselves explain the peculiar heightening of parent-youth conflict in our culture.

The fact is that most societies avoid the potential clash of old and young by using sociological position as a neutralizing agent. They assign definite and separate positions to persons of different ages, thereby eliminating competition between them for the same position and avoiding the competitive emotions of jealousy and envy. Also, since the expected behavior of old and young is thus made complementary rather than identical, the performance of cooperative functions as accomplished by different but mutually related activities suited to the disparate organic needs of each, with no coercion to behave in a manner unsuited to one's organic age. In our culture, where most positions are *theoretically* based on accomplishment rather than age, interage competition arises, superior organic propensities lead to a high evaluation of youth (the so-called "accent on youth"), a disproportionate lack of opportunity for youth manifests itself, and consequently, arrogance and frustration appear in the young, fear and envy, in the old.

PSYCHOSOCIAL DIFFERENCES: ADULT REALISM VS. YOUTHFUL IDEALISM

The decelerating rate of socialization . . . , when taken with rapid social change and other conditions of our society, tends to produce certain differences of orientation between parent and youth. . . .

Though both youth and age claim to see the truth, the old are more con-servatively realistic than the young, because on the one hand they take Utopian ideals less seriously and on the other hand take what may be called operating ideals, if not more seriously, at least more for granted. Thus, middle-aged people notoriously forget the poetic ideals of a new social order which they cherished when young. In their place, they put simply the working ideals current in the society. There is, in short, a persistent tendency for the ideology of a person as he grows older to gravitate more and more toward the status quo ideology, unless other facts (such as a social crisis or hypnotic suggestion) intervene. With ad-vancing age, he becomes less and less bothered by inconsistencies in ideals. He tends to judge ideals according to whether they are widespread and hence ef-fective in thinking about practical life, not according to whether they are logically consistent. Furthermore, he gradually ceases to bother about the *untruth* of his ideals, in the sense of their failure to correspond to reality. He assumes through long habit that, though they do not correspond perfectly, the discrepancy is not significant. The reality of an ideal is defined for him in terms of how many people accept it rather than how completely it is mirrored in actual behavior. Thus, we call him, as he approaches middle age, a realist.

The young, however, are idealists, partly because they take working ideals literally and partly because they acquire ideals not fully operative in the social organization. Those in authority over children are obligated as a requirement of their status to inculcate ideals as a part of the official culture given the new generation. The children are receptive because they have little social experience—experience being systematically kept from them (by such means as censorship, for example, a large part of which is to "protect" children). Consequently, young people possess little ballast for their acquired ideals, which therefore soar to the sky, whereas the middle-aged, by contrast, have plenty of ballast.

This relatively unchecked idealism in youth is eventually complicated by the fact that young people possess keen reasoning ability. The mind, simply as a logical machine, works as well at sixteen as at thirty-six.[1] Such logical capacity, combined with high ideals and an initial lack of experience, means that youth soon discovers with increasing age that the ideals it has been taught are true and consistent are not so in fact. Mental conflict thereupon ensues, for the young person has not learned that ideals may be useful without being true and con-sistent. As a solution, youth is likely to take action designed to remove incon-sistencies or force actual conduct into line with ideals, such action assuming one of several typical adolescent forms—from religious withdrawal to the militant support of some Utopian scheme—but in any case consisting essentially in serious allegiance to one or more of the ideal moral systems present in the culture. An illustration of youthful reformism was afforded by the Laval Uni-versity students who decided to "do something about" prostitution in the city of Quebec. They broke into eight houses in succession one night, "whacked

[1] F. K. Shuttleworth, "The Adolescent Period: A Graphic and Pictorial Atlas," *Monograph of the Society for Research in Child Development,* 1938, Vol. 3, No. 8, Figs. 16, 230, 232, 276, 285, 308.

naked inmates upon the buttocks, upset beds and otherwise proved their collegiate virtue. . . ." They ended by "shoving the few remaining girls out of doors into the cold autumn night" (*Time*, October 19, 1936).

A different, usually later reaction to disillusionment is the cynical or sophomoric attitude; for, if the ideals one has imbibed cannot be reconciled and do not fit reality, then why not dismiss them as worthless? Cynicism has the advantage of giving justification for behavior that young organisms crave anyway. It might be mistaken for genuine realism if it were not for two things. The first is the emotional strain behind the "don't care" attitude. The cynic, in his judgment that the world is bad because of inconsistency and untruth of ideals, implies that he still values the ideals. The true realist sees the inconsistency and untruth, but without emotion; he uses either ideals or reality whenever it suits his purpose. The second is the early disappearance of the cynical attitude. Increased experience usually teaches the adolescent that overt cynicism is unpopular and unworkable, that to deny and deride all beliefs which fail to cohere or to correspond to facts, and to act in opposition to them, is to alienate oneself from any group, because these beliefs, however unreal, are precisely what makes group unity possible. Soon, therefore, the youthful cynic finds himself bound up with some group having a system of working ideals, and becomes merely another conformist, cynical only about the beliefs of other groups.

While the germ of this contrast between youthful idealism and adult realism may spring from the universal logic of personality development, it receives in our culture a peculiar exaggeration. Social change, complexity, and specialization (by compartmentalizing different aspects of life) segregate ideals from fact and throw together incompatible ideologies while at the same time providing the intellectual tools for discerning logical inconsistencies and empirical errors. Our highly elaborated burden of culture, correlated with a variegated system of achieved vertical mobility, necessitates long years of formal education which separate youth from adulthood, theory from practice, school from life. Insofar, then, as youth's reformist zeal or cynical negativism produces conflict with parents, the peculiar conditions of our culture are responsible.

SOCIOLOGICAL DIFFERENCES: PARENTAL AUTHORITY

Since social status and office are everywhere partly distributed on the basis of age, personality development is intimately linked with the network of social positions successively occupied during life. Western society, in spite of an unusual amount of interage competition, maintains differences of social position between parent and child, the developmental gap between them being too clear-cut, the symbiotic needs too fundamental, to escape being made a basis of social organization. Hence, parent and child, in a variety of ways, find themselves enmeshed in different social contexts and possessed of different outlooks. The much publicized critical attitude of youth toward established ways, for example, is partly a matter of being on the outside looking in. The "established ways" under criticism are usually institutions (such as property, marriage, profession) which the adolescent has not yet entered. He looks at them from the point of view of the outsider (especially since they affect him in a restrictive manner), either failing to imagine himself finding satisfaction in such patterns or else feeling resentful that the old have in them a vested interest from which he is excluded.

Not only is there differential position, but also *mutually* differential position, status being in many ways specific for and reciprocal between parent and child. Some of these differences, relating to the birth-cycle and constituting part of the family structure, are universal. This is particularly true of the super- and sub-ordination summed up in the term *parental authority.*

Since sociological differences between parent and child are inherent in family organization, they constitute a universal factor potentially capable of producing conflict. Like the biological differences, however, they do not in themselves produce such conflict. In fact, they may help to avoid it. To understand how our society brings to expression the potentiality for conflict, indeed to deal realistically with the relation between the generations, we must do so not in generalized terms but in terms of the specific "power situation." Therefore, the remainder of our discussion will center upon the nature of parental authority and its vicissitudes in our society.

Because of his strategic position with reference to the new-born child (at least in the familial type of reproductive institution), the parent is given considerable authority. Charged by his social group with the responsibility of controlling and training the child in conformity with the mores and thereby insuring the maintenance of the cultural structure, the parent, to fulfill his duties, must have the privileges as well as the obligations of authority, and the surrounding community ordinarily guarantees both.

The first thing to note about parental authority, in addition to its function in socialization, is that it is a case of authority within a primary group. Simmel has pointed out that authority is bearable for the subordinate because it touches only one aspect of life. Impersonal and objective, it permits all other aspects to be free from its particularistic dominance. This escape, however, is lacking in parental authority, for since the family includes most aspects of life, its authority is not limited, specific, or impersonal. What, then, can make this authority bearable? Three factors associated with the familial primary group help to give the answer: (1) the child is socialized within the family, and therefore knowing nothing else and being utterly dependent, the authority of the parent is internalized, accepted; (2) the family, like other primary groups, implies identification, in such sense that one person understands and responds emphatically to the sentiments of the other, so that the harshness of authority is ameliorated; (3) in the intimate interaction of the primary group control can never be purely one-sided; there are too many ways in which the subordinated can exert the pressure of his will. When, therefore, the family system is a going concern, parental authority, however inclusive, is not felt as despotic.

A second thing to note about parental authority is that while its duration is variable (lasting in some societies a few years and in others a lifetime), it inevitably involves a change, a progressive readjustment, in the respective positions of parent and child—in some cases an almost complete reversal of roles, in others at least a cumulative allowance for the fact of maturity in the subordinated offspring. Age is a unique basis for social stratification. Unlike birth, sex, wealth, or occupation, it implies that the stratification is temporary, that the person, if he lives a full life, will eventually traverse all of the strata having it as a basis. Therefore, there is a peculiar ambivalence attached to this kind of differentiation, as well as a constant directional movement. On the one hand, the young person, in the stage of maximum socialization, is, so to speak, *moving into* the social organization. His social personality is expanding, i.e., acquiring an increased amount of the cultural heritage, filling more powerful and numerous positions. His future is before him, in what the older person is leaving behind. The latter, on the other hand, has a future before him only in the sense that the offspring represents it. Therefore, there is a disparity of interest, the young person placing his thoughts upon a future which, once the first stages of dependence are passed, does not include the parent, the old person placing his hopes vicariously upon the young. This situation, representing a *tendency* in every society, is avoided in many places by a system of respect for the aged and an imaginary projection of life beyond the grave. In the absence of such a religio-ancestral system, the role of the aged is a tragic one.

Let us now take up, point by point, the manner in which western civilization has affected this *gemeinschaftliche* and processual form of authority.

Conflicting Norms

To begin with, rapid change has, as we saw, given old and young a different social content, so that they possess conflicting norms. There is a loss of mutual identification, and the parent will not "catch up" with the child's point of view, because he is supposed to dominate rather than follow. More than this, social complexity has confused the standards *within* the generations. Faced with conflicting goals, parents become inconsistent and confused in their own minds in rearing their children. The children, for example, acquire an argument against discipline by being able to point to some family wherein discipline is less severe, while the parent can retaliate by pointing to still other families wherein it is firmer. The acceptance of parental attitudes is less complete than formerly.

Competing Authorities

We took it for granted, when discussing rapid social change, that youth acquires new ideas, but we did not ask how. The truth is that, in a specialized and complex culture, they learn from competing authorities. Today, for example, education is largely in the hands of professional specialists, some of whom, as college professors, resemble the sophists of ancient Athens by virtue of their work of accumulating and purveying knowledge, and who consequently have ideas in advance of the populace at large (i.e., the parents). By giving the younger generation these advanced ideas, they (and many other extrafamilial agencies, including youth's contemporaries) widen the intellectual gap between parent and child.

Steps in Parental Authority

Our society provides little explicit institutionalization of the progressive re-adjustments of authority as between parent and child. We are intermediate be-tween the extreme of virtually permanent parental authority and the extreme of very early emancipation, because we encourage release in late adolescence. Un-fortunately, this is a time of enhanced sexual desire, so that the problem of sex and the problem of emancipation occur simultaneously and complicate each other. Yet even this would doubtless be satisfactory if it were not for the fact that among us the exact time when authority is relinquished, the exact amount, and the proper ceremonial behavior are not clearly defined. Not only do different groups and families have conflicting patterns, and new situations arise to which old definitions will not apply, but the different spheres of life (legal, economic, religious, intellectual) do not synchronize, maturity in one sphere and im-maturity in another often coexisting. The readjustment of authority between individuals is always a ticklish process, and when it is a matter of such close authority as that between parent and child it is apt to be still more ticklish. The failure of our culture to institutionalize this readjustment by a series of well-defined, well-publicized steps is undoubtedly a cause of much parent-youth dis-sension. The adolescent's sociological exit from his family, via education, work, marriage, and change of residence, is fraught with potential conflicts of interest which only a definite system of institutional controls can neutralize. The parents have a vital stake in what the offspring will do. Because his acquisition of in-dependence will free the parents of many obligations, they are willing to re-linquish their authority; yet, precisely because their own status is socially identified with that of their offspring, they wish to insure satisfactory conduct on the latter's part and are tempted to prolong their authority by making the decisions themselves. In the absence of institutional prescriptions, the conflict of interest may lead to a struggle for power, the parents fighting to keep con-trol in matters of importance to themselves, the son or daughter clinging to per-sonally indispensable family services while seeking to evade the concomitant control.

Concentration Within the Small Family

Our family system is peculiar in that it manifests a paradoxical combination of concentration and dispersion. On the one hand, the unusual smallness of the family unit makes for a strange intensity of family feeling, while on the other, the fact that most pursuits take place outside the home makes for a dispersion of activities. Though apparently contradictory, the two phenomena are really interrelated and traceable ultimately to the same factors in our social structure. Since the first refers to that type of affection and antagonism found between relatives, and the second to activities, it can be seen that the second (dispersion) isolates and increases the intensity of the affectional element by sheering away common activities and the extended kin. Whereas ordinarily the sentiments of kinship are organically related to a number of common activities and spread over a wide circle of relatives, in our mobile society they are associated with only a few common activities and concentrated within only the immediate family. This makes them at once more instable (because ungrounded) and more intense. With the diminishing birth rate, our family is the world's smallest kinship unit, a tiny closed circle. Consequently, a great deal of family sentiment is directed toward a few individuals, who are so important to the emotional life that complexes easily develop. This emotional intensity and situational instability increase both the probability and severity of conflict.

In a familistic society, where there are several adult male and female relatives within the effective kinship group to whom the child turns for affection and aid, and many members of the younger generation in whom the parents have a paternal interest, there appears to be less intensity of emotion for any particular kinsman and consequently less chance for severe conflict.[2] Also, if conflict between any two relatives does arise, it may be handled by shifting mutual rights and obligations to another relative.

Open Competition for Socioeconomic Position

Our emphasis upon individual initiative and vertical mobility, in contrast to rural-stable regimes, means that one's future occupation and destiny are determined more at adolescence than at birth, the adolescent himself (as well as the parents) having some part in the decision. Before him spreads a panorama of possible occupations and avenues of advancement, all of them fraught with the uncertainties of competitive vicissitude. The youth is ignorant of most of the facts. So is the parent, but less so. Both attempt to collaborate on the future, but because of previously mentioned sources of friction, the collaboration is frequently stormy. They evaluate future possibilities differently, and since the decision is uncertain yet important, a clash of wills results. The necessity of choice at adolescence extends beyond the occupational field to practically every phase of life, the parents having an interest in each decision. A culture in which more of the choices of life were settled beforehand by ascription, where the possibilities were fewer and the responsibilities of choice less urgent, would have much less parent-youth conflict.[3]

Sex Tension

If until now we have ignored sex taboos, the omission has represented a deliberate attempt to place them in their proper context with other factors,

[2] M. Mead, "Social Organization of Manua," *Bernice P. Bishop Museum Bulletin*, Honolulu, 1930, No. 7; D. M. Spencer, "The Composition of the Family as a Factor in the Behavior of Children in Fijian Society," *Sociometry*, 1939, 2, pp. 47–55.
[3] M. Mead. *Coming of Age in Samoa*, Morrow, 1928, pp. 200 ff.

rather than in the unduly prominent place usually given them.[4] Undoubtedly, because of a constellation of cultural conditions, sex looms as an important bone of parent-youth contention. Our morality, for instance, demands both premarital chastity and postponement of marriage, thus creating a long period of desperate eagerness when young persons practically at the peak of their sexual capacity are forbidden to enjoy it. Naturally, tensions arise—tensions which adolescents try to relieve, and adults hope they will relieve, in some socially acceptable form. Such tensions not only make the adolescent intractable and capricious, but create a genuine conflict of interest between the two generations. The parent, with respect to the child's behavior, represents morality, while the offspring reflects morality *plus* his organic cravings. The stage is thereby set for conflict, evasion, and deceit. For the mass of parents, toleration is never possible. For the mass of adolescents, sublimation is never sufficient. Given our system of morality, conflict seems well-nigh inevitable.

Yet it is not sex itself but the way it is handled that causes conflict. If sex patterns were carefully, definitely, and uniformly geared with non-sexual patterns in the social structure, there would be no parent-youth conflict over sex. As it is, rapid change has opposed the sex standards of different groups and generations, leaving impulse only chaotically controlled.

The extraordinary preoccupation of modern parents with the sex life of their adolescent offspring is easily understandable. First, our morality is sex-centered. The strength of the impulse which it seeks to control, the consequent stringency of its rules, and the importance of reproductive institutions for society, make sex so morally important that being moral and being sexually discreet are synonymous. Small wonder, then, that parents charged with responsibility for their children and fearful of their own status in the eyes of the moral community, are preoccupied with what their offspring will do in this matter. Moreover, sex is intrinsically involved in the family structure and is therefore of unusual significance to family members *qua* family members. Offspring and parent are not simply two persons who happen to live together; they are two persons who happen to live together because of past sex relations between the parents. Also, between parent and child there stand strong incest taboos, and doubtless the unvoiced possibility of violating these unconsciously intensifies the interest of each in the other's sexual conduct. In addition, since sexual behavior is connected with the offspring's formation of a new family of his own, it is naturally of concern to the parent. Finally, these factors taken in combination with the delicacy of the authoritarian relation, the emotional intensity within the small family, and the confusion of sex standards, make it easy to explain the parental interest in adolescent sexuality. Yet because sex is a tabooed topic between parent and child, parental control must be indirect and devious, which creates additional possibilities of conflict.

    [4] L. K. Frank, "The Management of Tensions," *American Journal of Sociology*, 1928, 33, pp. 706–722; M. Mead, *Coming of Age in Samoa*, Morrow, 1928, pp. 216–217, 222–223.

SUMMARY AND CONCLUSION

Our parent-youth conflict thus results from the interaction of certain universals of the parent-child relation and certain variables the values of which are peculiar to modern culture. The universals are (1) the basic age or birth-cycle differential between parent and child, (2) the decelerating rate of socialization with advancing age, and (3) the resulting intrinsic differences between the old and young on the physiological, psychosocial, and sociological planes.

Though these universal factors *tend* to produce conflict between parent and child, whether or not they do so depends upon the variables. We have seen that the distinctive general features of our society are responsible for our excessive parent-adolescent friction. Indeed, they are the same features which are affecting *all* family relations. The delineation of these variables has not been systematic, because the scientific classification of whole societies has not yet been accomplished; and it has been difficult, in view of the interrelated character of societal traits, to seize upon certain features and ignore others. Yet certainly the following four complex variables are important: (1) the rate of social change; (2) the extent of complexity in the social structure; (3) the degree of integration in the culture; and (4) the velocity of movement (e.g., vertical mobility) within the structure and its relation to the cultural values.

Our rapid social change, for example, has crowded historical meaning into the family time-span, has thereby given the offspring a different social content from that which the parent acquired, and consequently has added to the already existent intrinsic differences between parent and youth, a set of extrinsic ones which double the chance of alienation. Moreover, our great societal complexity, our evident cultural conflict, and our emphasis upon open competition for socioeconomic status have all added to this initial effect. We have seen, for instance, that they have disorganized the important relation of parental authority by confusing the goals of child control, setting up competing authorities, creating a small family system, making necessary certain significant choices at the time of adolescence, and leading to an absence of definite institutional mechanisms to symbolize and enforce the progressively changing stages of parental power.

If ours were a simple rural-stable society, mainly familistic, the emancipation from parental authority being gradual and marked by definite institutionalized steps, with no great postponement of marriage, sex taboo, or open competition for status, parents and youth would not be in conflict. Hence, the presence of parent-youth conflict in our civilization is one more specific manifestation of the incompatibility between an urban-industrial-mobile social system and the familial type of reproductive institutions.

2 THE PEER GROUP

New forms of peer relationships are springing up in the typical college experience, according to the physician writing here. As a result, he notes, three sexual moralities are being intensely debated on college campuses today: the "new morality," amorality, and traditional morality. The dilemma of college officials who have no consistent mandate from parents, students, faculty or alumni for policy in this area is here presented. Understanding of issues rather than proliferation of rules is stressed.

Dana L. Farnsworth

Sexual Morality and the Dilemma of the Colleges*

During the last few years much interest has been focused on sexual practices in the colleges, an interest stimulated in part by the demands of students for greater freedom in this area together with confusion on the part of parents and college officials as to what should be the proper standards of behavior. It is quite difficult for parents and children to talk together frankly about sexual matters because of the great gulf in experience between the two generations. The background of our present college generation is very different from that of their parents. Social change was quite rapid during the time the parents of today were maturing but is even more so at present.

Communication between older and younger members of the college communities also is hampered by many influences, including lack of a consensus as to what the central issues are, criticism of those who become interested in the subject and lack of persons competent to hold discussion groups.

* Presented at the 1965 annual meeting of the American Orthopsychiatric Association, New York, New York.

The sexual behavior of college students may be changing in the direction of practices formerly attributed to members of lower socioeconomic groups.[1] Reliable data on which to base such an opinion is not yet conclusive, but all general observations suggest this to be true. Not only is there thought to be a qualitative change in sexual practices but also an acceleration in such behavior. What was thought to be characteristic behavior at 18 or 20 years of age may now be observed in persons 16 to 18 or even younger.

There appear to be three general points of view regarding sexual behavior which can be characterized as: (1) the traditional morality, (2) the new morality, and (3) amorality. In the first of these, the traditional morality, the following principles are considered important:

—Renunciation or control of instinctual gratification permits a reasonable degree of civilization (Freud).
—Restraint tends to aid in developing a capacity for thoughtfulness concerning the welfare of others, particularly in a parental sense. Restraint also is thought to aid in the sublimation of sexual energies.
—Marriage becomes one of life's most cherished institutions when sexual restraint is practiced.
—The total moral fiber of a society is strengthened if sexual standards are maintained and weakened when sexual standards are ignored.
—Young people need help in controlling their strong impulses during their formative years.

In the new morality:

—Fidelity and consideration of others occupy a very high place.
—Physical sex is supposed to occur only after the establishment of friendship and love.
—Exploitation of the sexual partner is very much opposed.
—A high ethical component is apparent in the thinking of those who adhere to this general view even though it may not be in accordance with views traditionaly held, nor with the views of many religious groups.

In the third general viewpoint, which is in effect a somewhat amoral one, the central belief is that no restrictions are needed. If sexual impulses are allowed free rein, tension, anxiety, and frustration will be lowered, and happiness, satisfaction in living and effectiveness increased. The main problem for those who hold this point of view is that of persuading other persons to accept this way of behaving.

Obviously, no one of these three viewpoints can be portrayed explicitly without some qualification. Any individual may move from one viewpoint to another, or he may adhere to one and act as if he upheld another. It is this discrepancy

[1] Kinsey, A. C., W. B. Pomeroy, C. E. Martin, and P. H. Gebhard, *Sexual Behavior in the Human Female*, Philadelphia: W. B. Saunders Co., 1953, pp. 293–296.

between outer appearance and private behavior that is confusing to many persons, young and old alike.

In the past sexual behavior has been regulated in varying degrees by religious teachings and customs based on them and by fear of disaster if something goes wrong, such as detection, disease, or pregnancy. These deterrents to free sexual behavior have become somewhat weakened, especially during the last few decades for reasons familiar to everyone. At the same time there does not appear to have been any major moral breakdown. This suggests that the present generation of young people is fully as moral as any in the past although for different reasons.

College officials are very much concerned about certain key issues with respect to sexual behavior. For example, pressures toward experience which the young person does not wish and for which he is not yet ready may be unduly effective. A certain "bandwagon" effect occurs when peer group pressures push young people into such behavior. Frequently these pressures become so strong that a young person subject to them may feel guilty for *not* indulging in behavior currently popular, just as he may feel guilty *for* doing so if his training has been conventional or idealistic.

Illegitimate pregnancies pose problems which are virtually insoluble in terms of the social, cultural, and legal framework within which colleges must operate. It is probable that those persons who become pregnant are more disturbed emotionally than those who manage their lives without this complication. A recent study at a British university confirmed this thesis clearly.[2] The loss of any student because of the failure to manage sexual life successfully is always keenly felt by college officials as well as by the student's family.

Parental attitudes in general are not consistent enough for any guidelines or policy. Although opinions regarding sexual behavior are usually very firmly held, they are sometimes favorable and at other times unfavorable toward free sexual expression. Furthermore, when college administrators are called upon to take definite action in a given situation, there is a considerable tendency to blame such officials for their attempts at restoring order rather than looking at the original source of difficulty.

Freedom of choice is desired for all students, but when peer group pressures and the bandwagon effect become too strong, the individual may be deprived of this freedom.

I believe it is correct to assert that most college administrators do not wish to have a series of complicated and specific rules regarding behavior in this area; they realize that attempts at enforcement create many new problems. They do not wish to develop a spy system since the main purpose of the college experience is to enable students to develop the ability to make their own decisions—hopefully wise decisions. Most administrators are averse to impose on others their

---

[2] Kidd, C. B., R Giel, and J. B. Brown, "The Antecedent Mental Health of Pregnant Unmarried Women " *Proceedings of the British Student Health Association,* Oxford, For private circulation, pp. 51–59, 1964.

personal views, varying as these do from person to person, institution to institution, and section to section in the country. Administrators also cannot and do not wish to ignore public sentiment in the communities surrounding the colleges.

The excessive emphasis on all aspects of sex and obscenity which is now prevalent in novels, plays, and the mass media of communication may enable parents, teachers, and others to become more honest about sexual education than has been possible up to now.

At the present time it seems to me that the following problems that are well nigh insoluble prevent the promotion of a satisfactory kind of sexual education. Religious views vary among sects as well as in different parts of the country. Contraception is not completely reliable no matter what assurances some people may give. For college students this reliability may be impaired by conscious maneuvering on the part of one partner to produce pregnancy. The strong views of parents either in the direction of freedom of sexual behavior or of control are not expressed in such a way as to be of much help. Those who have a vested interest in pornography are very ingenious in developing excellent arguments to prevent interference in their moneymaking activities. College administrators value freedom and dislike censorship. Drawing the line between these attitudes and the desire to be helpful in guiding the development of young people into channels which will not be destructive to their future is a very delicate matter. There is no consensus as to appropriate means of furthering sex education not only at the college level but at all stages of development. Variations in attitudes toward sexual education in different sections of the country make it almost impossible for any widespread program to be adopted. Not the least of the difficulties is that anyone working seriously for improved sexual adaptation almost invariably becomes the object of ridicule from his associates and others in the community.

Once a program is agreed upon, the question then arises as to who will carry it out. Should it be done by parents, physicians, members of the clergy, marital counselors, faculty members, or some other group? If persons in any of these groups are willing to undertake this task, then how shall they be trained? How is it possible to separate the giving of factual information from moralizing?

College officials may be reticent about imposing their views on others, but they do wish to make it crystal clear that they uphold high standards of personal behavior just as they uphold intellectual integrity. They want to encourage as much thoughtfulness in this area of behavior as in any other. They wish to develop the kind of behavior which will not bring unnecessary unhappiness or disaster to young people as they fashion a way of life which will strengthen rather than weaken family life.

In my opinion, no particular viewpoint can be forced on young people, but there should be full and frank discussion in families, in groups, between couples and between older and younger colleagues in the colleges. If students are given answers without any real awareness of the issues, they will not be helped very much. If, however, a program is developed which will enable them to get a keen awareness of the issues that are involved, I believe that they will come up with better answers than our generation has been able to evolve.

After all, the problem is of more significance to young people than to those of the older generation. It is up to them to determine what kind of a world they want their children to live in. As they discuss sexual issues, it is desirable that they recall the nature of the training they experienced and the embarrassing situations they encountered in their childhood and to relate these experiences to their present problems. Finally, they should project their thoughts into the future in terms of developing attitudes toward sex which will be helpful as they begin to raise their own children. This three-dimensional approach to the problem helps bring some objectivity in place of the rather intense urgency with which most young adolescents and early adults view such problems.

Unfortunately, those who guide the policies of institutions get little help from parents, as I have already stated, because of the confusion and variety of their views, but I fear that they get even less help from the faculty. There is a tendency to leave all such matters to the dean's office and to give inadequate support to the idea that integrity confined to intellectual matters is quite insufficient and should be extended to all facets of behavior.

Even though the colleges are not *in loco parentis* to their students in the literal sense, they do have a responsibility to encourage them to adopt reasonable standards of behavior. There is no compelling reason for college administrators to be intimidated by the accusation that they are "upholding middle-class morals." The standards of morality and how they are determined and transmitted from one generation to another are proper and necessary subjects for continuing discussion between students and faculty members.

For parents, religious leaders, college officials, and all others who have a responsibility for late adolescents and young adults in secondary schools and colleges, some standards or ideals of behavior are desirable. Let us first examine the principle, "All premarital sexual intercourse is undesirable." Deviations from that code of behavior have every imaginable variety, ranging from rape or the production of a child with illegitimate parents (at the most regrettable end of the spectrum of undesirable activities) to intercourse between engaged couples who expect to marry soon and who can marry at once if pregnancy occurs (at the least undesirable end). In each instance of departure from the ideal the individual knows of its undesirability and is aware of possible consequences If unpleasant developments follow, he is in a position to learn from his experience; there is no one on whom he can reasonably project blame.

Let us assume another principle: "Premarital sexual relations are undesirable for those who are immature or cannot undertake the responsibility for a possible child, but for those who are mature and responsible, they are enriching and ennobling." Immediately a couple considering such relations must classify themselves, just at the time when it is only logical that they should be optimistic. It is easy to guess what the decision will be. If tragedy ensues, as it occasionally does, who can wonder that they are confused about society's inconsistent attitudes toward them.

Until we resolve our own confusions, we will not be in a favorable position to help our younger colleagues thread their way through the devious paths to development of sexual maturity. The experiences in our college psychiatric and counseling services lead us to believe that those who ignore the conventional standards are no more happy or effective than those who observe them. In fact, I believe that they have more depression, anxiety, agitation, and other inhibiting emotional conflict than those who manage to adhere to their ideals.

A large proportion of the younger students who come from families with reasonable ideals feel more comfortable if limits are set, if some guidelines are evident, and if someone is present who cares enough about them to help them avoid disaster.

As college officials, we are more concerned with the quality of future marriages and the family life they make possible than with any particular physical act in which either partner may have been involved. Of course, this does not imply that the nature and extent of sexual activities before marriage is irrelevant to the success of that marriage

If we are to progress in making sense out of this important area of personal development, we will need the sympathetic understanding and support of parents, faculty members, and the students themselves. There should then follow innumerable personal discussions, seminars, and other procedures for transmitting accurate information. At the same time the complex issues associated with choice or behavior should be explored. Opinions concerning sexual behavior should be expressed, but not put forth as scientific facts.

Sexual education and the formation of standards of sexual morality are not separable from other aspects of personal maturation, nor should they be unduly circumscribed as they are pursued in the colleges. The goal should be that of aiding each student to develop a healthy personality in which sexuality plays a constructive and satisfying part rather than being considered undignified and regrettable.

Analyzing the literary tastes of contemporary youth for insights into the peer culture, the author finds two conflicting world views. Bob Dylan's "Desolation Row" appeals because it is more passive and comfortable than the real world, which is viewed as insane. Tolkien's trilogy seems to appeal as widely as Dylan's psychedelic lyrics but, in contrast, urges action, responsibility and growth.

Alvin E. Winder

Bob Dylan and J. R. R. Tolkien: Two World Views to Which Adolescents Respond

"Frodo Lives" is one of several slogans that began to appear on buttons conspicuously worn by American teenagers about two years ago. When questioned now they talk quietly but intensely about hobbits, orcs, and Sauron, the Dark Lord. Their conversation reflects a growing feeling that J. R. R. Tolkien, former Oxford don and specialist in Anglo-Saxon literature, has with his fantasy *The Lord of the Rings* struck an expressive chord in the adolescent psyche.

Tolkien's only serious rival as an interpreter of adolescent needs and dreams thus far in the 1960's is Bob Dylan, generally hailed as the most important folk artist in America today. Dylan's metier is the message song. A young fellow performer whose support also comes from the youth segment, Joan Baez, has stated, "Bobby is expressing what I—and many other young people—feel, what we want to say. Most of the 'protest' songs about the bomb and race prejudice and conformity are stupid. They have no beauty. But Bobby's songs are powerful as poetry and powerful as music."

Characteristic of the paradox of contemporary youth is their responsiveness to both Dylan's message songs and Tolkien's heroic quest. Dylan's listeners are asked to identify with his view of the world, which he characterizes in his "Eve of Destruction" as being close to annihilation. He further develops this theme in his long recording titled "Desolation Row." In the latter, the work world is described in a way reminiscent of Paul Goodman's "rat race." Agents of society and articulate spokesmen of the adult establishment are said to

> Come out and around up everyone
> That knows more than they do.
> Then they bring them to the factory
> Where the heart attack machine
> Is strapped across their shoulders.

Major ideologies of the adult world are satirized. Einstein, disguised as Robin Hood, emerges as a snivelling, drooling old man reciting the alphabet of destruction, $E = mc^2$. Once, chants Dylan, he was a human being, with feeling and compassion:

> You would not think to look at him
> But he was famous long ago
> For playing the electric violin on Desolation Row.

Freud has reduced the world to the size of a leather cup and as a result the whole effort of psychoanalysis, of the patient and psychotherapist working together, is likened by Dylan to "playing on a penny whistle."

Finally, the stock images of adult man and woman are likened to Cassanova and Ophelia. Dylan's characterization of Ophelia is that "her sin is her lifelessness." Her time is spent "peeking into Desolation Row" and wishing she could return. Cassanova too seeks to escape from the life-in-death sentence imposed upon him as the price of entry into the adult world. He must be "poisoned with words" so that he will not heed his natural impulse to flee back to Desolation Row. Only there can he find some sanctuary. It is a place of becoming, a place where Cinderella can sweep up the pieces for eternity but where she can never become a princess. Finally, the singer says at the end of his Odyssey through the real world:

> Don't send me no letters, no
> Not unless you mail them from Desolation Row.

Dylan himself behaves in life as if he were a citizen of Desolation Row. His vision of the adolescent "hang-up" differs considerably from the "beat" view of the 1950's or the "new religion" of Timothy Leary. He does not, in the words of Dr. Leary, "turn on, tune in, and opt out." The LSD or pot trip is not for him, nor the beat celebration of being on the road. Commenting on his own life, he has remarked, "Just because you're free to move doesn't mean you're free." Not free, he shies away from quest or commitment: "Most people," he says, "have some kind of vested interest in the way things are now. Me, I'm cool." And in his advice to others he says, "All I can do is *show* the people who ask me questions about how I live. All I can do is be me."

Like Desolation Row, Tolkien's Middle Earth is also populated with human-like creatures who have somehow become distorted: the evil orcs, goblins, necromancers, and the Dark Lord called Sauron. The sympathetic hobbits live not in Desolation Row, where one waits as in limbo for entry into a real world, but in the simple world of the latency-age child: a world of great charm where evil acts rarely go beyond common gossip, a small measure of envy, or bad manners.

The theme of a quest characteristic of adolescence is introduced in Tolkien's *The Hobbit*. A respectable hobbit named Bilbo Baggins is induced by the wizard Gandalf to embark on a treasure hunt with a group of dwarfs who are setting off to regain their ancient treasure from its present owner, an evil dragon named Smaug. The unsophistocated dwarfs, like Bilbo the hobbit, display no competence in dealing with the evil world of the Middle Earth. Like Bilbo, they are childlike. But Bilbo begins to grow in the knowledge of evil, while the dwarfs remain forever stunted—that is, forever children. The trilogy, *The Lord of the Rings*, opens when Gandalf, the wise adult, persuades Bilbo to give up a magic ring that he found on his quest with the dwarfs.

For an understanding of *The Hobbit* and *The Lord of the Rings*, it is necessary to understand the symbolism of the ring. Bilbo had come upon it deep in the heart of the Misty Mountains, where he used its magic powers to become invisible and escape its previous owner. He has used its magic sparingly, the only indication Tolkien gives us in *The Hobbit* that the ring's powers should not be flaunted by its possessor; later on in the trilogy, however, the reader learns from Gandalf that the ring is evil and that it has the power to corrupt its wearer. From then on, its possession draws its owner toward evil. Bilbo's young cousin Frodo is charged with the duty of actually destroying the ring, for should Sauron, the Dark Lord who forged the ring, recover it, darkness would cover the earth. So begins the second quest.

What, for the adolescent, is the significance of the magic ring? Its psychological meaning is revealed in the use to which Bilbo originally put it: to assist its possessor in escaping from overwhelming odds. The ring saves Bilbo from being and feeling powerless.

The psychological threat of individual powerlessness is evident in the early life of the child. Indeed, the young infant is totally powerless in the face of the mother's decisions to give or to withhold nourishment, comfort, and therefore life itself. Freudian psychology tells us that it is in this period of childhood that the genesis of magical thinking occurs. Its earliest form is the child's halucinated image of the mother, a false perception brought about through a synthesis among the young child's senses. This halucination serves the child's psychic need to control the sources of his supplies and relieve his fear of loss. When indulged in by the adolescent, however, magical thinking to reduce a sense of personal powerlessness is considered regressive. It makes unnecessary any struggle to come to grips with the world—to experience both good and evil and to develop techniques for dealing with them. Its use inhibits psychic growth, for although it helps the adolescent to ward off his feelings of powerlessness, it does so at the expense of his remaining a child. It is, therefore, evil for him to use magical thought, just as it is evil for Frodo to use the magic ring. Both Frodo and the adolescent must destroy this evil, lest it get control over them.

We see then that both Dylan's and Tolkien's worlds are familiar to adolescents. Tolkien's heroic quest is exciting for them because it is like their own search for identity, a journey that takes them from the safe confines of middle and late childhood into an uncharted world where each individual must measure himself against reality, even if this reality proves dangerous and treacherous. Dylan's Desolation Row is hardly so appealing as a happy childhood place, yet it is preferable to the adult world which offers only enslavement and banality. Because Dylan finds more honesty and fidelity in Desolation Row than outside of it, he counsels the adolescent to remain there. Tolkien's advice is just the opposite. In the guise of Gandalf, the wise and good wizard, he urges the hobbit to leave the safe haven of childhood, the Shire, and to pursue his quest. Both Bilbo and Frodo leave as children and return as men.

3 THE SCHOOL

America's public schools are here characterized as highly successful melting pots, from which students from a variety of distinctive environments emerge as standardized products. Adducing data from a study which compared creativity with high intelligence as each is encouraged by the schools, Professor Friedenberg contends that originality is suppressed in the school's attempt to hand down prevailing middle class values and styles. He suggests that non-public schools are valuable as they provide alternative educational experiences.

Edgar Z. Friedenberg

The School
as a Social Environment

Our free public high school has from the beginning discharged two paramount social functions, neither of which has burdened secondary education elsewhere to anything like the same extent. The first of these is to build a common pattern of values and responses among adolescents from a diversity of class and ethnic backgrounds; the high school is a very important unit in our traditional system of melting pots. The second has been to help youngsters, as we say, to better themselves. In most industrial countries this second function has by now assumed about as much importance as it has in the United States; but this is recent.

Until World War II secondary education of university preparatory quality in the rest of the world was essentially education for adolescents who had a reasonably high level of ascribed status. They came, as we used to say, from good homes; and, good or not, what they learned in school was culturally continuous with what they were used to at home. The same symbols had roughly the same meanings in both *ambiances*. In the United States, however, this was not true.

The public high school, being locally run, has generally deferred in various ways to the claims of status, devoting a preponderance of its resources and granting a preponderance of its rewards to solidly middle-class boys and girls to the relative neglect of lower-status youngsters, whom it often treats with great hostility. But its *own* folkways and traditions are not solidly middle-class; and if the higher-status youngsters are more favorably treated than their lower-status classmates, it must be recognized that the high school also extracts from them extra service as laboratory specimens for aspiring lower-status youth, and that the favor they receive is to some extent vitiated by the experience of immersion in a shabby-genteel and often envious environment for a period of years.

The melting pot and mobility functions of the high school are complementary. In combination, they are peculiarly potent. The atmosphere of the high school is permeated by the values they generate when combined. The combination is synergistic, and it really works. Taken as the high school directs, public education efficiently produces the kind of individual who can, and does, operate to sustain and augment his own position in a limitless variety of situations; and who does so with a characteristic American style regardless of his antecedents. This is just as true of rich antecedents as poor, and probably truer. The American ideal of equality is nowhere stronger than in public education; and if its administrators tend to be "realistic" about status, they nevertheless keep a school in which an upper-class vocabulary or accent is informally corrected as surely as that of the slum; and the *insouciance* and spontaneity of rich and poor alike is reduced to the guarded good humor of the executive. In metropolitan areas, at least, the high school dropout rates for upper- and lower-status students appear to be roughly comparable. Figures on this are not available to my knowledge, because schools do not directly record the social class of their students, and upper-status youngsters who leave public school for private school are not considered dropouts. But leave they do, in large proportions; and they are not always fleeing from the Negro. Even from the suburbs that have so far excluded Negroes, upper-class white parents manage to send their children to Chaminade or Country Day, and the Negroes they meet there may ask them home to dinner, if they like them.

Upper-class rejection of the public school of course reflects a variety of motives, including sheer snobbery and an often erroneous presumption that the private school selected can get its students into Ivy colleges. But it also reflects a search for what parents call higher standards. On examination these standards often turn out to be no higher than those of the public school, but decidedly different from them. No more and no better work may de demanded of students, but it is slightly different work, and it is demanded for different reasons. This is true, of course, only of those private schools that do, in fact, have a social function different from the public schools. To the extent that the school depends for patronage on the anxiety of ambitious and socially insecure parents, it will compound the defects of the public school and add a few of its own. All private schools in America, no doubt, receive many helpless adolescents from such sources; but there are still some schools in which these students do not set the tone and they may therefore find refuge and real help in working out the meaning of their own lives under the illumination of disciplined study. This is harder for the public school to provide under its twin mandate to serve as a melting pot and a rocket to the moon.

There is something to be learned from etymology. The original meaning of education as a "drawing-out" makes an important point about the process—the same point that John Dewey and the progressive education people, at their best, also made. Education, if it is to have any depth, must start with and be derived from the life-experience of the student, which is in some measure unique for every boy or girl. It must cultivate this experience with a disciplined and demanding use of the best resources offered by the humanities and the sciences—to help the individual understand the meaning of his own experience. The consequence of such education, though it clearly leads the student to share in a universal cultural heritage, is more fundamentally to *sharpen* his individuality, to clarify and emphasize to *him* the ways in which he is unique.

A school that serves as a melting pot must inhibit this process, not facilitate it. Its purpose is to establish a common response to certain key stimuli, regardless of how different the respondents started out to be. Not only the content becomes stereotyped; so do the values underlying it, for the function of the school is to make it unnecessary to take account of the differences that might have resulted from the heterogeneity of life. It often fails, of course, and the student's folder receives a notation that his personality is defective; that he underachieves or is immature or emotionally disturbed—perfectly true, too; regression and ritualized internal conflict are classical responses to unbearably painful pressure on the emerging self.

When, however, the mandate to contribute to social mobility is joined to the melting pot process, the result is far more inhibitory to education. The student now learns that it is no longer sufficient to give the same answer; he must learn to distinguish the *right* answer. And he must learn to do this reliably and, as nearly as possible, automatically while his inner voice continues to shriek that the answer is wrong. Of course, his inner voice gradually gets a lot softer and more plaintive, and may finally show up as nothing more than a symptom. At this juncture, however, it would be a little unfair to say that the student's values are stereotyped; a real value has emerged. It has become important to him to learn to give the right answer quicker and more often than the next boy, who now is seen as a competitor rather than a person. And the inner voice is no longer irrelevant. It becomes, instead, the voice of the betrayer.

Professors Jacob W. Getzels and Philip W. Jackson in their recent work on *Creativity and Intelligence* [1] illustrate this process statistically. They drew their sample from a private, university-affiliated high school which afforded them, I should judge, an unusually abundant supply of the kind of "far-out" youngster that their methodology defines as creative. Their independent variables—that is, the criteria by which they assigned individual youngsters to their "high-creative"

[1] Jacob W. Getzels and Philip W. Jackson, *Creativity and Intelligence*, New York: John Wiley & Sons, Inc., 1962.

group—are essentially measures of "divergent thinking," as Professor J. P. Guilford of the University of Southern California defines this kind of mental activity in contrast to the "convergent thinking" of conventional high IQ students. Getzels and Jackson, in other words, started out by setting up a procedure in which the kind of adolescent who is especially prone to find a wealth of unconventional meanings in familiar material, and to use these meanings to arrive at perfectly workable but sometimes shockingly original solutions to problems, was contrasted with the kind of adolescent who is adept at setting such meanings aside as distractions and marching with power and determination along the path of conventional wisdom.

From a sample of 449 private high school students with a mean IQ of 129, Getzels and Jackson selected 26 students who were in the top 20 per cent on their Guilford-type measures of creativity, but not in IQ; and 28 who were in the top 20 per cent in IQ, but not in creativity. The two groups were then compared with each other and with the total group of 449 on school performance as measured by standard achievement tests; teachers' preferences for having them, when identified by name, in class; and the quality and manner of their response to a series of pictures like those used in the Thematic Apperception Test.

Both groups did equally well on the subject-matter tests of school achievement, and better than the total group of 449. The teachers, however, preferred the high IQ students to both the "high creatives" and those who had not been included in either group; and though they did prefer the high creatives to the average student, the difference was too small to be statistically significant. It should be borne in mind that this was a private secondary school with an exceptionally intelligent student body, and teachers who, to some extent, had chosen to teach gifted students and were accustomed to them. But they nevertheless preferred school achievement to be expressed in conventional terms, which the creatives were unlikely to do.

Getzels and Jackson quote illustratively the following sample responses to one of their story-pictures.

One picture stimulus was perceived most often as a man in an airplane reclining seat returning from a business trip or conference. A high IQ student gave the following story: "Mr. Smith is on his way home from a successful business trip. He is very happy and he is thinking about his wonderful family and how glad he will be to see them again. He can picture it, about an hour from now, his plane landing at the airport and Mrs. Smith and their three children all there welcoming him home again." A high-creative subject wrote this story: "This man is flying back from Reno, where he has just won a divorce from his wife. He couldn't stand to live with her any more, he told the judge, because she wore so much cold cream on her face at night that her head would skid across the pillow and hit him in the head. He is now contemplating a new skid-proof face cream."

This is perhaps sufficient to illustrate the contrasting cognitive styles of Getzels' and Jackson's high creatives and high IQ's; and also to suggest what it is that teachers dislike about the former. The youngsters in their high-creative sample *do* disrupt the social environment. You can lead them to the pot; but they just don't melt, they burn. Intelligent and perceptive critics of Getzels' and Jackson's work have pointed out that the actual power of the creative students to create anything worthwhile remains, at their age, unestablished; but their prickliness, hostility, and aggression show up on nearly every instrument of the study. Getzels and Jackson included among their procedures one of having each subject draw whatever he liked on a sheet of paper captioned "Playing Tag in the School Yard." The drawings of the high IQ subjects are literal and humorless, "stimulus-bound"; the high creatives' drawings are fantastic and comical, with something of the quality of Till Eulenspiegel about them; but they are also gory. Combining Getzels' and Jackson's Tables 10 and 11,[2] we get the following statistics on these drawings as they rate them:

| | Type of Student | |
	High IQ	High creative
Number of students in sample	28	26
Humor present	5	14
Humor absent	23	12
Violence present	1	9
Violence absent	27	17

We do not, of course, know how this spiral of reciprocal hostility starts; whether the youngsters become hostile and sarcastic because they are punished for their originality, even though at first they express it openly, innocently, and warmly; or whether a youngster will only think and feel divergently if he starts with a certain detachment from and distrust of conventional, established attitudes and procedures. Most likely—say, on the basis of such a cogent analysis as that in Ernest G. Schachtel's brilliant and classic paper, "On Memory and Childhood Amnesia,"[3] the beginnings of creativity in the exploratory sensuality of childhood are quite free from hostility; they are innocent, though hardly chaste. But exploratory sensuality is punished long before the child gets to school, and certainly before he gets to high school. Among the initially gifted, the high creatives are perhaps those who have received enough affection through the total process that they can afford to respond to insult by getting angry and verbally swatting back. The high IQ's have been treated wholly as instruments of parental aspirations, even at home, and become anxious at any sign that they are getting off the track; anger and hostility are beyond their emotional means. The findings of Getzels and Jackson on the home background of their contrasting subjects bear this out.

[2] Jacob W. Getzels and Philip W. Jackson, *Creativity and Intelligence,* New York: John Wiley & Sons, Inc., 1962, p. 49. The tables indicate that the statistical probability of a chance difference between high IQ's and high creatives, as great as that shown here, is .02 or less.

[3] Ernest G. Schachtel, "On Memory and Childhood Amnesia," *Metamorphosis,* New York: Basic Books, Inc., 1959, pp. 279–322.

But their most poignant data were obtained from an instrument that they called the Outstanding Traits Test. This consisted of 13 thumbnail descriptions of such traits as social skill, goal-directedness and good marks, using phrases like "Here is the student who is best at getting along with other people"; "Here is the student who is best able to look at things in a new way and to discover new ideas"; "Here is the outstanding athlete in the school," and so forth. The students in their sample were asked to rank these 13 descriptions in three different ways: as "preferred for oneself," as "favored by teachers," and as "believed predictive of adult success." The rank-order correlations obtained between the high IQ and high creative students as to how these traits contributed to later success was *unity*; as to what teachers preferred, it was 0.98. The high creative and high IQ students, in short, were in absolute agreement as to what traits would make a person succeed in adult life; they were virtually agreed as to what teachers liked in students—though the two ratings were not identical. Nevertheless, the correlation between the two groups' ratings of these traits as "preferred for oneself" was only 0.41. This can only be interpreted to mean that one or both of these groups believed that pleasing teachers and becoming successful was just not worth what it cost, even though they agreed completely as to what that cost would be.

Which group rejected the image of success that both shared? The data clearly permit me to resolve this question and end your suspense. Here, instead of correlations *between* the high IQ's and the high creatives, we need, of course, correlations *within* each group for the three possible bases of sorting. Here they are:

Components of correlation	Students	
	High IQ	High creative
Personal traits believed "predictive of success" and "favored by teachers"	0.62	0.59
Personal traits "preferred for oneself" and "believed predictive of adult success"	0.81	0.10
Personal traits "preferred for oneself" and "believed favored by teachers"	0.67	−0.25

I would interpret these statistics to mean that the high creatives cannot bring themselves to be what they believe success requires, and are even more strongly repelled by what the teacher demands. The correlation coefficients on the two "favored by teachers" categories are really very curious and interesting across the board. I find a .6 correlation here astonishingly low for *both* groups—with these N's of 26 and 28 such a correlation has little statistical significance. While, for the high IQ's, the correlation between "preferred for oneself" and "predictive of success" is high, for the high creatives, it is negligible.

BOTH HIGH IQ's, HIGH CREATIVES SHOW A NEED TO ACHIEVE

All these data could be explained very satisfactorily by the hypothesis that the high creatives, spontaneous and joyful as the happy-go-lucky Negro slave of song and story, just don't give a damn; that this is their way of singing "Hallelujah, I'm a bum." But it won't do. Using two standard measures of the need to achieve, David McClelland's *need: achievement* and Fred L. Strodtbeck's *V-score*, Getzels and Jackson were unable to find any significant differences between the two groups, or between either group and the total population of 449; the figures given for the high creatives are actually slightly higher on both measures. So we must turn for our interpretation to the relationship between the students and the school itself.

Both groups, I infer, see the teacher as on the side of success, but being too naive and square to be a very reliable guide as to how to go after it. Since the high IQ's are determined to *be* the kind of person who succeeds, this reduces the relevance of the teacher to him, but not the relevance of the school. Or to put it another way, the importance of the school as the monitor of his progress is quite enough to bring the high IQ to terms with it; and the terms are generous enough not to demand that he listen to what it actually says. To the high creative, the whole experience is rather frustrating and annoying, and relevant only because there is no viable alternative to high school for a middle-class adolescent. Lower-class adolescents who are not interested in economic success or who feel the school too suffocating can just drop out, go off on a kick, and let the authorities conceal their relief while they pretend to search for them. But this kind of direct action would cost the middle-class youngster his role, and cause him too much anxiety to be a satisfactory alternative. Generally he stays, and looks for ancillary satisfactions in specialized relationships with his peers, in sports or hobbies or sometimes sex and even love, building up a credential while inwardly rejecting the qualities the credential symbolizes.

For both groups, however, the function of the school becomes essentially liturgical, not epistemological. It isn't supposed to make sense. It is not appropriate to believe, disbelieve, or test what one is taught in school. Instead, one *relates* to it; one tries to figure out why this line has been taken rather than another, to figure out what response is expected, and give it.

The result is a peculiar kind of moral vacuity; a limitation of responsible *perception*, and therefore, of moral behavior, to situations that are wholly concrete and immediate. The public school is not primarily an educational institution. I have forgotten who first said that most Christians would feel equal consternation at hearing Christianity denounced and at seeing it practised; it ought, presumably, to have been Mary. But I am quite sure that this could justly be said of most Americans with respect to public education. In many ways, the relationship of the school to the community is like that of a TV station that carries mostly network programs but that is largely dependent on local advertising for support. Like the TV station, the school has its own technical staff, and such autonomy as it possesses is derived from their custody of the mysteries and the records, rather than from any considerable measure of popular deference to their authority. The entertainment provided is frequently of high quality and shrewdly geared to the public taste. Concessions to the intellect and culture, provided as a public service, tend to be more ponderous, conventional, and unconvincing. Though the staff likes to boast about how much of this sort of thing they program, they are self-conscious about it, and rather fearful. The commercials for the local way of life are interminable, boring, and egregiously dishonest, and the audience knows it. But they are hard to change for they are the real basis for the support the school receives. And they are effective, as good commercials are, not so much in stimulating an active desire for the product as in convincing the audience that only a social misfit would be without it.

STUDENTS PREPARE FOR NEXT STEP

What the students learn best in high school is how to function in and uitilize a limited power network to achieve limited personal and social objectives. They learn how to get along and make ready for the next onward state. By the time they reach college, they are likely to be thoroughly impatient of anything else; and in our culture, college seldom tries their patience much; the process continues. To me, the most interesting finding in a recent study of medical students [4] is the righteous resentment with which the young medics respond to instruction in medical—to say nothing of social—theory. What they want from medical school is conventional knowledge and practical hints (what they call pearls) and a clear road to the practitioner's license. To get this they are willing to work like dogs; but they resist any suggestion that they work like a higher primate.

Doctors, of course, have notoriously high IQ's, and it is not astonishing that medical students should resemble Getzels' and Jackson's high IQ's in their characteristic cognitive style. But they are also quite creative, when they feel that circumstances and the American Medical Association permit; as are many high IQ's. Creativity and intelligence, like height and weight, are undoubtedly highly correlated. Getzels and Jackson adopted a classic design for their study to permit them to examine contrasts; just as biologists studying human metabolism might deliberately set out to study the differences between short, fat people and tall, thin ones. But both are exceptional, which is why the sample fell from 449 to 28 in one quadrant and 26 in the other. Had they chosen to study youngsters who were in the top 20 per cent in both creativity and IQ, they would probably have found 60 or so in the sample. How would *they* have fared in school?

Getzels and Jackson tell us nothing about this. My own understanding and observation of public education suggests that they would probably be very successful, indeed, and would be well received by the school and acquire a sub-

[4] Howard S. Becker, Blanche Geer, Everett S. Hughes, and Anselm L. Strauss, *Boys in White,* Chicago: University of Chicago Press, 1962.

stantial proportion of positions of leadership. We would accept them as our best young Americans—executive material. And the school would teach them to be discreet: not to let their creativity get the upper hand, not to jeopardize their chances by antagonizing persons more stupid than themselves who might nevertheless turn up later on some committee that was passing on them. The pitch would be made on a high moral plane—usually in terms of keeping their availability so as not to impair their usefulness—but the net effect would be to convince the youngster that he ought not to get out of line or speak out of turn, if he hoped ultimately to put his creativity to use in the service of, say, General Electric or the United States Food and Drug Administration.

A statistic frequently cited in the United States is that we spend a little more on hard liquor than we do on public education. I have just finished reading a book which seems to me more striking in its educational implications than any work directly *about* education since Martin Mayer's *The Schools.*[5] This book is Theodore H. White's *The Making of the President 1960;*[6] and after reading it I find that datum shocking. We ought to be spending a *lot* more on hard liquor. We are going to need it, and besides, it works. But I have introduced Mr. White's book into this discussion, not primarily as a vivid portrait of the failure of public education to instruct a trustworthy electorate—though that, according to James Madison, was its essential function—but to allude to one particular passage as a specific illustration of creativity and what happens to it. Mr. White gives a circumstantial account of Richard Nixon's suspiciousness of the press and ineptness in communicating with it, which made the job of the reporters assigned to cover his campaign—for papers primarily committed to his support—almost impossible. The reporters themselves came to dislike and distrust Mr. Nixon and his program. In their dispatches, no hint of their actual feelings or personal appraisal appeared.

But Mr. White reports:

> Then having done their duty, they began frivolously to write imaginary dispatches of what they felt would be a more accurate transcription of their private understanding. I reproduce here a few leads of such dispatches as illustrations of what happens when the press feels itself abused.
> Guthrie Center, Iowa (read one)—Vice-President Nixon said today farmers should eat their way out of the surplus problem. . . .
> Guthrie Center, Iowa (another)—Vice-President Nixon admitted today that the farm problem was too big for the Republican Party to handle. He said that if elected President, he would appoint Senator Hubert H. Humphrey as Secretary of Agriculture and let him wrestle with the problem. . . .
> Guthrie Center, Iowa (another)—Vice-President Nixon today called on Pope John XXIII for guidance in finding a solution to the troublesome farm problems which have plagued Catholic, Jew and Protestant alike. . . .[7]

[5] Martin Mayer, *The Schools,* New York: Harper & Brothers, 1960.
[6] Theodore H. White, *The Making of the President 1960,* Atheneum House, Inc., 1961.
[7] Theodore H. White, *The Making of the President 1960,* Atheneum House, Inc., 1961, pp. 274–275.

. My point is that Mr. White also illustrates what doesn't happen even when the press feels itself abused. These "imaginary dispatches" may well afford "a more accurate transcription of their private understanding" than what the reporters actually transmitted. Their responsibility as reporters, I should say, included that of letting the public know not only what Mr. Nixon had said but what they thought he was actually like, properly labeled, of course, as a subjective judgment. This they were too canny to release until too late for it to do any good.

It is self-evident, I believe, that the quality of these imaginary dispatches is identical with the quality of the picture stories produced by the high creatives in Getzels' and Jackson's study, but the factually correct dispatches are the kind of response the high IQ's produce. The reporters, then, must have been both; but they had learned better than to be both when the chips were down and people were watching. They were not deliberately taught this in school, but school is a very good place in which to learn it.

Mr. White further writes:

> One had to see Nixon entering a small Iowa village, the streets lined with schoolchildren, all waving American flags until it seemed as if the cavalcade were entering a defile lined by fluttering, peppermint-striped little banners . . . to see him at his best . . . These people were his natural constituency, his idiom their idiom . . . [8]
>
> . . . He woke in Marietta, Ohio, on Monday, October 25th, to begin his last 'peak' effort and it was clear from his first speech of the day that he was at one with his audience as he had not been since he had passed through the corn fields of Iowa in the first week of the campaign. A sign outside the courthouse of Marietta, Ohio, read: High School Debaters Greet World Debater—the sign was apropos, and of the essence of his last trip as he revived. For he *was* a high-school debater, the boy who had, some thirty years before, won a Los Angeles *Times* prize for his high-school oration on the Constitution. He was seeking not so much to score home a message as to win the hearts of his little audiences. . . .[9]

It *is* a little like entering a defile. Some of us would prefer to enter a demurrer. On the basis of cognitive style I would infer that this would include a disproportionate number of high creatives. But how, in the present public high school, does one go about it?

One of the traditional forms of demurrer in our society is to get up and slowly walk away. We have always counted on pluralism as our most effective weapon against conformity and, in de Tocqueville's phrase, "the tyranny of the majority"; and I think it is one of the best social instruments that could be devised and inherent in the nature of democracy. For that reason, I am very much in favor of private and parochial schools. As a matter of social policy, I think they should receive some tax support. I am not a constitutional lawyer, and I cannot judge the legal merits of the argument that aid to church schools, granted at their request, would constitute the Congress making a law respecting an establishment of religion. Personally, I think this is a ridiculous interpretation of the First

[8] Theodore H. White, *The Making of the President 1960*, Atheneum House, Inc., 1961, p. 277.
[9] Theodore H. White, *The Making of the President 1960*, Atheneum House, Inc., 1961, p. 300.

Amendment; but, then, the First Amendment has always been my favorite passage of the Constitution, and I am naturally reluctant to believe that it is against anything that I favor.

I am convinced that private schools—and in this country many of these are church-supported—contribute more to the general welfare even than they do to their own constituency. We so desperately need alternative life-styles and *ethical models that are related to a particular community and to the experience of life within it*, rather than recipes for tearing away from one's roots and learning to function smoothly among successively more affluent groups of strangers. As to the risk of encountering God, well, it is true that He can be very tricky. But I doubt if the encounter can be altogether avoided. It would certainly not harm any youngster—rather in the spirit of the New England gentlewoman who took up the study of Hebrew at the age of eighty-five—to learn how to confront Him and thrash out those issues on which they were in disagreement. Adolescents generally get along very well with God, anyhow. The Creation is exactly the kind of thing they can imagine having done themselves, and they can sympathize with the kind of trouble He got himself into by acting out His creative impulse. It is only in later life, the image having become somewhat tarnished, that the meeting tends to be rather embarrassing to both.

It is difficult to suggest practical ways in which the public school might represent and support a greater diversity of values and a less purely instrumental conception of learning. At present, the public high school lacks dignity. It is often incoherent. Whatever is learned of graciousness and leisure in English or art class—and it isn't likely to be much—is undercut by the food and the noise and standing in line in the cafeteria. The social studies class may discuss civil liberty, but the students still need a pass to walk through the hall and school disciplinary procedures are notably lacking in due process. The students are encouraged to get together in groups to discuss important issues, as long as there is somebody to represent all sides and the criticism doesn't go too deep. But there isn't any place to do it that is out of reach of the public address system announcing when you have to go to get your yearbook picture taken or directing Tom Brown to report to the principal's office *at once;* the efficiency of the p.a. system depends on the fact that you can't get away from it.

All these are trivia; what is not trivial is the continuous experience, day after day and year after year, of triviality itself; of being treated like a tiny unit in an administrative problem. So, really, it does add up; this is *how* you are taught not to take yourself too seriously. This is where you learn that whatever may be officially said, actual official decisions are made with the short-run purpose of getting the job done and keeping out of trouble. This is where you learn to keep your conversation brief, friendly, and to the point, instead of getting all hung up on ideas like an egghead or an Oxbridge don.

Of course, these things and worse occur in many private schools which can also be barren and stultifying. But when they are, there is at least the theoretical possibility of appealing to an explicit educational tradition that transcends

American middle-class practice to try and change them. These *are* basic American middle-class values, however; so there is not much use appealing there, though a smart public school administrator may develop considerable skill in identifying subgroups in his community that take education and youngsters more seriously. But it is a laborious and dangerous process. Public school administrators who try to give their communities better education than they are used to have a very short life expectancy. If you wish to see a case study of such a situation in detail, *Small Town in Mass Society*,[10] contains a superb one. But you know it already.

There is nothing wrong with the school as a social environment, except what is wrong with America. One of the sailors in my company when I was in the Navy during World War II had a stock proposal that he used to make with reference to any of our mates who was seriously annoying him. "Let's ostracize him," he said. "You hold him, and I'll do it." Technically, what Coleman proposes is the exact contrary. But I am afraid it comes to the same thing in the end.

It seems to me, then, that I have no choice but to conclude on a note of satisfaction. As a social environment the public high school, by and large, functions very effectively. It is expected to socialize adolescents into the American middle-class, and that is just what it does. You can actually see it doing it. If that isn't what you want, go fight Livingston Street.*

[10] Arthur J. Vidich and Joseph Bensman, *Small Town in Mass Society,* Princeton, New Jersey: Princeton University Press, 1958.
* [The offices of the New York City Board of Education are at 110 Livingston Street.]

Stepping back from the school system to examine its products as they interact with the culture at large, Paul Goodman finds youth isolated in a restrictive subculture. In this article he focuses on the speech of that subculture—its vocabulary, its content and its roots in the speech of adult society—and concludes that the hip, semi-articulate speech of adolscents is at the bottom a substitute for other, more meaningful questions they cannot ask.

Paul Goodman

The Universe of Discourse in Which They Grow Up

Let us now consider the interaction of school and the general culture as a climate of communication and ask:

What happens to the language and thought of young Americans as they grow up toward and through adolescence?

In the institutional speech, a child hears only one world-view. In the nature of the case, every mass-medium caters to a big common-denominator of opinion and taste, but even more influential is that the mass-media interlock. "News," for instance, is what is selected as newsworthy by two or three news services; three almost identical broadcasting networks abstract from the same; and the same is again abridged for the *Junior Scholastic*. Even for this news, only 60 towns in America now have competing newspapers (in 1900 there were 600). Similarly, the "standard of living," the way to live respectably and decently, is what is shown in the ads in a few mass-circulation magazines and identically in the TV commercials. Movie-sets of respectable life come from the same kind of engineers. Similarly, "political thought" is the platforms of two major parties that agree on all crucial issues, like the Cold War and the Expanding Economy, and that get practically all of the coverage by the same newspapers and broadcasters.

Much of this public speech is quite meaningless. The ads compete with high rhetoric but the commodities are nearly the same, and a child can see that our lives are not *quite* so vastly occupied by soap, cigarettes, and beer. Politicians are very polemical, but they avoid any concrete issues that might differentiate the candidates and lose votes. The real meaning of the speeches, the goal of profits and power, is never stated. By age 11 or 12, bright children, perhaps readers of *Mad* magazine, recognize that most of the speech is mere words.

The interlocking of the schools into the system is more serious, for here the children have to work at it and cooperate. The story is the same. The galloping increase of national tests guarantees that the class-work will become nothing but preparation for these same tests. Corporation talent-scouts hover in the high schools, and even the primary schools are flooded with corporation brochures. Excellent scientists in Washington who chart courses in science and mathematics understand that there must be leeway for individuality and guesswork; but in the hands of incompetent teachers, the national standard naturally becomes an inflexible ruler. And TV and machine-teaching are formal statements that *everybody apperceives in the same way, with no need for dialogue.*

Apart from family, children have little speech with any adults except schoolteachers. But the crowding and scheduling in school allow little chance or time for personal contact. Also, increasingly in grade schools as well as in colleges, the teachers have abdicated their personal role to specialist counselors and administrators, so that confiding and guidance tend to occur only in extreme situations. One must be "deviant" to be attended to as a human being.

This public speech cannot easily be tested against direct observation or experience. Urban and suburban children do not see crafts and industries. Playthings are prefabricated toys; there is little practical carpentry, plumbing, or mechanics; but there are do-it-yourself kits. The contrast of city and country vanishes in endless conurbation. Few children know animals. Even basic foods are packaged and distributed, and increasingly precooked, in the official style.

And a child hears less of any rival style or thought. The rival world-view of (even hypocritical) religion is no longer influential. Children do not know the Bible. Eccentric classical children's literature is discouraged by librarians because it does not fit educators' word-lists and is probably unhygienic. The approved books are concocted according to the official world-view. Other more exciting reading, like comic books, does not contrast to life but withdraws from it, is without reality or feeling. The movies are the same more insidiously, because they are apparently adult and real. Finally, the ideal models of careers with their characters and philosophies—scientist, explorer, nurse, writer—have been normalized to TV stereotypes: they are all the same Organization Man, though they wear various costumes.

Nevertheless, this one system of meaning, although homogeneous and bland, is by no means sparse or quiet. On the contrary, the quantity of public speech, plays, information, cartoons is swamping. The tone is jumpy and distracting. In the schools, exposure occurs with intense pressure of tests for retention and punishment for failure to retain.

No one can critically appreciate so many images and ideas; and there is very little solitude or moratorium to figure them out. A child is confused. And he is also anxious, because if the information is not correctly parroted, he will fall off the school ladder and be a drop-out; or he will not be hep among his little friends.

At a childish level, all this adds up to brainwashing. The components are (a) a uniform world-view, (b) the absence of any viable alternative, (c) confusion about the relevance of one's own experience and feelings, and (d) a chronic anxiety, so that one clings to the one world-view as the only security. This *is* brainwashing.

Of course, in all societies and periods of history small children are subject to brainwashing, for they are weak, ignorant, economically dependent, and subject to bullying. In some ways in our society the brainwashing of children is not so pernicious as it has been at other times, for there is less corporal punishment, less extreme poverty, less fear of death, and less brutal toilet-training and sexual disciplining. On the other hand, the ideological exposure is unusually swamping, systematic, and thorough. Profit societies, like garrison states, invade every detail of life. But worst of all is that parents are as baffled as the children; since the areas of choice and initiative are so severely limited, they too lose touch with personal and practical information.

Thus, despite our technology of surplus, our civil peace(?), and so much educational and cultural opportunity, it is hard for an American child to grow toward independence, to find his identity, to retain his curiosity and initiative, and to acquire a scientific attitude, scholarly habits, productive enterprise, poetic speech.

Unfortunately, the pervasive philosophy to which children are habituated as they grow up is the orthodoxy of a social machine not interested in persons, except to man and aggrandize itself. Especially not young persons.

Then what happens when, with this background of impersonal and stereotyped language, the child becomes adolescent: awkward and self-conscious, sexually hungry and falling in love, searching for identity, metaphysical, shaken in religious faith or undergoing religious conversion, his Oedipus-complex reviving, making a bid for freedom from home, grandiosely ambitious, looking for a vocation, eager to be serviceable as a human being? At best, in organic communities, rational communication breaks down and the community has recourse to rites of passage.

The American world-view is worse than inadequate; it is irrelevant and uninterested, and adolescents are spiritually abandoned. They are insulated by not being taken seriously. The social machine does not require or desire its youth to find identity or vocation; it is interested only in aptitude. It does not want new initiative, but conformity. Our orthodoxy does not bear metaphysics. Religious troubles are likely to be treated as psychotic; they are certainly disruptive of urban order and scholastic scheduling. Many, maybe most, of the careers that are open are not services to humanity; that is not why businesses are run, nor why bombs are stockpiled. Idealism is astonishingly without prestige.

The adolescent sexual situation is peculiarly ambiguous. We are in a transitional phase of the sexual revolution and there is a breakdown of repression (keeping out of mind) and also less inhibition of sexual behavior. Yet neither in the economy, the housing, nor the family pattern is there any provision for the changed mores. Quite the contrary, the years of tutelage even tend to lengthen, especially for middle-class youth in colleges whose administrations regard themselves as *in loco parentis*. The official mental-hygienic ideology bears little relation to the stormy images and imperative demands of adolescent love. In the elementary and junior high schools, sexual facts do not officially exist. But an adolescent is supposed to be sexual or there is alarm.

Embarrassment—the inability to express or reveal one's needs and feelings to the others—is universal among adolescents. But in our society it is especially problematic. The embarrassment contains or will contain hostility to those who will not pay attention or will put one down; and also despair at the futility of trying to make oneself clear. For there is not even a common language relevant to one's burning private facts—how pathetic it is to hear adolescents using the language of TV marriage-counselors, or of movies! Inevitably, silent hostility is retroflected as self-denigration. An adolescent ceases to believe in the rightness of his own wants, and soon he even doubts their existence. His rebellious claims seem even to himself to be groundless, immature, ridiculous.

Broadly speaking, the difficulties of adolescent communication, both in speaking and listening, are kinds of embarrassment. Let us here discuss adolescent speechlessness, in-group language and sub-culture, and how adolescents finally give up their own meaning and swallow the official adult philosophy hook, line, and sinker.

Embarrassment may be grounded in too strong desire and confusion, or in hostility and fear.

Paling and blushing embarrassment in expressing lust or aspiration is largely due to confusion caused by powerful feelings that have been untried, or vague new ideas that seem presumptuous. It is akin to ingenuous shame, which is exhibition suddenly inhibited because it is (or might be) unacceptable. With courage and encouragement, such speechless embarrassment can falter into sweet or ringing poetic speech, by which the youth explains himself, also to himself. More common with use, however, is for the youth to inhibit his stammering and to brazen out the situation with a line imitated from the mass-media or salesmanship. For example, the strategy is to "snow" the girl rather than talk to her. Thereby he proves that he is grownup, has an erection etc., but he sacrifices feeling, originality, the possibility of growth, and the possibility of love.

The speechless embarrassment of hostility is fear of retaliation if one reveals oneself. Suppose a youth is reprimanded, advised, or perhaps merely accosted by an authoritative adult, e.g. a guidance counselor; he will maintain a sullen silence and not give the adult the time of day. His presumption is that the adult is setting a trap, could not understand, does not care anyway. The youth cannot adopt a breezy line, as with a peer, for the adult has more words. He will be taken as fresh, hostile, or in bad taste. Therefore it is best to say nothing, expressing (perhaps unconsciously) a blazing contempt. In this situation, the youth's interpretation is not too erroneous, except that the authority is usually not malevolent but busy and perhaps insensitive.

Suppose, however, the adult is a good teacher who does care for the young persons and would like to reach them in meaningful terms, not the orthodoxy. Then, as Frank Pinner has pointed out, it is likely that the teacher's dissenting ideas will be met by a wall of silence that makes communication impossible. The young are so unsure, and their distrust is such, that in the crisis of possible contact they prefer to cling to safe conformity, even though among themselves they may bitterly attack these same conformist ideas.

Even worse, there is an hermetic silence about anything deeply felt or threatening; such things are unspeakable even to one's peers, no less to adults. One may boast to a friend about a sexual conquest or fret about poor grades, but one may not reveal that one is in love or has a lofty aspiration. Or to give a tragic example: Puerto Rican boys will chatter endless small talk and one-up one another, but nobody will mention that one of their number has just been sent to jail or that one has just died of an overdose of heroin. If the forbidden subject is mentioned, they do not hear it. They cannot psychologically afford to relate themselves, their verbal personalities, to the terrible realities of life. (Incidentally, I have heard from teachers in the New York schools that there is a similar cleavage in many young Puerto Rican's knowledge of the English language. They seem to talk English fluently as long as the subject is superficial and "grown-up"; but they are blank in many elementary words and phrases, and are quite unable to say, in English, anything that they really want or need.)

To diminish embarrassment, since communication with the adults is cut off, there is developed an increasingly exaggerated adolescent "sub-culture," with its jargon, models, authors, and ideology. Let us first distinguish between a "sub-culture" and a "sub-society."

An intense youth sub-society is common in most cultures. In our culture, the interest in sexual exploration, dancing, simple exciting music, athletics, cars and races, clubs and jackets, one-upping conversation, seems to be natural to youth— just as many adult interests are naturally irrelevant and boring to them. Also, the sharing of secrets, often mysterious even to themselves, is everywhere a powerful bond of union among adolescents; and certainly their business is nobody else's business. The Youth Houses of some primitive communities institutionalize all this rather better than our own boarding-schools and colleges, which are too ridden with *in loco parentis* regulations.

The development of such a sub-society into a full-blown sub-culture, however, is not normal, but reactive. It signifies that the adult culture is hostile to adolescent interests, or is not to be trusted; that parents are not people and do not regard their children as people; that the young are excluded from adult activities that might be interesting and, on the other hand, that most adult activities are *not* worth growing up into as one becomes ready for them. Rather, on the contrary, the adults are about to exploit the young, to pressure them into intrinsically boring careers, regardless of proper time or individual choice.

Normally there is not a "youth culture" and an "adult culture," but youth is the period of growing up in the one culture. With us, however, youth feels itself to be almost out-caste, or at least manipulated. It therefore has secrets, jargon, and a lore of sabotage and defense *against* the adult culture.

But then, since the intellectual life of callow boys and girls in isolation from the grown-up economy and culture is thin gruel, youth interests are vastly puffed up into fads, disk-jockeys, politically organized gangs and wars, coterie literature, drugs and liquor, all frantically energized by youthful animal spirits—and cleverly managed by adult promoters. The teen-age market is more than $10 billions a year, in jackets, portable radios, sporting goods, hair-dos, bikes, and additional family cars. Needless to say, this secondary development is simply a drag on the youthful spirit. It is largely frivolous and arbitrary, yet it is desperately conservative and exerts a tremendous pressure of blackmail against nonconformers or those ignorant of the latest, who will be unpopular. It makes it hard to talk sense to them, or for them to talk sense, whether adolescent or adult. And of course there is no chance for intelligent dissent from the official philosophy and standard of life. Naturally, too, especially in the middle class, the regressed adults play at and sponsor every teen-age idiocy.

Inevitably, the high school—with its teen-age majority and adult regime—becomes a prime area for sabotage and other fun and games. I have heard James Coleman, who has most studied these phenomena, express the opinion that the average adolescent is really *in* school, academically, for about ten minutes a day! Not a very efficient enterprise.

A certain number of the young gang up and commit defiant delinquencies. These are partly the revolt of nature—for there is much in our society that is insulting and intolerably frustrating. They are partly reactive against *whatever* happens to constitute "correct" behavior. And they are partly a pathetic bid for attention, as it is said, "We're so bad they give us a Youth Worker."

A pathetic characteristic of recent middle-class adolescent sub-culture is taking on the language and culture of marginal groups, Negroes and Latin Americans, addicts, Beat drop-outs from the colleges and the Organized System. This is appropriate, for these others too are abused and disregarded; they are in the same case as the adolescents. But such a culture is hardly articulate. Also, there is something exploiting about imitation authentic out-caste people, who live as they do not by choice but by necessity.

Nevertheless, for many of the woefully embarrassed, this semi-articulate speech—saying "man" and "cat" and "like, man"—makes conversation possible. The adolescent culture is something to talk about and this is a style to talk in. The words of one syllable of jive, the thoughts of one syllable of Beat, the content of kicks, movies, and high school dances, are not a wide discourse, but they foster being together, and everybody can democratically participate.

Unfortunately, the small talk drives out real talk. It is incredibly snobbish and exclusive of sincerity and originality. Embattled against the adult world that must inexorably triumph, adolescent society jealously protects itself against meaning.

To adolescents of sixteen, the adult world must seem like a prison door slamming shut. Some must get jobs which are sure not to fit them and in which they will exercise no initiative whatever. Others must engage in the factitious competition for college-entrance. Either process is formidable with forms and tests. The kids are ignorant of the ropes and ignorant of what they want. Disregarded by the adults, they have in turn excluded adult guidance or ideas looking toward the future. But their adolescent bravado is now seen to be unrealistic and even ridiculous. Having learned nothing, nor fought any battles, they are without morale.

Their weakness can be observed vividly on college campuses. Students gripe about the moral rules by which they are still absurdly harassed at 18 and 19 years of age. It's ironical; if they had quit school and were assembly-line workers, they would be considered responsible enough to come and go, have sex, and drink.—Yet it comes to nothing but griping; they do not feel justified to enforce their demands, for they have never had this issue, or any issue, out with their parents. Similarly, they are unhappy about the overcrowded classes, the credits, the grading; they know they are disappointed in the education they are getting; yet they are so confused about what they do want that they are speechless.

And just in the colleges, which are supposed to be communities of scholars, face-to-face communication is diminished. The adolescent sub-culture that persists is irrelevant to the business going on, except to sabotage it, but the adolescent community is *not* replaced by close acquaintance with learned adults. The teachers hold the students off and, as I argued in *The Community of Scholars*, it is a chief function of orderly administration to keep the students out of contact with the teachers and the teachers out of contact with one another. Naturally, as long as the students are isolated with one another, they can be treated as immature, which they are.

The dialogue with the subject-matter, with Nature and History, is as skimpy as with the teacher. Colleges are not interested in such things any more—it has little Ph.D. value. The sudent is told the current doctrine and is trained to give it back accurately. And still proving his masculinity and doing a snow-job, the student thinks that the purpose of a course is to "master the subject." Necessarily, in the conflict with the adult world, the young suffer a crushing defeat. There are various ways of surviving it. Some give up on themselves and conform completely—a few indeed become more royalist than the king (but these are often psychopathic, middle-class delinquents). Others make rationalizations: they will return to the fray later when they are "better prepared." Or, "The most important thing is to get married and raise a normal family," they will hold onto feeling and meaning for their family life, or perhaps for their "personal" behavior. A surprising number tell you that the goal of life is $50,000 a year.

The psychology of the introjection is evident: defeated, they identify with what has conquered them, in order to fill the gap with some meaning or other. Once they have made the new identification, they feel strong in it, they defend it by every rationalization.

An alternative philosophy that has recommended itself to some older adolescents is hipsterism. A hipster cushions the crushing defeat by society by *deliberately* assuming convenient roles in the dominant system, including its underworld, to manipulate it for his own power or at least safety. The bother with this idea—it is the argument of Thrasymachus in Plato's *Republic*—is that the hipster cannot afford to lose himself, or even to become un-selfconscious. He must be ahead of every game. Then he cannot grow by loving or believing anything worthwhile, and he exhausts himself in business with what he holds in contempt, deepening his own cynicism and self-contempt. But hipsterism does provide a satisfaction of mastery and victory which ward off his panic of powerlessness, passivity, and emasculation. It is a philosophy for chronic emergency, during which communication consists inevitably of camouflage and secrecy, "playing it cool," or of gambits of attack to get the upper hand.

The conditions that I have been describing, and the youthful responses to them, sadly limit human communication and even the concept of it. "Communication" comes to be interpreted as the transfer of a processed meaning from one head to another which will privately put it in a niche in its own system of meanings. This system is presumably shared with the others—one can never know. And in this presumptive consensus, the exchanged information adds a detail or a specification, but it does not disturb personality or alter characteristic behavior, for the self has not been touched. At most, the information serves as a signal for action from the usual repertory.

Among Americans, this sentiment of consensus, "understanding," is so important that much speech and reading does not even give new information, but is a ritual touching of familiar bases. (This is evident in much newspaper reading, in after-dinner speeches, and so forth.) But the case is not much different with active speech that is supposed to affect choice, e.g. in politics, for no disturbing issues are broached, nor anything that one would have to think new thoughts about. The underlying consensus is assumed—is signalled by the usual words— and no important alternative is offered.

The consensus is *presumably* shared, but any dialectic to test this assumption is in bad form, just as it is impolite to question a loose generalization made in small talk, and say "Prove it." In ideal cybernetic theory, the exchange of information is supposed to alter the organisms conversing, since they must make internal readjustments to it; but my observation is that no such alteration occurs. The chief meaning of conversation is its own smooth going on.

By contrast, the active speech of salesmanship is more lively, because it is meant importantly to change behavior, toward buying something; it is not meant merely to soothe. Thus, strikingly, TV commercials are the only part of TV that makes novel use of the medium itself, employing montage and inventive music, playing with the words, images and ideas. The pitch of a salesman is likely to be *ad hominem*, in bad form, both flattering and threatening. (Needless to say, there is no dialogue; the hearer is passive or dumbly resistant.) But of course, in salesmanship, apart from the one pre-thought transaction, the consensus is powerfully protected; the TV ad and the program that it sponsors avoid anything that might surprise, provoke, or offend any single person in an audience of millions.

Consider what is lost by this narrow concept of communication as the exchange of processed information with which each communicant copes internally.

(a) The function of speech as the shaping expression of pre-verbal needs and experiences, by which a speaker first discovers *what* he is thinking. Such speech cannot be entirely pre-thought and controlled; it is spontaneous. (b) The function of speech as personally initiating something by launching into an environment that is *unlike* oneself. Initiating, one presumes there is no consensus; otherwise why bother speaking? (c) Most important of all, the function of speech as dialogue between persons *committed to the conversation*—or between a person and a subject-matter in which he is absorbed. This results in change of the persons because of the very act of speaking; they are not fixed roles playing a game with rules.

Speaking is a way of making one's identity, of losing oneself with others in order to grow. It depends not on prior consensus with the others, but on trust of them. But, in my opinion, the speech defined in most contemporary communication theory is very like the speech of the defeated adolescents I have been describing. It is not pragmatic, communal, poetic, or heuristic. Its function is largely to report in a processed *lingua franca*.

Speech cannot be personal and poetic when there is embarrassment of self-revelation, including revelation to oneself, nor when there is animal diffidence and communal suspicion, shame of exhibition and eccentricity, clinging to social norms. Speech cannot be initiating when the chief social institutions are bureaucratized and pre-determine all procedures and decisions, so that in fact individuals have no power anyway that is useful to express. Speech cannot be exploratory and heuristic when pervasive chronic anxiety keeps people from risking losing themselves in temporary confusion and from relying for help precisely *on* communicating, even if the communication is Babel.

As it is, people have to "think" before they speak, rather than risking speaking and finding out what they mean by trying to make sense to others and themselves. In fact, they finally speak English as though they were in school.

One publication to examine the direction provided youth by the public high school has been The Educational Decision-Makers *by sociologists Aaron Cicourel and John I. Kitsuse (Bobbs-Merrill, 1963). In his review of the book for a scholarly journal, Professor Friedenberg underscores the authors' conclusion that a highly effective counseling bureaucracy has assumed full charge of students' educational development. The reviewer suggests that adolescents' freedom and dignity may in this way be compromised.*

Edgar Z. Friedenberg

The Dignity of Youth and Other Atavisms

This short paperback is a thoroughly penetrating and highly significant study of a new aspect of American educational practice, the values underlying it, and its long-range social implications. *The Educational Decision-Makers* is a case study of the function and activities of counselors in a 3600-student high school in a mainly upper-middle-class high school in Chicago's North Shore suburbs. Median family income for the community in 1960 was $9193; the median male had completed half a year of college. Eighty per cent of the parents expect their children to go on to college, and 75 per cent of Lakeshore's graduates do, in fact, go.

This is what makes the counselor's function in the school decisively important. At Lakeshore, their decisions and the dossier they compile determine what, if any, college will admit a graduate. Moreover, their placement of entering freshmen determines whether the student will finish high school with or without the courses required for college admission. Parents, Cicourel and Kitsuse find, know little or nothing about the details of college entrance requirements and make no substantial effort to learn; 97 per cent of the parents from the top three social classes in their sample simply assumed that their children would go to college; and this assumption was independent of their children's entering grade-average from elementary school and their tested scholastic aptitude.

The result is to leave the high school student's future educational career almost entirely to the discretion of Lakeshore's counselors, and to make their perception of him paramount in determining his opportunities. Lakeshore, apparently, does not offer separate general, commercial, and academic tracks. But it does have what are called, in the language of 1984, "opportunity courses" for students deemed less able and "honors courses" for more able students, as well as regular sections for well-rounded students. High grades in "opportunity" sections, and low grades in "honors" sections are both discounted in determining grade averages for recommendations to college; and the "opportunity courses" do not as a rule meet specific college entrance requirements in any case. At Lakeshore, then, a student whom counselors assign on entrance to a program of primarily college-preparatory courses virtually has it made from the beginning; those whom they bar from or counsel out of such courses may find it impossible to get into college at all, however well they do in the program.

Cicourel and Kitsuse demonstrate that counselors' assignment of students cannot be accounted for on the basis of entering grades or SCAT scores alone; there are important residual factors. They never succeed in quite identifying these, though they are nothing so simple as social class attributes alone. The authors' extensive quotations from interviews with counselors suggest that no greater precision is possible; the counselors themselves are not that clear about what they are doing.

What is frightening about this new bureaucracy is not prejudice or ill-will, but the zeal with which it assigns students to categories designed to justify its own *raison d'etre*. "Underachievers" and—surely a remarkable concept in itself —"overachievers" are canvassed and disposed of in order to give substance to the counselor's function. As the authors state (pp. 81–82):

> In their attempts to define a professional domain, therefore, school counselors have been concerned with establishing a claim to what we may term "surface" problems that students may encounter in their day-to-day school and extracurricular activities. It should be noted, however, that in a highly bureaucratized school system the counselor occupies a position in which he coordinates the referral of students to the various special services, including those of the psychologists and social workers. . . . In this position of interprofessional rivalry, the counselor seeks to develop his own definitions of problem types that will not conflict with or overlap those used by social workers, psychologists, and psychiatrists.

The expansion of the counseling function in American schools is a consequence both of our extreme emphasis on the school as the instrument of social mobility and of our recently increased concern for developing talent that might be overlooked by less formal processes of search and seizure. But, as Cicourel and Kitsuse rather drily observe (p. 136):

> The advances and setbacks in the process of mobility in such a system are governed less by the folk norms of the larger society than by the doctrines and practices of a professionalized bureaucracy. Insofar as the rationalization and bureaucratization of procedures imply greater "objectivity" in the evaluation of performance and distribution of rewards, it might be argued that the application of such organizational techniques represents an institutionalization of the folk norms of contest mobility. Our materials do not support such an argument.

And the danger resulting from these doctrines and practices cannot be stated better than they state it (p. 147):

> It would not be an exaggeration to state that the high school as a "talent farm" pro-

duces its own problems, and that it has developed a "clinic" to deal with them. . . . Suspending the question of the validity of interpretations of student problems made by the counseling personnel and the modes of treatment that are prescribed and practiced, the issue which must be addressed is whether or not the school is or should be authorized to engage in such activities. We do not doubt that from a psychiatric point of view the behavior of some students may be diagnosed as serious problems that call for specialized treatment. . . . We do question, however, the propriety of a procedure that routinely assigns students to counselors who not only monitor their progress but actively seek and probe for "problems." This is an invasion of privacy, however disguised it may be by an ideology of service and "help," and an invasion during a period when maintaining the privacy of unique personal experience may be critical for the adolescent's awareness of his own individuality. What is even more disturbing is the prospect that this solicitous treatment will produce a new generation of youth socialized to the practice of easy confessions and receptive to "professional" explanations of who they are and what they aspire to become.

Indeed, Cicourel and Kitsuse do not exaggerate the peril. In collaboration with Carl Nordstrom, I have recently completed an intensive study of nine secondary schools in their observable effect on student values, dealing specifically with the issue these authors raise. Nearly all our student subjects accept as legitimate any invasion of their private life the school may undertake in the name of "helping" and declare that it is very important for their parents to co-operate with the school when this occurs. What these youngsters have lost in freedom, sad as it is, may be less than what they have renounced in dignity. Unfortunately, the record of our life as a people since Tocqueville's time and before hardly suggests that we have ever been greatly devoted to either.

A concluding note on the school is sounded here by a psychologist. Bruno Bettelheim warns that most questions about education are non-questions. Rather than ask what schools should teach, he believes, we should ask what values will be needed by the next generation of adults. He raises an issue which some have designated our higher illiteracy: the prevalence of individuals who can read but cannot relate their ideas to the world around them.

Bruno Bettelheim

Notes on the Future of Education

The most significant problem facing any society that is conscious of itself is to determine what values it wishes to live by, and how to translate those values into everyday social action. Since I also believe that the preconditions for acquiring values start with the educational experience from birth on, and since this is my main field of interest, I shall focus my remarks on education.

I believe that the present widespread concern with education deliberately addresses itself to pseudo-problems, so as to avoid the real ones. Or, as my friend Sidney Harris, in discussing some of my writings, put it—much better than I could—we are asking "non-questions" to avoid coming to grips with what are the real questions so that we won't be forced to act on what are the real answers. For example, most discussions of our schools, and of the training or retraining of our youth, approach these issues by asking the non-question of "what they should learn," while the real question would be "what persons they should be." Witness the complaint that our schools fail to teach our children to read and write and spell. The real problem is, why don't we give, even to those of our children who do know how to read, reading matter that would equip them to know how to live in this world. Remember that Lee Harvey Oswald knew how to read and write, and Hitler was the author of a book.

A non-question I am often asked is: "Should my child do certain chores around the house?" To answer, "yes, he should do them," would imply forcing the child, which will only arouse resentment. But "no" would imply that a child should never be expected to help around the house. The true problem behind the non-question about chores might be several connected convictions and worries. One of them might be: "If I do not hold my child to certain tasks from an early age on, he will later in life shirk his duties." Or else: "The example of how I attend to my own duties is not enough to set a pattern which my child will later copy, because he likes me, and the way I do things." Thus, what looks like a question may turn out to be an expression of a parent's worry about how good an example he is setting, and whether his child will follow it even if no force is applied.

Another example of a non-question is "How can we beautify our cities and our superhighways?" The real question should be: "Why do we live in ways that make our cities so incredibly ugly?" We ask the non-question "How can we add beauty to our lives?" instead of asking "Why is our life so devoid of it?" Art in the museums, theatres, or even in our public places is not much more than sugarcoating of the real question of why beauty and dignity are lacking in our homes, in our schools, in the relations between us and our children.

I believe most questions raised about education are non-questions, asked as a defense against recognizing the true questions, because the true questions would force us to radically change our thinking about ourselves, the world, and the education of our children. These questions are: "What kind of world do we really want to live in? What kind of person do we want our children to be, so that they will create a world very different from ours, a world in which they can live in accordance with their full potentialities, instead of having most of them stunted by the age they reach school?"

Up to now Western man, bent on conquering poverty and illness, has concentrated on finding out how to deal with the external world. But the end of this period is fast approaching. Although poverty is still with us, I think it is right to say it is still with us only because we have not yet decided in all seriousness to do away with it.

In the meantime our educational system still concentrates on teaching "know-how" and is woefully deficient in teaching "why?" and "what-for?" "Know-how" is a technological solution; the "why" and "what-for" are scientific and human questions. It remains an underlying assumption of much of our education that we shall be dropped on a desert island when we graduate, with nothing to rely on but the factual knowledge we acquired in school. Actually, most factual knowledge is readily available to us in reference sources, and the job for which a student acquired skills in school will, as likely as not, be obsolete by the time he graduates. The important task is to develop in our students the ability to ask the penetrating questions that the new reconstruction of man and society will require.

We are well into the scientific revolution, but we have hardly begun the psychological revolution. In order to use the new freedoms made possible by technology we must gain a much deeper understanding of ourselves and our world. Our education deals too much with things. When it deals with people it too often deals with them as things too. We pipe knowledge into classrooms and expect wisdom and maturation to bloom. We are so ill-prepared to deal with mass society and automation, even in the classrooms where we teach about them, that it takes student revolts such as those of Berkeley to shock us alert. At least I hope it has made us aware that many of our best students feel so alienated in society today that, in what is less a deliberate and more a desperate effort, they resort to four-letter words. They think in this way they will finally provoke us to some action, so that they, and we too, will become real to them. Without knowing it, and motivated by their unconscious, they select words that refer, they believe, to something real, so as to make us aware how unreal and futile they feel is what we offer them in our schools.

At our own University too, students ask again and again: "Why were we never told in school what life in our cities is really like? Why weren't we told about the inner conflicts we dimly felt in ourselves but could not grapple with, because nobody taught us the skill?"

This they can ask openly, but only in secret do they ask the more devastating questions: "Why am I so lonely? Why can I not come close to anyone in my feelings? Why am I afraid of my own feelings, desires, fantasies? Why are we so afraid to give freely of ourselves? Why can't we get close even to those who love us, and whom we love? Why do we suppress our sensitivities?"

I think one pressing problem of the coming decade is to change our educational system so that all these perturbing questions will be asked, and those about the inequities still in the world, their causes, and why we do not apply remedies that already exist. Most of all, the schools ought to teach the true nature of man, teach about his troubles with himself, his inner turmoils, and about his difficulties in living with others. They should teach the prevalence and the power of both man's social and asocial tendencies, and how the one can domesticate the other, without destroying his independence or self-love.

I hope it is clear by now that I am talking about the acquisition of values as more important than the acquisition of knowledge and skills. What is sorely lacking in our education, and will have to stand in the center of all educational efforts in the future, is the education of the emotions. And those cannot be educated without clear values. Certainly the emotions cannot be educated by machines, nor in classes of thirty or forty, nor by teachers who are forced to spend most of their time in filling out forms, or in giving and checking assignments. Nor by teachers who stay with a child for only a few months instead of several years, nor by an educational system that is vilified in the press and by self-appointed public spokesmen. In short, it will have to be an education that makes man less concerned with an ever-increasing production of power, and more concerned with the purpose for which he means to put that power to use.

Such radical reform of our educational system will require that we give up worrying about the drawing of school district boundaries and the composition of the classroom. It will require us, instead, to concern ourselves with the quality of teaching, a teaching that will not be hamstrung by having to adhere to textbooks which contain mainly pseudo-information, or which are directed toward college entrance examinations which tell nothing about the true merits of a student. What I suggest, then, is that in the decade to come we take teaching seriously instead of being mainly concerned with matters of educational administration. To take teaching seriously means, as even the most mixed-up students at Berkeley realized, having schools organized on a small, that is, human scale. It means high schools, for example, of only a few hundred students. It means small classes of only twelve to fifteen students, so that the teacher can know them all personally and well. It means teachers who will stay for several years with what then will be *their* boys and girls, so that meaningful educational and human relations can develop. Most of all, it means teachers who will be free to spend all their time in class, teaching. If we so organize our education, we won't have to worry about dropouts, or under-achievers, because it will be much more exciting to stay in class, and to learn. True, such programs will be expensive, but much less so than the present poverty programs—which we then won't need, since a so educated generation will not be confronted with problems of poverty because it will not permit poverty in its midst. And it will be incredibly less expensive than putting a man on the moon. Instead of a man on the moon it would give us a generation of truly educated, truly moral, and truly autonomous men and women right on this earth.

Dr. Bettelheim, you have referred to man's technological progress, his growing ability to eliminate poverty. Eventually man will not be concerned with working to sustain himself physically. My question is this: if we relieve man of this stimulus, what do we substitute—human psychology being what it is—to keep him from becoming a total parasite?

This has, of course, worried many of us, because it really means a radical change in the capitalistic ethic, or whatever you want to call it. I don't worry too much about it for my generation and the generation of our children, because they will have plenty to do in distributing our affluence more equitably in this country and the rest of the world—and I think we both agree that this would be desirable. One might hope that if they really do that, they will find the service rendered to their fellow men much more rewarding than any accumulation for themselves. If I may wax theological: the spiritual satisfaction of such an enterprise of helping one's fellow man, first economically, and later also emotionally, will be so much more rewarding that every man on earth will grow into an autonomous being, enjoying security and human dignity. This will be so much more rewarding that they won't go back to striving for those other earthly rewards which can be gained by the methods of an acquisitive society.

4 WORK

This article examines economic, industrial and social factors that shape the work and career possibilities available to American adolescents. Although new statistics accumulate daily, and technological innovations change the face of industry at a more dramatic pace than seemed possible even a few years ago, Dr. Dansereau's thesis of the "culture shock" experienced by adolescents when moving from academic to industrial life remains relevant.

H. Kirk Dansereau

Work and the Teen-Ager

Adults frequently complain that today's teen-ager does not know what work is, that his only interest is in having a good time, that his sometimes bizarre behavior emphasizes these truths. One father complains that if there were work or play to be performed at the same time, his son would choose the play every time. "The only time he works is when he needs money to play."

Differences between adults and adolescents are not unique to this culture. Murray and Kluckhohn point out that major discrepancies exist in all cultures between the ideal patterns enacted by members of different age groups. Different behaviors are rewarded by different age groups, and antagonism between adults and adolescents is due partly to "conflicting culture patterns which arise and are transmitted at the adolescent level." [1] In our society, part of the difference in viewpoints about work results, in addition, from adult edict, and the persistence of the difference is due, in large measure, to the extension of the adolescent period by adults themselves. The protraction is related to at least two factors, namely, emphasis on more extensive formal education and closure of the labor market to the teen-ager, to be discussed below.

[1] Clyde Kluckhohn and Henry A. Murray (eds.), *Personality in Nature, Society, and Culture* (New York: Alfred A. Knopf, Inc., 1948), p. 22.

DEVELOPMENTAL TASKS AND PART-TIME WORK

As a matter of fact, many teen-agers do work, some, of course, because they must, but others because they actually want to. Sometimes the teen-ager works for the money he earns, because within his peer group, the lack of money may be a status detractor; the expenditure—the more frivolous the better—may have an additive quality, since recognition may be obtained from bizarre spending. But money alone does not dictate what jobs teen-agers will seek any more than it dictates the work adults will seek. Desire to be with one's friends, desire for new experience, or a desire to be protected from the rain may be just as important. Even how long the teen-ager believes he must continue in a given task is in part a determinant of whether he will accept it.

Many teen-agers work extremely hard at their hobbies, developing remarkable dexterity and satisfying active curiosity. Sometimes work can be like a game. Vincent and Mayers elaborate this point: "Some work and play cannot be clearly separated; much play or part of it is work-like, and some work play-like." [2]

That teen-agers themselves are aware of the developmental tasks served by their part-time employment and the money they earn is illustrated by the following list. In order of frequency mentioned, they were the establishing of economic independence, the achieving of emotional independence of parents and other adults, the acceptance of proper sex roles and new relations with peers, the acceptance, desiring, and achieving of socially responsible behavior, and the selection and preparation for an occupation.[3] Referring to his own research, Hutson states: [4]

> Work experience has deep meaning for the pupil, meanings which guidance workers must understand if they are to help these young workers to make good judgments. Important as it is to prevent these adolescents from pursuing their self exploitation at the expense of their self development, the satisfactions which they derive from work for pay must be recognized. To youth these values seem so substantial that they are sought not only by the financially impoverished but by many whose families can well take care of their financial needs.

The truth of the last statement is evidenced by the behavior of the son of a college dean who, much to his father's chagrin, took a job as helper on a local garbage truck.

The actual use of the money is, of course, determined by individual exigencies. The function of the teen-age worker of the eighteenth century—assistance to the family—is considerably less important today. It is likely to be peer group values which now determine whether the young casual worker spends his income for fun or saves it toward going to college. Incidentally, job opportunities them-

[2] Melvin J. Vincent and Jackson Mayers, *New Foundations for Industrial Sociology* (Princeton: D. Van Nostrand Co., 1959), p. 13.
[3] Percival W. Hutson, *The Guidance Function in Education* (New York: Appleton-Century-Crofts, 1958), p. 370.
[4] Percival W. Hutson, *The Guidance Function in Education* (New York: Appleton-Century-Crofts, 1958), p. 370.

selves often hinge on overt expression of need for money to go to college, regardless of the actual intended use of the income.

KEEP OUT! MEN AT WORK

But, despite the desire for and appreciation of work by teen-agers, the truth of the matter is, as Jane Warters has flatly stated, that "except in time of war, the employment of youth is generally not needed or wanted." [5] The youngster who wants work experience finds that work is basically one aspect of the adult world not open for him; the absence of noteworthy expansion of the economy and a concurrent increase in automation makes it likely to remain so.

Child labor laws also limit the number of opportunities for teen-age workers. Such laws exist in every state, and the federal Fair Labor Standards Act contains provisions which apply to the employment of minors in interstate and foreign commerce. Where state standards for protection of the young worker are more stringent, they supersede the federal standards. Such laws require possession of a certificate in order to work. This requirement forces the teen-ager who wants to work to face a bureaucratic gatekeeper, a confrontation which many a youth is reluctant to endure; in this respect, he differs little from many adults.

Even granting that he is able to overcome this initial hurdle, the teen-ager finds himself in an age group which is discriminated against. We hear a good deal about discrimination against the older worker; however, we hear much less about the equally extensive discrimination against the younger one. As a matter of fact, as Gross points out, in the work world, "youth . . . tends to be a status depressant. . . . On the whole, experience is accorded greater prestige than is education per se." [6]

But how is experience to be accumulated in the absence of genuine work responsibilities? The necessary experience for jobs which teen-agers consider worth while may not be accumulated until the aspiring employee is already trapped in what is to him an undesirable occupation. Such, for example, was the case of the coed who did typing as summer work because she could not get experience in industrial recreation. Or it may be available only to those with connections; one young woman entered college during the summer not necessarily to finish in three years but rather, as she put it, because she might as well be here since she could not get a job in her home town, her father not owning a store.

Even if experience were available, however, the very fact of youth would mitigate against the chances of the teen-ager. The youth, either in a position of authority or at the head of the work flow, is, in essence, setting the pace for his elders, and, no matter how competent he may be, he is in an anomalous position. [7] Indeed, because of the culturally defined low status of youth in the

---

[5] Jane Warters, *High School Personnel Work Today* (2d ed.; New York: McGraw-Hill, 1956, p. 8

[6] Edward Gross, *Work and Society* (New York: Thomas Y. Crowell Co., 1958), pp. 435, 437.

[7] Delbert C. Miller and William H. Form, *Industrial Sociology: An Introduction to the Sociology of Work Relations* (New York: Harper and Brothers, 1951), pp. 823–824.

industrial structure, such a position may be ruinous to production and likewise to the self of both the younger and the older worker.

Unable to overcome the age-grade nature of the occupational structure, the teen-ager is, as a result, frequently relegated to the meanest tasks. The Dictionary of Occupational Titles, in its section on casual work experience, after-school and vacation-type employment, presents some of the jobs the teen-ager may reasonably anticipate. Aside from basic military training, these are bus boy (or girl), delivery boy, farm hand, gas station worker, house-to-house canvassing, housework (female or male), newsboy, soda dispensing, store worker (grocery or variety), store worker (specialty or department store), telegraph messenger work, truck helper, and ushering.[8] A similar situation obtains for permanent jobs. And it is accentuated when social class is taken into consideration. As Schneider states, ". . . . the 'lower'-ranking occupations of industry are the first to be entered by adolescents, and these occupations are filled by working-class youth. The more desirable jobs are filled later, by and large from youth of other classes."[9] Gross has shown that men twenty-four or older experience preferential treatment in hiring as compared to that received by workers who are younger. Those in the lower class grouping could be found in semiskilled, other service, and semi-professional as well as in unskilled classifications.[10] But it would seem that the unskilled category is the only one for which the teen-ager could usually offer much competition. Younger workers in general—not teen-agers alone—are at a competitive disadvantage. Dubin says "the 'middle age' dominance in the labor force tends to favor those past 35 years as against younger workers."[11]

The net effect of all the factors here considered is to extend the status of childhood far into adolescence. Ruth Benedict points out that children are thought of as wanting to play while adults are considered as having to work. While her statements pertain to the child, a similar philosophy of behavior now pervades the adolescent period also.

A child does not make any labor contribution to our industrial society except as it competes with an adult; its work is not measured against its own strength and skill but against high-geared industrial requirements. . . . The child is praised because the parents feel well disposed, regardless of whether the task is well done by adult standards, and the child acquires no sensible standard by which to measure its achievement.[12]

---

[8] War Manpower Commission, *Dictionary of Occupational Titles*, Part IV: Entry Occupational Classification (Rev. ed.; Washington, D. C.: United States Government Printing Office, 1944), pp. 168–173.

[9] Eugene V. Schneider, *Industrial Sociology: The Social Relations of Industry and the Community* (New York: McGraw-Hill, 1957), p. 448.

[10] Eugene V. Schneider, *Industrial Sociology: The Social Relations of Industry and the Community* (New York: McGraw-Hill, 1957), p. 199.

[11] Robert Dubin, *The World of Work: Industrial Society and Human Relations* (Englewood Cliffs, New Jersey: Prentice-Hall, 1958), p. 163.

[12] "Continuities and Discontinuities in Cultural Conditioning," in Logan Wilson and William L. Kolb, *Sociological Analysis: An Introductory Text and Case Book* (New York: Harcourt, Brace, 1949), p. 225.

The marginality of the teen-ager therefore continues; the concomitant anomie is conducive to his pursuit of norms other than those of the adult work world. The value-system vacuum may be filled by peer group standards and their correlative behavior patterns. These are the patterns which are often characterized as weird, strange, unnatural, or bizarre. Perhaps these descriptive adjectives are applied to rock-and-roll addicts and beats only because prior comparable age-grade behavior patterns were so common and so in conformity to adult norms—flagpole sitting, goldfish swallowing, dance marathons, zoot suits, and panty raids.

COME BACK!

Because the absence of an imaginative alternative to a job other than the traditional school, when the lure of quick employment and economic reward does inveigle a teen-age student to discontinue his education and he succeeds in getting a job, educators become greatly concerned to win him back. New York City, for example, has proposed a three-week campaign prior to the beginning of the school year aimed at reducing the number of school dropouts. The drive is intended to continue throughout the school year. The facts which sparked such action are that 900,000 pupils dropped out of school during the 1960–1961 year and that, of these, an estimated 70 per cent had the ability to finish high school and probably the ability to go on to college. Further, it is estimated that there will be 7,500,000 dropouts during the next ten years. The dropout rate appears to be declining, but so, too, is the number of jobs which do not require a high school diploma. The New York City dropout rate for both public and private schools combined is 30 per cent.[13] Thus, it can seen that both bright and dull students drop out, adding to the number who are destined to the unskilled, poor paying, low status jobs.[14] A survey of these facts lends credence to Thomas' assertion that the occupation is more likely to choose the individual than vice versa and that the individuals are most likely to fall into those jobs which are most available and require least training and preparation.[15]

PREFERENCES AND ASPIRATIONS

These are not the jobs teen-agers necessarily want. Much has been written on what constitutes a good job. Reynolds, for example, specifies the physical nature of the job, the amount and nature of supervision, level of wages, fairness

[13] Gene Currivan, "City Starts Drive to Keep Students," New York Times, August 16, 1961.
[14] Jane Warters, High School Personnel Work Today (2d ed.; New York: McGraw-Hill, 1956), p. 27; Eugene V. Schneider, Industrial Sociology: The Social Relations of Industry and the Community (New York: McGraw-Hill, 1957), p. 447.
[15] Lawrence G. Thomas, The Occupational Structure and Education (Englewood Cliffs, New Jersey: Prentice-Hall, 1956), p. 236.

of treatment, relations with others, regularity of employment, presence of a union, hours of work, shift, and physical conditions.[16] While these reflect adult criteria, a marked similarity exists between them and the variables and sources of work satisfaction expressed by younger members of our society, namely: working conditions, advancement opportunities, prospective income, fair treatment, job tenure, independence in making decisions, and the like.[17] As Thomas points out, youth expresses preference for occupations which are high in both income and prestige, important and popular values in American culture, thus demonstrating "a keen and accurate sensitivity to the nation's cultural values."[18]

The teen-ager frequently aspires to jobs which he may never achieve. Exposure to occupational rankings of a socioeconomic nature may contribute to this phenomenon. Students, as recipients of adult values, have often been the subjects of inquiry relative to the ranking of occupations. The assumptions underlying these scales attest to the degree of adult influence. Caplow has listed five such assumptions, namely, white-collar work is superior; self-employment is superior; clean occupations are superior; the importance of a business occupation depends upon the size of the business; personal service is degrading—better to be employed by an enterprise than to do the same work for an individual.[19] It is somewhat tautological to subject the student to rankings which are frequently his "own."

It should not be unexpected, then, that a study of seventh- through twelfth-grade students in twelve states revealed that boys expressed a desire to be engineers, farmers, physicians, lawyers, and, less frequently, mechanics; or that girls showed a preference for clerical work and nursing.[20] The reasons stated for making such choices—aside from a liking for the work or its attractiveness, financial reward, and belief in their fitness for it—reflected adult rather than primarily peer-group pressures—parental influence, the influence of teachers and relatives as well as of friends.

Without claiming causal nexus, Baer and Roeber list numerous factors which appear to be related to youth's career planning. Many of these also reflect adult influence. Their list includes interests, abilities, parents, friends, desire for upward mobility, opportunity for quick employment, opportunity for advancement, attitudes toward education, identification with certain individuals, age, sex role, ego strength, need satisfaction, economic conditions, personality development, economic rewards, and security.[21]

[16] Lloyd G. Reynolds, *Labor Economics and Labor Relations* (New York: Prentice-Hall, Inc., 1949), pp. 42–49.

[17] Lawrence G. Thomas, *The Occupational Structure and Education* (Englewood Cliffs, New Jersey: Prentice-Hall, 1956), pp. 236–245.

[18] Lawrence G. Thomas, *The Occupational Structure and Education* (Englewood Cliffs, New Jersey, 1956), p. 238.

[19] Theodore Caplow, *The Sociology of Work* (Minneapolis: University of Minnesota Press, 1954), pp. 42–43.

[20] Carroll H. Miller, *Foundations of Guidance* (New York: Harper & Brothers, 1961), pp. 235–236.

[21] Max F. Baer and Edward C. Roeber, *Occupational Information* (2d ed.; Chicago: Science Research Associates, 1958), p. 355.

Still, even though the teen-ager may have serious career plans, these may be upended by the actualities of the occupational structure referred to above—a major determinant of the kind of job he can really get.

ANOMALIES

But let us assume that the teen-ager has now cleared all the hurdles put in the way of serious participation in the work world. He is now faced with a set of anomalies that, singly or together, often amount to culture shock. Miller and Form have given careful attention to the problems faced by the neophyte worker.[22] Five contradictions in work values assail him. The young worker must learn to accept responsibility; yet he cannot get a job which requires responsibility. He must work hard, says the norm; he notes that this is not necessary today. He must learn to get along with others; but he must be aggressive to get ahead. He must learn the value of money; but no one gets rich by pinching pennies. He must learn to hold a job; but the way to get ahead is by moving around.[23] In addition, or as a result, there is the phenomenon which Miller and Form label culture shock, the revulsion the young worker feels against the routine of repetitive work, the fatigue of hard work, the commands of an authoritarian supervisor, dishonest business procedures, the deviant personal habits of fellow workers, and the insecurity of work.[24] These factors may have their impact upon both prepared and unprepared new workers. It is little wonder that younger workers tend to engage in "shopping around" for jobs. Workers' mobility from job to job is age related, stability becoming characteristic only during the worker's thirties. It is worth noting that Dubin has estimated the number of jobs held during a forty-six-year work life at twelve.[25] Such interjob traffic must account partially for the fact that the majority of American workers are performing occupational functions for which they were not specifically trained.

TRANSITION

Certainly, what is needed for the adolescent's smooth transition to the world of work, in order to minimize culture shock, is a realistic and continuous socialization process. Frequently, the transition is so abrupt as to compound rather than to mitigate the conditions conducive to culture shock.

The teen-ager, by way of better preparation for real life, needs an opportunity to assume some responsibility even more than he needs the chance to develop

[22] Delbert C. Miller and William H. Form, *Industrial Sociology: An Introduction to the Sociology of Work Relations* (New York: Harper and Brothers, 1951), Chaps. 16, 17.
[23] Delbert C. Miller and William H. Form, *Industrial Sociology: An Introduction to the Sociology of Work Relations* (New York: Harper and Brothers, 1951), p. 574.
[24] Delbert C. Miller and William H. Form, *Industrial Sociology: An Introduction to the Sociology of Work Relations* (New York: Harper and Brothers, 1951), pp. 627–631.
[25] Robert Dubin, *The World of Work: Industrial Society and Human Relations* (Englewood Cliffs, New Jersey: Prentice-Hall, 1958), p. 266.

the routine movements associated with manual dexterity. While some high school shop and commercial courses and apprenticeship programs have such a goal, many do not.

Even with respect to manual skills, not to mention responsibility, "most high school shop courses," says Spaulding, "are not really designed to produce craftsmen, and (one study reports that) many of the 1,216,142 students taking typing were not expecting to use it as the key to a job." [26] Thus, not even in these courses was a bridge being built between the teen-ager's world and the world of work.

Apprenticeship programs may be no better. Spaulding states that even when such programs are available, the young man may be taught only "enough to allow him to perform some particular job and will then be used as cheap labor." [27] Apprenticeship programs have become overly standardized, and Scott and his associates express concern over this. In some cases, four years are not necessary—two or three would be sufficient or four or five years might be required.[28]

If cultural values emphasize the importance of a smooth transition and if the recent past is indicative of the future, the preliminaries must begin early; for, by the time the teen-agers reach eighteen or nineteen years of age, a large proportion of both males and females will be in the labor force. The males will be predominantly operatives and the females clerks. It is likewise important that the adolescent's training, either formal or informal, should provide time and opportunity for job "shopping" to permit him to learn of various job requirements and to provide him with some criteria for evaluating his own capabilities.

FUNCTIONALITY

Adults sometimes raise questions as to whether teen-age culture prepares the teen-ager for adult work life or whether, contrariwise, it tends to make him unfit for it. More specifically, the question is whether the teen-ager's emphasis on such values as athletics, popularity, and fun really have an adult payoff. This is but another one of those adult questions about teen-agers which virtually defies dogmatic answers. But some interesting implications are revealed in considering them.

Emphasis on athletics, particularly for a boy, is frequently held over from the father's past, from either his achievements or his frustrations. Yet, the old arguments in favor of athletics—learning how to win, how to lose, or even how to memorize signals—may have a modicum of validity. Even as many athletic endeavors are group phenomena, so is a good deal of actual work. Further, learning

[26] Charles B. Spaulding, *An Introduction to Industrial Sociology* (San Francisco: Chandler Publishing Company, 1961), p. 585.

[27] Charles B. Spaulding, *An Introduction to Industrial Sociology* (San Francisco: Chandler Publishing Company, 1961), p. 586.

[28] Walter Dill Scott, Robert C. Clothier, and William R. Spriegel, *Personnel Management: Principles, Practices, and Point of View* (5th ed.; New York: McGraw-Hill, 1954), pp. 321–322.

how men and women are expected to behave under varying competitive conditions may have implications which extend beyond mere recreational situations.

Teen-age emphasis on popularity likewise has its adult counterpart. Popularity in American society is not sought by teen-agers only. Thus, perhaps the question is what makes for teen-age popularity. If it should be found to stem from family background, talent, initiative, or success, the parents of a popular teen-ager would probably ask no further. Popularity is undoubtedly a better than average indication of one's degree of belonging; teen-agers as well as adults are prone to seek the security related to that attribute. If the teen-ager learns to handle rather than to exploit popularity, such ability could become a valuable adult asset, for, with regard to work, it is redundant to repeat the fact that among adults the chief cause of job separation is the inability to get along with others. High school students argue that the school should teach "useful things in everyday life—like meeting people every day."[29] The teen-ager's drive for popularity may, thus, afford him that experience which he claims the school neglects.

But, more basically, the fun orientation of teen-age culture may conceivably prove to be the best possible preparation for a future in which work will contribute less and less to human satisfactions. Historically, there have been two basic views of work. One, the Renaissance view, stressed the intrinsic value of the work itself; the other, related to Protestantism, emphasized work as a key to religious salvation. C. Wright Mills contends that today neither of these points of view has wide acceptance.[30] Rather, it seems, the more pervasive modern view is that work is a necessary evil. "Work is split from the rest of life," says Mills "especially from the spheres of conscious enjoyment; nevertheless, most men and many women must work." Further, he says, "each day men sell little pieces of themselves in order to try to buy them back each night and weekend with the coin of 'fun.' "[31] "Fun," not work, becomes the core around which one builds his personality. There is, to be sure, a contrary point of view which, on the basis of the effects of unemployment and retirement on workers, argues that work is still a basic value for most men; but it would be worth while to know more about the extent to which such elements as the strength of work-group ties and economic de-grading are related to the difficulty associated with withdrawal from the labor force. Such considerations could well outweigh the individual's desire to stay on the job per se, to keep the mind and body occupied in specific required tasks. But even if it were true that work remains a basic source of satisfaction today, automation is relentlessly erasing much of it from the industrial scene. Whether due to the quality of work today or to its diminishing availability, work may no longer be available as a source of life satisfactions.

Returning, then, to the earlier question about the functionality of teen-age culture, we may well conclude that the teen-ager's design for living, organized

[29] Jane Warters, *High School Personnel Work Today* (2d ed.; New York: McGraw-Hill, 1956), pp. 43, 57.
[30] C. Wright Mills, *White Collar: The American Middle Classes* (New York: Oxford University Press, 1951), pp. 218-219.
[31] C. Wright Mills, *White Collar: The American Middle Classes* (New York: Oxford University Press, 1951), p. 237.

as it is around leisure-time pursuits and fun, rather than around work, may be a prototype of the adult world of the future when automation has deprived many people of work—as adult patterns have for so long deprived teen-agers—as a source of life satisfactions.

The discontinuity between adolescence and the assumption of adult roles is stated by Paul Goodman in an adolescent's terms: "during my productive years I will spend eight hours a day doing what is no good." Stressing man's need to do something worthwhile, the author analyzes career models offered by modern technological America. He concludes that adolescents shun work when they see its outcome as, for example, brilliantly-produced rigged quiz shows.

Paul Goodman

Jobs

It's hard to grow up when there isn't enough man's work. There is "nearly full employment" (with highly significant exceptions), but there get to be fewer jobs that are necessary or unquestionably useful; that require energy and draw on some of one's best capacities; and that can be done keeping one's honor and dignity. In explaining the widespread troubles of adolescents and young men, this simple objective factor is not much mentioned. Let us here insist on it.

By "man's work" I mean a very simple idea, so simple that it is clearer to ingenuous boys than to most adults. To produce necessary food and shelter is man's work. During most of economic history most men have done this drudging work, secure that it was justified and worthy of a man to do it, though often feeling that the social conditions under which they did it were *not* worthy of a man, thinking, "It's better to die than to live so hard"—but they worked on. When the environment is forbidding, as in the Swiss Alps or the Aran Islands, we regard such work with poetic awe. In emergencies it is heroic, as when the bakers of Paris maintained the supply of bread during the French Revolution, or the milkman did not miss a day's delivery when the bombs recently tore up London.

At present there is little such subsistence work. In *Communitas* my brother and I guess that one-tenth of our economy is devoted to it; it is more likely one-twentieth. Production of food is actively discouraged. Farmers are not wanted and the young men go elsewhere. (The farm population is now less than 15 per cent of the total population.) Building, on the contrary, is immensely needed. New York City needs 65,000 new units a year, and is getting net, 16,000. One would think that ambitious boys would flock to this work. But here we find that building, too, is discouraged. In a great city, for the last twenty years hundreds of thousands have been ill housed, yet we do not see science, industry, and labor enthusiastically enlisted in finding the quick solution to a definite problem. The promoters are interested in long-term investments, the real estate men in speculation, the city planners in votes and graft. The building craftsmen cannily see to it that their own numbers remain few, their methods antiquated, and their rewards high. None of these people is much interested in providing shelter, and nobody is at all interested in providing new manly jobs.

Once we turn away from the absolutely necessary subsistence jobs, however, we find that an enormous proportion of our production is not even unquestionably useful. Everybody knows and also feels this, and there has recently been a flood of books about our surfeit of honey, our insolent chariots, the follies of exurban ranch houses, our hucksters and our synthetic demand. Many acute things are said about this useless production and advertising, but not much about the workmen producing it and their frame of mind; and nothing at all, so far as I have noticed, about the plight of a young fellow looking for a manly occupation. The eloquent critics of the American way of life have themselves been so seduced by it that they think only in terms of selling commodities and point out that the goods are valueless; but they fail to see that people are being wasted and their skills insulted. (To give an analogy, in the many gleeful onslaughts on the Popular Culture that have appeared in recent years, there has been little thought of the plight of the honest artist cut off from his audience and sometimes, in public arts such as theater and architecture, from his medium.)

What is strange about it? American society has tried so hard and so ably to defend the practice and theory of production for profit and not primarily for use that now it has succeeded in making its jobs and products profitable and useless.

Consider a likely useful job. A youth who is alert and willing but not "verbally intelligent"—perhaps he has quit high school at the eleventh grade (the median), as soon as he legally could—chooses for auto mechanic. That's a good job, familiar to him, he often watched them as a kid. It's careful and dirty at the same time. In a small garage it's sociable; one can talk to the customers (girls). You please people in trouble by fixing their cars, and a man is proud to see rolling out on its own the car that limped in behind the tow truck. The pay is as good as the next fellow's, who is respected.

So our young man takes this first-rate job. But what when he then learns that the cars have a built-in obsolescence, that the manufacturers do not want them to be repaired or repairable? They have lobbied a law that requires them to provide spare parts for only five years (it used to be ten). Repairing the new cars is often a matter of cosmetics, not mechanics; and the repairs are pointlessly expensive—a tail fin might cost $150. The insurance rates therefore double and treble on old and new cars both. Gone are the days of keeping the jalopies in good shape, the artist-work of a proud mechanic. But everybody is paying for foolishness, for in fact the new models are only trivially superior; the whole thing is a sell.

It is hard for the young man now to maintain his feelings of justification, sociability, serviceability. It is not surprising if he quickly becomes cynical and time-serving, interested in a fast buck. And so, on the notorious *Reader's Digest* test, the investigators (coming in with a disconnected coil wire) found that 63 percent of mechanics charged for repairs they didn't make, and lucky if they didn't also take out the new fuel pump and replace it with a used one (65 per cent of radio repair shops, but *only* 49 per cent of watch repairmen "lied, overcharged, or gave false diagnoses").

There is an hypothesis that an important predisposition to juvenile delinquency is the combination of low verbal intelligence with high manual intelligence, delinquency giving a way of self-expression where other avenues are blocked by lack of schooling. A lad so endowed might well apply himself to the useful trade of mechanic.

Most manual jobs do not lend themselves so readily to knowing the facts and fraudulently taking advantage oneself. In factory jobs the workman is likely to be ignorant of what goes on, since he performs a small operation on a big machine that he does not understand. Even so, there is evidence that he has the same disbelief in the enterprise as a whole, with a resulting attitude of profound indifference.

Semiskilled factory operatives are the largest category of workmen. (I am leafing through the U.S. Department of Labor's *Occupational Outlook Handbook,* 1957.) Big companies have tried the devices of applied anthropology to enhance the loyalty of these men to the firm, but apparently the effort is hopeless, for it is found that a thumping majority of the men don't care about the job or the firm; they couldn't care less and you can't make them care more. But this is *not* because of wages, hours, or working conditions, or management. On the contrary, tests that show the men's indifference to the company show also their (unaware) admiration for the way the company has designed and manages the plant; it is their very model of style, efficiency, and correct behavior. (Robert Dubin, for the U.S. Public Health Service.) Maybe if the men understood more, they would admire less. The union and the grievance committee take care of wages, hours, and conditions; these are the things the workmen themselves fought for and won. (Something was missing in that victory, and we have inherited the failure as well as the success.) The conclusion must be that workmen are indifferent to the job because of its intrinsic nature: it does not enlist worthwhile capacities, it is not "interesting"; it is not his, he is not "in" on it; the product is not really useful. And indeed, research directly on the subject, by Frederick Herzberg on Motivation to Work, shows that it is defects in the intrinsic aspects of the job that make workmen "unhappy." A survey of the literature (in Herzberg's *Job Attitudes)* shows that Interest is second in importance only to Security, whereas Wages, Conditions, Socializing, Hours, Ease, and Benefits are far less important. But foremen, significantly enough, think that the most important thing to the workman is his wages. (The investigators do not seem to inquire about the usefulness of the job—as if a primary purpose of *working* at a job were not that it is good *for* something! My guess is that a large factor in "Security" is the resigned reaction to not being able to take into account whether the work of one's hands is useful for anything; for in a normal life situation, if what we do is useful, we feel secure about being needed. The other largest factor in "Security" is, I think, the sense of being needed for one's unique contribution, and this is measured in these tests by the primary importance the workers assign to being "in" on things and to "work done being appreciated." (Table prepared by Labor Relations Institute of New York.)

Limited as they are, what a remarkable insight such studies give us, that men want to do valuable work and work that is somehow theirs! But they are thwarted.

Is not this the "waste of our human resources"?

The case is that by the "sole-prerogative" clause in union contracts the employer has the sole right to determine what is to be produced, how it is to be produced, what plants are to be built and where, what kinds of machinery are to be installed, when workers are to be hired and laid off, and how production operations are to be rationalized. (Frank Marquart.) There is *none* of this that is inevitable in running a machine economy; but *if* these are the circumstances, it is not surprising that the factory operatives' actual code has absolutely nothing to do with useful service or increasing production, but is notoriously devoted to "interpersonal relations"; (1) don't turn out too much work; (2) don't turn out too little work; (3) don't squeal on a fellow worker; (4) don't act like a big-shot. This is how to belong.

Let us go on to the Occupational Outlook of those who are verbally bright. Among this group, simply because they cannot help asking more general questions—e.g., about utility—the problem of finding man's work is harder, and their disillusion is more poignant.

> He explained to her why it was hard to find a satisfactory job of work to do. He had liked working with the power drill, testing the rocky envelope of the shore, but then the employers asked him to take a great oath of loyalty.
>
> "What!" cried Rosalind. "Do you have scruples about telling a convenient fib?"
>
> "No, I don't. But I felt uneasy about the sanity of the director asking me to swear to opinions on such complicated questions when my job was digging with a power drill. I can't work with a man who might suddenly have a wild fit."
>
> ... "Why don't you get a job driving one of the big trucks along here?"
>
> "I don't like what's in the boxes," said Horatio sadly. "It could just as well drop in the river—and I'd make mistakes and drop it there."
>
> "Is it bad stuff?"
>
> "No, just useless. It takes the heart out of me to work at something useless and I begin to make mistakes. I don't mind putting profits in somebody's pocket—but the job also has to be useful for something."
>
> ... "Why don't you go to the woods and be a lumberjack?"
>
> "No! They chop down the trees just to print off the *New York Times!*"
>
> (*The Empire City*, III, i, 3.)

The more intelligent worker's "indifference" is likely to appear more nakedly as profound resignation, and his cynicism may sharpen to outright racketeering.

"Teaching," says the *Handbook*, "is the largest of the professions." So suppose our now verbally bright young man chooses for teacher, in the high school system or, by exception, in the elementary schools if he understands that the elementary grades are the vitally important ones and require the most ability to teach well (and of course they have less prestige). Teaching is necessary and useful work; it is real and creative, for it directly confronts an important subject matter, the children themselves; it is obviously self-justifying; and it is ennobled by the arts and sciences. Those who practice teaching do not for the most part succumb to cynicism or indifference—the children are too immediate and real for the teachers to become callous—but, most of the school systems being what they are, can teachers fail to come to suffer first despair and then deep resignation? Resignation occurs psychologically as follows: frustrated in essential action, they nevertheless cannot quit in anger, because the task is necessary; so the anger turns inward and is felt as resignation. (Naturally, the resigned teacher may then put on a happy face and keep very busy.)

For the job is carried on under impossible conditions of overcrowding and saving public money. *Not* that there is not enough social wealth, but first things are not put first. Also, the school system has spurious aims. It soon becomes clear that the underlying aims are to relieve the home and keep the kids quiet; or, suddenly, the aim is to produce physicists. Timid supervisors, bigoted clerks, and ignorant school boards forbid real teaching. The emotional release and sexual expression of the children are taboo. A commercially debauched popular culture makes learning disesteemed. The academic curriculum is mangled by the demands of reactionaries, liberals, and demented warriors. Progressive methods are emasculated. Attention to each case is out of the question, and all the children —the bright, the average, and the dull—are systematically retarded one way or another, while the teacher's hands are tied. Naturally the pay is low—for the work is hard, useful, and of public concern, all three of which qualities tend to bring lower pay. It is alleged that the low pay is why there is a shortage of teachers and why the best do not choose the profession. My guess is that the best avoid it because of the certainty of miseducating. Nor are the best *wanted* by the system, for they are not safe. Bertrand Russell was rejected by New York's City College and would not have been accepted in a New York grade school.

Next, what happens to the verbally bright who have no zeal for a serviceable profession and who have no particular scientific or artistic bent? For the most part they make up the tribes of salesmanship, entertainment, business management, promotion, and advertising. Here of course there is no question of utility or honor to begin with, so an ingenuous boy will not look here for a manly career. Nevertheless, though we can pass by the sufferings of these well-paid callings, much publicized by their own writers, they are important to our theme because of the model they present to the growing boy.

Consider the men and women in TV advertisements, demonstrating the product and singing the jingle. They are clowns and mannequins, in grimace, speech, and action. And again, what I want to call attention to in this advertising is not the economic problem of synthetic demand, and not the cultural problem of Popular Culture, but the human problem that these are human beings working as clowns; that the writers and designers of it are human beings thinking like idiots; and the broadcasters and underwriters know and abet what goes on—

> Juicily glubbily
> Blubber is bubbily
> delicious and nutritious
> —eat it, Kitty, it's good.

Alternately, they are liars, confidence men, smooth talkers, obsequious, insolent, etc., etc.

The popular-cultural content of the advertisements is somewhat neutralized by *Mad* magazine, the bible of the twelve-year-olds who can read. But far more influential and hard to counteract is the *fact* that the workmen and the patrons of this enterprise are human beings. (Highly approved, too.) They are not good models for a boy looking for a manly job that is useful and necessary, requiring human energy and capacity, and that can be done with honor and dignity. They are a good sign that not many such jobs will be available.

The popular estimation is rather different. Consider the following: "As one possible aid, I suggested to the Senate subcommittee that they alert celebrities and leaders in the fields of sports, movies, theater and television to the help they can offer by getting close to these (delinquent) kids. By giving them positive 'heroes' they know and can talk to, instead of the misguided image of trouble-making buddies, they could aid greatly in guiding these normal aspirations for fame and status into wholesome progressive channels." (Jackie Robinson, who was formerly on the Connecticut Parole Board.) Or again: when a mass cross-section of Oklahoma high school juniors and seniors was asked which living person they would like to be, the boys named Pat Boone, Ricky Nelson, and President Eisenhower; the girls chose Debbie Reynolds, Elizabeth Taylor, and Natalie Wood.

The rigged Quiz shows, which created a scandal in 1959, were a remarkably pure distillate of our American cookery. We start with the brute facts that (a) in our abundant expanding economy it is necessary to give money away to increase spending, production, and profits; and (b) that this money must not be used for useful public goods in taxes, but must be plowed back as "business expenses," even though there is a shameful shortage of schools, housing, etc. Yet when the TV people at first tried simply to give the money away for nothing (for having heard of George Washington), there was a great Calvinistic outcry that this was demoralizing (we may gamble on the horses only to improve the breed). So they hit on the notion of a real contest with prizes. But then, of course, they could not resist making the show itself profitable, and competitive in the (also rigged) ratings with other shows, so the experts in the entertainment-commodity manufactured phony contests. And to cap the climax of fraudulence, the hero of the phony contests proceeded to persuade himself, so he says, that his behavior was educational!

The behavior of the networks was correspondingly typical. These business organizations claim the loyalty of their employees, but at the first breath of trouble they were ruthless and disloyal to their employees. (Even McCarthy was loyal to his gang.) They want to maximize profits and yet be absolutely safe from any risk. Consider their claim that they knew nothing about the fraud. But if they watched the shows that they were broadcasting, they could not *possibly*, as professionals, not have known the facts, for there were obvious type-casting, acting, plot, etc. If they are not professionals, they are incompetent. But if they don't watch what they broadcast, then they are utterly irresponsible and on what grounds do they have the franchises to the channels? We may offer them the choice: that they are liars or incompetent or irresponsible.

The later direction of the investigation seems to me more important, the inquiry into the bribed disk-jockeying; for this deals directly with our crucial economic problem of synthesized demand, made taste, debauching the public and preventing the emergence and formation of natural taste. In such circumstances there cannot possibly be an American culture; we are doomed to nausea and barbarism. And *then* these baboons have the effrontery to declare that they give the people what the people demand and that they are not responsible for the level of the movies, the music, the plays, the books!

Finally, in leafing through the *Occupational Outlook Handbook*, we notice that the armed forces employ a large number. Here our young men can become involved in a world-wide demented enterprise, with personnel and activities corresponding.

Thus, on the simple criteria of unquestioned utility, employing human capacities, and honor, there are not enough worthy jobs in our economy for average boys and adolescents to grow up toward. There are of course thousands of jobs that are worthy and self-justifying, and thousands that can be made so by stubborn integrity, especially if one can work as an independent. Extraordinary intelligence or special talent, also, can often carve out a place for itself—conversely, their usual corruption and waste are all the more sickening. But by and large our economic society is *not* geared for the cultivation of its young or the attainment of important goals that they can work toward.

This is evident from the usual kind of vocational guidance, which consists of measuring the boy and finding some place in the economy where he can be fitted; chopping him down to make him fit; or neglecting him if they can't find his slot. Personnel directors do not much try to scrutinize the economy in order to find some activity that is a real opportunity for the boy, and then to create an opportunity if they can't find one. To do this would be an horrendous task; I am not sure it could be done if we wanted to do it. But the question is whether anything less makes sense if we mean to speak seriously about the troubles of the young men.

Surely by now, however, many readers are objecting that this entire argument is pointless because people in *fact* don't think of their jobs in this way at all. *Nobody* asks if a job is useful or honorable (within the limits of business ethics). A man gets a job that pays well, or well enough, that has prestige, and good conditions, or at least tolerable conditions. I agree with these objections as to the fact. (I hope we are wrong.) But *the question is what it means to grow up into such a fact as: "During my productive years I will spend eight hours a day doing what is no good."*

Yet, economically and vocationally, a very large population of the young people are in a plight more drastic than anything so far mentioned. In our society as it is, there are not enough worthy jobs. But if our society, being as it is, were run more efficiently and soberly, for a majority there would soon not be any jobs at all. There is at present nearly full employment and there may be for some years, yet a vast number of young people are rationally unemployable, useless. This paradox is essential to explain their present temper.

Our society, which is not geared to the cultivation of its young, *is* geared to a profitable expanding production, a so-called high standard of living of mediocre value, and the maintenance of nearly full employment. Politically, the chief of these is full employment. In a crisis, when profitable production is temporarily curtailed, government spending increases and jobs are manufactured. In "normalcy"—a condition of slow boom—the easy credit, installment buying, and artificially induced demand for useless goods create jobs for all and good profits for some.

Now, back in the Thirties, when the New Deal attempted by hook or crook to put people back to work and give them money to revive the shattered economy, there was an outcry of moral indignation from the conservatives that many of the jobs were "boondoggling," useless made-work. It was insisted, and rightly, that such work was demoralizing to the workers themselves. It is a question of a word, but a candid critic might certainly say that many of the jobs in our present "normal" production are useless made-work. The tail fins and built-in obsolescence might be called boondoggling. The $64,000 Question and the busy hum of Madison Avenue might certainly be called boondoggling. Certain tax-dodge Foundations are boondoggling. What of business lunches and expense accounts? fringe benefits? the comic categories of occupation in the building trades? the extra stagehands and musicians of the theater crafts? These jolly devices to put money back to work no doubt have a demoralizing effect on somebody or other (certainly on me, they make me green with envy), but where is the moral indignation from Top Management?

Suppose we would cut out the boondoggling and gear our society to a more sensible abundance, with efficient production of quality goods, distribution in a natural market, counterinflation and sober credit. At once the work week would be cut to, say, twenty hours instead of forty. (Important People have already mentioned the figure thirty.) Or alternately, half the labor force would be unemployed. Suppose too—and how can we not suppose it?—that the automatic machines are used generally, rather than just to get rid of badly organized un-skilled labor. The unemployment will be still more drastic.

(To give the most striking example: in steel, the annual increase in productivity is 4 per cent, the plants work at 50 per cent of capacity, and the companies can break even and stop producing at *less than 30 per cent* of capacity. These are the conditions that forced the steel strike, as desperate self-protection. (Estes Kefauver, quoting Gardiner Means and Fred Gardner.)

Everybody knows this, nobody wants to talk about it much, for we don't know how to cope with it. The effect is that we are living a kind of lie. Long ago, labor leaders used to fight for the shorter work week, but now they don't, be-cause they're pretty sure they don't want it. Indeed, when hours are reduced, the tendency is to get a second, part-time job and raise the standard of living, *because* the job is meaningless and one must have something; but the standard of living is pretty meaningless, too. Nor is this strange atmosphere a new thing. For at least a generation the maximum sensible use of our productivity could have thrown a vast population out of work, or relieved everybody of a lot of useless work, depending on how you take it. (Consider with how little cutback of useful civilian production the economy produced the war goods and main-tained an Army, economically unemployed.) The plain truth is that at present very many of us are useless, not needed, rationally unemployable. It is in this paradoxical atmosphere that young persons grow up. It looks busy and expansive, but it is rationally at a stalemate.

These considerations apply to all ages and classes; but it is of course among poor youth (and the aged) that they show up first and worst. They are the most unemployable. For a long time our society has not been geared to the cultivation of the young. In our country 42 per cent have graduated from high school (pre-dicted census, 1960); less than 8 per cent have graduated from college. The high school trend for at least the near future is not much different: there will be a high proportion of drop-outs before the twelfth grade; but *markedly more* of the rest will go on to college; that is, the stratification will harden. Now the schooling in neither the high schools nor the colleges is much good—if it were better more kids would stick to it; yet at present, if we made a list we should find that a large proportion of the dwindling number of unquestionably useful or self-justifying jobs, in the humane professions and the arts and sciences, re-quire education; and in the future, there is no doubt that the more educated will have the jobs, in running an efficient, highly technical economy and an ad ministrative society placing a premium on verbal skills.

(Between 1947 and 1957, professional and technical workers increased 61 per cent, clerical workers 23 per cent, but factory operatives only 4½ per cent and laborers 4 percent.—Census.)

For the uneducated there will be no jobs at all. This is humanly most unfor-tunate, for presumably those who have learned something in schools, and have the knack of surviving the boredom of those schools, could also make some-thing of idleness; whereas the uneducated are useless at leisure too. It takes application, a fine sense of value, and a powerful community-spirit for a people to have serious leisure, and this has not been the genius of the Americans.

From this point of view we can sympathetically understand the pathos of our American school policy, which otherwise seems so inexplicable; at great expense compelling kids to go to school who do not want to and who will not profit by it. There are of course unpedagogic motives, like relieving the home, controlling delinquency, and keeping kids from competing for jobs. But there is also this desperately earnest pedagogic motive, of preparing the kids to take *some* part in a democratic society that does not need them. Otherwise, what will become of them, if they don't know anything?

Compulsory public education spread universally during the nineteenth century to provide the reading, writing, and arithmetic necessary to build a modern industrial economy. With the overmaturity of the economy, the teachers are struggling to preserve the elementary system when the economy no longer requires it and is stingy about paying for it. The demand is for scientists and technicians, the 15 per cent of the "academically talented." "For a vast majority (in the high school)," says Dr. Conant in *The Child, the Parent, and the State*, "the vocational courses are the vital core of the program. They represent something related directly to the ambitions of the boys and girls." But somehow, far more than half of these quit. How is that?

Let us sum up again. The majority of young people are faced with the following alternative: Either society is a benevolently frivolous racket in which they'll manage to boondoggle, though less profitably than the more privileged; or society is serious (and they hope still benevolent enough to support them), but they are useless and hopelessly out. Such thoughts do not encourage productive life. Naturally young people are more sanguine and look for man's work, but few find it. Some settle for a "good job"; most settle for a lousy job; a few, but an increasing number, don't settle.

I often ask, "What do you want to work at? If you have the chance. When you get out of school, college, the service, etc."

Some answer right off and tell their definite plans and projects, highly approved by Papa. I'm pleased for them, but it's a bit boring, because they are such squares.

Quite a few will, with prompting, come out with astounding stereotyped, conceited fantasies, such as becoming a movie actor when they are "discovered" —"like Marlon Brando, but in my own way."

Very rarely somebody will, maybe defiantly and defensively, maybe diffidently but proudly, make you know that he knows very well what he is going to do; it is something great; and he is indeed already doing it, which is the real test.

The usual answer, perhaps the normal answer, is "I don't know," meaning, "I'm looking; I haven't found the right thing; it's discouraging but not hopeless."

But the terrible answer is, "Nothing." The young man doesn't want to do anything.

—I remember talking to half a dozen young fellows at Van Wagner's Beach outside of Hamilton, Ontario; and all of them had this one thing to say: "Nothing." They didn't believe that what to work at was the kind of thing one *wanted.* They rather expected that two or three of them would work for the electric company in town, but they couldn't care less. I turned away from the conversation abruptly because of the uncontrollable burning tears in my eyes and constriction in my chest. Not feeling sorry for them, but tears of frank dismay for the waste of our humanity (they were nice kids). And it is out of that incident that many years later I am writing this book.

5 SOCIOPOLITICAL ACTION

This first article on the role adolescents can play in changing society suggests that possibilities for social change in a culture derive from the status enjoyed by its youth. Citing several non-literate societies, the author presents a far-reaching hypothesis concerning alienated youth and a society in transition: societies affording low status to youth create a deviant group open to social experimentation; conversely, youth with high status tend to perpetuate the status quo.

Frank Musgrove

Youth and Social Change

FRUSTRATION AND INNOVATION

When, in the days of World War II, Karl Mannheim looked forward to a reconstructed post-war Britain, he emphasized the important role that youth must play if progress and change were to be achieved. "I believe that static societies which develop only gradually, and in which the rate of change is relatively slow, will rely mainly on the experience of the old." [1] A dynamic society, on the other hand, would accord youth a high status: a frustrated and stagnant Britain had failed to give youth "its proper place and share in public life." [2] Although Mannheim was aware that the driving force of the young originated in large measure from their "outsider" position, [3] he saw no inconsistency in urging that they should become insiders: "the dynamic societies which want to make a new start, whatever their social or political philosophy may be, will rely mainly on the co-operation of youth. They will organize their vital resources

[1] Karl Mannheim, *Diagnosis of Our Time* (1943), p. 33.
[2] Karl Mannheim, *Diagnosis of Our Time* (1943), p. 43.
[3] Karl Mannheim, *Diagnosis of Our Time* (1943), p. 36.

138

and will use them in breaking down the established direction of social development."

The truth is probably the opposite of Mannheim's thesis. It is true that high status of young people is often closely associated with a heightened tempo of social change; but it is frequently a consequence rather than a cause. Eisenstadt has pointed to great social and political movements in nineteenth-century Europe which were closely associated with the energies of young people—Mazzini's "Young Italy," the German youth movements following the rapid transformation which took place during the post-Bismarckian era, and the nationalist movements in the Near and Far East today which have relied heavily on students and young army officers.[4] But the latter have achieved importance after the social and political revolutions and not before: it was their low status in the traditional, familistic setting, in which the authority of the elders was paramount, which must be seen as an important cause of social change; their subsequent high status is a result. It is likely that revolutionary change which owes much to such circumstances will fail to maintain its forward momentum.[5] The middle- and upper-class young women of late-Victorian and Edwardian England, whose status frustrations led to the militant Suffragette movement, have been succeeded in mid-twentieth-century Britain by an enfranchised adult female population unremarkable at any social level for vigorous, let alone revolutionary, political activity.

The causes of social change are complex, and the low status of youth only one factor which merits attention. But it is a factor which has been comparatively little examined. When the modes of social change which have occurred among non-literate peoples in contact with the West are compared, the position of the young in the indigenous societies provides at least a partial explanation of the nature of the response. It is now many years since Fortes argued that a comparative sociology of culture contact was needed "without which we can never hope to perceive the causes of social change."[6] In this chapter nothing so ambitious is attempted; but a variety of circumstances in which social change has occurred —or has been resisted—will be compared, and as far as possible the status of the young isolated and examined for its bearing on the processes of resistance and change.

The argument advanced in this chapter is this: that in those societies in which the status of adolescents and young adults (particularly the males) is high, change will tend to be slow, the blandishments of an elaborate and alien civilization resisted; where their status is low, and their seniors can effectively block their access to adult statuses and impede their assumption of adult roles, then there is likely to be a predisposition to change, to social innovation and experimentation, to a ready response to the opportunities which may be offered by an alien,

---

[4] S. N. Eisenstadt, *From Generation to Generation* (1956), pp. 171–174.

[5] Cf. A. J. P. Taylor's interpretation of the failure of German liberals in 1848—because they had succeeded, as students, in the movement of national liberation in 1813: "The revolution of 1848 was not the explosion of new forces, but the belated triumph of *Burschenschaft*, the students of the war of liberation who were now men in their fifties . . . dependent on the princes for their salaries or pensions as civil servants." See *The Course of German History* (1945), p. 69.

[6] Meyer Fortes, "Culture Contact as a Dynamic Process," *Africa* (1936), 9.

intrusive culture to follow alternative and quicker routes to power and importance. When the young are segregated from the adult world, held in low esteem, and delayed in their entry into adult life, they are likely to constitute a potentially deviant population; but when they are segregated from the adult world in a position of high status and power (for instance, in warrior groups), a conservative society is the probable result. High status and a sense of importance may be achieved by the young through integration with, rather than segregation from, the adult world: they may share their seniors' work and responsibilities, their pleasures and pastimes; in this case, too, resistance to change is likely to be strong.

While British anthropologists of the "functional" school have resolutely refused to invoke psychology to account for the processes of culture change, finding sufficient explanation in "social facts," in the inter-relations of institutions and their capacity or incapacity to satisfy "needs," American anthropologists have looked for light in personality- and in learning-theory. "A well-developed learning theory," Hallowell has maintained, "is relevant to promoting further knowledge of the whole process of cultural transmission as well as the processes involved in acculturation and culture change."[7] The new learning which takes place when social change occurs, it is argued, is explicable only in terms of the personality organization which facilitates or impedes adjustment to new circumstances: in the process of social change, "a crucial variable may be the kind of personality structure of the people undergoing acculturation."[8]

While it is true that sociological explanations imply at least rudimentary psychological assumptions—usually somewhat crudely hedonistic views of learning and motivation—it is possible to look for the social correlates of change without venturing into the wide sea of personality-and-culture theory. The position of the young in a society's social structure can be shown to have an intimate connection with that society's stability and response to changing external circumstances. It is true that throughout the world today non-literate societies are changing whatever may be the power enjoyed by their young; but their rates and modes of change differ, and their readiness or proneness to change have varied widely at the "zero point of contact" (in Lucy Mair's phrase), even when the alien impact was similar in range, intensity, organization, and content. The standardized policy of America's Indian Affairs Department in the later nineteenth century met with a wide variety of reactions from the Indian tribes: the Makah[9] were remarkable for their degree of assimilation to American culture while remaining active and vigorous; the Sioux,[10] treated to an essentially similar programme of education and Americanization, rejected the alien culture, without vigour, only with dispirited apathy. The tribes of Africa have shown a similar

---

[7] A. Irving Hallowell, "Culture, Personality, and Society," in A. L. Kroeber, *Anthropology Today* (1953), p. 599.
[8] A. Irving Hallowell, "Culture, Personality, and Society," in A. L. Kroeber, *Anthropology Today* (1953), pp. 613–614.
[9] See Elizabeth Colson, *The Makah Indians* (1953).
[10] See G. MacGregor, *Warriors Without Weapons* (1946).

variety of response to the endeavours of European missionaries, labour recruiters, and government officials.

Change may be voluntary or forced,[11] but however reluctant in their first encounter, tribal societies throughout the world are undergoing change, at varying rates. The size and concentration of their populations, their proximity to or remoteness from European institutions and settlements, the administrative policies of imperial powers, are all relevant circumstances. Tribes in which the cultivation of cash crops has been successfully introduced have probably made the most important and positive changes in adapting tribal life to a new political and economic context;[12] tribes which supply migrant labour to distant European enterprises have often changed less; those with neither cash cropping nor migrant labourers have generally persisted in a traditional way of life. But at the zero point of impact, tribal societies showed marked differences in their proneness to change, even when the impact was similar in nature and extent.

When Her Majesty's Special Commissioner made his preliminary report on the Uganda Protectorate in 1900, he was struck by the different responses of tribes within a relatively small region of Africa. "Among the naked Nilotic negroes of the eastern half of the Protectorate missionary propaganda seems at the present time to be absolutely impossible. . . . On the other hand, the Bantu-speaking natives are well inclined to religious inquiry."[13] The egalitarian Lango and Iteso, without marked distinctions of rank or political authority ("it is sometimes difficult to find a man who does not profess to be a 'somebody' "[14]), were contemptuous of alien ideas, institutions, and customs, tenacious of their own; the hierarchical, centralized states like the Baganda, among whom distinctions of rank and age were marked, and the track of seniority long, were more ready to learn alien ways. From the very first days of contact they showed themselves not only predisposed to learn a new religion,[15] but were "greedy for cloth and for almost every manufactured article up to a phonograph and a brougham."[16]

When a social system presents blockages and delays to the satisfaction of needs, particularly the urgently felt social and sexual needs of young men, the institutions of an alien civilization may be eagerly embraced. The new institutions may, indeed, create new needs,[17] but initially they offer the chance of satisfying existing needs more quickly and directly. "An individual adopts an innovation of his own free will only when he has become convinced that it offers him some kind of reward—perhaps greater efficiency, or more security,

[11] For a useful discussion of this distinction, see Ian Hogbin, *Social Change* (1958), pp. 98–99.
[12] See A. Southall, "Social Change, Demography and Extrinsic Factors" in A. Southall (ed.), *Social Change in Modern Africa* (1961), pp. 1–13.
[13] *Preliminary Report of Her Majesty's Special Commissioner on the Uganda Protectorate* (1901), cd. 671, p. 6.
[14] A. L. Kitching, *On the Backwaters of the Nile* (1912), p. 160.
[15] Even at the price of martyrdom at the hands of political superiors who interpreted the new learning as a threat to their authority. See R. P. Ashe, *Two Kings of Uganda* (1899), pp. 215–231, for an account of kabaka Mwanga's persecution of native Christians ("readers") in Buganda.
[16] *Preliminary Report of Her Majesty's Special Commissioner on the Uganda Protectorate* (1901).
[17] See the author's study, "A Uganda School as a Field of Culture Change," *Africa* (1952), 22, for an examination of an African school as an institution which meets "emergent needs" which have no strict counterpart in either the indigenous or the intrusive culture.

or enhanced status." [18] An established value may now be realized more effectively in a new way; [19] thus whereas security, land, status, and the brideprice
could eventually be attained by young men throughout most of Melanesia
through service to maternal uncles, Western contact offered an alternative and
quicker route to independence and fully adult status: work for wages in European
enterprises. The result is to undermine the authority of age: "the senior men are
in a quandary.... The tendency is therefore towards a loosening of the ties binding the two age-groups together." [20]

New institutions may be accepted because they seem to lend support to existing social values; but their long term effect may be to undermine them. Thus
European-type schools have often been supported by African parents because
their immediate effect has been to discipline the young and maintain the authority of seniority. In the nineteen-thirties Lucy Mair found in the villages of
Buganda that:

> The parents themselves are anxious to have their children go to school; there is no
> question of the children being taken from their influence against their will... The
> parents do not themselves feel that European education is likely to make their children
> disrespectful. Indeed I remember one father declaring that children were better kept
> in order at school than at home....[21]

But the boys themselves may welcome school not because it supports (some of)
the traditional values of the indigenous social order, but because it subverts
them. As the author reported from Uganda in the nineteen-fifties: "The school
appears to be most effective (with its pupils) when it is not attempting to take
over the functions of tribal institutions: it is most effective not in shoring up the
deficiences of tribal institutions, but when it is on wholly new ground, dealing
with subjects outside the sphere of traditional instruction and pursuits." [22]

The Wilsons presented a cataclysmic view of social change under conditions
of culture contact. Seeing pre-contact African societies as coherent systems ("To
deny the assumption of social coherence would be to abandon all hope of analysis in history..." [23]), albeit with "normal opposition" which could be contained
—between a boy and his mother's brother, between co-wives or a wife and her
husband's people—they argued that culture contact introduced "radical opposition," fundamental and irreconcilable conflict between law and law, logic and
logic, convention and convention. Social change was disequilibrium: thus
Christianity and monogamy raised complex opposition within the society of the

[18] Ian Hogbin, *Social Change* (1958), p. 57.
[19] Ian Hogbin, *Social Change* (1958), p. 94. Cf. B. Malinowski, *The Dynamics of Culture Change* (1945): "One kind of institution can be replaced by another which fulfils a similar function" (p. 52). "The ultimate reality in culture change thus hinges on the fact that corresponding institutions in two cultures satisfy analogous needs in different ways and with different techniques...."
[20] Ian Hogbin, *Social Change* (1958), p. 94.
[21] L. P. Mair, *An African People in the Twentieth Century* (1934), pp. 68–69.
[22] F. Musgrove, "Some Refections on the Sociology of African Education," *African Studies* (1952), II. See also the author's study of African children's play: "(they) do not of their own accord bring traditional games into the school": "Education and the Culture Concept," *Africa* (1953), 23.
[23] G. and M. Wilson, *Analysis of Social Change* (1945), p. 23.

Nyakyusa: the traditional value of hospitality by the wealthy was incapable of realization with such institutions. "The opposition can only be removed by social change, economic or religious." [24]

But social change had already occurred—when some, at least, of the Nyakyusa adopted Christianity and monogamy: what the Wilson's are perhaps explaining is *further* social change. The initial acceptance of new institutions—which may have unforeseen consequences in the future—when it is voluntary, is a solution to existing tensions and frustrations. When marriage is an important sign of adult status, and when the conditions of marriage are closely controlled by the older age groups, change may be accepted because it promotes an existing value (status through marriage) while undermining another (the authority of the old). At least for the young the balance of advantage is on the side of change: they have not even necessarily learned new ideas and values, but have only found support for ideas and values which already existed, but were perhaps experimental and disreputable. Discontent with the authority of their seniors was already present. "Every real society consists of a core of orthodox norms and conforming actions round the margins of experiment that changing norms and actions emerge into sanctioned acceptance." [25]

Societies which have shown an initial proneness to change have often been characterized by the frustrations of young men whose chance of marriage is jeopardized by the power of elderly polygymists. The Mende of Sierra Leone and the Azande of the Sudan have been differently involved in contact with the West: the former have had a more sustained and intimate contact, the latter are geographically remote. Both are societies hierarchical in their social and political organization, both give power to older men, and both have been noted for their inclination to social innovation and their ready acceptance of change. Formerly among the Azande "The older men had a monopoly of wives, and in the past it was difficult for young men to marry. The need of food and the hope of acquiring a sufficient number of spears with which to marry anchored a youth to his family and kin. The father of a family exercised great control over his sons who treated him with deep respect." [26] Similarily with the Mende: "Married persons constitute a definite and more senior category to those who are unmarried irrespective of the actual age of the latter." "In the old days, few men had the opportunity of obtaining a wife before they were 30, or even 35 years of age, and had proved their hardihood and diligence. Nowadays . . . a man has more opportunities to secure the amount of bridewealth through his own efforts and so achieve a wife while still in his early twenties." [27] In such circumstances the

---

[24] G. and M. Wilson, *Analysis of Social Change* (1945), p. 126.

[25] A. W. Southall, "Norms and Status Symbols" in A. W. Southall (ed.), *Social Change in Modern Africa* (1961), p. 14.

[26] E. E. Evans-Pritchard, *Witchcraft and Oracles Among the Azande* (1937), p. 16. "We shall find that social status intrudes into every phase of Azande life" (p. 14), but "it is unusually easy for the European to establish contact with them. . . . (they) are always ready to copy the behaviour of those they regard as their superiors in culture and to borrow new modes of dress, new weapons and utensils, new words, and even new ideas . . ." (p. 13).

[27] K. L. Little, *The Mende of Sierra Leone* (1951), p. 140.

young have every reason to enter the mission school, European factory and mine.

SEGREGATION WITH HIGH STATUS

The societies which have shown themselves particularly resistant to change at least in the early phases of their contact with the culture of the West have commonly been those in which the young had a high and assured status and importance either through their close involvement in adult affairs or through segregated age-group institutions which exercised social, political, or military power. Segregated age-group organizations of this kind are to be found in tribes widely different in their political and social structures; and the precise functions of the age-groups are themselves extremely various. They are found in "segmentary tribes" without central governmental institutions—the Nuer, the Nandi, the Plains Indians, the Lango, and the Masai; they are found in centralized kingdoms like the Zulu and the Ashanti. The structure and the functions of the age-groups [28] vary: the age-range embraced, their internal sub-divisions and organization, their political, educational, military or social activities and purposes. Thus the Nandi age-set [29] of young men has military significance, but the age-set system of the Nuer of the Sudan has neither a military nor a political purpose: it is a major determinant of social relationships and domestic behaviour.[30] But in all cases initiation is associated with the legitimate entry into heterosexual relationships; membership of the age-group promotes status in the total community (as opposed to the family or other local group) and so functions as an integrative mechanism for the entire society. Although the anthropological evidence on change in these different tribes is often difficult to compare, and the ways of *measuring* social change so various as to make comparison particularly difficult, these societies do appear to have shown unusual persistence in their traditional ways even under considerable external pressure. Speaking of such societies Eisenstadt has observed: "The existing data fully warrant the assumption that no *structural* tendencies toward deviancy can be discerned in these age groups....[31]

The Nandi and the Nuer are both tribes whose conservatism has been fully attested and whose age-group organizations have been thoroughly and meticulously investigated and described. Nuer youths are initiated at the age of 14 to 16; they then jump "from the grade of boyhood to the grade of manhood, and the character of their social life is correspondingly transformed...." "After initiation a lad takes on the full privileges and obligations of manhood in work, play, and

---

[28] "Age-set" refers to persons who have been initiated during the successive annual ceremonies of a single initiation period; "age-group" refers more generally to any division of a population by age. Political duties may be allocated on the basis of age: the age-sets then pass through the successive age-grades of warrior and elder.

[29] See G. W. B. Huntingford, *The Nandi of Kenya* (1953).

[30] See E. E. Evans-Pritchard, *The Nuer* (1940).

[31] S. N. Eisenstadt, *From Generation to Generation* (1956), p. 280.

war. Above all, he gives himself whole-heartedly to winning the favours of the maidens of the neighbourhood." [32] Adult status is not dependent on marriage. Sons are married by seniority, and after one has married the family herd must reach its former strength before cattle are available for the marriage of the next. Thus a young man may not marry until his mid-twenties. In the meantime, however, he will have no problem of access to women.

Age-group membership, and particuarly initiation, has been held to account more than anything else for the character and social attitudes of the Nuer: their sensitivity, pride and arrogance, their stubbornness and independence, their impatience of authority. [33] They have in the past shown no sense of inferiority in the presence of the white man, no inclination to adopt his institutions and way of life.

Similarly with the Nandi of Kenya. Proud and conservative, with a long history of resistance to British administration, they have been unwilling to change the customs, beliefs and outlook of their ancestors. Without chiefs or any form of central authority, the warrior age-set exercises great power. The age-range within an age-set might be 7 or 8 years. 10 to 15 years might elapse between the completion of one set and the opening of another. The initiates attain full adult status after a few months' seclusion; they have no need to wait until the completion of the 4-year initiation period. As warriors they can marry and make love to unmarried girls, they are responsible for military operations and enjoy wide social privileges. The younger boys' age-sets dance attendance on them, but they in their turn are assured of succession when power is formally handed over. [34]

The close connection between the power of the young and social stability is seen among the Comanche Indians when they moved from the Plateau to the Plains. In their earlier, inhospitable plateau environment they were a potentially unstable society. Dominated by the old, the young of very little account, the transformation of their culture has been described as a "striking lesson in social change." [35]

As a brigand tribe of the Plains, the young warriors on whom prosperity depended enjoyed a dominant social position; institutions evolved which promoted their cohesion and solidarity—wife-sharing, the equal distribution of spoils, the limited tenure of positions of leadership. "These men exercised no formal civil authority, but they possessed great power through prestige. In reality they managed the tribe." "Top rank in Comanche society was attained by the fine warrior. . . . When he was past the fighting age, his status declined quickly." [36]

Forcible change was eventually brought to the Comanche ("they were retired under government protection" [37]). But until this happened, they had a stability which has been attributed largely to the fact that "the individuals are not blocked

[32] E. E. Evans-Pritchard, *Kinship and Marriage Among the Nuer* (1951), p. 51.
[33] See E. E. Evans-Pritchard, *The Nuer* (1940).
[34] G. W. B. Huntingford, *The Nandi of Kenya* (1953).
[35] Abram Kardiner, *The Psychological Frontiers of Society* (1945).
[36] Abram Kardiner, *The Psychological Frontiers of Society* (1945), pp. 55–56.
[37] Abram Kardiner, *The Psychological Frontiers of Society* (1945), p. 96.

in development, and the individual can contribute to the common good and participate in it according to his talents. It is a true democracy." [38]

Other societies have accorded less power to organized youth but, while they have retained the direction of affairs in the hands of the elders, they have nevertheless given to youth a sense of importance and social usefulness. Among the Nyakyusa of Tanganyika the unique institution of the age-village segregates young males from adult society from the age of 9 or 10. The original members of the age-village remain together throughout life. Although in their early youth they are economically dependent on their fathers, whose fields they hoe, they have a sense of solidarity and power; they value good fellowship and cooperation; and although they are commoners, at least as they reach mature years they constitute a social and political force of which hereditary chiefs must take serious account.

The tension between the uprising and the mature generation is minimal. Intergeneration accusations of witchcraft are very rare.[39] Eisenstadt surprisingly includes the Nyakyusa among the "familistic societies" in which, "since these age groups arise as a result of strong tension between the generations, a somewhat stronger deviant potential is indicated." [40] If the Nyakyusa age-groups originated in strong inter-generation tension, they have proved a most effective social mechanism for reducing it.[41]

The Ngoni of Nyasaland also segregate their young males; and here the connection between the pride and sense of importance of young men on the one hand, and the society's conservatism on the other, is perhaps easier to see. It is true that the proud, hierarchical Ngoni, with their keen sense of social distinction and precedence, are changing: economic developments have been beyond their control, and "The economic foundations of political power and social prestige have been to a large extent undermined by the abolition of war and slavery and the exodus of men to the south for work in mines and on farms." [42] But change has for long been resisted. The initial reaction was one of "pronounced antipathy to European contact." The traditional values and customs have been overwhelmed rather than willingly surrendered. The ancient virtues of dignity, self-control and correct deportment are still valued and achieved in a changing social order.

[38] Abram Kardiner, The Psychological Frontiers of Society (1945), p. 423.
[39] See Monica Wilson, Good Company (1951).
[40] S. N. Eisenstadt, From Generation to Generation (1956), p. 249.
[41] Cf. the argument that societies in which, because of child-rearing arrangements, young males are particularly hostile to their fathers and dependent on their mothers often resolve the conflict either through initiation ceremonies or through a change of residence for the boys at puberty. The Nuer, for example, are held to be an illustration of the former practice, the Nyakyusa of the latter: "change of residence serves the same functions that we have posited for initiation ceremonies, for example, by establishing male authority, breaking the bond with the mother, and ensuring acceptance of the male role." The absence of both initiation ceremonies and of residential change for adolescent males among the Tallensi, for example, is explained according to this theory by different methods of infant care, particularly the shorter period of exclusive mother-son sleeping arrangements. See J. W. M. Whiting, R. Kluckhohn and A. Anthony, "The Function of Male Initiation Ceremonies at Puberty," in E. E. Maccoby, T. M. Newcomb and E. L. Hartley (eds), Readings in Social Psychology (3rd ed. 1958).
[42] Margaret Read, Native Standards of Living and African Culture Change (1938).

Personal dignity and self-esteem are in large measure the outcome of life in the boys' dormitory, which young males enter at the age of 6. Although the age-range in the dormitories was formerly very wide, spanning more than a dozen years, and internal distinctions of status were sharp, life in them promoted a sense of solidarity and high morale. The boys were not segregated in futile dependency: they had a valued contribution to make to the life and economy of the nation.

They were of sufficient importance to be allowed into the discussions of high affairs conducted by the senior men at the kraal gate; in caring for cattle they did a responsible job from which they gained a strong notion of their own importance. Although marriage among the Ngoni was formerly comparatively late—usually little short of 30 for men—adolescent and young adult males seem to have had no frustration or resentment against their elders. "The seeming absence of frustration and overt rebellion in the years just after puberty was due to the social recognition by relatives and by the village community of the new stage reached by boys and girls, and to the increasing responsibility required of them for carrying out allotted tasks and for preparing for their future careers." [43]

INTEGRATION WITH HIGH STATUS

Adolescents and young men may achieve a sense of high importance not from segregation in age-sets or looser age-groups associations which confer high status, power or privilege, but from close connection with the lives and affairs of adults. Eisenstadt suggests that this absence of age-group organization is a feature of those societies—often "segmentary" tribes—in which the kin group is a virtually self-sufficient social unit, in which the young can learn all the role dispositions necessary for adult life. Seniority may play an important part in the regulation of behaviour, but the young have an integral role in the social order.

The Tallensi of northern Ghana, the Tikopia of Polynesia, and perhaps the Samoans, are examples of societies which are on the whole conservative and in which the young have importance through social integration. The young of Tikopia in the nineteen-twenties, although before puberty they generally went around in independent little bands, were early involved in the central concerns of the island's economy. "The child soon comes to take part in the work of the community, and so useful is it that a household without one is at a distinct loss. At first it goes out with a relative to the cultivations and intersperses its play with fetching and carrying things. Gradually most of the economic minutiae are allotted to it by its elders, including others than parents, and its performances, small in themselves, act as the emollient which allows the household machinery to run smoothly." [44] Although marriage was relatively late and the authority of elders respected, Firth found no evidence of revolt or deviation among the

---

[43] Margaret Read, *Children of their Fathers* (1959), p. 170.
[44] R. Firth, *We, the Tikopia* (1957 ed.), p. 150.

young, who found ample compensation in their way of life and accepted the social institutions in which they were increasingly involved—mourning obligations, affinal regulations, and duties to chiefs.

A quarter of a century later Firth found the Tikopia remarkably little changed in spite of their widening contacts with the outer world. In 1929 they had shown little inclination to go abroad to work for wages; by 1952 migrant labor was more common. But the influence of the West was incorporated into the existing social structure without appreciably changing it. "The reaction was one of incorporation—to keep the fabric of the culture intact while using in it as many foreign elements as possible. 'We, the Tikopia,' wished to remain the Tikopia." [45] Between 1929 and 1952 they had even "incorporated" the use of money, using the white man's currency for dealing with the white man, the traditional currency (bark-cloth) for transactions among themselves.

In spite of the continued efforts of Christian missionaries there was as much polygamy in 1952 as in 1929 (though the proportion of polygamous marriages was small at both dates). There was no change in the actual quantity of marriage: while there had been an increase of 33 per cent in spouses of all kinds, the population had grown by 35 per cent. Marriage was still relatively late, but the sex intrigues of young unmarrieds were still common form. The system of descent was little changed, and young men still choose their brides from a very limited geographical range: in 1952 as in 1929 one-sixth of all marriages took place between people of the same village. Although Firth senses the likelihood of imminent widespread social change, little had in fact occurred since the time of his original field-work in the twenties.

Another Polynesian people, the Samoans, accord their young a position in society similar to that in Tikopia; and while they have proved a flexible and adaptable society, like the Tikopians they incorporated Western influence without undergoing drastic social transformation. When Margaret Mead investigated their social life in the twenties, she found that the young were given tasks, according to their strength and abilities, which were functionally related to the work of the adult world. Marriage was neither a prerequisite of fully adult status nor a necessary condition of sexual experience. Margaret Mead contrasted the Samoan condition with that often found in Pacific communities: "In many parts of the South Seas contact with white civilization has resulted in the complete degeneration of native life, the loss of native techniques and traditions, and the annihilation of the past. In Samoa this is not so." [46]

The Tallensi of Ghana provide a final example of the integration of the young and social stability and conservatism which seem to be closely associated with it. Although the Tallensi desire some of the material products of Western civilization, and are prepared, as migrant labourers, to work for them, they "still preserve the culture bequeathed to them by their forefathers and the social structure of their own, homogeneous society." [47]

The Tallensi are a "segmentary" and extremely egalitarian society, although

[45] R. Firth, *Social Change in Tikopia* (1959), p. 46.
[46] Margaret Mead, *Coming of Age in Samoa* (Pelican Books 1954), p. 216.
[47] Meyer Fortes, *The Dynamics of Clanship among the Tallensi* (1945), p. 12.

they enjoin respect for age and seniority. But the young do not enter institutionalized age-groups with concerns distinct from those of their elders: "the
social sphere of adult and child is unitary and undivided." [48] Children and
adolescents share in the work of their elders as they are able; they have in consequence a sense of social purpose and importance, and of rights to which they
are properly entitled. Young people learn their social and economic roles from
close association with their parents or older siblings. "The child is from the beginning oriented towards the same reality as its parents. . . . The interests, motives
and purposes of children are identical with those of adults, but at a simpler level
of organization. Hence the children need not be coerced to take a share in
economic and social activities. They are eager to do so."

The Tallensi have resisted fundamental changes in their social system. Even
the returning labourer-migrants, bringing back foreign ideas and exotic information, "have made no appreciable impression on the native scheme of values and
beliefs, or in their practical knowledge. . . . Though they are one of the influences modifying the strict letter of custom in minor respects, they are not a
disintegrating ferment in the native social order." [49]

It is the contention of this chapter that such social resilience, conservatism and
stability are directly causally related to the status and importance accorded to
adolescents and young adults. There are undoubtedly circumstances in which
a society with "integrated" youth may succumb to, or even readily accept, profound social change. The Ovimbundu of Angola may be such a people. Childs
has described how, from later childhood, boys and girls assume a definite role in
the work of the adult community. A boy at this age may make his first trip with
a trading caravan, and will help his father in the fields. From the period of later
childhood an Ovimbundu is a responsible person: he assumes considerable, and
growing, economic responsibility, and is accounted legally responsible for his
actions.[50]

More recent studies have shown profound changes in Umbundu society. The
position of the Ovimbundu as traders and their deep involvement in the economic
life of Europeans may be important factors in "the very rapid social change" [51]
that has occurred. But the change does not appear to be a vigorous and vital
response to new opportunities: "The present Umbundu social system deprived
of any form of public life ticks over, as a man who has been paralysed may
continue to live." [52]

SEGREGATION WITH LOW STATUS

Segregated age-group institutions do not necessarily confer high status on the
young or promise certain progress towards it. They may, on the contrary, sig-

[48] Meyer Fortes, *Social and Psychological Aspects of Education in Taleland* (1938), p. 8.
[49] Meyer Fortes, *The Dynamics of Clanship among the Tallensi* (1945), p. 12.
[50] See G. M. Childs, *Umbundu Kinship and Character* (1949).
[51] A. C. Edwards, *The Ovimbundu under Two Sovereignties* (1962), p. 155.
[52] A C. Edwards, *The Ovimbundu under Two Sovereignties* (1962), p. 160.

nalize the rejection of the young from the central concerns of a society, underline their inferior standing, suggest their futility, and direct their attention to matters irrelevant to the major pre-occupations of the adult world. Such age-groups will be potentially deviant or at least experimental in new social forms which may provide an escape from the blockages from which their members suffer.[53]

Among the Tiv of Nigeria age-mates formerly constituted a mutual aid society for (largely ineffectual) protection against their elders, particularly fathers and senior brothers. The latter possessed *tsav* by virtue of their age: supernatural power which ensured potency and skill, and was augmented by eating human flesh. The victim was provided by some other person, and the man who ate the flesh incurred a "flesh-debt" which could be discharged only by supplying a close relative as an exchange victim.

Elders rich in *tsav* were consequently a serious menace to their younger kin. They were also powerful through their control over their sons' possibilities of marriage. Fully adult status was impossible until a man was married; but marriage could take place only when his father (or older married brother) supplied him with one of his daughters to give in exchange for a bride. The institution of exchange marriage placed a young man's advance to adult status at the caprice of his elders.

The younger Tiv had always been noted for their willingness for social experimentation, but the possibilities for this in the traditional society were limited. In 1927 an edict of the colonial government forbade exchange marriage and at a blow opened the floodgates of social change. The edict was resisted by the old, since it undermined the very basis of their power. But the young accepted it with eagerness, "in fact these had been consulted and had been enthusiastically in its favour."[54] Change now "ramified in every aspect of the culture." Freed from the tyranny of the old, young men fortified their position by working for wages in railway developments and other European enterprises. Henceforth, "A man could get a wife through his own efforts, without waiting his turn, which depended on the priority of claims within the group, and without dependence on his father."

Still more dramatic was the social change among the Manus of New Guinea in the interval between Margaret Mead's original study of them in the nineteen-twenties and her return visit twenty-five years later. The sheer weight of the Western impact, particularly in the shape of the American Army, must be held largely responsible for the fact that the Manus are "a people who have moved

---

[53] Eisenstadt has argued that such potentially deviant age-groups, which do not function as mechanisms of social integration, are likely to arise in "familistic societies": it is one of his major hypotheses that "Age groups tend to arise when the structure of the family or descent group blocks the younger members' opportunities for attaining social status within the family (a) because the older members block the younger ones' access to the facilities which are prerequisites of full adult roles, and/or (b) the sharpening of incest taboos and restrictions on sexual relations within the family unit postpones the younger members' attainment of sexual maturity": S. N. Eisensadt, *From Generation to Generation* (1956), p. 248.

[54] See Margaret Mead (ed.), *Culture Patterns and Technical Change* (1953), pp. 114–143.

faster than any people of whom we have records, a people who have moved in fifty years from darkest savagery to the twentieth century, men who have skipped over thousands of years of history in just the last twenty-five. . . ." [55]

A money economy has become established among the Manus, the clothing and calendar of the West, American-type marriage "for love". Old "avoidances" (for example of mothers-in-law) have disappeared. But most significant of all, the position of the young in Manus society has changed, their importance has increased through Western education and more direct involvement in adult affairs. The sullen, aggressive, and brittle human relationships of the past seemed to have been generally superseded by easy and harmonious social intercourse.

Change had not been accepted with reluctance: "the great avidity with which they seized on new situations" [56] had been the striking feature of their response to the massive contact of the West. In their traditional society the young had constituted an outsider group: trained in physical skills, prudery and respect for property, they were otherwise left to their own devices. Manus society was characterized by the cultural non-participation of the young, marked cultural discontinuity between the generations. "There is no attempt to induct the child into this alien adult world," wrote Margaret Mead in 1928. "He is given no place in it and no responsibilities." [57] "Manus children live in a world of their own, a world from which adults are wilfully excluded, a world based on different premises from those of adult life." [58] The result was latent deviance and a marked predisposition to seek in a new way of life personal significance unattainable in the old.

REWARDS AND PENALTIES

Latent deviance is likely to become actual when the rewards of change are sufficiently attractive, when they promise a real solution to the status difficulties of the young. (If the high rewards for the new behaviour continue, *further* change is likely to be impeded.) Similar educational techniques aimed specifically at fundamental culture-change will have widely different results if the social rewards of change are markedly different. It has commonly been observed that a new member of an organization, society, or nation learns the new behaviour required of him more rapidly if he enjoys, or is promised, a position of high status; if his position is more lowly, although he is exposed to similar influences, he is more likely to cling to his former attitudes, values and customs. New recruits to the armed services, business institutions, neighbourhoods, more readily learn the speech idioms, methods of deportment and characteristic modes of behaviour, when they have success in the society's activities and are rewarded with enhanced prestige and formal standing. There is considerable evidence

[55] Margaret Mead, *New Lives for Old* (1956), p. 8.
[56] Margaret Mead, *New Lives for Old* (1956), p. 158.
[57] Margaret Mead, *Growing up in New Guinea* (Pelican Books 1942), p. 78.
[58] Margaret Mead, *Growing up in New Guinea* (Pelican Books 1943), p. 66.

from American studies of immigrants that those who are rewarded with high status positions quickly become "acculturated"; those of lower occupational rank cling more tenaciously to their former style of life (and tend, where possible, to occupy the same residential areas). If social change is to be effectively promoted among immigrants, they must be offered suitable rewards in the new system. As an American sociologist has recently concluded: "if we are interested in acculturating immigrants to the United States, our social structure must be sufficiently open to offer them upward occupational mobility." [59]

One of the most striking contrasts in the history of social change is that between the response of the Dakota Indians and the Janissaries of the Ottoman Empire to essentially similar methods of (forcible) "re-education." The resounding success in the case of the latter and the dismal failure in the case of the former, are intelligible in terms of the social penalties and rewards attendant on the "new learning."

The remarkable educational institutions of the Ottoman Turks, in which Christian slaves, the "Tribute of Blood," were prepared for the work of defending, extending, and ruling the domains of their masters, are not only among the most spectacular, but the most successful, in the history of education. For at least two centuries after the Turks captured Constantinople in 1453, slaves taken from the "familistic" peasant societies of Greece, Albania, Serbia, Bosnia and Bulgaria, were successfully inducted into the Mohammedan culture which they triumphantly carried half way to Dover.

The sons of shepherds and herdsmen were taken from their Greek Orthodox homes and trained to rule an Islamic Empire. Every boy was aware that he was a potential Grand Vizier. "The Ottoman system deliberately took slaves and made them ministers of state. It took boys from the sheep-run and the plough-tail and made them courtiers and the husbands of princesses; it took young men whose ancestors had borne the Christian name for centuries, and made them rulers of the greatest Muhammedan states, and soldiers and generals in invincible armies whose chief joy was to beat down the Crown and elevate the Crescent." [60]

The Christians were not taken as young children but at or a little before puberty, between the age of 10 and 14. They had learned one way of life and must now learn another. They had every inducement to do so. Their material needs were well cared for: the commanding officer of a battalion was the "Soup Maker," the second-in-command the "Head Water Carrier"; the regimental colours were the soup cauldron itself.

[59] S. Alexander Weinstock, "Role Elements: A Link between Acculturation and Occupational Status", British Journal of Sociology (1963), p. 14. It is also the case that the role which goes with high occupational status spills over into wider areas of life, only marginally connected with work, than is commonly the case with a more lowly occupation. A wider area of life is necessarily changed for the immigrant corporation lawyer than for the doorman.

[60] See H. H. Lybyer, The Government of the Ottoman Empire at the Time of Soleyman the Magnificent (1913). Cf. the sentimental and psychologically unreal version of H. A. L. Fisher, A History of Europe (1936), p. 402: "The Janissary was a slave. The affections which sweeten the character, the interests which expand the mind, the ideals which give elevation to the will, were denied him. An iron discipline effaced the past and impoverished the future . . . he went forth to slay the enemies of the Sultan and of Allah with the inflamed and contracted fanaticism of a monk."

The majority were destined for a military career in which the top command positions were open to them. A carefully selected minority were embarked on a 14-year course of training and education, with rigorous weeding out along the route, for posts in the civil administration. The best entered the Palace School of the Grand Seraglio (there were usually some 300 pages, 600 during the reign of Soleyman the Magnificent in the sixteenth century). Three auxiliary schools (and later a fourth) each contained a similar number.

Those who passed with distinction through the first six or eight years of the course entered upon more specialized training in the Hall of the Expeditionary Force, the Hall of the Commissariat, the Hall of the Treasury, or the Hall of the Bedchamber. The liberal arts, the arts of government and of war, were the subjects studied under notable scholars, mathematicians, and musicians who enjoyed royal patronage. Though technically "slaves," and debarred from handing on wealth or position to their children, they had social and political eminence. Out of 60 Grand Viziers who have been traced in Turkish history, 48 were trained at the Palace School (the remaining 12, slaves also, started less promisingly in the artisan schools).[61]

Machiavelli and the Imperial Ambassador to Constantinople in the mid-sixteenth century have left contemporary testimony to the success of the system, to the stability and durability of a social and political order which, in the high prestige and power which it gave to young warriors and administrators, albeit of alien origin, had a built-in safeguard against deviation. (It was only with the establishment of hereditary offices in the civil and military hierarchies that the system failed to work effectively after the seventeenth century. The revolutionary "Young Turks" of the twentieth century were the outcome of an increasingly closed and rigid social system.)

Machiavelli had offered no hope of internal support to the would-be invader of the Turkish state. He could not "expect his enterprise to be aided by the defection of those whom the sovereign has around him.... Whosoever, therefore, attacks the Turk must reckon on finding a united people...." Attacks against the kingdoms of Western Europe were much more hopeful "since you will always find in them men who are discontented and desirous of change...."[62]

Busbecq, who was Imperial Ambassador to Constantinople intermittently between 1555 and 1562 analysed this stability and high morale in greater detail:

No distinction is attached to birth among the Turks; the deference to be paid to a man is measured by the position he holds in the public service... honours, high posts and judgeships are the rewards of great ability and good service. If a man be dishonest, or lazy, or careless, he remains at the bottom of the ladder, an object of contempt, for such qualities there are no honours in Turkey. This is the reason that they are successful in their undertakings, that they lord it over others, and are daily extending the bounds of their empire. These are not our (European) ideas; with us there is no opening left for

[61] See Barnette Miller, The Palace School of Muhammad the Conqueror (1941), pp. 6–7.
[62] N. Machiavelli, The Prince, trans. N. H. Thomson (1913), Bk. 4, pp. 24–25.

merit; birth is the standard for everything; the prestige of birth is the sole key to advancement in the public service.[63]

The Federal authorities of America attempted, in the later-nineteenth and early-twentieth centuries, to induct the youth of the Indian tribes into the culture of white America. Their methods—enforced and prolonged schooling of the young away from their parents, an "immensely thoughtful and costly experiment in federal Indian education" [64]—nowhere met with the resounding success of the remarkably similar institutions of the Ottoman Turks, and often with pathetic failure. This was not because the American soldiers, administrators, and educators lacked the thoroughness, ruthlessness, resources or pedagogical skills of the Turks in the days of Soleyman the Magnificent. The Indian children had learned one culture; they refused to learn another. Whereas the Turks offered boundless social rewards for social change and new learning, the Americans offered not top command posts in the army, civil administration and business corporations; but only life as marginal men and second-class citizens on the reserves.

There were some tribes for whom even this was an escape from the social blockages and frustrations of the indigenous order. Thus the Makah, formerly characterized by rigid social stratification, were more successfully assimilated than most: as fishermen they found rewards in the prosperity of wider American markets. And re-education was ruthless: "Parents who refused to send their children to school were imprisoned until they saw the uselessness of refusal." [65] But a similar technique and equal ruthlessness left the once vigorous and self-confident Dakota only apathetic, listlessly discarding the new values and customs they were taught.

The proud and virile Dakota had hunted buffalo across the prairie: an egalitarian society, "a hunter democracy, levelling every potential dictator and every potential capitalist." [66] The young male was accorded prestige and importance. "Every educational device was used (by the Dakota) to develop in the boy a maximum of self-confidence. . . . He was to become a hunter after game, woman and spirit." In his upbringing, emphasis was placed on "his right to autonomy and on his duty of initiative." [67] The federal authorities aimed to bring about change to the American way of life through systematic teaching. "Children were virtually kidnapped to force them into government schools, their hair was cut and their Indian clothes thrown away. They were forbidden to speak in their own language. . . . Parents who objected were also jailed. Where possible, children were kept in school year after year to avoid the influence of their families." [68] These measures failed. The American cowboy culture was an inadequate recompense for the best of a vanished tribal life.

[63] Quoted C. T. Forster and F. H. B. Daniell, *The Life and Letters of Ogier Ghiselin de Busbecq* (1881), vol. I, pp. 152–155.
[64] Erik H. Erikson, *Childhood and Society* (1951), p. 98.
[65] Elizabeth Colson, *The Makah Indians* (1953), p. 20.
[66] E. H. Erikson, *Childhood and Society (1951),* p. 101.
[67] E. H. Erikson, *Childhood and Society (1951),* p. 128.
[68] See G. MacGregor, *Warriors Without Weapons* (1946).

THE BEST OF BOTH WORLDS

Poised between the old world and the new, the young in non-literate tribal societies have often been able to use the new world to perpetuate the old. Savings from wages earned as migrant labourers have enabled them to return to their traditional societies not to change them, but to secure with their wealth a valued status within the traditional framework. They have a sociological significance not unlike that of the eighteenth-century nabobs who returned from India to buy positions in English society which, in the majority of cases could not have been theirs if they had remained at home. Far from aiming to transform the society to which they returned after exotic experiences abroad, they attained significance precisely by supporting the social structure which gave them the chance to buy a place in the squirearchy, the exclusive clubs, and the most expensive and exclusive of them all, the House of Commons.

Inevitably the enriched tribesman changes his society to some extent when he returns. He belongs to a class of *nouveaux riches* which threatens established political and social authorities. He enjoys independence of paternal (and avuncular) authority. And yet if such men desire status in terms of the social order in which they grew up, they will seek to preserve it, to minimize the effect that they themselves have upon it. There is no gain in buying one's way into an aristocracy which has been undermined and is in a state of decay.

Young men of the Tonga tribe on the shores of Lake Nyasa regard it as normal to spend some part of their early lives working in the Rhodesias or South Africa. "Young men consider their stay in the village, before they go off to the towns, as a period of marking time." [69] But even while they are away, they manoeuvre for office and position within the traditional social structure. They are concerned to maintain the traditional values and social order, and "when they return from an urban life abroad they settle again in the pattern of Tonga life which is still dominated by traditional values. There are no obvious signs of social disorganization and the Tonga still hold together as a tribal unit distinct from other such units around them."

Similarly with the Tikopia and the Tallensi. The young men of Tikopia who go abroad to work retain their rights and interests in the homeland. Though clearly they are a potential threat to established authorities when they return with comparative wealth, they seek not to overthrow traditional authorities but to enter into alliance with them. By the late nineteen-thirties the young men of Taleland were also leaving home in large numbers to work elsewhere for wages. But "labour migrants remain strongly attached to their families and natal settlements, and it is always assumed that they will eventually return ... and when they do return they resume the traditional way of life." [70]

The *nouveaux riches* among the Ngoni have used the wealth they earned in European work to buy social status in traditional terms. They have converted

[69] See J. Van Velsen, "Labour Migration as a Positive Factor in the Continuity of Tonga Tribal Society," in A. Southall, *Social Change in Modern Africa* (1961).
[70] Meyer Fortes, *The Dynamics of Clanship Among the Tallensi* (1945), p. 11.

cash into cows. If they were formerly cultivators, without cattle, the mere possession of cows will not in itself bring high social status. "But if he goes with
due deference to the older men who own cattle to ask for advice and technical
help about building his kraal and breeding in his herd, in course of time they
will include him in their discussions about cattle when they sit in the men's
talking place."[71] But what he cannot do for himself he can do for his sons. His
cattle can secure them well-connected brides, and his grandchildren at least will
be assured of the highest social standing through the dignity of birth on the
mother's side. Social change is impeded by contact with the West.

In all these instances young men had a position of some importance or significance even in the "pre-contact" social order; they were not potential deviants
looking for an escape from their frustrations in the opportunities of a new civilization. The new civilization has enabled them to become even more important in
traditional terms; they are even less inclined to deviate from old standards, customs and values. It may be one of the ironies of the human condition that any
society must choose between social conservatism and rigidity, or the oppression
of its young.

*Unlike pre-literate societies, contemporary America yields many statements by members
of its youth culture. In her commencement address at San Francisco State College,
Rochelle Gatlin attempted to express the attitudes that led many of her generation toward social action like that which took place at the University of California at Berkeley
in the mid 1960's. Today's students, she stated, are becoming disenchanted with an older
liberal rhetoric which they feel to be almost irresponsible in the nuclear age.*

Rochelle Gatlin

A Radical Frame of Mind

College students of the 1960's are different from those of ten years ago.
Specific issues in which questions of ethics are sharply defined have impelled
them to reject the beat-style withdrawal of the 1950's. To paraphrase Crane
Brinton, "Many of the new generation have thrown themselves into movements
like the Peace Corps, civil rights, disarmament, and international government.
They do this often to the accompaniment of words of despair and anger, but
their deeds belie their words." Many of the same students who heroically went
to Mississippi last summer were carried out of Sproul Hall* last winter. Although

[71] Margaret Read, *Native Standards of Living and African Culture Change* (1938), p. 32.
* Center of the Berkeley student demonstrations.

the Berkeley Free Speech Movement contained a few hipsters and revolutionary zealots, there was a surprisingly large proportion of what U.C. graduate Michael Miller calls the most intellectually serious and morally alert students on campus, who demand the most from the university, who are concerned with putting knowledge of the past to work in the present and who believe that the educational process should provide a continuum between ideas and social action.

Fortunately demonstrations, sit-ins, and arrests are not the only ways to affect university and social reform. The Free Speech Movement was a dramatic event that occasioned sensational headlines, but at other institutions less publicized programs have been initiated. For example, the Committee for an Ideal Campus at Brandeis University in Massachusetts is an officially recognized organization, which receives a budget from the associated student body. Some of the programs of this committee include: compiling a critique of professors and courses, tabulating a student-faculty poll intended to ascertain what issues concern the campus community, making plans for a national convention of similar student groups, and initiating the Spinoza Institute—which will offer nongraded courses and seminars next fall in the Modern Cinema, Eastern Thought, Psychedelic Stimulants, and the History of Peace Movements.

In its first Statement of Purpose, the Committee for an Ideal Campus summed up principles which are advanced by student reformers and university critics all over the country. This statement says in part:

> We believe that the ideal university is an intellectual community of teachers and students. . . knowledge is advanced as a force which is personally relevant and meaningful, not as a commodity which is produced and marketed. . . .
> By virtue of its intellectual freedom, the university can serve society as a center of independent thought and criticism. The members of the university may challenge undesirable customs and values, offer suggestions for their improvement, and exercise their rights as citizens to participate in social and political action.

Obviously the constant scrutiny of university and social practices found in the above declaration may lead to unrest, but I do not believe that unrest is something that can or should be "remedied" by suppression. To state this positively, the effect of current student unrest may be a critical analysis—even expose—of hypocritical practices in relation to traditional American values of peace, equality, and individual freedom. For example, it took the Freedom Riders and the registering of disenfranchised Southern Negroes—and unfortunately the murder of a few white Northerners—to focus the country's attention on the wide discrepancy between the ideal and the practice of equality.

One characteristic of socially alert students is their dissatisfaction with and even discarding of the liberalism of Woodrow Wilson, Franklin Roosevelt, and Clark Kerr. Stanley Kauffmann has expressed the growing irrelevance of liberalism with its optimistic belief in progress by saying that although liberal sentiments are unimpeachable, they are almost irresponsible in the light of existing conditions—the contemporary equivalent of a hundred Hail Marys to avert the Black

Plague. To many students, there is something ineffectual about the liberal bureaucrat with his tools of mediation and compromise. Furthermore, (as Michael Miller has said in a recent article in *Dissent*), "the more militant students regard liberalism with something less than satisfaction. They believe it to be somehow implicated, if only by default, in the heritage of nightmares that compose modern history—Auschwitz, Hiroshima, the Cold War, McCarthyism."

But student radicals do not look to bureaucratic, puritanical Russia or to unindustrialized, overpopulated, and poverty-ridden China as models. Not Marx, but Gandhi and Thoreau are their mentors. Their goal is to eliminate the divorce between the political and the personal; no definite programs, no slogans, only a direct emotional response to hypocrisy and injustice.

This graduating class joins with others throughout the country in facing tasks that require a radical and experimental frame of mind, guided by generous social impulses. We must find workable ideas to replace the myths that have been outrun by technology and social upheaval; we must develop a social vision less shallow than the duty to spend money to keep the economy going; and we must emphasize that although education might *sometimes* produce practical innovations beneficial to our health and material comfort, it should *always* produce greater understanding of the human condition and promise.

Taking the student revolt at the Berkeley campus of the University of California as its starting point, this article goes on to suggest psychological reasons underlying student activism at large. The author raises the question whether contemporary youth can work with college and university personnel to fashion a new cultural response to threats which youth perceives against its own survival.

Alvin E. Winder

The Restless Undergraduates

Recent student demonstrations at the Berkeley campus of the University of California have touched off widespread speculation about today's undergraduates. Some have offered the explanation that their restlessness is generated by a small cadre of student leaders whose participation in the civil rights movement has made them strongly politically minded. Others have written of a generally repressive atmosphere throughout our mass educational institutions which gives evidence of the administrations' attempt to pass on lower-middle-class values generally identified as hoary admixtures of insecurity clothed with respectability.

Those who advance this explanation believe that student restlessness is a reaction to an extreme conformity imposed through this "don't rock the boat" philosophy of administration.

It is my belief, as a teacher and counselor of undergraduates for the past several years, that to understand the restless student we must understand the psychology of adolescents in a world which offers them no certain and identifiable future. Nearly forty years ago in his appraisal of civilization and its discontents, Freud raised as the most significant question of the twentieth century the dramatic uncertainty of man's future. He said:

> Men have brought their powers of subduing the forces of nature to such a pitch that by using them they could now very easily exterminate one another to the last man. They know this—hence arises a great part of their current unrest, their dejection, their mood of apprehension.

Since 1930, when the above paragraph was published, the crisis attendant on human survival has deepened. For Freud wrote before the development of both the awesome weapons of contemporary warfare and the uncanny systems for delivering them which have resulted in a world that is so often described as maintaining itself in a balance of terror.

Why should the adolescent be even more anxious than his elders in the face of an uncertain future? Erik Erikson, whose major work in recent years has centered on the adolescent coming of age in modern western culture, has stated that the primary need of every adolescent is to be able to pledge his fidelity to the future: that is, to believe that there is a future to which he can realistically commit his energies, his dreams, and his plans. The adolescent seeks continuously to question those around him about the validity of this future.

Another great psychologist, Shakespeare, has masterfully evoked the futility of youth's attempt to probe for real values behind the words of those in authority who purport to know best. It would be hard to find a better maxim on character-building anywhere in literature than in Polonius' instruction to his son, Laertes: "This above all, to thine own self be true, and it must follow as the night the day, thou canst not then be false to any man." Yet the playwright soon lets us see how easily Polonius ignores his own credo. For in the very next scene he sends his servant, Reynaldo, off to "play false" with Laertes by spying on him. Modern adolescents are quick to compare Polonius' high-sounding phrases with his unprincipled behavior and to categorize him as, in modern adolescent terms, "a fink."

A fine example of one modern institution which has capitalized on this preoccupation of today's youth with adult world double-talk is *Mad Magazine*. Often called the bible of the literate twelve-year-old, *Mad* may indeed be said to play a major role in this culture's *rite de passage* from the trust of childhood to the search for meaning in adolescence. For its young readers, this sardonic slap at established society, produced in the familiar comic strip format of childhood, seems to serve as a consensual validation of the adolescent's dawning awareness of adults' double standards. *Mad* is sold in college bookstores, although students of college age have usually gone on to prefer its more sophisticated counterparts in such novels as Joseph Heller's *Catch 22*.

How has the professional educator responded to the undergraduate adolescent's troubled search for guidelines to a valid future? More specifically, has the professional educator, the college president, or the university administrator shared with his students so candid a view of man's present condition as Freud set forth in *Civilization and Its Discontents*? Further, has he offered youth educational goals which will permit them even to begin to approach what clearly will constitute the central problem of their generation?

A fine example of one modern institution which has capitalized on the pre- the contemporary educator approaches his dialogue with students. He is willing to ask the student to live by the values of the Judeo-Christian tradition, and he is willing to point the student toward the military or corporate recruiter, but he is not willing to confront the student with the reality of a world that must turn to the immediate task of insuring its own survival. H. Levi, provost of the University of Chicago, in a recent memorandum on the University College, has defined the colleges' responsibility as "a mission to carry forward through their students a mastery of our culture and increasingly an understanding of other societies and their traditions." Similarly, former University of California President Clark Kerr in the 1963 Godkin lectures stated that the university produces ideas in the form of research, and idea men in the form of graduates, for the use of the military, industry, and the government.

The much-quoted educational statesman, Dr. James Conant, has expressed concern that "attention has been centered for so long on the individuality of each child that [educators] resist any idea that a new national concern might be an important factor in planning a high school program." The new national concern to which Dr. Conant refers is national defense against the Soviet Union, and the solution he proposes is the planning of an educational program that will make youth more effective warriors in the cold war.

But undoubtedly the best example of the double standard of communication upon which modern educational leaders rely was the statement in which Clark Kerr paralleled Polonius' famous statement with his own maxim on academic freedom. In the 1963 Godkin lectures, Kerr stated: "There are some things that should not be compromised. . . . Then the mediator [the college president] needs to become a gladiator."

Not long after this, students on the Berkeley campus of the University of California chose to confront President Kerr with an issue they felt should not be compromised. Writing in the December 21, 1964, issue of *The Nation*, reporter Jean Marine described Berkeley's Student Free Speech Movement members as insisting upon the right of students to openly advocate their political beliefs on the campus. Marine further reported that University administrators and faculty insisted that the issue was not negotiable. Unwilling to negotiate, President Kerr emerged as neither gladiator nor mediator in the eyes of the students.

Shortly thereafter, the University President concurred with California's Governor Brown in a decision to order the State Police onto the Berkeley campus to deal with student demonstrators. This action caused Kerr to be branded as an unscrupulous opportunist by large segments of collegiate youth. Like Polonius, when called upon to act, he seemed to place his personal prestige as a sound administrator above a commitment to stated ideals.

If the Berkeley demonstrations are examined in the light of the psychology of adolescence, then the basic issue on the campus was not free speech or students' freedom to participate in civil rights activities. Both these issues did serve importantly as a vehicle for the expression of discontent. But still more important was how those issues served as a vehicle for posing a more basic question. That question as framed by the students was—not, "Are you, the administration and the faculty, for or against the civil rights movement?"—but rather: "Are you for or against us? We the students who know that we must discard the illusion that the human race has a privileged status in the universe, know also that it is possible in our time for malignant forces to release hydrogen bombs that can destroy all human life. For if you answer in the affirmative, 'Yes, we are for you,' then you, the faculty and administration, must help to provide an educational climate and experience that will help us cope with this problem." Indeed, the student questioners went further, urging that faculty and administration give up the passive stance of today's academic man.

Provost Levi's mission to develop mastery of this and other cultures is thus rejected as inadequate to academe's new task, as is President Kerr's objective of producing idea men for an existing military-industrial complex. Instead, students ask that all members of the academic community—students, faculty, and administrators—become partners in creating a new culture: one that will attend to the threats against survival and thereby make possible a meaningful future.

It seems probable that, so long as American youth continue to perceive their future as chaotic and uncertain, American colleges and universities will see more demonstrations such as those at Berkeley; the next decade may well be characterized by a growing tide of open student rebellions on some college and university campuses. Should this occur, it is to be hoped that the pattern of reacting by force and indifference that prevailed at Berkeley will not be resorted to again. To refuse to engage in a frank dialogue with adolescents who are eager to talk about the world they are inheriting—and, even more significant, adolescents who are restless to begin acting on that world in an attempt to improve its chances for survival—would seem to constitute a nearly fatal blow to the future of this and later generations.

DISCUSSION TOPICS

1. Discuss the implications for adolescent development of the following trends in American family life:
   a. an increase in individual activities over family activities
   b. the growing isolation of grandparents from the family unit

c. the decline of family influence on occupational choice

d. increased mobility

2. What is meant by the *status* of adolescents as a group? What roles do adults play in determining the content of the adolescent subculture? Is today's adolescent subculture truly rebellious toward the values of adults?

3. Discuss ways in which the school tends to enforce and encourage conformity among adolescents. Are apparently trivial dress and hairstyle regulations of any significance in this connection? It is possible for the school to support the ideal of the unique personal identity and excellence of all students?

4. What are the ramifications for adolescent development of the increasing isolation of work from other facets of life? Is a firm self concept desirable from the standpoint of employers? Why has there been a tendency in recent years for college graduates to turn away from high-paying, secure jobs in giant corporations in favor of more socially useful activity such as service in the Peace Corps or Vista?

5. How healthy is adolescents' increasing participation in forms of social and political action such as demonstrations, sit-ins, and strikes? Discuss this question from the standpoint, first, of identity formation and, second, of social stability. Taking into account the fact that over half of the United States population is under twenty-five years of age, at what point should youth begin to have a significant voice in the management of their own affairs? If youth were to become a major force in determining the directions of social change, what impact would this have on their own development?

6. Does the increasing use of psychological and social services in the schools constitute a threat to the privacy of adolescents? Is it important that adolescents have a sense of privacy? What may be the meaning in this connection of the increasing suicide rate among persons under twenty-one?

III THE DISADVANTAGED ADOLESCENT

We have seen that contradictions and ambiguities in many of our basic institutions make it difficult for contemporary middle- and working-class youth to carve out a firm and confident self-identity. The problem is greatly compounded when we turn to a consideration of the impact of the same institutions on disadvantaged youth. For although the struggle to separate from one's family, make one's way into suitable educational patterns, and find appropriate work and a compatible mate is difficult for all youth, in the case of mainstream adolescents it is at least undergirded by a continuity of values and a life-style that is familiar and reassuring. For young people outside the dominant social strata, the process is discontinuous and dysfunctional in the extreme. This part of our collection examines the major institutions of this society as they are experienced by youth whose lower socioeconomic roots tend to isolate them from the mainstream.

It has often been noted that the nature of family life among the poor can differ markedly from the common American pattern. Impoverished Appalachian whites who find their way to Northern cities attempt to maintain extended family ties in conflict with the expectations of the public school system and other aspects of urban life. The Mexican-American family, on the other hand, is often strongly patriarchal, giving children and adolescents little or no independence in decision-making. Puerto-Ricans are ill-prepared to cope with race prejudice on the mainland because marriage patterns in Puerto Rico are virtually unaffected by skin color.

Northern urban-ghetto Negro families tend toward matriarchal patterns born of a high incidence of separation between husbands and wives, leading in turn to absent fathers and illegitimacy. Isolated from the rest of American society, the Negro has evolved a peculiar set of practices by which to adapt to his situation. It is Lee Rainwater's thesis, in the first article following, that the character of Negro slum families is the result of a highly predictable pattern beginning with peer-group activity, running through premarital pregnancy, and ending in marriage. In the Negro slum culture, marriage is a negative experience, though it provides the chief context of early socialization for children. Because the family has such a profound effect on its young members, one author, Wiltse, has suggested that the Aid to Dependent Children program, which brings mental health professionals into contact with these families, offers a potent but little-used tool by which to understand the personal toll of social and economic deprivation.

The extreme social alienation of disadvantaged youth often shows itself most clearly in peer-group activities. Popular conceptions of the group life of poor youth have taken their content from the urban neighborhood gang wars of the 1950's—which supported the idea of a delinquent subculture. Miller points out in this connection that the values and attitudes underlying gang behavior are not as antisocial as they may appear, when it is realized that so-called delinquent behavior is quite in keeping with the values of lower-class Negro adults. In fact it may be that the Negro gangs' values are not so discontinuous with those of their elders as are the attitudes of middle-class adolescents when compared with middle-class adult attitudes. Though teachers, social workers, police, and others who work with poor youth often consider them extremely hostile and rebellious, their behavior is actually highly functional and life-affirming within their own social and physical milieu, which gives high status to youth who are tough, smart, love excitement and act directly to satisfy their needs. To make their way in the larger society, disadvantaged youth would have to renounce the values of peer groups *and* family—an alternative few mainstream youth face. The program described by Bakal et al is an attempt to replace alienation with self-regulation as a basis for developing the motivation to learn among youth outside the dominant social strata.

Volumes have been written about the school-related difficulties of disadvantaged youth. Here we wish to call attention primarily to the fact that school success usually demands a renunciation of many of the materials out of which self concept is formed. Today's schools are increasingly caught up in a serious conflict between turning out more and better mathematicians, scientists, and linguists, on the one hand, and simply keeping unemployed teen-agers off the streets. As a result, Negro youth with inadequate educational backgrounds find the tone of the school is for them one of regimentation and policing. School records of the misbehaviors of disadvantaged youth are the beginning of a life-long dossier that is a substitute for true self-identity and an indictment of the capacity of the American high school to serve as an agent of social mobility. Kvaraceus believes that schools can have a salutary effect on these youth only after the creation of a non-threatening, therapeutic climate in which the interaction between Negro youth and their teachers will be considerably altered. Kraft finds much lacking in present programs for disadvantaged children which have been established under the assumption that extended education is the key to success in this society.

In explaining the high unemployment rate among minority groups, it is common to cite a lack of educational preparation. Yet this is at best only half the answer. Recently, the median yearly income in a large Northern city for whites with an eighth-grade education was higher than that for Negroes with one to three years of college. Such trends are not unperceived by Negro adolescents.

If their vocational aspirations fall below those of their more fortunate age mates it is not entirely because they misunderstand the role of education in the world of work.

Employment counselors have long been aware that the likelihood of finding a job is much greater for middle-class than for lower-class youth. U. S. Department of Labor studies confirm that the unemployment rate for dropouts is twice that for high school graduates and that dropouts earn less money than graduates, even in the same jobs.

Disadvantaged segments of the population have been alienated from political processes for some time. But recent signs seem to hint that the poor may be finding their voice. The tempered idealism of youth who have taken up the civil rights cause—their seeming gaiety and hope for the future, together with an utter seriousness of purpose and a resolve to right old social and political wrongs—appears to have caught fire among some of the disadvantaged whom they have befriended. Such radicalism may serve, according to Zinn, to usher in a nonviolent, but sweeping, revolution.

What avenues these activities may open up for the discovery of new adolescent models among political leaders remains conjecture. At present, it appears that adults who exert the greatest influence on alienated young people are those who represent ethnicity or racial pride. Such models can be useful in helping disadvantaged adolescents acquire a sense of self. Yet in the long run their impact may be to further alienate youth from the dominant social and political climate. Thus much of the energy that might otherwise be channeled into constructive social and political action would be drained off into hostile and aggressive acts against the majority. From the standpoint of adolescent development, this means wasted human potential.

The present decade has witnessed a more concerted effort to assist those in deprived circumstances than any other period except perhaps the 'Thirties. Michael Harrington's *The Other America* has awakened the country to the fact that one third of the population of the "affluent society" meets the criteria of poverty. Yet virtually all federally initiated programs designed to wage war on poverty have drawn sharp criticism as attempts by a middle-class staff of experts to assimilate the poor into the mainstream of American life. The five documents which conclude this part are one response to this situation. They seem to imply that the disadvantaged can articulate their own needs and programs, but that the larger society is as yet unresponsive to this new form of sociopolitical activity.

At the moment, therefore, the dilemma of the disadvantaged adolescent remains largely unchanged. He must either renounce his family, friends and familiar surroundings and try to develop an identity out of the unfamiliar values of middle-class America, or he must be prepared to continue in social and economic deprivation for the rest of his life.

1 THE FAMILY

This analysis of family processes among lower-class Negroes grew out of the author's studies of Negro ghetto life. He theorizes that socioeconomic exploitation of Negroes by the white community has caused them to view themselves as victims fated to suffer. In turn, Rainwater believes, they transfer their own suffering to their kin, thereby giving to Negro children both negative self-concepts and highly defined models for victim roles.

Lee Rainwater

Crucible of Identity: The Negro Lower-Class Family

As long as Negroes have been in America, their marital and family patterns have been subjects of curiosity and amusement, moral indignation and self-congratulation, puzzlement and frustration, concern and guilt, on the part of white Americans.[1] As some Negroes have moved into middle-class status, or

[1] This paper is based in part on research supported by a grant from the National Institutes of Mental Health, Grant No. MH-09189, "Social and Community Problems in Public Housing Areas." Many of the ideas presented stem from discussion with the senior members of the Pruitt-Igoe research staff—Alvin W. Gouldner, David J. Pittman, and Jules Henry—and with the research associates and assistants on the project. I have made particular use of ideas developed in discussions with Boone Hammond, Joyce Ladner, Robert Simpson, David Schulz, and William Yancey. I also wish to acknowledge helpful suggestions and criticisms by Catherine Chilman, Gerald Handel, and Marc J. Swartz. Although this paper is not a formal report of the Pruitt-Igoe research, all of the illustrations of family behavior given in the text are drawn from interviews and observations that are part of that study. The study deals with the residents of the Pruitt-Igoe housing projects in St. Louis. Some 10,000 people live in these projects which comprise forty-three eleven-story buildings near the downtown area of St. Louis. Over half of the households have female heads, and for over half of the households the principal income comes from public assistance of one kind or another. The research has been in the field for a little over two years. It is a broad community study which thus far has relied principally on methods of participant observation and open-ended interviewing. Data on families come from repeated interviews and observations with a small group of families. The field workers are identified as graduate students at Washington University who

acquired standards of American common-man respectability, they too have shared these attitudes toward the private behavior of their fellows, sometimes with a moral punitiveness to rival that of whites, but at other times with a hard-headed interest in causes and remedies rather than moral evaluation. Moralism permeated the subject of Negro sexual, marital, and family behavior in the polemics of slavery apologists and abolitionists as much as in the Northern and Southern civil rights controversies of today. Yet, as long as the dialectic of good or bad, guilty or innocent, overshadows a concern with who, why, and what can be, it is unlikely that realistic and effective social planning to correct the clearly desperate situation of poor Negro families can begin.

This paper is concerned with a description and analysis of slum Negro family patterns as these reflect and sustain Negroes' adaptations to the economic, social, and personal situation into which they are born and in which they must live. As such it deals with facts of lower-class life that are usually forgotten or ignored in polite discussion. We have chosen not to ignore these facts in the belief that to do so can lead only to assumptions which would frustrate efforts at social reconstruction, to strategies that are unrealistic in the light of the actual day-to-day reality of slum Negro life. Further, this analysis will deal with family patterns which interfere with the efforts slum Negroes make to attain a stable way of life as working- or middle-class individuals and with the effects such failure in turn has on family life. To be sure, many Negro families live *in* the slum ghetto, but are not *of* its culture (though even they, and particularly their children, can be deeply affected by what happens there). However, it is the individuals who succumb to the distinctive family life style of the slum who experience the greatest weight of deprivation and who have the greatest difficulty responding to the few self-improvement resources that make their way into the ghetto. In short, we propose to explore in depth the family's role in the "tangle of pathology" which characterizes the ghetto.

The social reality in which Negroes have had to make their lives during the 450 years of their existence in the western hemisphere has been one of victimization "in the sense that a system of social relations operates in such a way as to deprive them of a chance to share in the more desirable material and non-material products of a society which is dependent, in part, upon their labor and loyalty." In making this observation, St. Clair Drake goes on to note that Negroes are victimized also because "they do not have the same degree of access which others have to the attributes needed for rising in the general class system—money, education, 'contacts,' and 'know-how.' " [2] The victimization

have no connection with the housing authority or other officials, but are simply interested in learning about how families in the project live. This very intensive study of families yields a wealth of information (over 10,000 pages of interview and observation reports) which obviously cannot be analyzed within the limits of one article. In this article I have limited myself to outlining a typical family stage sequence and discussing some of the psychosocial implications of growing up in families characterized by this sequence. In addition, I have tried to limit myself to findings which other literature on Negro family life suggests are not limited to the residents of the housing projects we are studying.

[2] St. Clair Drake, "The Social and Economic Status of the Negro in the United States," *Daedalus* (Fall 1965), p. 772.

process started with slavery; for 350 years thereafter Negroes worked out as best they could adaptations to the slave status. After emancipation, the cultural mechanisms which Negroes had developed for living the life of victim continued to be serviceable as the victimization process was maintained first under the myths of white supremacy and black inferiority, later by the doctrines of gradualism which covered the fact of no improvement in position, and finally by the modern Northern system of ghettoization and indifference.

When lower-class Negroes use the expression, "Tell it like it is," they signal their intention to strip away pretense, to describe a situation or its participants as they really are, rather than in a polite or euphemistic way. "Telling it like it is" can be used as a harsh, aggressive device, or it can be a healthy attempt to face reality rather than retreat into fantasy. In any case, as he goes about his field work, the participant observer studying a ghetto community learns to listen carefully to any exchange preceded by such an announcement because he knows the speaker is about to express his understanding of how his world operates, of what motivates its members, of how they actually behave.

The first responsibility of the social scientist can be phrased in much the same way: "Tell it like it is." His second responsibility is to try to understand why "it" is that way, and to explore the implications of what and why for more constructive solutions to human problems. Social research on the situation of the Negro American has been informed by four main goals: (1) to describe the disadvantaged position of Negroes, (2) to disprove the racist ideology which sustains the caste system, (3) to demonstrate that responsibility for the disadvantages Negroes suffer lies squarely upon the white caste which derives economic, prestige, and psychic benefits from the operation of the system, and (4) to suggest that in reality whites would be better rather than worse off if the whole jerry-built caste structure were to be dismantled. The successful accomplishment of these *intellectual* goals has been a towering achievement, in which the social scientists of the 1920's, '30's, and '40's can take great pride; that white society has proved so recalcitrant to utilizing this intellectual accomplishment is one of the great tragedies of our time, and provides the stimulus for further social research on "the white problem."

Yet the implicit paradigm of much of the research on Negro Americans has been an overly simplistic one concentrating on two terms of an argument:

White cupidity —————————→ Negro suffering.

As an intellectual shorthand, and even more as a civil rights slogan, this simple model is both justified and essential. But, as a guide to greater understanding of the Negro situation as human adaptation to human situations, the paradigm is totally inadequate because it fails to specify fully enough the *process* by which Negroes adapt to their situations as they do, and the limitations one kind of adaptation places on possibilities for subsequent adaptations. A reassessment of previous social research, combined with examination of current social research on Negro ghetto communities, suggests a more complex, but hopefully more vertical, model:

White cupidity
creates
Structural Conditions Highly Inimical to Basic Social Adaptation (low-income availability, poor education, poor services, stigmatization)
to which Negroes adapt
by
Social and Personal Responses which serve to sustain the individual in his punishing world but also generate aggressiveness toward the self and others
which results in
Suffering directly inflicted by Negroes on themselves and on others.

In short, whites, by their greater power, create situations in which Negroes do the dirty work of caste victimization for them.

The white caste maintains a cadre of whites whose special responsibility is to enforce the system in brutal or refined ways (the Klan, the rural sheriff, the metropolitan police, the businessman who specializes in a Negro clientele, the Board of Education). Increasingly, whites recruit to this cadre middle-class Negroes who can soften awareness of victimization by their protective coloration. These special cadres, white and/or Negro, serve the very important function of enforcing caste standards by whatever means seems required, while at the same time concealing from an increasingly "unprejudiced" public the unpleasant facts they would prefer to ignore. The system is quite homologous to the Gestapo and concentration camps of Nazi Germany, though less fatal to its victims.

For their part, Negroes creatively adapt to the system in ways that keep them alive and extract what gratification they can find, but in the process of adaptation they are constrained to behave in ways that inflict a great deal of suffering on those with whom they make their lives, and on themselves. The ghetto Negro is constantly confronted by the immediate necessity to suffer in order to get what he wants of those few things he can have, or to make others suffer, or both—for example, he suffers as exploited student and employee, as drug user, as loser in the competitive game of his peer-group society; he inflicts suffering as disloyal spouse, petty thief, knife- or gun-wielder, petty con man.

It is the central thesis of this paper that the caste-facilitated infliction of suffering by Negroes on other Negroes and on themselves appears most poignantly within the confines of the family, and that the victimization process as it operates in families prepares and toughens its members to function in the ghetto world, at the same time that it seriously interferes with their ability to operate in any other world. This, however, is very different from arguing that "the family is to blame" for the deprived situation ghetto Negroes suffer; rather we are looking at the logical outcome of the operation of the widely ramified and interconnecting caste system. In the end we will argue that only palliative results can be expected from attempts to treat directly the disordered family patterns to be described. Only a change in the original "inputs" of the caste system, the structural conditions inimical to basic social adaptation, can change family forms.

Almost thirty years ago, E. Franklin Frazier foresaw that the fate of the Negro family in the city would be a highly destructive one. His readers would have little reason to be surprised at observations of slum ghetto life today:

> . . . As long as the bankrupt system of southern agriculture exists, Negro families will continue to seek a living in the towns and cities. . . . They will crowd the slum areas of southern cities or make their way to northern cities where their families will become disrupted and their poverty will force them to depend upon charity.[3]

IDENTITY PROCESSES IN THE FAMILY

Now we want to examine the effect that growing up in the slum ghetto has in terms of socialization and personality development.

Household groups function for cultures in carrying out the initial phases of socialization and personality formation. It is in the family that the child learns the most primitive categories of existence and experience, and that he develops his most deeply held beliefs about the world and about himself.[4] From the child's point of view, the household *is* the world; his experiences as he moves out of it into the larger world are always interpreted in terms of his particular experience within the home. The painful experiences which a child in the Negro slum culture has are, therefore, interpreted as in some sense a reflection of this family world. The impact of the system of victimization is transmitted through the family; the child cannot be expected to have the sophistication an outside observer has for seeing exactly where the villains are. From the child's point of view, if he is hungry it is his parents' fault; if he experiences frustrations in the streets or in the school it is his parents' fault; if that world seems incomprehensible to him it is his parents' fault; if people are aggressive or destructive toward each other it is his parents' fault, not that of a system of race relations. In another culture this might not be the case; if a subculture could exist which provided comfort and security within its limited world and the individual experienced frustration only when he moved out into the larger society, the family

---

[3] E. Franklin Frazier, *The Negro Family in the United States*, (Chicago, 1939), p. 487,

[4] Talcott Parsons concludes his discussion of child socialization, the development of an "internalized family system" and internalized role differentiation by observing, "The internalization of the family collectivity as an object and its values should not be lost sight of. This is crucial with respect to . . . the assumption of representative roles outside the family on behalf of it. Here it is the child's family membership which is decisive, and thus his acting in a role in terms of its values for 'such as he.' " Talcott Parsons and Robert F. Bales, *Family, Socialization and Interaction Process* (Glencoe, Illinois, 1955), p. 113.

might not be thought so much to blame. The effect of the caste system, however, is to bring home through a chain of cause and effect all of the victimization processes, and to bring them home in such a way that it is often very difficult even for adults in the system to see the connection between the pain they feel at the moment and the structured patterns of the caste system.

Let us take as a central question that of identity formation within the Negro slum family. We are concerned with the question of who the individual believes himself to be and to be becoming. For Erikson, identity means a sense of continuity and social sameness which bridges what the individual *"was* as a child and what he is *about to become* and also reconciles his *conception of himself* and his community's recognition of him." Thus identity is a "self-realization coupled with a mutual recognition." [5] In the early childhood years identity is family-bound since the child's identity is his identity *vis-a-vis* other members of the family. Later he incorporates into his sense of who he is and is becoming his experiences outside the family, but always influenced by the interpretations and evaluations of those experiences that the family gives. As the child tries on identities, *announces* them, the family sits as judge of his pretensions. Family members are both the most important judges and the most critical ones, since who he is allowed to become affects them in their own identity strivings more crucially than it affects anyone else. The child seeks a sense of valid identity, a sense of being a particular person with a satisfactory degree of congruence between who he feels he is, who he announces himself to be, and where he feels his society places him.[6] He is uncomfortable when he experiences disjunction between his own needs and the kinds of needs legitimated by those around him, or when he feels a disjunction between his sense of himself and the image of himself that others play back to him.[7]

"Tell it like it is."

When families become involved in important quarrels the psychosocial underpinnings of family life are laid bare. One such quarrel in a family we have been studying brings together in one place many of the themes that seem to dominate identity problems in Negro slum culture. The incident illustrates in a particularly forceful and dramatic way family processes which our field work, and some other contemporary studies of slum family life, suggests unfold more subtly in a great many families at the lower-class level. The family involved, the Johnsons, is certainly not the most disorganized one we have studied; in some respects their

[5] Erik H. Erikson, "Identity and the Life Cycle," *Psychological Issues*, Vol. 1, No. 1 (1959).

[6] For discussion of the dynamics of the individual's *announcements* and the society's *placements* in the formation of identity, see Gregory Stone, "Appearance and the Self," in Arnold Rose, *Human Behavior in Social Process* (Boston, 1962), pp. 86–118.

[7] The importance of identity for social behavior is discussed in detail in Ward Goodenough, *Cooperation and Change* (New York, 1963), pp. 176–251, and in Lee Rainwater, "Work and Identity in the Lower Class," in Sam B. Warner, Jr., *Planning for a Nation of Cities* (Cambridge, Massachusetts, 1966). The images of self and of other family members is a crucial variable in Hess and Handel's psychosocial analysis of family life; see Robert D. Hess and Gerald Handel, *Family Worlds* (Chicago, 1959), especially pp. 6–11.

way of life represents a realistic adaptation to the hard living of a family nine-teen years on AFDC* with a monthly income of $202 for nine people. The two oldest daughters, Mary Jane (eighteen years old) and Esther (sixteen) are preg-nant; Mary Jane has one illegitimate child. The adolescent sons, Bob and Richard, are much involved in the social and sexual activities of their peer group. The three other children, ranging in age from twelve to fourteen, are apparently also moving into this kind of peer-group society. When the argument started Bob and Esther were alone in the apartment with Mary Jane's baby. Esther took exception to Bob's playing with the baby because she had been left in charge; the argument quickly progressed to a fight in which Bob cuffed Esther around, and she tried to cut him with a knife. The police were called and subdued Bob with their nightsticks. At this point the rest of the family and the field worker arrived. As the argument continued, these themes relevant to the analysis which follows appeared:

(1) The sisters said that Bob was not their brother (he is a half-brother to Esther and Mary Jane's full brother). Indeed, they said their mother "didn't have no husband. These kids don't even know who their daddies are." The mother defended herself by saying that she had one legal husband, and one common-law husband, no more.

(2) The sisters said that their fathers had never done anything for them, nor had their mother. She retorted that she had raised them "to the age of womanhood" and now would care for their babies.

(3) Esther continued to threaten to cut Bob if she got a chance (a month later they fought again, and she did cut Bob, who required twenty-one stitches).

(4) The sisters accused their mother of favoring their lazy brothers and asked her to put them out of the house. She retorted that the girls were as lazy, that they made no contribution to maintaining the household, could not get their boy friends to marry them or support their children, that all the support came from her AFDC check. Mary Jane retorted that "the baby has a check of her own."

(5) The girls threatened to leave the house if their mother refused to put their brothers out. They said they could force their boy friends to support them by taking them to court, and Esther threatened to cut her boy friend's throat if he did not co-operate.

(6) Mrs. Johnson said the girls could leave if they wished but that she would keep their babies; "I'll not have it, not knowing who's taking care of them."

(7) When her thirteen-year-old sister laughed at all of this, Esther told her not to laugh because she, too, would be pregnant within a year.

* [Aid for Dependent Children, now Aid to Families with Dependent Children, a federal program providing welfare benefits for children deprived of support and living with a relative.]

(8) When Bob laughed, Esther attacked him and his brother by saying that both were not man enough to make babies, as she and her sister had been able to do.

(9) As the field worker left, Mrs. Johnson sought his sympathy. "You see, Joe, how hard it is for me to bring up a family. . . . They sit around and talk to me like I'm some kind of a dog and not their mother."

(10) Finally, it is important to note for the analysis which follows that the following labels—"black-assed," "black bastard," "bitch," and other profane terms—were liberally used by Esther and Mary Jane, and rather less liberally by their mother, to refer to each other, to the girls' boy friends, to Bob, and to the thirteen-year-old daughter.

Several of the themes outlined previously appear forcefully in the course of this argument. In the last year and a half the mother has become a grandmother and expects shortly to add two more grandchildren to her household. She takes it for granted that it is her responsibility to care for the grandchildren and that she has the right to decide what will be done with the children since her own daughters are not fully responsible. She makes this very clear to them when they threaten to move out, a threat which they do not really wish to make good nor could they if they wished to.

However, only as an act of will is Mrs. Johnson able to make this a family. She must constantly cope with the tendency of her adolescent children to disrupt the family group and to deny that they are in fact a family—"He ain't no brother of mine"; "The baby has a check of her own." Though we do not know exactly what processes communicate these facts to the children it is clear that in growing up they have learned to regard themselves as not fully part of a solidary collectivity. During the quarrel this message was reinforced for the twelve-, thirteen-, and fourteen-year-old daughters by the four-way argument among their older sisters, older brother, and their mother.

The argument represents vicious unmasking of the individual members' pretenses to being competent individuals.[8] The efforts of the two girls to present themselves as masters of their own fate are unmasked by the mother. The girls in turn unmask the pretensions of the mother and of their two brothers. When the thirteen-year-old daughter expresses some amusement they turn on her, telling her that it won't be long before she too becomes pregnant. Each member of the family in turn is told that he can expect to be no more than a victim of his world, but that this is somehow inevitably his own fault.

In this argument masculinity is consistently demeaned. Bob has no right to play with his niece, the boys are not really masculine because at fifteen and sixteen years they have yet to father children, their own fathers were no goods

---

[8] See the discussion of "masking" and "unmasking" in relation to disorganization and re-equilibration in families by John P. Spiegel, "The Resolution of Role Conflict within the Family," in Norman W. Bell and Ezra F. Vogel, A Modern Introduction to the Family (Glencoe, Illinois, 1960), pp. 375–377.

who failed to do anything for their family. These notions probably come originally from the mother, who enjoys recounting the story of having her common-law husband imprisoned for nonsupport, but this comes back to haunt her as her daughters accuse her of being no better than they in ability to force support and nurturance from a man. In contrast, the girls came off somewhat better than the boys, although they must accept the label of stupid girls because they have similarly failed and inconveniently become pregnant in the first place. At least they can and have had children and therefore have some meaningful connection with the ongoing substance of life. There is something important and dramatic in which they participate, while the boys, despite their sexual activity, "can't get no babies."

In most societies, as children grow and are formed by their elders into suitable members of the society they gain increasingly a sense of competence and ability to master the behavioral environment their particular world presents. But in Negro slum culture growing up involves an ever-increasing appreciation of one's shortcomings, of the impossibility of finding a self-sufficient and gratifying way of living.[9] It is in the family first and most devastatingly that one learns these lessons. As the child's sense of frustration builds he too can strike out and unmask the pretentions of others. The result is a peculiar strength and a pervasive weakness. The strength involves the ability to tolerate and defend against degrading verbal and physical aggressions from others and not to give up completely. The weakness involves the inability to embark hopefully on any course of action that might make things better, particularly action which involves cooperating and trusting attitudes toward others. Family members become potential enemies to each other, as the frequency of observing the police being called in to settle family quarrels brings home all too dramatically.

The conceptions parents have of their children are such that they are constantly alert as the child matures to evidence that he is as bad as everyone else. That is, in lower-class culture human nature is conceived of as essentially bad, destructive, immoral.[10] This is the nature of things. Therefore any one child must be inherently bad unless his parents are very lucky indeed. If the mother can keep the child insulated from the outside world, she feels she may be able to prevent his inherent badness from coming out. She feels that once he is let out into the larger world the badness will come to the fore since that is his nature. This means that in the identity development of the child he is constantly exposed to identity labeling by his parents as a bad person. Since as he grows up he does not experience his world as particularly gratifying, it is very easy for him to conclude that this lack of gratification is due to the fact that something is wrong with him. This, in turn, can readily be assimilated to the definitions of being a

---

[9] See the discussion of self-identity and self-esteem in Thomas F. Pettigrew, *A Profile of the Negro American* (Princeton, New Jersey, 1964), pp. 6–11.

[10] Rainwater, Coleman, and Handel, *Workingman's Wife* (New York, 1959), pp. 44–51. See also the discussion of the greater level of "anomie" and mistrust among lower-class people in Ephriam Mizruchi, *Success and Opportunity* (New York, 1954). Unpublished research by the author indicates that for one urban lower-class sample (Chicago) Negroes scored about 50 per cent higher on Srole's anomie scale than did comparable whites.

bad person offered him by those with whom he lives.[11] In this way the Negro slum child learns his culture's conception of being-in-the-world, a conception that emphasizes inherent evil in a chaotic, hostile, destructive world.

Blackness

To a certain extent these same processes operate in white lower-class groups, but added for the Negro is the reality of blackness. "Black-assed" is not an empty pejorative adjective. In the Negro slum culture several distinctive appellations are used to refer to oneself and others. One involves the terms, "black" or "nigger." Black is generally a negative way of naming, but nigger can be either negative or positive, depending upon the context. It is important to note that, at least in the urban North, the initial development of racial identity in these terms has very little directly to do with relations with whites. A child experiences these identity placements in the context of the family and in the neighborhood peer groups; he probably very seldom hears the same terms used by whites (unlike the situation in the South). In this way, one of the effects of ghettoization is to mask the ultimate enemy so that the understanding of the fact of victimization by a caste system comes as a late acquisition laid over conceptions of self and of other Negroes derived from intimate, and to the child often traumatic, experience within the ghetto community. If, in addition, the child attends a ghetto school where his Negro teachers either overtly or by implication reinforce his community's negative conceptions of what it means to be black, then the child has little opportunity to develop a more realistic image of himself and other Negroes as being damaged by whites and not by themselves. In such a situation, an intelligent man like Mr. Wilson * can say with all sincerity that he does not feel most Negroes are ready for integration—only under the experience of certain kinds of intense personal threat coupled with exposure to an ideology that places the responsibility on whites did he begin to see through the direct evidence of his daily experience.

To those living in the heart of a ghetto, black comes to mean not just "stay back," but also membership in a community of persons who think poorly of each other, who attack and manipulate each other, who give each other small comfort in a desperate world. Black comes to stand for a sense of identity as no better than these destructive others. The individual feels that he must embrace an unattractive self in order to function at all.

We can hypothesize that in those families that manage to avoid the destructive identity imputations of "black" and that manage to maintain solidarity against such assaults from the world around, it is possible for children to grow up with a sense of both Negro and personal identity that allows them to socialize them-

[11] For a discussion of the child's propensity from a very early age for speculation and developing explanations, see William V. Silverberg, *Childhood Experience and Personal Destiny* (New York, 1953), pp. 81 ff.

* [A young blue collar worker, one of 10,000 people living in the Pruitt-Igoe housing projects in St. Louis, interviewed as part of the research effort described in the note at the beginning of this article.]

selves in an anticipatory way for participation in the larger society.[12] This broader sense of identity, however, will remain a brittle one as long as the individual is vulnerable to attack from within the Negro community as "nothing but a nigger like everybody else" or from the white community as "just a nigger." We can hypothesize further that the vicious unmasking of essential identity as black described above is least likely to occur within families where the parents have some stable sense of security, and where they therefore have less need to protect themselves by disavowing responsibility for their children's behavior and denying the children their patrimony as products of a particular family rather than of an immoral nature and an evil community.

In sum, we are suggesting that Negro slum children as they grow up in their families and in their neighborhoods are exposed to a set of experiences—and a rhetoric which conceptualizes them—that brings home to the child an understanding of his essence as a weak and debased person who can expect only partial gratification of his needs, and who must seek even this level of gratification by less than straight-forward means.

Strategies for Living

In every society complex processes of socialization inculcate in their members strategies for gratifying the needs with which they are born and those which the society itself generates. Inextricably linked to these strategies, both cause and effect of them, are the existential propositions which members of a culture entertain about the nature of their world and of effective action within the world as it is defined for them. In most of American society two grand strategies seem to attract the allegiance of its members and guide their day-to-day actions. I have called these strategies those of *the good life* and of *career success*.[13] A good life strategy involves efforts to get along with others and not to rock the boat, a comfortable familism grounded on a stable work career for husbands in which they perform adequately at the modest jobs that enable them to be good providers. The strategy of career success is the choice of ambitious men and women who see life as providing opportunities to move from a lower to a higher status, to "accompish something," to achieve greater than ordinary material well-being, prestige, and social recognition. Both of these strategies are predicated on the assumption that the world is inherently rewarding if one behaves properly and does his part. The rewards of the world may come easily or only at the cost of great effort, but at least they are there.

In the white and particularly in the Negro slum worlds little in the experience that individuals have as they grow up sustains a belief in a rewarding world. The strategies that seem appropriate are not those of a good, family-based life or of a career, but rather *strategies for survival*.

[12] See Ralph Ellison's autobiographical descriptions of growing up in Oklahoma City in his *Shadow and Act* (New York, 1964). . . .
[13] Lee Rainwater, "Work and Identity in the Lower Class," in Sam B. Warner, Jr., *Planning for a Nation of Cities* (Cambridge, Massachusetts, 1966).

Much of what has been said above can be summarized as encouraging three kinds of survival strategies. One is the strategy of the *expressive life style* which I have described elsewhere as an effort to make yourself interesting and attractive to others so that you are better able to manipulate their behavior along lines that will provide some immediate gratification.[14] Negro slum culture provides many examples of techniques for seduction, of persuading others to give you what you want in situations where you have very little that is tangible to offer in return. In order to get what you want you learn to "work game," a strategy which requires a high development of a certain kind of verbal facility, a sophisticated manipulation of promise and interim reward. When the expressive strategy fails or when it is unavailable there is, of course, the great temptation to adopt a *violent strategy* in which you force others to give you what you need once you fail to win it by verbal and other symbolic means.[15] Finally, and increasingly as members of the Negro slum culture grow older, there is the *depressive strategy* in which goals are increasingly constricted to the bare necessities for survival (not as a social being but simply as an organism).[16] This is the strategy of "I don't bother anybody and I hope nobody's gonna bother me; I'm simply going through the motions to keep body (but not soul) together." Most lower-class people follow mixed strategies, as Walter Miller has observed, alternating among the excitement of the expressive style, the desperation of the violent style, and the deadness of the depressed style.[17] Some members of the Negro slum world experiment from time to time with mixed strategies that also incorporate the stable working-class model of the good American life, but this latter strategy is exceedingly vulnerable to the threats of unemployment or a less than adequate pay check, on the one hand, and the seduction and violence of the slum world around them, on the other.

Remedies

Finally, it is clear that we, no less than the inhabitants of the ghetto, are not masters of their fate because we are not masters of our own total society. Despite the battles with poverty on many fronts we can find little evidence to sustain our hope of winning the war given current programs and strategies.

The question of strategy is particularly crucial when one moves from an examination of destructive cultural and interaction patterns in Negro families to the question of how these families might achieve a more stable and gratifying

---

[14] Lee Rainwater, "Work and Identity in the Lower Class," in Sam B. Warner, Jr., *Planning for a Nation of Cities* (Cambridge, Massachusetts, 1966).

[15] Short and Strodtbeck see violent behavior in juvenile gangs as a kind of last resort strategy in situations where the actor feels he has no other choice. See James F. Short, Jr., and Fred L. Strodtbeck, *Group Process and Gang Delinquency* (Chicago, 1965), pp. 248–264.

[16] Wiltse speaks of a "pseudo depression syndrome" as characteristic of many AFDC mothers. Kermit T. Wiltse, "Orthopsychiatric Programs for Socially Deprived Groups," *American Journal of Orthopsychiatry*, Vol. 33, No. 5 (October 1963), pp. 806–813. [Wiltse's article follows the present paper in this collection.]

[17] Walter B. Miller, "Lower Class Culture as a Generating Milieu of Gang Delinquency," *Journal of Social Issues*, Vol. 14, No. 3 (1958), pp. 5–19. [pp. 189–204 in this collection]

life. It is tempting to see the family as the main villain of the piece, and to seek to develop programs which attack directly this family pathology. Should we not have extensive programs of family therapy, family counseling, family-like education, and the like? Is this not the prerequisite to enabling slum Negro families to take advantage of other opportunities? Yet, how pale such efforts seem compared to the deep-seated problems of self-image and family process described above. Can an army of social workers undo the damage of three hundred years by talking and listening without massive changes in the social and economic situations of the families with whom they are to deal? And, if such changes take place, will the social-worker army be needed?

If we are right that present Negro family patterns have been created as adaptations to a particular socioeconomic situation, it would make more sense to change that socioeconomic situation and then depend upon the people involved to make new adaptations as time goes on. If Negro providers have steady jobs and decent incomes, if Negro children have some realistic expectation of moving toward such a goal, if slum Negroes come to feel that they have the chance to affect their own futures and to receive respect from those around them, then (and only then) the destructive patterns described are likely to change. The change, though slow and uneven from individual to individual, will in a certain sense be automatic because it will represent an adaptation to changed socioeconomic circumstances which have direct and highly valued implications for the person.

It is possible to think of three kinds of extra-family change that are required if family patterns are to change; these are outlined below as pairs of current deprivations and needed remedies:

Deprivation Effect of Caste Victimization	Needed Remedy
I. Poverty	Employment income for men; income maintenance for mothers
II. Trained incapacity to function in a bureaucratized and industrialized world	Meaningful education of the next generation
III. Powerlessness and stigmatization	Organizational participation for aggressive pursuit of Negroes' self-interest
	Strong sanctions against callous or indifferent service to slum Negroes
	Pride in group identity, Negro and American

Unless the major effort is to provide these kinds of remedies, there is a very real danger that programs to "better the structure of the Negro family" by direct intervention will serve the unintended functions of distracting the country from the pressing needs for socioeconomic reform and providing an alibi for the failure to embark on the basic institutional changes that are needed to do anything about abolishing both white and Negro poverty. It would be sad, indeed, if, after the Negro revolt brought to national prominence the continuing problem of poverty, our expertise about Negro slum culture served to deflect the national impulse into symptom-treatment rather than basic reform. If that happens, social scientists will have served those they study poorly indeed.

Let us consider each of the needed remedies in terms of its probable impact on the family. First, the problem of poverty: employed men are less likely to leave their families than are unemployed men, and when they do stay they are more likely to have the respect of their wives and children. A program whose sole effect would be to employ at reasonable wages slum men for work using the skills they now have would do more than any other possible program to stabilize slum family life. But the wages must be high enough to enable the man to maintain his self-respect as a provider, and stable enough to make it worthwhile to change the nature of his adaptation to his world (no one-year emergency programs will do). Once men learn that work pays off it would be possible to recruit men for part-time retraining for more highly skilled jobs, but the initial emphasis must be on the provision of full-time, permanent unskilled jobs. Obviously it will be easier to do this in the context of full employment and a tight labor market.[18]

For at least a generation, however, there will continue to be a large number of female-headed households. Given the demands of socializing a new generation for non-slum living, it is probably uneconomical to encourage mothers to work. Rather, income maintenance programs must be increased to realistic levels, and mothers must be recognized as doing socially useful work for which they are paid rather than as "feeding at the public trough." The bureaucratic morass which currently hampers flexible strategies of combining employment income and welfare payments to make ends meet must also be modified if young workers are not to be pushed prematurely out of the home.

Education has the second priority. (It is second only because without stable family income arrangements the school system must work against the tremendous resistance of competing life-style adaptations to poverty and economic insecurity.) As Kenneth Clark has argued so effectively, slum schools now function more to stultify and discourage slum children than to stimulate and train them. The capacity of educators to alibi their lack of commitment to their charges is protean. The making of a different kind of generation must be taken by educators as a stimulating and worthwhile challenge. Once the goal has been accepted they must be given the resources with which to achieve it and the flexibility necessary to experiment with different approaches to accomplish the goal. Education must

---

[18] This line of argument concerning the employment problems of Negroes, and poverty war strategy more generally, is developed with great cogency by James Tobin, "On Improving the Economic Status of the Negro," *Daedalus* (Fall 1965), and previously by Gunnar Myrdal, in his *Challenge to Affluence* (New York, 1963), and Orville R. Gursslin and Jack L. Roach, in their "Some Issues in Training the Employed," *Social Problems*, Vol. 12, No. 1 (Summer 1964), pp. 68–77.

be broadly conceived to include much more than classroom work, and probably more than a nine-months schedule.[19]

If slum children can come to see the schools as representing a really likely avenue of escape from their difficult situation (even before adolescence they know it is the only *possible* escape) then their commitment to school activities will feed back into their families in a positive way. The parents will feel proud rather than ashamed, and they will feel less need to damn the child as a way to avoid blaming themselves for his failure. The sense of positive family identity will be enriched as the child becomes an attractive object, an ego resource, to his parents. Because he himself feels more competent, he will see them as less depriving and weak. If children's greater commitment to school begins to reduce their involvement in destructive or aimless peer-group activities this too will repercuss positively on the family situation since parents will worry less about their children's involvement in an immoral outside world, and be less inclined to deal with them in harsh, rejecting, or indifferent ways.

Cross-cutting the deprivations of poverty and trained incapacity is the fact of powerlessness and stigmatization. Slum people know that they have little ability to protect themselves and to force recognition of their abstract rights. They know that they are looked down on and scape-goated. They are always vulnerable to the slights, insults, and indifference of the white and Negro functionaries with whom they deal—policemen, social workers, school teachers, landlords, employers, retailers, janitors. To come into contact with others carries the constant danger of moral attack and insult.[20] If processes of status degradation within families are to be interrupted, then they must be interrupted on the outside first.

One way out of the situation of impotence and dammed-up in-group aggression is the organization of meaningful protest against the larger society. Such protest can and will take many forms, not always so neat and rational as the outsider might hope. But, coupled with, and supporting, current programs of economic and educational change, involvement of slum Negroes in organizational activity can do a great deal to build a sense of pride and potency. While only a small minority of slum Negroes can be expected to participate personally in such movements, the vicarious involvement of the majority can have important effects on their sense of self-respect and worth.

Some of the needed changes probably can be made from the top, by decision in Washington, with minimal effective organization within the slum; but others can come only in response to aggressive pressure on the part of the victims themselves. This is probably particularly true of the entrenched tendency of service personnel to enhance their own sense of self and to indulge their middle-class *ressentiment* by stigmatizing and exploiting those they serve. Only effective protest can change endemic patterns of police harassment and brutality, or

---

[19] See Chapter 6 (pages 111–153) of Kenneth Clark, *Dark Ghetto* (New York, 1965), for a discussion of the destructive effects of ghetto schools on their students.

[20] See the discussion of "moral danger" in Lee Rainwater, "Fear and the House-as-Haven in the Lower Class," *Journal of the American Institute of Planners*, February 1966.

teachers' indifference and insults, or butchers' heavy thumbs, or indifferent street cleaning and garbage disposal. And the goal of the protest must be to make this kind of insult to the humanity of the slum-dweller too expensive for the perpetrator to afford; it must cost him election defeats, suspensions without pay, job dismissals, license revocations, fines, and the like.

To the extent that the slum dweller avoids stigmatization in the outside world, he will feel more fully a person within a family and better able to function constructively within it since he will not be tempted to make up deficits in self-esteem in ways that are destructive of family solidarity. The "me" of personal identity and the multiple "we" of family, Negro, and American identity are all inextricably linked; a healthier experience of identity in any one sector will repercuss on all the others.

Dr. Wiltse discusses kinds of psychological disturbances he found among urban families receiving Aid to Dependent Children funds. He suggests that symptoms from which these individuals suffer although not the result of classic maternal deprivation are nevertheless similar to those that result from maternal deprivation and can probably be traced to extreme social and economic deprivation. He analyses how such social ills are transmitted within the family from generation to generation.

Kermit T. Wiltse

Orthopsychiatric Programs for Socially Deprived Groups

Preventive and restorative mental health work is never done in a vacuum. If done at all, it is through specific social service programs that touch significantly the lives of those children and their parents whose mental health is an object of concern. My proposition is that the Aid to Dependent Children (ADC) program, administered by more than 3,000 local public welfare departments, affects the lives of more children and holds the potential to affect their lives more profoundly than all other social welfare and mental health programs combined.

SOCIAL DEPRIVATION

"Social deprivation" is a relative term. In a money-oriented society, financial deprivation is certainly a social deprivation. Nearly two and one-half million children in more than three-quarters of a million families covered by this national program live at or below a minimum standard of health and decency. Most live in cities, usually in the areas of poorest housing and most limited resources for education and socialization. Eligibility for this public aid hinges on the death, incapacity or continued absence from home of the family breadwinner. This means that ADC families are fatherless, or, in approximately 10 per cent of the cases, the present father is unable to carry a crucial aspect of the father role. In the most obvious respects, these families are socially deprived from a mental health standpoint: The children are deprived of a present or functioning father as an object of love and identification and as a source of economic security, and the mothers, deprived of the emotional fulfillment of a husband, are also endeavoring to cope with the demands of a dual parent role in an atmosphere of economic deprivation and insecurity.

Certain social characteristics of ADC families suggest that individuals with poor ego functioning tend to sift into the caseload. Actually, since very little systematic study of even the "counting" variety has been completed, we lack a clear profile of the typical ADC family and the range of its problems. The recent study by Greenleigh Associates [1] of the ADC program in Chicago and Cook County found that approximately 70 per cent of the ADC families included one or more children born out of wedlock; the frequency of repetition of this personally and socially destructive behavior is particularly impressive. Most of the families were "multiproblem" in the sense that they were laboring under interrelated physical, emotional and social problems. This and other studies show that the typical urban ADC parent is usually poorly equipped educationally and socially for meeting the demands of modern urban living, is burdened by discrimination stemming from a combination of race and social class factors and is beset by constellations of physical and psychological problems.

My thesis is that the ADC program provides a significant but little-used vantage point from which the professions concerned with mental health can observe what social deprivation really means in the lives of people, and that it provides an operating structure of agencies plus policies and resources that can be used, or certainly much better used than it is at present, to achieve mental health objectives for socially deprived urban children.

I am frankly desirous that more people, particularly psychiatrists, social workers, psychologists, and related mental health workers, become actively interested in the ADC program. The implementation of such an active interest will be discussed further on.

I want now to develop a more definitive picture of the mental health problems of this ADC segment of socially deprived urban people as a springboard for considering treatment approaches based on what we know, and research approaches to extend our knowledge.

During the academic year 1958–1559, I was in charge of a pilot project in the

---

[1] "Facts, Fallacies, and Future: A Study of the Aid to Dependent Children Program of Cook County, Illinois," 1960, Greenleigh Associates, Inc., New York, New York.

San Francisco Department of Public Welfare. Its purpose, broadly conceived, was to learn more about the Aid to Dependent Children caseload in that city regarding the types of problems presented by individual recipients, the specific kinds of social services they need and how to offer such services so that the typical ADC family could understand their meaning and use them. More specifically, we used individual, family and group methods to study the problems of ADC families and to examine and test techniques of helping them. Help was defined as improvement in role functioning on the part of each family member, with particular attention to the mother's performance of child-care functions and household management, and to the children's performance in school and peer relationships.

The project design called for each of the two project social workers to carry a small caseload of families receiving ADC, for intensive study and the provision of specific services, including financial assistance and family and individual counseling. Each worker was also to develop a discussion group of ADC recipient mothers, which would be both a means of studying the ADC client and her sub-culture and a method of treatment of the problems she manifested.

CHARACTERISTICS OF ADC FAMILIES

In reading the agency case records of numerous families from which we selected those for the project caseload, we were repeatedly impressed with the extent and quality of pathology in this cross-section sampling of an urban, socially deprived group. Since nine out of ten ADC families have no father in the home, references to ADC parents are usually to the mother. At a superficial level these mothers are poorly educated, itself an indication of a history of social deprivation. "Social" in this context refers to all the socioeconomic factors that determine who shall be educated in our society and who shall not be. Typically these mothers have little or no significant work history; hence they have experienced neither work satisfactions nor the identity-forming influences of such experience. Additionally, they lack work skills and therefore employment opportunities that would provide them with a source of income and pride in their accomplishment. The Greenleigh Associates study already cited gives the real impact of social deprivation in terms of actual deficiencies in education and in occupational and social skills—deficiencies that must be overcome if these parents are to achieve any part of the "better life for their children" of which this report shows they dream.

Such data represent the tangible characteristics of the caseload. Less tangible, but more important to this discussion, are the psychological characteristics of this group. A cross section of the case histories of ADC families, especially the backgrounds of the parents, shows an impressive history of deprivation. A large proportion were the children of homes broken by death or desertion; many were themselves born out of wedlock; a surprising number spent many years in orphanages and foster homes, with all the emotional deprivation this experience represents. Extreme poverty is characteristic of many more childhood backgrounds. The impact of such case analysis is impossible to escape. It is axiomatic in our understanding of human behavior that a human being can give only as he has received. Hence we are frequently working with parents who have little to give their children, a reflection of their own history of deprivation.

The initial reading of a sample of case records in a public welfare department such as that in San Francisco is likely to be a depressing experience. One is confronted intimately with so much pathos, so much deprivation, so many frustrated hopes and shattered dreams. More important to our consideration here, one comes away thinking the ADC caseload is heavily weighted by sick people—sick psychologically and displaying a myriad of physical symptoms and complaints. Our initial reading of case records left us with just such an impression—that we were dealing with a very sick group of people for whom the potentialities for quick improvement in personal and social functioning were limited. I hasten to point out that this initial impression was not substantiated; they were not as ill as they first seemed, and improvement in their functioning as a result of our efforts was greater than expected.

THE PSEUDO DEPRESSION SYNDROME

Out of individual interviews and particularly out of group discussion with this sample of ADC parents, a picture of psychological functioning and social behavior gradually emerged that it seemed appropriate to identify as "pseudo depression syndrome." It was characteristic of many of the ADC parents in varying degrees of severity. This syndrome was similar to typical clinical depression in symptom manifestation. We found a combination of immobilization with regard to effective activity, isolation from social relationships, depressed appearance, weight loss, poor appetite and chronic health problems. These manifestations were general, but I want to make a particular point of our observation that this behavior was highly characteristic of this socially deprived segment of urban families. Although the behavior is identified as pseudo depression, to distinguish it from the clinically recognized depression of psychiatric literature, I must caution immediately that the qualifying word "pseudo" carries no implication that the characteristic symptoms described were affected or consciously assumed.

This cluster of behavior symptoms is distinguished from true clinical depression by its very different origins and response to treatment. Depression as we deal with it in psychiatric clinics stems from early and severe maternal deprivation. The typical clinical depression syndrome may be triggered by a current incident or failure in interpersonal relationships, but its severity is always completely out of proportion to the reality of daily living. In fact, people sometimes go into depression at that moment when they are most free of reality demands, or when the circumstances of their lives appear most easy and secure. The pattern of immobilization, isolation and withdrawal from effective engagement with the environment that we so consistently observed in our ADC families was quite the opposite. Their behavior seemed a reasonable response to the buffetings of a series of singularly destructive environmental experiences, coming on the heels of poor ego formation.

It is impossible to argue sensibly which was cause and which effect. The destructive and ego-diminishing factors in their situation were emphatic and real. They were "on relief" in a society where that carries clear connotations of inadequacy, immorality and worthlessness. They lived a hand-to-mouth existence at or below a minimum level of health and decency in a society that bombarded them on every side with the mandate to spend money and to own material possessions, a society that says all too clearly that what you have is a measure of what you are. They felt themselves to be—and this came out so clearly in their communications—the pawns of the agencies of the community and of the authorities in those agencies: the public welfare agency, the social workers, the county hospital, the doctor, the police department and the juvenile court. This feeling of vulnerability to the "structure" of society was especially marked. They spent long hours waiting for attention in county hospitals, clinics, welfare departments and district attorneys' offices, often feeling they were at the mercy of the whims of the authority figures of the community or, as often as not, unable to make their needs known with sufficient clarity and force to gain appropriate attention. Content analysis of verbatim records taken of the group discussions we held provided much of the detailed data from which we developed our concept of pseudo or, perhaps more accurately stated, situational depression syndrome.

Not only are these people subject to the buffeting of the urban environment in which they live their economically and socially deprived lives, but their diminished egos must also constantly cope with the implications of their own obvious failures. They have been failures as husbands or wives, often several times, as evidenced by their records of desertion and divorce. They have been economic failures, as evidenced by their being on relief. At least three-fifths of them in San Francisco are of a racial minority subject to many open as well as obscure forms of discrimination. Discrimination with its implication of "less worth" usually seems to leave some residue of an inner feeling of worthlessness in the individual object of discrimination. Many have failed as parents, as evidenced by citations for neglect or pressure by welfare workers to improve their standard of child care. The newspapers are full of stories of the malfeasance and immorality of ADC mothers, and they cannot but feel it is partly deserved—after all, one-third to one-half of their children are illegitimate, and, under economic pressure, many at one time or another resort to petty fraud. A significant number of mothers had repetitive illegitimate pregnancies and were constantly confronted with their own stupidity or ineptitude.

In some instances the client's sense of failure and inadequacy had been clearly enhanced by the assistance agency's making demands upon him that he was unable to meet. Some had spent much time seeking employment. Repeated rejection by employers was experienced as an additional defeat, which they vaguely felt they may have deserved. Some had repeatedly been told by medical agencies that there was nothing wrong with them, although they felt constantly ill and in pain.

The following three quotations from the verbatim records of group discussions illustrate the client's conception of himself as a person who is inadequate to the demands of his environment—a victim of inner pressure and outer demands neither of which he can understand or control:

> Every time I seem as if I'm trying to get ahead it's always something that pushes me back. So I guess I'm a little bit overanxious. . . . I tried a couple of times at my work but it seemed as if I always get sick or something. I have my troubles, a skin allergy, dermatitis, it don't start until I work, so probably that's one of my problems there, you see. But I mean, I think everyone wants to be independent. I mean, I know for myself that's what I want to be, but it seems like you always have to fall back on what you don't want to be, do, I mean.

> I get nervous, and I just quit everything and go lay down, because I can't afford to think, because I've had so much trouble I can't afford to think too fast, it makes me too sick . . . my stomach . . . and if that check wasn't in the mailbox.

> The reason I can say it is because I suffered all sorts of things, I was passing out, dying, everything else. But I'll tell you one that that [sic] really brings the nervousness is when you're alone with the children and have husband affairs, and they try you and you hate to see little children cry. You want to reach out and do for them and give to them and you can't. Well, then that builds up—you're just like a wounded lion or tiger; you know if you hurt him he will get back in a corner and strike back? Well, that's the way I felt. Anyone that said anything to me I just wanted to strike back, because you know, I was wounded as from hurt, it looked like everything was against me.

I have dwelt on this concept of a pseudo depression syndrome as characteristic of many within the ADC segment of urban population because I have found it an increasingly useful concept in considering both mental health needs and treatment approaches. In passing, I note that we received empirical verification of our subjective observations from quite a different study. In connection with a project conducted in the Alameda Department of Public Welfare of California, the California Personal Inventory Test, a projective test, was given to a sample of ADC mothers. The C.P.I. protocols revealed in an objective way a typical depressive syndrome with aggressive features that could be inferred as primarily utilized by the personality to cover up the underlying depression.[2] A vast amount of research and literature in the broad field of dynamic psychology supports the observation that rage and hostility tend to be the basic defenses against depression in the individual personality. When directed against other people and the environment, they are usually described as representing an inappropriate or mis-

---

[2] Irving Piliavin, Alvin Rudoff and Robert Kennedy. Presented at the American Public Welfare Association Regional Conference, Berkeley, California, October 15–18, 1961.

directed aggression, meaning that it is not aggression directed toward appropriate social goals by appropriate means, but toward inappropriate goals and by generally self-defeating methods.

A KEY TO AID AND TREATMENT

I have come to the general hypothesis that psychological depression, situationally related as I have described it here, is the single most important problem of the socially deprived urban parent as represented by the ADC segment. Much research is needed to elaborate and verify this general hypothesis. Speaking generally, most socially deprived urban people living economically marginal lives in urban slum environments seem to exist under a more or less constant state of situationally related depression. Their children grow up in this atmosphere of depression and isolation from that mainstream of life wherein the American dream of faith in the future and in one's self seems justified. The poor in our society no longer have such sharply etched oppressors as overlords or political bosses upon whom to project the fault for their situations. The cause of their poverty and misfortune is felt to lie within themselves, because the social conditions underlying poverty in American urban environments are so complex and ill-defined. For the individual that experiences it, such poverty is all the more anachronistic because he is surrounded in urban environments by the symbols of affluence and comfort, and economic and social deprivation become the more difficult to bear as the number of really poor people becomes proportionally smaller.

I am sure this theme of situationally derived psychological depression with concomitant reactive behavior as typical of the socially deprived segment of the urban community, is neither very new nor very original. Yet I believe it provides a concept that gives a frame of reference for mental health research and a means of visualizing restorative and preventative mental health programs. The more I have studied and worked along this line, the more clearly it has appeared to me that the term psychological depression expresses in individual terms what such captions as "socially depressed," "socially deprived," and "social dynamite" express in group terms. In other words, psychological depression, situationally derived, is both the cause and effect in individual human beings of whatever is meant by these terms when applied to groups.

IMPROVEMENT OF PUBLIC AID

Within this framework adequate assistance grants have meaning, for they not only provide minimum comfort but also carry the implication of society's concern for the individual's welfare. Through them, the public assistance social worker symbolizes a concerned and giving parent figure, rather than an unloving and withholding one. This point needs to be emphasized, since deep within the

American cultural pattern lies the fallacious attitude that hardship and deprivation toughen and strengthen a person, and that our society cannot risk decent public health and welfare standards because it will weaken the "moral fiber" of the people. Public social policy is nowhere more confused and confusing than when it attempts to deal with problems of providing adequate financial aid to the needy. I believe the fear of the impulse toward dependency, which each of us senses within himself, is projected into the social scene, leading us to fear and hate dependency when we think we see it displayed by others. If this hypothesis is sound, then a major mental health task is to reduce this all-pervasive fear, to make possible a more sane and rational disposition of the public social policy issues that surround the provision of adequate financial aid to the economically deprived. Specifically, this means that mental health workers have an obligation to understand the financial aid programs, particularly those providing for families and children, so that they know how to cope with the fear that adequate relief programs will create dependency. Armed with this knowledge, mental health workers can take leadership in many different ways in their own communities to support better standards of public aid.

Returning for a moment to our project in San Francisco, I have already emphasized the manner in which discussion groups of ADC mothers were used to gain insight into the "relief subculture." The records of these discussions are a rich source of insight into economic and social deprivation in our urban culture. Without further elaboration of the specific accomplishments of these discussion groups for the individual members, let me point out that there is open before us a very large, new field of operations for the development of group approaches in a variety of patterns. The public welfare agencies have been essentially untouched by the rapid extension of group methods in such types of social agencies as mental hygiene clinics, hospitals, and correctional agencies.

The Federal Government, through the force of its grant-in-aid program, is putting increasing pressure upon state public welfare agencies and, in turn, upon local county departments to improve their services for families and children. The Aid to Dependent Children program is gradually emerging as a broadly gauged family and child welfare program, and the local agencies administering both it and other assistance programs must eventually become multiplefunction social agencies, staffed to provide the kind and quality of services that will help the individual family overcome such personal-social problems as have already been enumerated. This calls for Herculean efforts to upgrade the quality of current staffs of public welfare agencies and to attract imaginative and educationally qualified people to public welfare careers.

Money is becoming available through federal and state governments for general and for demonstration research. It can be anticipated that opportunities will increase for testing or demonstrating any idea that holds promise of enhancing our knowledge of the problems or of dealing more effectively with these problems of the socially deprived segment of the community that comes under the purview of public welfare agencies.

2 THE PEER GROUP

This report on one type of lower-class Negro peer group—the delinquent street-corner gang—is based on the author's longitudinal study of Negro adolescent groups. Miller identifies six "focal concerns" of all urban lower-class Negroes that he believes are dominant motivations of the delinquent segment. He concludes that Negro youths' delinquent behavior should be viewed not as an expression against white middle-class values but as the logical outgrowth of their own motivations.

Walter B. Miller

Lower Class Culture as a Generating Milieu of Gang Delinquency

The etiology of delinquency has long been a controversial issue, and is particularly so at present. As new frames of reference for explaining human behavior have been added to traditional theories, some authors have adopted the practice of citing the major postulates of each school of thought as they pertain to delinquency, and going on to state that causality must be conceived in terms of the dynamic interaction of a complex combination of variables on many levels. The major sets of etiological factors currently adduced to explain delinquency are, in simplified terms, the physiological (delinquency results from organic pathology), the psychodynamic (delinquency is a "behavioral disorder" resulting primarily from emotional disturbance generated by a defective mother-child relationship), and the environmental (delinquency is the product of disruptive forces, "disorganization," in the actor's physical or social environment).

This paper selects one particular kind of "delinquency" [1]—law-violating acts committed by members of adolescent street corner groups in lower class communities—and attempts to show that the dominant component of motivation underlying these acts consists in a directed attempt by the actor to adhere to forms of behavior, and to achieve standards of value as they are defined within that community. It takes as a premise that the motivation of behavior in this situation can be approached most productively by attempting to understand the nature of cultural forces impinging on the acting individual as they are perceived *by the actor himself*—although by no means only that segment of these forces of which the actor is consciously aware—rather than as they are perceived and evaluated from the reference position of another cultural system. In the case of "gang" delinquency, the cultural system which exerts the most direct influence on behavior is that of the lower class community itself—a long-established, distinctively patterned tradition with an integrity of its own—rather than a so-called "delinquent subculture" which has arisen through conflict with middle class culture and is oriented to the deliberate violation of middle class norms.

The bulk of the substantive data on which the following material is based was collected in connection with a service-research project in the control of gang delinquency. During the service aspect of the project, which lasted for three years, seven trained social workers maintained contact with twenty-one corner group units in a "slum" district of a large eastern city for periods of time ranging from ten to thirty months. Groups were Negro and white, male and female, and in early, middle, and late adolescence. Over eight thousand pages of direct observational data on behavior patterns of group members and other community residents were collected; almost daily contact was maintained for a total time period of about thirteen worker years. Data include workers' contact reports, participant observation reports by the writer—a cultural anthropologist—and direct tape recordings of group activities and discussions.[2]

FOCAL CONCERNS OF LOWER CLASS CULTURE

There is a substantial segment of present-day American society whose way of life, values, and characteristic patterns of behavior are the product of a dis-

[1] The complex issues involved in deriving a definition of "delinquency" cannot be discussed here. The term "delinquent" is used in this paper to characterize behavior or acts committed by individuals within specified age limits which if known to official authorities could result in legal action. The concept of a "delinquent" individual has little or no utility in the approach used here; rather, specified types of *acts* which may be committed rarely or frequently by few or many individuals are characterized as "delinquent."

[2] A three year research project is being financed under National Institutes of Health Grant M-1414, and administered through the Boston University School of Social Work. The primary research effort has subjected all collected material to a uniform data-coding process. All information bearing on some seventy areas of behavior (behavior in reference to school, police, theft, assault, sex, collective athletics, etc.) is extracted from the records, recorded on coded data cards, and filed under relevant categories. Analysis of these data aims to ascertain the actual nature of customary behavior in these areas, and the extent to which the social work effort was able to effect behavioral changes.

tinctive cultural system which may be termed "lower class." Evidence indicates that this cultural system is becoming increasingly distinctive, and that the size of the group which shares this tradition is increasing.[3] The lower class way of life, in common with that of all distinctive cultural groups, is characterized by a set of focal concerns—areas or issues which command widespread and persistent attention and a high degree of emotional involvement. The specific concerns cited here, while by no means confined to the American lower classes, constitute a distinctive *patterning* of concerns which differs significantly, both in rank order and weighting from that of American middle class culture. The following chart presents a highly schematic and simplified listing of six of the major concerns of lower class culture. Each is conceived as a "dimension" within which a fairly wide and varied range of alternative behavior patterns may be followed by different individuals under different situations. They are listed roughly in order of the degree of *explicit* attention accorded each, and, in this sense represent a

CHART 1: Focal Concerns of Lower Class Culture

Area	Perceived Alternatives (state, quality, condition)	
1. Trouble:	law-abiding behavior	law-violating behavior
2. Toughness:	physical prowess, skill; "masculinty"; fearlessness, bravery, daring	weakness, ineptitude; effeminacy; timidity, cowardice, caution
3. Smartness:	ability to outsmart, dupe, "con"; gaining money by "wits"; shrewdness, adroitness in repartee	gullibility, "con-ability"; gaining money by hard work; slowness, dull-wittedness, verbal maladroitness
4. Excitement:	thrill; risk, danger; change, activity	boredom; "deadness," safeness; sameness, passivity
5. Fate:	favored by fortune, being "lucky"	ill-omened, being "unlucky"
6. Autonomy:	freedom from external constraint; freedom from superordinate authority; independence	presence of external constraint; presence of strong authority; dependency, being "cared for"

[3] Between 40 and 60 per cent of all Americans are directly influenced by lower class culture, with about 15 per cent, or twenty-five million, comprising the "hard core" lower class group —defined primarily by its use of the "female-based" household as the basic form of child-rearing unit and of the "serial monogamy" mating pattern as the primary form of marriage. The term "lower class culture" as used here refers most specifically to the way of life of the "hard core" group; systematic research in this area would probably reveal at least four to six major subtypes of lower class culture, for some of which the "concerns" presented here would be differently weighted, especially for those subtypes in which "law-abiding" behavior has a high overt valuation. It is impossible within the compass of this short paper to make the finer intracultural distinctions which a more accurate presentation would require.

weighted ranking of concerns. The "perceived alternatives" represent polar positions which define certain parameters within each dimension. As will be explained in more detail, it is necessary in relating the influence of these "concerns" to the motivation of delinquent behavior to specify *which* of its aspects is oriented to, whether orientation is *overt* or *covert*, *positive* (conforming to or seeking the aspect), or *negative* (rejecting or seeking to avoid the aspect).

The concept of "focal concern" is used here in preference to the concept "value" for several interrelated reasons: (1) It is more readily derivable from direct field observation. (2) It is descriptively neutral—permitting independent consideration of positive and negative valences as varying under different conditions, whereas "value" carries a built-in positive valence. (3) It makes possible more refined analysis of subcultural differences, since it reflects actual behavior, whereas "value" tends to wash out intracultural differences since it is colored by notions of the "official" ideal.

Trouble

Concern over "trouble" is a dominant feature of lower class culture. The concept has various shades of meaning; "trouble" in one of its aspects represents a situation or a kind of behavior which results in unwelcome or complicating involvement with official authorities or agencies of middle class society. "Getting into trouble" and "staying out of trouble" represent major issues for male and female, adults and children. For men, "trouble" frequently involves fighting or sexual adventures while drinking; for women, sexual involvement with disadvantageous consequences. Expressed desire to avoid behavior which violates moral or legal norms is often based less on an explicit commitment to "official" moral or legal standards than on a desire to avoid "getting into trouble," e.g., the complicating consequences of the action.

The dominant concern over "trouble" involves a distinction of critical importance for the lower class community—that between "law-abiding" and "non-law-abiding" behavior. There is a high degree of sensitivity as to where each person stands in relation to these two classes of activity. Whereas in the middle class community a major dimension for evaluating a person's status is "achievement" and its external symbols, in the lower class, personal status is very frequently gauged along the law-abiding–non-law-abiding dimension. A mother will evaluate the suitability of her daughter's boyfriend less on the basis of his achievement potential than on the basis of his innate "trouble" potential. This sensitive awareness of the opposition to "trouble-producing" and "non-trouble-producing" behavior represents both a major basis for deriving status distinctions, and an internalized conflict potential for the individual.

As in the case of other focal concerns, which of two perceived alternatives— "law-abiding" or "non-law-abiding"—is valued varies according to the individual and the circumstances; in many instances there is an overt commitment to the "law-abiding" alternative, but a covert commitment to the "non-law-abiding." In certain situations, "getting into trouble" is overtly recognized as prestige-conferring; for example, membership in certain adult and adolescent primary groupings ("gangs") is contingent on having demonstrated an explicit commitment to the law-violating alternative. It is most important to note that the choice between "law-abiding" and "non-law-abiding" behavior is still a choice *within* lower class culture; the distinction between the policeman and the criminal, the outlaw and the sheriff, involves primarily this one dimension; in other respects they have a high community of interests. Not infrequently brothers raised in an identical cultural milieu will become police and criminals respectively.

For a substantial segment of the lower class population "getting into trouble" is not in itself overtly defined as prestige-conferring, but is implicitly recognized as a means to other valued ends, e.g., the covertly valued desire to be "cared for" and subject to external constraint, or the overtly valued state of excitement or risk. Very frequently "getting into trouble" is multi-functional, and achieves several sets of valued ends.

Toughness

The concept of "toughness" in lower class culture represents a compound combination of qualities or states. Among its most important components are physical prowess, evidenced both by demonstrated possession of strength and endurance and athletic skill; "masculinity," symbolized by a distinctive complex of acts and avoidances (bodily tatooing; absence of sentimentality; non-concern with "art," "literature," conceptualization of women as conquest objects, etc.); and bravery in the face of physical threat. The model for the "tough guy"—hard, fearless, undemonstrative, skilled in physical combat—is represented by the movie gangster of the thirties, the "private eye," and the movie cowboy.

The genesis of the intense concern over "toughness" in lower class culture is probably related to the fact that a significant proportion of lower class males are reared in a predominantly female household, and lack a consistently present male figure with whom to identify and from whom to learn essential components of a "male" role. Since women serve as a primary object of identification during pre-adolescent years, the almost obsessive lower class concern with "masculinity" probably resembles a type of compulsive reaction-formation. A concern over homosexuality runs like a persistent thread through lower class culture. This is manifested by the institutionalized practice of baiting "queers," often accompanied by violent physical attacks, an expressed contempt for "softness" or frills, and the use of the local term for "homosexual" as a generalized pejorative epithet (e.g., higher class individuals or upwardly mobile peers are frequently characterized as "fags" or "queers"). The distinction between "overt" and "covert" orientation to aspects of an area of concern is especially important in regard to "toughness." A positive overt evaluation of behavior defined as "effeminate" would be out of the question for a lower class male; however, built into lower class culture is a range of devices which permit men to adopt behaviors and concerns which in other cultural milieux fall within the province of women, and at the same time to be defined as "tough" and manly. For example, lower class men can be professional short-order cooks in a diner and still be regarded as "tough." The highly intimate circumstances of the street corner gang involve the recurrent expression of strongly affectionate feelings towards other men. Such expressions, however, are disguised as their opposite, taking the form of ostensibly aggressive verbal and physical interaction (kidding, "ranking," roughhousing, etc.).

Smartness

"Smartness," as conceptualized in lower class culture, involves the capacity to outsmart, outfox, outwit, dupe, "take," "con" another or others, and the concomitant capacity to avoid being outwitted, "taken," or duped oneself. In its essence, smartness involves the capacity to achieve a valued entity—material goods, personal status—through a maximum use of mental agility and a minimum use of physical effort. This capacity has an extremely long tradition in lower class culture, and is highly valued. Lower class culture can be characterized as "non-intellectual" only if intellectualism is defined specifically in terms of control over a particular body of formally learned knowledge involving "culture" (art, literature, "good" music, etc.), a generalized perspective on the past and present, conditions of our own and other societies, and other areas of knowledge imparted by formal educational institutions. This particular type of mental attainment is, in general, overtly disvalued and frequently associated with effeminacy; "smartness" in the lower class sense, however, is highly valued.

The lower class child learns and practices the use of this skill in the street corner situation. Individuals continually practice duping and out-witting one another through recurrent card games and other forms of gambling, mutual exchanges of insults, and "testing" for mutual "con-ability." Those who demonstrate competence in this skill are accorded considerable prestige. Leadership roles in the corner group are frequently allocated according to demonstrated capacity in the two areas of "smartness" and "toughness"; the ideal leader combines both, but the "smart" leader is often accorded more prestige than the "tough" one—reflecting a general lower class respect for "brains" in the "smartness" sense.[4]

The model of the "smart" person is represented in popular media by the card shark, the professional gambler, the "con" artist, the promoter. A conceptual distinction is made between two kinds of people: "suckers," easy marks, "lushes," dupes, who work for their money and are legitimate targets of exploitation; and sharp operators, the "brainy" ones, who live by their wits and "getting" from the suckers by mental adroitness.

Involved in the syndrome of capacities related to "smartness" is a dominant emphasis in lower class culture on ingenious aggressive repartee. This skill, learned and practiced in the context of the corner group, ranges in form from

[4] The "brains-brawn" set of capacities are often paired in lower class folk lore or accounts of lower class life, e.g., "Brer Fox" and "Brer Bear" in the Uncle Remus stories, or George and Lennie in "Of Mice and Men."

the widely prevalent semi-ritualized teasing, kidding, razzing, "ranking," so characteristic of male peer group interaction, to the highly ritualized type of mutual insult interchange known as "the dirty dozens," "the dozens," "playing house," and other terms. This highly patterned cultural form is practiced on its most advanced level in adult male Negro society, but less polished variants are found throughout lower class culture—practiced, for example, by white children, male and female, as young as four or five. In essence, "doin' the dozens" involves two antagonists who vie with each other in the exchange of increasingly inflammatory insults, with incestuous and perverted sexual relations with the mother a dominant theme. In this form of insult interchange, as well as on other less ritualized occasions for joking, semi-serious, and serious mutual invective, a very high premium is placed on ingenuity, hair-trigger responsiveness, inventiveness, and the acute exercise of mental faculties.

Excitement

For many lower class individuals the rhythm of life fluctuates between periods of relatively routine or repetitive activity and sought situations of great emotional stimulation. Many of the most characteristic features of lower class life are related to the search for excitement or "thrill." Involved here are the highly prevalent use of alcohol by both sexes and the widespread use of gambling of all kinds— playing the numbers, betting on horse races, dice, cards. The quest for excitement finds what is perhaps its most vivid expression in the highly patterned practice of the recurrent "night on the town." This practice, designated by various terms in different areas ("honky-tonkin' "; "goin' out on the town"; "bar hoppin' "), involves a patterned set of activities in which alcohol, music, and sexual adventuring are major components. A group or individual sets out to "make the rounds" of various bars or night clubs. Drinking continues progressively throughout the evening. Men seek to "pick up" women, and women play the risky game of entertaining sexual advances. Fights between men involving women, gambling, and claims of physical prowess, in various combinations, are frequent consequences of a night of making the rounds. The explosive potential of this type of adventuring with sex and aggression, frequently leading to "trouble," is semi-explicitly sought by the individual. Since there is always a good likelihood that being out on the town will eventuate in fights, etc., the practice involves elements of sought risk and desired danger.

Counterbalancing the "flirting with danger" aspect of the "excitement" concern is the prevalence in lower class culture of other well established patterns of activity which involve long periods of relative inaction, or passivity. The term "hanging out" in lower class culture refers to extended periods of standing around, often with peer mates, doing what is defined as "nothing," "shooting the breeze," etc. A definite periodicity exists in the pattern of activity relating to the two aspects of the "excitement" dimension. For many lower class individuals the venture into the high risk world of alcohol, sex, and fighting occurs regularly once a week, with interim periods devoted to accommodating to possible consequences of these periods, along with recurrent resolves not to become so involved again.

Fate

Related to the quest for excitement is the concern with fate, fortune, or luck. Here also a distinction is made between two states—being "lucky" or "in luck," and being unlucky or jinxed. Many lower class individuals feel that their lives are subject to a set of forces over which they have relatively little control. These are not directly equated with the supernatural forces of formally organized religion, but relate more to a concept of "destiny," or man as a pawn of magical powers. Not infrequently this often implicit world view is associated with a conception of the ultimate futility of directed effort towards a goal: if the cards are right, or the dice good to you, or if your lucky number comes up, things will go your way; if luck is against you, it's not worth trying. The concept of performing semi-magical rituals so that one's "luck will change" is prevalent; one hopes that as a result he will move from the state of being "unlucky" to that of being "lucky." The element of fantasy plays an important part in this area. Related to and complementing the notion that "only suckers work" (Smartness) is the idea that once things start going your way, relatively independent of your own effort, all good things will come to you. Achieving great material rewards (big cars, big houses, a roll of cash to flash in a fancy night club), valued in lower class as well as in other parts of American culture, is a recurrent theme in lower class fantasy and folk lore; the cocaine dreams of Willie the Weeper or Minnie the Moocher present the components of this fantasy in vivid detail.

The prevalence in the lower class community of many forms of gambling, mentioned in connection with the "excitement" dimension, is also relevant here. Through cards and pool which involve skill, and thus both "toughness" and "smartness"; or through race horse betting, involving "smartness"; or through playing the numbers, involving predominantly "luck," one may make a big killing with a minimum of directed and persistent effort within conventional occupational channels. Gambling in its many forms illustrates the fact that many of the persistent features of lower class culture are multi-functional—serving a range of desired ends at the same time. Describing some of the incentives behind gambling has involved mention of all of the focal concerns cited so far—Toughness, Smartness, and Excitement, in addition to Fate.

Autonomy

The extent and nature of control over the behavior of the individual—an important concern in most cultures—has a special significance and is distinctively patterned in lower class culture. The discrepancy between what is overtly valued and what is covertly sought is particularly striking in this area. On the overt level there is a strong and frequently expressed resentment of the idea of external controls, restrictions on behavior, and unjust or coercive authority. "No one's gonna push *me* around," or "I'm gonna tell him he can take the job and shove it . . ." are commonly expressed sentiments. Similar explicit attitudes are maintained to systems of behavior-restricting rules, insofar as these are perceived as representing the injunctions, and bearing the sanctions of superordinate authority. In addition, in lower class culture a close conceptual connection is made between "authority" and "nurturance." To be restrictively or firmly controlled is to be cared for. Thus the overtly negative evaluation of superordinate authority frequently extends as well to nurturance, care, or protection. The desire for personal independence is often expressed in such terms as "I don't need *nobody* to take care of me. I can take care of myself!" Actual patterns of behavior, however reveal a marked discrepancy between expressed sentiment and what is covertly valued. Many lower class people appear to seek out highly restrictive social environments wherein stringent external controls are maintained over their behavior. Such institutions as the armed forces, the mental hospital, the disciplinary school, the prison or correctional institution, provide environments which incorporate a strict and detailed set of rules defining and limiting behavior, and enforced by an authority system which controls and applies coercive sanctions for deviance from these rules. While under the jurisdiction of such systems, the lower class person generally expresses to his peers continual resentment of the coercive, unjust, and arbitrary exercise of authority. Having been released, or having escaped from these milieux, however, he will often act in such a way as to insure recommitment, or choose recommitment voluntarily after a temporary period of "freedom."

Lower class patients in mental hospitals will exercise considerable ingenuity to insure continued commitment while voicing the desire to get out; delinquent boys will frequently "run" from a correctional institution to activate efforts to return them; to be caught and returned means that one is cared for. Since "being controlled" is equated with "being cared for," attempts are frequently made to "test" the severity or strictness of superordinate authority to see if it remains firm. If intended or executed rebellion produces swift and firm punitive sanctions, the individual is reassured, at the same time that he is complaining bitterly at the injustice of being caught and punished. Some environmental milieux, having been tested in this fashion for the "firmness" of their coercive sanctions, are rejected, ostensibly for being too strict, actually for not being strict enough. This is frequently so in the case of "problematic" behavior by lower class youngsters in the public schools, which generally cannot command the coercive controls implicitly sought by the individual.

A similar discrepancy between what is overtly and covertly desired is found in the area of dependence-independence. The pose of tough rebellious independence often assumed by the lower class person frequently conceals powerful dependency cravings. These are manifested primarily by obliquely expressed resentment when "care" is not forthcoming rather than by expressed satisfaction when it is. The concern over autonomy-dependency is related both to "trouble" and "fate." Insofar as the lower class individual feels that his behavior is controlled by forces which often propel him into "trouble" in the face of an explicit determination to avoid it, there is an implied appeal to "save me from myself." A solution appears to lie in arranging things so that his behavior will be coercively restricted by an externally imposed set of controls strong enough to forcibly restrain his inexplicable inclination to get in trouble. The periodicity observed in connection with the "excitement" dimension is also relevant here; after involvement in trouble-producing behavior (assault, sexual adventure, a "drunk"), the individual will actively seek a locus of imposed control (his wife, prison, a restrictive job); after a given period of subjection to this control, resentment against it mounts, leading to a "break away" and a search for involvement in further "trouble."

FOCAL CONCERNS OF THE LOWER CLASS
ADOLESCENT STREET CORNER GROUP

The one-sex peer group is a highly prevalent and significant structural form in the lower class community. There is a strong probability that the prevalence and stability of this type of unit is directly related to the prevalence of a stabilized type of lower class child-rearing unit—the "female-based" household. This is a nuclear kin unit in which a male parent is either absent from the household, present only sporadically, or, when present, only minimally or inconsistently involved in the support and rearing of children. This unit usually consists of one or more females of child-bearing age and their offspring. The females are frequently related to one another by blood or marriage ties, and the unit often includes two or more generations of women, e.g., the mother and/or aunt of the principal child-bearing female.

The nature of social groupings in the lower class community may be clarified if we make the assumption that it is the *one-sex peer unit* rather than the two-parent family unit which represents the most significant relational unit for both sexes in lower class communities. Lower class society may be pictured as comprising a set of age-graded one-sex groups which constitute the major psychic focus and reference group for those over twelve or thirteen. Men and women of mating age leave these groups periodically to form temporary marital alliances, but these lack stability, and after varying periods of "trying out" the two-sex family arrangement, gravitate back to the more "comfortable" one-sex grouping, whose members exert strong pressure on the individual *not* to disrupt the group by adopting a two-sex household pattern of life.[5] Membership in a stable and solidary peer unit is vital to the lower class individual precisely to the extent to

---

[5] Further data on the female-based household unit (estimated as comprising about 15 per cent of all American "families") and the role of one-sex groupings in lower class culture are contained in Walter B. Miller, "Implications of Urban Lower Class Culture for Social Work," *Social Service Review*, 1959, 33, No. 3.

which a range of essential functions—psychological, educational, and others, are not provided by the "family" unit.

The adolescent street corner group represents the adolescent variant of this lower class structural form. What has been called the "delinquent gang" is one subtype of this form, defined on the basis of frequency of participation in law-violating activity; this subtype should not be considered a legitimate unit of study per se, but rather as one particular variant of the adolescent street corner group. The "hanging" peer group is a unit of particular importance for the adolescent male. In many cases it is the most stable and solidary primary group he has ever belonged to; for boys reared in female-based households the corner group provides the first real opportunity to learn essential aspects of the male role in the context of peers facing similar problems of sex-role identification.

The form and functions of the adolescent corner group operate as a selective mechanism in recruiting members. The activity patterns of the group require a high level of intra-group solidarity; individual members must possess a good capacity for subordinating individual desires to general group interests as well as the capacity for intimate and persisting interaction. Thus highly "disturbed" individuals, or those who cannot tolerate consistently imposed sanctions on "deviant" behavior cannot remain accepted members; the group itself will extrude those whose behavior exceeds limits defined as "normal." This selective process produces a type of group whose members possess to an unusually high degree both the *capacity* and *motivation* to conform to perceived cultural norms, so that the nature of the system of norms and values oriented to is a particularly influential component of motivation.

Focal concerns of the male adolescent corner group are those of the general cultural milieu in which it functions. As would be expected, the relative weighting and importance of these concerns pattern somewhat differently for adolescents than for adults. The nature of this patterning centers around two additional "concerns" of particular importance to this group—concern with "belonging," and with "status." These may be conceptualized as being on a higher level of abstraction than concerns previously cited, since "status" and "belonging" are achieved *via* cited concern areas of Toughness, etc.

Belonging

Since the corner group fulfills essential functions for the individual, being a member in good standing of the group is of vital importance for its members. A continuing concern over who is "in" and who is not involves the citation and detailed discussion of highly refined criteria for "in-group" membership. The phrase "he hangs with us" means "he is accepted as a member in good standing by current consensus"; conversely, "he don't hang with us" means he is not so accepted. One achieves "belonging" primarily by demonstrating knowledge of and a determination to adhere to the system of standards and valued qualities defined by the group. One maintains membership by acting in conformity with valued aspects of Toughness, Smartness, Autonomy, etc. In those instances where conforming to norms of this reference group at the same time violates norms of other reference groups (e.g., middle class adults, institutional "officials"), immediate reference group norms are much more compelling since violation risks invoking the group's most powerful sanction: exclusion.

Status

In common with most adolescents in American society, the lower class corner group manifests a dominant concern with "status." What differentiates this type of group from others, however, is the particular set of criteria and weighting thereof by which "status" is defined. In general, status is achieved and maintained by demonstrated possession of the valued qualities of lower class culture—Toughness, Smartness, expressed resistance to authority, daring, etc. It is important to stress once more that the individual orients to these concerns *as they are defined within lower class society*; e.g., the status-conferring potential of "smartness" in the sense of scholastic achievement generally ranges from negligible to negative.

The concern with "status" is manifested in a variety of ways. Intragroup status is a continued concern, and is derived and tested constantly by means of a set of status-ranking activities; the intra-group "pecking order" is constantly at issue. One gains status within the group by demonstrated superiority in Toughness (physical prowess, bravery, skill in athletics and games such as pool and cards), Smartness (skill in repartee, capacity to "dupe" fellow group members), and the like. The term "ranking," used to refer to the pattern of intra-group aggressive repartee, indicates awareness of the fact that this is one device for establishing the intra-group status hierarchy.

The concern over status in the adolescent corner group involves in particular the component of "adultness," the intense desire to be seen as "grown up," and a corresponding aversion to "kid stuff." "Adult" status is defined less in terms of the assumption of "adult" responsibility than in terms of certain external symbols of adult status—a car, ready cash, and, in particular, a perceived "freedom" to drink, smoke, and gamble as one wishes and to come and go without external restrictions. The desire to be seen as "adult" is often a more significant component of much involvement in illegal drinking, gambling, and automobile driving than the explicit enjoyment of these acts as such.

The intensity of the corner group member's desire to be seen as "adult" is sufficiently great that he feels called upon to demonstrate qualities associated with adultness (Toughness, Smartness, Autonomy) to a much greater degree than a lower class adult. This means that he will seek out and utilize those avenues to these qualities which he perceives as available with greater intensity than an adult and less regard for their "legitimacy." In this sense the adolescent variant of lower class culture represents a maximization or an intensified manifestation of many of its most characteristic features.

Concern over status is also manifested in reference to other street corner groups. The term "rep" used in this regard is especially significant, and has broad connotations. In its most frequent and explicit connotation, "rep" refers to the "toughness" of the corner group as a whole relative to that of other groups; a "pecking order" also exists among the several corner groups in a given interactional area, and there is a common perception that the safety or security of the group and all its members depends on maintaining a solid "rep" for toughness vis-a-vis other groups. This motive is most frequently advanced as a reason for involvement in gang fights: "We *can't* chicken out on this fight; our rep would be shot!"; this implies that the group would be relegated to the bottom of the status ladder and become a helpless and recurrent target of external attack.

On the other hand, there is implicit in the concept of "rep" the recognition that "rep" has or may have a dual basis—corresponding to the two aspects of the "trouble" dimension. It is recognized that group as well as individual status can be based on both "law-abiding" and "law-violating" behavior. The situational resolution of the persisting conflict between the "law-abiding" and "law-violating" bases of status comprises a vital set of dynamics in determining whether a "delinquent" mode of behavior will be adopted by a group, under what circumstances, and how persistently. The determinants of this choice are evidently highly complex and fluid, and rest on a range of factors including the presence and perceptual immediacy of different community reference-group loci (e.g., professional criminals, police, clergy, teachers, settlement house workers), the personality structures and "needs" of group members, the presence in the community of social work, recreation, or educational programs which can facilitate utilization of the "law-abiding" basis of status, and so on.

What remains constant is the critical importance of "status" both for the members of the group as individuals and for the group as a whole insofar as members perceive their individual destinies as linked to the destiny of the group, and the fact that action geared to attain status is much more acutely oriented to the fact of status itself than to the legality or illegality, morality or immorality of the means used to achieve it.

LOWER CLASS CULTURE AND
THE MOTIVATION OF DELINQUENT BEHAVIOR

The customary set of activities of the adolescent street corner group includes activities which are in violation of laws and ordinances of the legal code. Most of these center around assault and theft of various types (the gang fight; auto theft; assault on an individual; petty pilfering and shoplifting; "mugging"; pocketbook theft). Members of street corner gangs are well aware of the law-violating nature of these acts; they are not psychopaths, nor physical or mental "defectives"; in fact, since the corner group supports and enforces a rigorous set of standards which demand a high degree of fitness and personal competence, it tends to recruit from the most "able" members of the community.

Why, then, is the commission of crimes a customary feature of gang activity? The most general answer is that the commission of crimes by members of adolescent street corner groups is motivated primarily by the attempt to achieve ends, states, or conditions which are valued, and to avoid those that are disvalued within their most meaningful cultural milieu, through those culturally available avenues which appear as the most feasible means of attaining those ends.

The operation of these influences is well illustrated by the gang fight—a prevalent and characteristic type of corner group delinquency. This type of activity comprises a highly stylized and culturally patterned set of sequences. Although details vary under different circumstances, the following events are generally included. A member or several members of group A "trespass" on the claimed territory of group B. While there they commit an act or acts which group B defines as a violation of its rightful privileges, an affront to their honor, or a challenge to the "rep." Frequently this act involves advances to a girl associated with group B; it may occur at a dance or party; sometimes the mere act of "trespass" is seen as deliberate provocation. Members of group B then assault members of group A, if they are caught while still in B's territory. Assaulted members of group A return to their "home" territory and recount to members of their group details of the incident, stressing the insufficient nature of the provocation ("I just *looked* at her! Hardly even said anything!"), and the unfair circumstances of the assault ("About *twenty* guys jumped just the *two* of us!"). The highly colored account is acutely inflammatory; group A, perceiving its honor violated and its "rep" threatened, feels obligated to retaliate in force. Sessions of detailed planning now occur; allies are recruited if the size of group A and its potential allies appears to necessitate larger numbers; strategy is plotted, and messengers dispatched. Since the prospect of a gang fight is frightening to even the "toughest" group members, a constant rehearsal of the provocative incident or incidents and the essentially evil nature of the opponents accompanies the planning process to bolster possibly weakening motivation to fight. The excursion into "enemy" territory sometimes results in a full scale fight; more often group B cannot be found, or the police appear and stop the fight, "tipped off" by an anonymous informant. When this occurs, group members express disgust and disappointment; secretly there is much relief; their honor has been avenged without incurring injury; often the anonymous tipster is a member of one of the involved groups.

The basic elements of this type of delinquency are sufficiently stabilized and recurrent as to constitute an essentially ritualized pattern, resembling both in structure and expressed motives for action classic forms such as the European "duel," the American Indian tribal war, and the Celtic clan feud. Although the arousing and "acting out" of individual aggressive emotions are inevitably involved in the gang fight, neither its form nor motivational dynamics can be adequately handled within a predominantly personality-focused frame of reference.

It would be possible to develop in considerable detail the processes by which the commission of a range of illegal acts is either explicitly supported by, implicitly demanded by, or not materially inhibited by factors relating to the focal concerns of lower class culture. In place of such a development, the following three statements condense in general terms the operation of these processes:

(1) Following cultural practices which comprise essential elements of the total life pattern of lower class culture automatically violates certain legal norms.

(2) In instances where alternate avenues to similar objectives are available, the non-law-abiding avenue frequently provides a relatively greater and more immediate return for a relatively smaller investment of energy.

(3) The "demanded" response to certain situations recurrently engendered within lower class culture involves the commission of illegal acts.

The primary thesis of this paper is that the dominant component of the motivation of "delinquent" behavior engaged in by members of lower class corner groups involves a positive effort to achieve states, conditions, or qualities valued within the actor's most significant cultural milieu. If "conformity to immediate reference group values" is the major component of motivation of "delinquent" behavior by gang members, why is such behavior frequently referred to as negativistic, malicious, or rebellious? Albert Cohen, for example, in *Delinquent Boys* (Glencoe: Free Press, 1955) describes behavior which violates school rules as comprising elements of "active spite and malice, contempt and ridicule, challenge and defiance." He ascribes to the gang "keen delight in terrorizing 'good' children, and in general making themselves obnoxious to the virtuous." A recent national conference on social work with "hard-to-reach" groups characterized lower class corner groups as "youth groups in conflict with the culture of their [sic] communities." Such characterizations are obviously the result of taking the middle class community and its institutions as an implicit point of reference.

A large body of systematically interrelated attitudes, practices, behaviors, and values characteristic of lower class culture are designed to support and maintain the basic features of the lower class way of life. In areas where these differ from features of middle class culture, action oriented to the achievement and maintenance of the lower class system may violate norms of middle class culture and be perceived as deliberately non-conforming or malicious by an observer strongly cathected to middle class norms. This does not mean, however, that violation of the middle class norm is the dominant component of motivation; it is a by-product of action primarily oriented to the lower class system. The standards of lower class culture cannot be seen merely as a reverse function of middle class culture—as middle class standards "turned upside down"; lower class culture is a distinctive tradition many centuries old with an integrity of its own.

From the viewpoint of the acting individual, functioning within a field of well-structured cultural forces, the relative impact of "conforming" and "rejective" elements in the motivation of gang delinquency is weighted preponderantly on the conforming side. Rejective or rebellious elements are inevitably involved, but their influence during the actual commission of delinquent acts is relatively small compared to the influence of pressures to achieve what is valued by the actor's most immediate reference groups. Expressed awareness by the actor of the element of rebellion often represents only that aspect of motivation of which he is explicitly conscious; the deepest and most compelling components of motivation—adherence to highly meaningful group standards of Toughness, Smartness, Excitement, etc.—are often unconsciously patterned. No cultural pattern as well-established as the practice of illegal acts by members of lower class corner groups could persist if buttressed primarily by negative, hostile, or rejective motives; its principal motivational support, as in the case of any persisting cultural tradition, derives from a positive effort to achieve what is valued within that tradition, and to conform to its explicit and implicit norms.

This article reports on one of many federally sponsored, privately administered programs currently being conducted with disadvantaged youth throughout the country. The authors describe a two-pronged educational model that was used in a residential setting to develop motivation to learn, among a group of alienated youth. The role of intensive group counseling and the evolution of a democratic student government are outlined.

Yitzhak Bakal, William Madaus and Alvin E. Winder

A Motivational Approach to Compensatory Education[1]

The area of compensatory education is generally thought of as furthering the equality of educational achievement so that educationally disadvantaged youngsters can use this means to move into the mainstream of American society. The need for compensatory education for the children of the poor is adequately documented by the Zacharias Panel on Educational Research and Development:

> By all known criteria, the majority of urban and rural slum schools are failures. In neighborhood after neighborhood across the country more than half of each age group fails to complete high school, and 5 per cent or fewer go on to some form of higher

[1] A partial report on an Upward Bound Project at the University of Massachusetts, Amherst, Massachusetts.

education. In many schools the average measured IQ is under 85, and it drops steadily as the children grow older. Adolescents depart from these schools ill-prepared to lead a satisfying, useful life or to participate successfully in the community.[2]

Gordon has identified eight approaches found in a wide variety of current programs. These are the development of new reading and language teaching methods, curriculum innovations with the dual aim of individualizing instruction and increasing the relevance of classroom materials, extracurricular innovations involving extending the school's influence into non-school time, parental involvement, community involvement, special techniques of teacher recruitment and training, guidance and counseling, and the development and utilization of special personnel for working with the culturally disadvantaged.[3] All of these approaches, with the exception of counseling and guidance, have environmental manipulation as their principal method of encouraging the student to participate in the learning process. The counseling approach is unique in that it has as its principal assumption that the student traumatized by his previous educational experience has responded with reactive stupidity, rigidity, and anti-social behavior. The counseling situation is so designed that he can make use of the protective sanction of an understanding adult to work through his intense feelings from which he is protecting himself either by assuming a stance of defensive stupidity or by turning away from an educational experience. Only then will his natural curiosity motivate him towards learning. Counseling, as used here, signifies a number of direct contacts with the client with the aim both of making him aware of, and of offering him assistance in, changing his attitudes and behavior. This view of counseling, current in some educational circles, was also felt to be broad enough to reflect a concept of behavioral change found in other helping disciplines.

This paper emphasizes the counseling approach because it believes that an understanding of motivation is a key that can bring about changes in human behavior. While the concept of intrinsic motivation has not been central in educational circles, those who have come to education from the mental health field, Redl and Wattenberg,[4] Anna Freud,[5] and A. S. Neill,[6] have applied this concept successfully to education.

It is indeed in the field of residential treatment that mental health concepts of motivation have made significant contributions to education in a residential setting (see Bettelheim,[7] Redl, et al.[8]).

[2] J. Zacharias, "Innovation and Experiment in Education," A progress report of the Panel of Educational Research and Development, U.S. Government Printing Office, Washington, D.C.
[3] Edmund W. Gordon, "Programs of Compensatory Education," *American Journal of Orthopsychiatry*, Vol. 25, No. 4 (July 1965), pp. 640–650.
[4] Fritz Redl and William Wattenberg, *Mental Hygiene in Teaching*, New York: Harcourt, Brace & World, Inc., 1951.
[5] Anna Freud, *Psychoanalysis for Teachers and Parents*, Boston: Beacon Press, 1960.
[6] A. S. Neill, *Summerhill*, New York: Hart Publishing Company, 1960.
[7] Bruno Bettelheim, *Love Is Not Enough*, Glencoe Illinois: Free Press, 1950.
[8] Fritz Redl and William Wattenberg, *Mental Hygiene in Teaching*, New York: Harcourt, Brace & World, Inc. 1951.

The present paper is based upon a summer's experience with an Upward Bound Project at the University of Massachusetts in Amherst and is concerned with that aspect of the program that enhanced student motivation. Students did meet daily in small classes to study mathematics, English, and social studies. The academic side of the program will be referred to in this paper only as it has direct bearing on motivational aspects of the program.

THE PROJECT

The Upward Bound Project is composed of a student body of approximately one hundred ninth and tenth grade students, the majority of whom possess above average mental ability but for a variety of reasons have achieved limited school success. The students come from a low socio-economic background, have low educational aspirations, and, in spite of their good scholastic potential, most have experienced failure in school. A high percentage (22%) of the students come from fatherless homes, and 45% of the families are welfare recipients. Thus, these students have suffered not only monetary but also psychological deprivation. Illness due to insufficient medical attention, deaths, reports of alcoholism, and marital difficulties, as well as physical wants, are present in many of their home situations.

SOME BASIC ASSUMPTIONS
CONCERNING THE STUDENT POPULATION

The primary purpose of the counseling component is to increase realistically the student's level of aspiration and to motivate him for educational goals, and by accomplishing this purpose to make it possible for him to utilize the classroom and curriculum to develop increased competence and skills in the areas of English, mathematics, and social studies. There are three problematic areas that have to be handled effectively in order to produce meaningful attitudinal changes towards education. They are:

(1) The student's negative attitude towards authority and his consequent alienation. This alienation results both from the student's feeling of estrangement from the educational goals of the school and from his sense of having no promise of a tangible career involving an educational commitment.

(2) The student's low capacity for verbalization and self-expression.

(3) The student's lack of role models for educational goals.

It has been briefly shown that most of these students experienced traumatic home situations. Their first encounters with authority were mainly ones of either rejection or punishment, or both. Authority, therefore, was perceived by these individuals in a negative sense, and the neighborhood culture continually reinforced this negative attitude. This culture views all accepted authority figures as middle-class agents whose main goals are to subjugate and deprive those who are less fortunate in this respect.

It became apparent from our contact with some of the students that their distrust and fear of authority brought about the following types of behavior: either total compliance, or overt and aggressive acting out. Consequently, the students were either timid, submissive, and withdrawn or they were hostile, defiant, and aggressive. These feelings towards authority which were manifest in the two types of behavior did not permit the students to function effectively in the public schools. The public school system is a middle-class institution. Its classroom size and its inflexible curriculum tend to make it a highly structured authoritarian establishment. Therefore, the public schools increased the students' feelings of alienation. They remained on the periphery, almost completely cut off from the school culture. For these reasons they rejected traditional public school education with its middle-class values and authoritarian postures.

These students confirm the research and speculations of others that individuals from low socio-economic backgrounds have limited powers of verbalization.[9, 10] Because of this deficiency in verbalization, they have a strong tendency to act, and they do so rather than talk. Their capacity to verbalize and express strong feelings, such as anger, is limited. This deficiency stems not only from their attitude towards authority, but is also due to the social, economic, and educational deprivation they have suffered. They have seldom been provided with an educational experience that allowed them to express freely their feelings and opinions. Since they cannot talk out their feelings, they act them out in a detrimental way. They become truant, cut classes, join gangs, or indulge in other delinquent forms of behavior. Their purpose is to avenge or to get even with society.

Students from low socio-economic backgrounds, engaged as they are in a constant struggle, are frequently not committed to educational goals. They are committed, instead, to a "cult of immediacy," a daily attempt to meet basic needs—and in some cases this involves a desperate struggle for survival. The opportunity to bridge the gap between the "cult of immediacy" and the longer term educational goals through knowing people committed to education is usually denied them, for there is usually in their environment a paucity of such individuals with whom they could identify. Because many of the Upward Bound students in this program came from very large families (50% came from families of five or more dependents), their parents—even if they appreciate education—had little time to invest in their children's learning. Consequently, the useless-

[9] Kenneth B. Clark, "Educational Stimulation of Racially Disadvantaged Children," *Education in Depressed Areas*, A. Henry Passow (ed.), New York Bureau of Publications, Teachers College, Columbia University, 1963.

[10] Robert J. Havighurst and Lindley J. Stiles, "A Statement of National Policy for Alienated Youth," *Phi Delta Kappan*, April 1961.

ness and unimportance of education was communicated to the child. This served to decrease his motivation to learn and to decrease his aspirations for educational goals. Even though a majority of the students expressed interest in a college education, it became apparent that their ideas about colleges and how to gain admission to one were extremely vague.

STRUCTURE

In order to create within the student meaningful attitudinal changes towards education three major forms of organization were built into the structure of the counseling part of the program. They were the student government, the committee for evaluation of dismissal, and the group counseling.

The Student Government

The first of these organizations was the student government. The idea of self-government was presented to the students early in the program, but it was adopted only after positive student reaction was evident. There were no preconceived plans or rigid guidelines. The students were allowed to assume the responsibility for their own student council, and counselors merely responded to their initiative. The responsibility, powers, and duties of the student council were established through the students' frank discussion with the administration. The administration included the director of the Program, the assistant director, and the head counselor; all other counselors and teachers were considered staff. In general, they were given the authority to exercise broad power in almost every area of the program, except that which was strictly academic. Counselors encouraged mutual involvement where both administration and student body could raise issues of mutual concern. The students, however, after evaluating the counselors' opinions, were free to make the final decisions themselves.

In order to secure a better overall representation, the following mechanism was developed. Twelve student representatives were elected through dormitory elections. Two resident counselors out of the twelve in the program were elected by the students to the council. The head counselor, who represented the administration, was present at council meetings. Since he was not a voting member, only two votes out of fourteen represented the staff. As a result of this pattern of representation, the student council was run mainly by the students, with the administration acting in an advisory capacity. The first issue undertaken by the student council involved extension of the curfew one half-hour on week-days and one additional hour on weekends. This seemed to students to be a real test of the counselors' resolve to give them genuine decision-making responsibility. Although there was some initial administrative opposition to the merits of extending the curfew, it was realized that the more important question was whether or not counselors could assign students this type of responsibility and still abide by their decisions.

Reassurance on the part of students that the staff was sincere in letting them have this authority opened the way for full cooperation based on mutual trust between the student council and the administration. The student council fully assumed the responsibility in the area of discipline, contributed to the area of recreational activity, and worked to increase the individuals' commitment to both learning and the goals of the program. The student council also assumed the responsibility of public relations. Student representatives showed the ability to explain both their commitment to the program and the program's functioning to a Community Action group. It should be emphasized that the student government was autonomous and functioned with little direction. This fact increased its initiative. But students' acceptance of the council's authority did not evolve easily. There was initial resentment on the part of the student body at accepting the discipline that was meted out by peers. As one student said, "I resent the fact that I have to be judged by my friends." However, when the student body observed that counselors were supporting their opinions and backing their decisions, they began to accept the idea of student authority.

The fact that the staff conveyed the idea that they had full confidence in the council's decisions greatly increased the prestige of the council. However, in the beginning, not all staff members supported the idea of self-government by the students. Initially there were ambivalent feelings about giving the students genuine authority. Questions were raised both about the ability of the students to make sound judgments and about whether they possessed enough maturity to assume responsibility for these judgments. There was also some unrealistic fear that the student government might take over and leave the staff powerless. These ambivalent feelings surfaced whenever the staff was confronted with a major crisis that involved the acting out of students. At critical times such as these, some of the staff felt that the administration should take back the control and power that they had delegated to the students.

The continuous support of the council by the administration, however, produced a change in attitude towards the council by many members of the staff, notably the resident counselors, and this change was towards the acceptance of the student council's authority. This resulted in the student council emerging as an asset to the entire student body and had the effect of producing a close identification between the students and the goals of the program.

The Committee for Evaluation of Dismissal

The second mechanism which provided for the growth of responsible behavior in the students was the creation of a staff committee for evaluation of students for whom dismissal had been suggested. There were several factors which contributed to the idea that a staff committee for dismissal was necessary, and its prudent utilization as an aid to the program was essential. The first factor in this decision was that there were no effective criteria for dismissal. The second factor was the students' fear that the staff or administration might act impulsively without a thorough evaluation. The third factor was an attempt to involve the staff in administrative decisions. Four members of the staff—a teacher, a group counselor, and two resident counselors—volunteered to assume this responsibility. A teacher was chosen as the chairman. In the five weeks that the committee functioned, eleven students were brought before it. In most cases their appearance before the committee produced a change in attitude which made it unnecessary for the committee to see the student a second time. In only one case did the committee concur on a need for dismissal, but even in this case the student and his parents had the option to initiate action to have him reinstated. Thus, the committee functioned primarily to raise motivation rather than to dismiss. The committee evaluated several aspects of each student's behavior: his learning, his classroom attendance and participation, his relations with peers, and his feeling towards authority. However, the primary concern in evaluating him was whether he had real commitment to the program and to its educational goals.

One brief example of the manner in which the staff committee functioned might give a better insight into why it was an important component of the program. One of the resident counselors referred a student to the committee. The boy continually missed classes and refused to complete homework, and his relations with his peers were deteriorating. When the boy was brought before the committee it was discovered that he actually hoped that he would be dismissed from the program. The expectation of punishment was the boy's own self-punishment. Instead of acting on his need to be rejected, the committee did the opposite and firmly told him that they could not allow him to run away. When the boy found that the committee was not going to reject him, he talked readily. He stated that many of his peers had turned against him and he felt that even many of his teachers were disinterested with his progress in the program. The counseling staff believed that underlying his behavior was a sense of guilt caused by his feeling of responsibility for the death of a relative. He sought the help of one of the counselors in the program. For the last week of the program his educational output increased, and he had begun to work through those problems that had been retarding his educational growth.

Group Counseling

The group counseling was conceived as having as a major goal the creation of an atmosphere in which the members would feel free to express their conflicting attitudes over the selecting or rejecting of an educational future. By this expression, we refer to the process of intercommunication between the group members themselves and the group leader, about problems arising from this conflict. The role of the group counselor was to facilitate this communication within the group through his shared interaction with them. Through this process, it was felt, a major part of students' conflicts could be resolved, and attitudinal changes could be brought about. When the repeated communication of specific problems dominated many sessions, they were referred to as group themes.

Another purpose of group counseling was to provide a setting in which the students could work through their alienation to school and their feelings towards authority. The group counselor, as an authority figure, was consciously and unconsciously perceived by the students as a representative of society, that is, a teacher, a school system, or a parent. The group served as an arena where transference relationships to the group counselor, resident counselor, or other group members were formed. The permissive atmosphere of the group encouraged the expression of feelings and allowed the students, through their expression, to work through their problems. The group counselor was an individual who could deal with a hostile group without becoming angry. He could deal with strong feelings without being threatened, and he could control the group without punishment. For all the students this was probably a unique experience, and it facilitated the working through of feelings of alienation and attitudes towards authority.

The groups were composed of eleven students, usually seven boys and four girls. The fact that both boys and girls were present during group counseling was a great aid to the therapeutic process that was taking place. A resident counselor who acted as an observer or recorder was also present. The students attended group counseling four times a week for fifty minutes. The administration decided to make attendance at group counseling compulsory in order to control the acting out of students by providing a setting in which the verbalization of strong feelings could take place. It was found, however, after approximately one week of group counseling that mandatory attendance was probably not necessary. When good group solidarity was formed and the students began talking about themselves in a confidential setting, attendance was not a problem. When the initial silences caused by the unstructured setting of group counseling had been overcome, the group exerted control over individual members. For example, tardy or absent members were confronted with this behavior and asked to explain it to members of their group. There was not one case of chronic absenteeism in any of the groups.

Several themes were dealt with during the program. The students' sense of alienation assumed several interesting symbolic forms and shapes during the life of the group. Initially, these feelings of alienation were expressed by the groups' questioning the group counselors' feelings and attitudes about them. Feelings were also expressed in symbolic discussions of backward and underdeveloped nations. The students seemed to be asking the counselors, "Are we backward?" "Are we really hopeless?" The counselors' acceptance of their feelings gave the students reassurance that they were not backward and that the staff attached much worth and importance to them.

Later, when the same theme of poverty programs or disadvantaged youngsters reappeared, the group members expressed very strong feelings. The counselor viewed this as progress because the group members were now struggling against and defying the low self-esteem which they felt accompanied their status as disadvantaged youth. The theme of alienation appeared again when they discussed school systems. In the initial sessions these feelings were expressed in statements of hopelessness and frustration. In later sessions, they were able to handle their problem more constructively through challenges and criticisms of the program and the schools. These criticisms stemmed not from feelings of alienation, but from a real desire to belong.

The subject of sex was another theme which was discussed in all groups. In many of the discussions the student's need to assert himself sexually was evident. Every time the boys were challenged by the girls they showed a real desire to assert their masculinity, which took many forms. One way of asserting themselves was the occasional use of obscenities. Another was by relating their past experience with the opposite sex, with alcohol, gangs, or other masculine activities in which they had engaged.

They also made remarks calculated to embarrass the mother-figure of the group, the resident counselor. It became evident that girls in the group were demanding that the boys assume a responsible masculine role. The boys responded at first by acting out a pseudo-masculinity (aggression against smaller boys, and obscenities). This attitude of pseudo-masculinity was definitely linked in the boys' minds with their attitudes towards the school and education. For example, it was considered masculine to reject studying, to engage in conflict with school authorities, to derogate teachers, and to create disturbances in the educational institution. At this point, the counselors were able to confront the group with this pseudo-masculinity, thus supporting the girls' demands that the boys assume responsible masculine behavior. Much progress was evident in this area. This theme was effectively handled within the groups.

In addition, counselors encouraged the students to bring the subject of sex to the group and discuss it freely. This free discussion greatly limited any sexual acting out that might have taken place if the group counseling component had been absent from the program. There was, in fact, little, if any, sexual acting out during the eight weeks. Instead, the staff witnessed normal, healthy relationships between sexes that increased student commitment towards the program's educational objectives. The presence of members of both sexes seemed an important factor in motivating the students for both increased study and behavioral change. Dramatic changes in many students' performance and behavior were witnessed when they started to date, while before dating these students had been hostile and uninvolved.

Another theme that was handled frequently within the groups was the students' relationships with parents and siblings. Initially, this theme was presented by the students in a way that minimized their needs for parents. Since the student population was adolescent, the group found this a common ground, and each individual received mutual support whenever the question of parental relations was brought up. They were able to learn from the related experiences of other group members that their problems and difficulties with parents were certainly not unique. Like all adolescents, they were seeking independence but they were constantly struggling with different methods of freeing themselves.

They came to realize that they resembled one another in their need to be independent, and the group feeling they experienced gave them this opportunity. The communication of this theme led to feelings of increased independence on the part of the group; the members became increasingly sure of the uniqueness of their own self-definitions. They began to see themselves as individuals who could commit themselves to learning as a means of furthering their own future occupational identities. As has been stated, many of these students came from extremely difficult home backgrounds. These home conditions were frequently taken up in group counseling, and the free discussion of these problems gave the students a better capacity to verbalize their feelings as well as some temporary relief from their home situations.

Although the focus during group counseling was on the group as a whole, and though there was not sufficient opportunity to explore individual problems, many of the latter found their way into group discussion. The confidential highly personal problems to the group. Two examples will illustrate how individual problems were handled in group counseling. The first concerns a seventeen-year-old Negro student who was the second of eight children and who came from a slum area. In his home environment he was active with several of his brothers in a neighborhood gang. While he was in the program, his elder brother was stabbed and killed by a rival gang. Although this student refrained from talking about this event, the group counselor brought the topic up for discussion and the boy was encouraged to talk about it. The group empathized with him when he related the manner in which his brother was killed, and fears concerning the act were expressed by the group. Some of the group members were concerned about their inability to prevent a similar occurrence and this made them more keenly aware of death. They expressed disappointment in authority, the police, who could not prevent this type of tragic occurrence. When the student expressed the need to take revenge, he was sitting tensely in the group, opening and closing a large knife. The group members expressed concern for both him and his future because of his determination to carry out an act of vengeance. The group was able to handle his feelings and thus calm his fears of his own destructive impulses. Much affect was expressed by the student, and at the end of the session he confided to his resident counselor that he was glad to be able to bring this problem to the group. He did not act upon his plan for vengeance. Instead, the staff saw him grow and become more committed to the program. This discussion had its benefits for the whole group as well; their handling of the boy's anger further strengthened their sense of being capable and independent.

Another example of individual help concerned a sixteen-year-old student who was an extremely shy, withdrawn individual who never participated in group counseling. He came from a background of extreme poverty. His mother was a possessive, strict, and domineering woman who made him feel that his opinions were useless and unimportant. In one session the group was discussing their home situations and asked the student to explain some of his experiences at home. The student replied, "You really wouldn't be interested." The group counselor used his authority to reassure him that his opinions were worthwhile. The student responded and received group encouragement and support. This helped greatly to enhance the student's self-esteem. His increased self-esteem and capacity to verbalize carried over into the academic area, where this student became far more interested and responsive.

As has been emphasized, the main objectives of the group counseling were to work through the students' feelings of alienation and their negative attitudes towards authority, and to increase their sense of self-definition. A great deal of progress was achieved in these areas. The breakdown in their feelings of alienation gave students an impetus to explore relationships in many areas that had educational significance. An example is the interracial project developed through the students' initiative and carried out with the assistance of a social studies teacher. No longer fully alienated, the students were able to ask themselves important questions about racial prejudice, such as the nature of the relationship between themselves and the adult world within the context of an interracial situation. The students decided that they would send out prearranged mixed couples, Negroes and whites, into the local communities. These mixed couples visited stores and other public places while other individuals in the project acted as observers. The students were able to observe the apparent as well as subtle revelations of prejudice, and this caused them to become more keenly aware of its existence. It also brought them closer to one another in their willingness to combat these attitudes. As one of the students said, "This project proved that Negroes and whites can fight together for one cause. The cause is equal rights for all." This project was successfully carried out by the students and the staff and thus helped to form a closer bond between the student body and the teaching staff.

As a result of the lessening of feelings of alienation, the students were able to explore relationships of a cooperative nature with the University personnel. The students heard that some University personnel not connected with Upward Bound needed assistance in the construction of a building to house an art exhibit. They volunteered their services, and almost forty students were involved in the construction work during their leisure time: an exciting by-product of the students' activity.

SUMMARY

This program was initiated in order to offer a group of disadvantaged teenagers an experience in compensatory education with the objective of preparing them for college. The summer residential program described and analyzed in this paper had as its objective creating the attitudinal and motivational change that must occur if these youngsters are to commit themselves to learning academic skills. Self-regulation is the key principle that underlies all the activity of this program. The major objective of the staff was to provide both a structure and an emotional climate in order to communicate to the students that the two most important things that adults can give teenagers are freedom and care.

Three major aspects of the structure of the program geared to provide this sense of freedom and care were the student government, the committee for evaluation and dismissal, and the group counseling.

That an atmosphere encouraging freedom led the youngsters to cultivate self-regulation is seen by the way they were able to ask important questions within the framework of classes and an academic curriculum. The project on prejudice initiated by the students within the social studies curriculum is an excellent example of this point.

The encouraging response of the students to the summer residential program suggests that this approach to compensatory education has a bearing on certain larger issues in the field. First, this program, by placing the students on a university campus, removed them from the stigma of poverty that is part of their life in their home communities. Secondly, the students were not asked to passively accept society's educational goals as represented to them by their public schools; rather, they were encouraged to actively explore both these goals and the possibilities of making their own choices. Thirdly, this was an interracial program where the contacts between youngsters were based upon their having equal status in the program. Fourth, the contacts between University and secondary school personnel and disadvantaged youngsters in a residential setting does a great deal to break down communication barriers between educators and students from a background of poverty. Fifth and finally, the use of a dynamically oriented treatment approach was instrumental in facilitating the principle of self-regulation, a principle basic to the successful raising and partial resolution of the above issues.

3 THE SCHOOL

In this thoroughgoing review of the many factors that are part of the Negro school experience, William Kvaraceus stresses conditions he believes must change in order to make
the schooling of Negroes a positive force for the improvement of their lives. He outlines
not only a new set of objectives for the schools but specific techniques that research and
observation have indicated are effective in achieving each objective.

William C. Kvaraceus

Negro Youth and Social Adaptation: The Role of the School as an Agent of Change

THE POSITION PAPER

Commenting on his own school experiences, James Baldwin brings our topic
into sharp focus. He writes: "School began to reveal itself, therefore, as a child's
game that one could not win, and boys dropped out and went to work. My
father wanted me to do the same. I refused, even though I no longer had any
illusions about what an education could do for me."[1] Today Negro youth
continues to fall out only to face the additional problem: there is less work
opportunity.

Digging even deeper to the taproots of the major problems facing Negro
youth, Baldwin insightfully admonishes us: "But the dispute has actually nothing
to do with education, as some among the eminently uneducated know. It has
to do with political power and it has to do with sex. And this is a nation which,

[1] James Baldwin, The Fire Next Time, New York: The Dial Press, Inc., 1963, pp. 32–33.

216

most unluckily, knows very little about either." [2] Since Dr. Grambs's paper is more closely related to sex and Dr. Seasholes's is directly concerned with political participation,* a discussion of the role of the school agency may appear to be less relevant, but hardly superfluous. Obviously, politics and sex represent a very heady mixture to be swallowed by American schools. But both are issues that must be faced.

Nevertheless, the compulsory classroom represents the universal vehicle—often the only vehicle—to self-realization, to achievement, to jobs, and to status for Negro youth. In mobilizing community forces to assist the culturally disadvantaged, social planners intuitively look to the school as a major—if not a central—resource. For the schools have all the children of all the people; they receive the child early and maintain close and intimate relationships with him for a long period of time; they have trained personnel (who are further trainable) to deal with children and youth; they aim to develop integrated and socially effective citizens; and they are found in every community. The school, then, as one of the community institutions that comes in close and prolonged contact with children and youth, enjoys a unique and strategic responsibility and opportunity for assisting culturally disadvantaged youth.

But the school's direct contribution in a community-wide program aimed to identify and assist the culturally disadvantaged will be realized only as "good schools" become "better schools." In this sense, the school's responsibility to the Negro student is no different from its responsibility to any other learner in the classroom, advantaged or disadvantaged, white or nonwhite—albeit his learning problems remain more concentrated and more complex.

The exact nature of the school's role (there are many role patterns) in assisting the culturally deprived Negro students will depend upon a clear differentiation of individual needs, interests, and capacities, as must be done with white students. In program planning at every grade level, we will need to consider the special problems of: (1) the Negro students who are already "well on their way" and who may try to out-middle-class their middle-class academic comrades; (2) those students who are in ferment—who are making the upward effort, but who are blocked and for whom there appears no legitimate means to chosen goals; and (3) those Negroes who are stable and are staying in the submilieu representing often the hard core of the defeated, the paralyzed, and the unmotivated.

Studies of the Negro pupil as a learner in the big-city school systems have frequently revealed him to be standing in a poor school posture if not in educational bankruptcy. His readiness for learning seldom reaches as high as the school anticipates. His nonverbal and non-academic sets create a difficult motivational problem and perhaps call for a different teaching-learning style than is found in the conventional classroom. His reading and language skills fall far below the level of his grade placement. He is more often truant and more fre-

[2] James Baldwin, *Nobody Knows My Name,* New York: Dell Publishing Co., Inc., 1961, pp. 101–102.
  * [Other papers presented on the occasion when this was first delivered.]

quently counted among the delinquent. Thus, suffering accumulated frustration due to failure, boredom, and constant pressure of the preposterous academic task, school becomes a place of confinement and the age of leaving looms like a welcomed escape hatch and a solution to his troubles. Although the Negro student is often viewed as a severe headache or burden to the school, the school represents an even greater headache and a heavier burden to him. And too often it is with a sigh of relief that the school may see him off to the street.

There are limitations on what the school apparatus can accomplish with and for disadvantaged youth. In the life space of the culturally disadvantaged, the school inserts itself only after much learning has already taken place. And always there are other powerful forces—family, housing, neighborhood, peer groups, labor organizations, mass media, the social and economic order—that impinge, in addition to the school experiences, on the growth and development of the young. Just what can the school agency do to maximize its positive influence with the young Negro?

The school agency will achieve its maximum effectiveness with the disadvantaged Negro to the degree to which it satisfies four major contingencies: first, if the teachers themselves provide good role models with whom many youngsters readily identify; second, if the curriculum of the school includes aims, methods, materials, and climate conducive to learning; third, if ancillary services, including testing, counseling, job placement, case work, and health services, are available and accessible to the youngster at the time of need; and fourth, if the school becomes a member of the community team and meshes its services with other public and private agencies that work closely with Negro youth and their families.

SCHOOL AS AN EGO-SUPPORTING INSTITUTION

Children in the big city who enter the public schools in heavily populated neighborhoods are immediately absorbed in a massive educational system. Although the big-city school system accepts all children, it does so on its own terms. These terms frequently demand some renunciation of differences—personal, social, and cultural—and a constant submission to the processes of conformity and standardization. Most schools achieve their goals at the price of some loss of privacy, personal identity, and individuality. They require submission to external controls and to the pressures of the group; they invoke the severe competitive processes of selection and survival of the academically fit; and all too frequently they produce an artificial separation between the classroom and the life stream of everyday problems and activities.

These demands of the large-city school system are most destructive to the egos of the culturally deprived. Children and youth who are unable or unwilling to submit frequently join the ranks of the school failures, the troubled and troublesome, the truants, and the early school dropouts. They may even set up their own ego-supporting institutions in the form of juvenile gangs. It is imperative that the school, in working to achieve its goals, operate always as an ego-supporting institution. The destructive nature of the school experiences of many unadapted youngsters, Negro and white, shows up vividly in studies of school failure, dropouts, youth unemployment, and delinquency. How can the total school effort, via the curriculum, the relationship with the teacher, and the special services, combine to reinforce and strengthen the self-concept of Negro youth and aid in their social adaptation?

THE CURRICULUM OF THE SCHOOL

There are two curricula that will be found in every school. First, there is the overt curriculum which is made up of all the teacher-planned (in some cases, teacher-pupil planned) activities in which the young learners are engaged and which lead, hopefully, to some agreed-upon goals. But as Alice Miel noted at the 1960 White House Conference, the school curriculum represents "a changing assemblage of opportunities for educational experience." In a fast-changing world, the American schools have not changed fast enough. This educational lag between the outside world and the classroom has been handicapping to all categories of learners, both advantaged and disadvantaged. Second, there is the covert, or subliminal, curriculum to be found in the cuture and subcultures of the school which sets up normative ways to behave and how not to behave. We shall consider special aspects of both curricula as they pertain to the school life of the Negro.

The Formal and Visible Curriculum

For many Negro youngsters, the curriculum experiences appear irrelevant and pointless. There is very little apparent connection between what goes on in school and the present or future life of the learner. In addition to the traditional function of transmitting the culture, school activities must connect with the child's present and his future. To ensure relevancy, school goals must be specified in terms of expected changes or modifications in behavior or in terms of the acquisition of new and desirable modes of behavior. As the behavior of masses of children undergoes modification, it may thus be possible to change the way of life and to improve the less effective cultural practices of the disadvantaged. School attendance and involvement in learning activities should make a discernible difference. This difference, broadly speaking, should be observable in the acquisition of new behavior or the changes in behavior of the learner. Such changes might be seen in the pupil's leisure-time activities, in his job competencies, in the management of his day-to-day home economics activities, in his decision-making and problem-solving behavior, in his maintenance of health and physical well-being, in the reading he does for information or pleasure, and in his capacity for further learning. Unless the pupil's behavior has been modified and improved and unless new and desirable behavior has been established, learning cannot be said to have taken place.

To illustrate this principle, consider first, the traditional learning experience in English literature in the high school. A youngster is required to read carefully (if not with pleasure) a number of books from the "recommended reading list." A detailed appraisal of his reading reveals his recall of plot, character, setting, and theme. Having answered all or a sufficient number of questions to the satisfaction of the teacher, the young learner seldom or never reads another book. Yet he may receive a "passing mark" in literature, although his nonreading behavior has not changed. Or consider, second, the pupil in social studies who has learned to recite the Bill of Rights, chapter and verse, but whose behavior and conduct as a youth now or as an adult later reflect no understanding of the meaning or implications of these articles in his personal, political, social, or business life. The expected and desired change in behavior has not taken place. The youngster has not learned.

To reiterate, in planning a variegated curriculum to meet the different needs of all pupils, the course objectives, insofar as possible, should be stated as concrete and visible modes of new behavior or as improvements or changes in established and less effective ways of behaving. As this is done, curriculum planners will need to consider three related problems.

First, there is the current danger, already cited, of mass education that will lead to a standardization of the Negro learner in the stereotype of the "middle-class citizen and parent" or into a regimented array of "correct" opinions, purchases, leisure-time pursuits, and occupations. Stated conversely, the maverick, the independent thinker or performer, or the divergent creator should be carefully sought out among children and youth who are born and who live within the estate of lower-classness. How to educate—literally, to lead out or draw out —the Negro child from his subculture into middle-class milieus, if the school's objectives so demand, and yet preserve and develop elements of individuality, divergency, and independence represents a major problem facing the curriculum planners. Unfortunately the curriculum planners seldom consult the youth— white or nonwhite—or with their parents either in curriculum development or in curriculum implementation.

On this point, Anna Freud has made an astute observation:

> Educators, that is to say those adults who form the environment of the child, always want to make him what suits them, which consequently differs according to the century, position, rank, class, etc., of the adults. But all these varying aims have one feature in common. The universal aim of education is always to make out of the child a grown-up person who shall not be very different from the grown-up world around him.[3]

What the dominant society demands for and of the Negro often makes little sense either to him or to his parents. This is especially true of the nonmobile

---

[3] Anna Freud, *Psychoanalysis for Teachers and Parents* (Barbara Low, Translator), Boston: The Beacon Press, 1960, p. 45. [Copyright Emerson Books, Inc.]

Negro who is stable and is staying in the subculture. Inarticulate and nonverbal as the youngster may appear (yet note the richness and creativity of his own hipster tongue), the dialogue concerning the aims and objectives of the school and the aims and objectives of the youngster and his family must be started even before he comes to school.

Anna Freud also indicated that an educator—unlike the child-caring mother—always wants something from the child. Many Negro children perceive this, and they appear afraid, unwilling, or unable to give back to the demanding authority. We need to inquire in schools why this is so.

Second, there is the constant threat of confining the Negro student and the potential or actual dropout to those educational experiences aimed exclusively in the direction of objectives that are immediate, extrinsic, utilitarian, and practical. Preoccupation with these goals runs the risk of placing a low ceiling on courses offered or chosen. The danger to the upwardly mobile Negro youth, whether on-their-way or in-ferment, is great. This is not to overlook what Riessman [4] has on several occasions pointed out: the need for concreteness and "down-to-earth learning by doing," especially in the initial stages and with the culturally less mobile Negro. Although accent on self and creativity may be alien to the culture of many deprived children, ideational goals should be held aloft and clearly visible, especially for the upwardly mobile and ultimately, through progression, for the less mobile. To diminish in any way the ideational goals in the education of Negro youth is to derogate. The current emphases on expansion of occupational training programs and on the development of marketable skills in many schools, as valuable as they may be, can in the long run further disadvantage the disadvantaged, whose educational sights may be lowered or whose stay in school may be shortened through the pursuit of terminal courses. Equal emphasis must be given to the development of school programs that place the accent on cultural enrichment, general education, and instructional improvement. Implicit in the differential student-course matching is the need for pupil personnel services, including counseling, testing, and job placement. To these we shall return later; but we have recognized at this point of goal determination that very careful consideration should be given to course selections as an aspect of career planning.

Third, to ensure desirable modifications in behavior or the development of new and improved modes of behavior, the school must provide richer opportunities to practice such behavior as a part of the learning experience and as an expression of the product of learning. This calls for the development of practice opportunities and laboratory experiences in school and community. Too much of school experience is theoretical, abstract, or, at best, vicarious. What is sorely needed in the curriculum of the secondary school is a graduated series of real-life experiences in problem solving and decision making, in participation within the social, political, and economic life of the in-school and out-of-school society. Most youth are cut out of the mainstream of community activities. They

[4] Frank Riessman, "Teaching the Culturally Deprived," *NEA Journal*, April 1963, p. 22.

have minimal function. The exile, the disenfranchisement, the rejection are most severe and complete with Negro youth. At least, white youth have some cosmetic value in the dominant adult community. In contrast, few adults swell with pride at the sight of norm-conforming Negro youth. To be a nothing, to have no function, is hard for all youth; but it is doubly hard for Negro youth.

Courses of study in problems of democracy, for example, should be centered on the study of local community problems, as well as planning for their solution and actually solving them. It is true that only youth can solve the youth problem. The energies of American youth, white and nonwhite, have seldom been tapped for social and civic benefit. That Negro youth have the initiative, the inspiration, and the commitment to high social purpose cannot be questioned as one views their strong role now in the steady drive to freedom and job opportunity. Energies expended in demonstrations, sit-ins, and freedom marches can also be directed to goals of self-realization and social betterment. The question to be explored here is: "What kinds of laboratory experiences and practices can the

Goals of Education as Projections of Self-Image

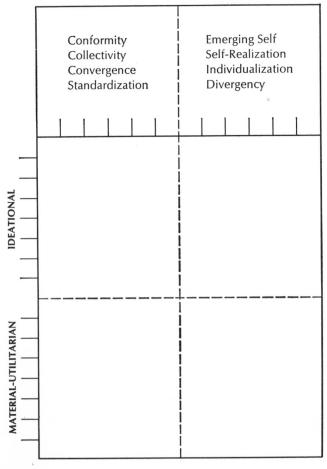

local school establish as an integral part of the regular curriculum to lend reality and significance to the focus of learning and to fix habits of behavior as explicated in the educational goals of the school?"

Now to point up our discussion of educational goals stated in terms of behavioral outcomes. The objectives of the school should be established and revised through continuous discussion with parents and with Negro youth themselves. These dialogues between school and home must be carried on a bivariate screen. On the following diagram we can scale the objectives of the school and of Negro youth on two dimensions. The horizontal axis represents a bipolar dimension of objectives on a scale ranging from conformity to divergency; the vertical axis represents a scale ranging from material-utilitarian to ideational. The bivariate chart invites consideration of current emphasis in programs now being offered to culturally deprived youth; it also offers material for reflection to curriculum planners as well as for those who run the courses. It is suggested that the participants in this Conference plot the objectives of current school programs that have been implemented, using the suggested schemata or some adaptation of the two dimensions.

But the goals of the school cirrucula are more than ordinary goals. They are projections of the future self-concept; they can promise a better future and a better self-concept, and they can beckon the learner to run the hard course of change.

A few selected comments are in order concerning the "materials and methods" of curricula with reference to the Negro student.

Motivation is one of the major problems that every teacher faces with the culturally disadvantaged. The pragmatic attitude and the anti-intellectualism typical of lower-class living lead to objectives that are predominantly utilitarian, with special emphasis on job procurement, as we have noted earlier. Ausubel,[5] however, makes a strong case for intrinsic motivation (the acquisition of knowledge for its own sake) as "the most promising motivational strategy" which can be adopted in teaching the culturally deprived learner or nonlearner. He points out that "meaningful school learning is more potent, relevant, durable and easier to arouse than its extrinsic counterpart." When successful, it furnishes its own reward. Also, since much of school learning cannot be easily rationalized as necessary for the everyday demands of living, only cognitive drive becomes the one immediately relevant motivation. He points out in addition that intrinsic motivation, unlike extrinsic motif, is not so likely to lose its potency or relevance in later life when utilitarian and career advancements are less and less a dominant life consideration. Ausubel suggests that

... it is not necessary to postpone learning activities until appropriate interests and motivations have been developed. Frequently the best way of motivating an unmotivated pupil is to ignore his motivational state for the time being and to concentrate on

[5] David P. Ausubel, "How Reversible Are the Cognitive and Motivational Effects of Cultural Deprivation? Implications for Teaching the Culturally Deprived Child," Urbana, Illinois: University of Illinois Bureau of Educational Research, p. 15. (Paper presented at the Conference on the Teaching of the Culturally Deprived Child, Buffalo, New York, March 28–30, 1963.)

teaching him as effectively as possible. Much to his surprise and to his teacher's, he will learn despite his lack of motivation; and from the satisfaction of learning he will characteristically develop the motivation to learn more.

Paradoxically, therefore, we may discover that the most effective method of developing intrinsic motivation to learn is to focus on the cognitive rather than on the motivational aspects of learning, and to rely on the motivation that is developed retroactively from successful educational achievement. This is particularly true when a teacher is able to generate contagious excitement and enthusiasm about the subject he teaches, and when he is the kind of person with whom culturally deprived children can identify. Masculinizing the school and dramatizing the lives and exploits of cultural, intellectual, and scientific heroes can also enhance the process of identification. At the same time, of course, we can attempt to combat the anti-intellectualism and lack of cultural tradition in the home through programs of adult education and cultural enrichment.[6]

The Subliminal Curriculum

The school is more than an agent of organized society; the school represents a small and, for many culturally disadvantaged youngsters, a strange and separate society.

I have already pointed out, and perhaps overstated, that the formal curriculum of the school provides planned and systematic experiences through which new behaviors and/or modifications of behavior are developed. This curriculum operates in most schools in a monotonous routine and ritual of lesson assigning, lesson hearing, and lesson marking. In an earlier study,[7] from which I shall borrow freely, I have pointed out that there is also a second and perhaps more powerful curriculum which is to be found in the culture of the school. This is the way of life of the school, providing a normative structure of how to act and how not to act. This subliminal curriculum, like the hidden but major portion of an iceberg, is in a sense a natural extension of the visible and formal curriculum of the school. Though hidden, it may represent for behavior and misbehavior the more formidable and sometimes more effective—if not hazardous —aspect of the school's program in developing real and significant changes in the behavior of high school youth.

The importance of this less visible aspect of the curriculum can be ascertained from the current protests centered on segregation in the New Rochelles, Englewoods, Bostons, and Birminghams. Intuitively, the lay public, including whites and nonwhites, appreciate the fact that the ethos of a high school with 90 percent Negro enrollment and the ethos of a high school in the same city with 90 percent white enrollment do represent a wide range of differences in the styles of

---

[6] David P. Ausubel, "How Reversible Are the Cognitive and Motivational Effects of Cultural Deprivation? Implications for Teaching the Culturally Deprived Child," Urbana, Illinois: University of Illinois Bureau of Educational Research, pp. 15–16. (Paper presented at the Conference on the Teaching of the Culturally Deprived Child, Buffalo, New York, March 28–30, 1963.)

[7] William C. Kvaraceus, "The Behavioral Deviate in the Culture of the Secondary School," Frontiers of Secondary Education (III), Paul M. Halverson (ed), Syracuse, New York: Syracuse University Press, 1958, pp. 18–27.

———. "Helping the Socially Inadapted Pupil in the Large City Schools," Exceptional Children, April 1962, pp. 399–404.

school living and learning. The climate of the "students" of one school may award status and prestige to the truant, the non-achiever, the recalcitrant learner, and the early dropout. The climate of student opinion of another school may award status and prestige to the high achiever, the college-bound, and the activities leader. Those who seek to ensure a preferred value system through the mathematical criterion involving "better balance" of white and Negro students will be disappointed. For the answer lies in the focal concerns or points of reference representing values and norms of the effective reference group, and more particularly within the leadership of the effective group.

There is no such thing as "the culture" of the American public secondary school. A wide variety of cultures and subcultures exist and can be found in different high schools and in different communities. The ways of life in the large inner-city high school will differ substantially from the way of living in the more homogeneous upper-middle-class models found in the clean and neat suburban school; and these, in turn, will differ from the patterns visible in the small high schools that are now fast disappearing from the rural scene. Margaret Mead has explored some of these significant variants in her Inglis Lecture, *The School in American Culture.*[8] At the same time, it must be recognized that the structure of school society, not unlike the structure of the society outside of school, consists of a number of subgroups, each with its own somewhat distinct cultural characteristics. In the high school, these may cluster around class status of the family, college-going intentions, course elections, ethnic aspects of the neighboring community, etc.

Behavior and, of course, misbehavior frequently are only manifestations or reflections of the cultural imperatives of the school. The cultural imperatives of the secondary school are powerful and pervasive. They may and frequently do neutralize and even supersede the forces operating in the formal and planned experiences of the visible curriculum.

My purpose here is to analyze some common imperatives culled from the cultural milieus of the secondary school that frequently tend to shape or determine personality (modes of adjustment). We must recognize, of course, that behavior and misbehavior represent always an interaction of the organism and the external environment referred to here in a cultural sense. Since the factors within the culture are more often overlooked than the factors under the skin in studying behavior and misbehavior, this discussion focuses exclusively on the more common cultural imperatives which have been distilled from many different secondary schools. All of these cultural imperatives can serve to predispose the high school student to misbehavior and social inadaptation, since they expose him to frustration, ego disintegration, stress, anxiety, weak imitative example, and lowered self-estimate.

The American high school is unique in many ways when compared with many of its European counterparts. A point of greatest difference can frequently be

[8] Margaret Mead, *The School in American Culture,* Cambridge, Massachusetts: Harvard University Press, 1951.

found in the free-and-easy boy-girl relationships best symbolized by the insurance policy carried in the form of the steady date or the isolated couple at the school dance united in romantic embrace.

The sexiest spot in any American town today can be found in its high school. This is especially true in smaller communities and most visible in suburbia, perhaps more so than in the inner city. This theme has been caught in the melodrama of *Peyton Place,* where even the high school principal is hardly immune to the sexually oriented climate of his own institution and eventually capitulates. The identical theme is burlesqued in the Grade B Hollywood celluloid, "High School Confidential," which recently played the wide screens of the local movie houses. In this caricature of the high school, seniors (maybe they were only sophomores) speak frequently and glibly of the stag and stud roles of the male "students."

In a sense, the sex-crossed activities of the high school provide an important part of the practicum for the future husband-wife companion role but without verbalization and without theoretical orientation to the phenomenon and meaning of sex. Hence the young adult may somehow master the developmental task and mature into an expert craftsman by the time the male or female family role is undertaken. But until the transition is from the *how* to the *why*, youth will seldom attain a professional level of their husband-wife roles. What is sorely needed in the American secondary school is the opportunity to talk it out rather than just act it out, even though the acting may be done without injury and on the symbolic level. The heavy curtain of official silence that hangs around sex in an institution replete with sex-crossed activities presents the modern educational paradox. It is hoped that talking it out will develop restraint, good sense, and moral principle rather than further accentuating an overaccentuated subject.

How much of this sex orientation is attributable to the unrealistic adult romanticism of youth and love and adult fantasies and fears in regard to Negroes and adolescents could be explored profitably by research teams from sociology, anthropology, psychology, and education. For it is the high schools that house the teen-agers who are regarded by adults, as Edgar Friedenberg has pointed out, as a "hot-blooded minority." They are, he says, "in the process of being denatured; of becoming under social stress, something more acceptable to dominant society, but essentially different from what its own growth and experience would lead to." [9] Friedenberg continues:

> In the most formal sense, then, the adolescent is one of our second class citizens. But the informal aspects of minority status are also imputed to him. "The teen-ager," like the Latin or Negro, is seen as joyous, playful, lazy, and irresponsible, with brutality lurking just below the surface and ready to break into violence. All these groups are seen as childish and excitable, imprudent and improvident, sexually aggressive, and dangerous, but possessed of superb and sustained power to satisfy sexual demands. [10]

[9] Edgar Z. Friedenberg, "The Image of the Adolescent Minority," *Dissent*, Spring 1963, p. 148.
[10] Edgar Z. Friedenberg, "The Image of the Adolescent Minority," *Dissent*, Spring 1963, p. 150.

The functional aspects of this teen-age stereotype for adults and teachers also need to be investigated, and the implications for teacher recruitment, training, and placement need to be drawn out. In this search we may find some answers to *de facto* (and other types of) segregation and to why a special effort must be made to recruit teachers for the inner-city schools, and also why high school dances are so closely and anxiously supervised. "The Black Board Jungle" made capital of adult fears, fantasies, and titillations by equating adolescence, delinquency, and aggressive sexuality in a high school setting for adult viewing. Front-page stories such as that of the marriage of Charlayne Hunter, the Negro co-ed who broke the color barrier at the University of Georgia, to Walter Stovall, a white Georgian, will always make exciting reading for some adults.

The fact that most private or independent secondary schools hold to their monolithic sex structure testifies that they continue to meet the needs of apprehensive parents who consciously or unconsciously seek out those school organizations which "protect" their young adolescents from the sex-crossed activities of the public high school. The presence of Negro students often underscores their apprehension. This is not to deny that there are other reasons, good and bad, that motivate anxious parents to send their maturing youngsters to private all-male or all-female schools. Integration has made a profitable business out of many bad private schools that were hardly solvent a few years ago.

Contrary to the practicum in relating to the opposite sex with its lack of information and discussion, the rest of the school's program at the high school level can best be described as information without application or implementation. For the period of his high school career, the learner is cut off from the stream of real-life problems. He finds himself in a deep freeze. The activities in which he must engage appear irrelevant to the Negro student's past, present, or future—especially the present. Since the high school is careful to skirt and detour around real-life problems and controversial issues involving race relations, alcoholism, materialism, religion, politics, collectivism, consumer competencies, marriage, and family life, it involves the learner in a type of artificially contrived busywork and shadowboxing that either lulls the adolescent into a stupor or drives him in his resentment out of school to overt aggression. In protecting youth from real-life problems, the school enters into a tragic conspiracy of irresponsible retreat from reality. The perversion of the high school curriculum to neutral and petty purposes emasculates the school program and distintegrates the ego. The complaints [11] of youth today are that the school experiences are stale and flat. Boredom in school is what drives many youths, Negro and white, to retaliatory and nonconforming behavior, to chronic truancy, and eventually to withdrawal. The best therapeutic device available for

[11] James S. Coleman, *The Adolescent Society*, New York: The Free Press of Glencoe, 1961. Note here the prestige values attached to sports and popularity over the academic, and Edgar Z. Friedenberg's interpretation in a recent issue of the *College Board Review* vindicating the adolescents' value systems against the reality of the academic requirement of high school [page 111 in this collection].

the noisy and retreating part of our adolescent society is an interesting, meaningful, and vital high school curriculum.

Nowhere is the listless play-acting more visible than in the so-called student governments in the high school. Seldom are youth trusted to make their own decisions and to experience the learning that can come from making moral choices or socioeconomic-political decisions on their own. The direction and supervision exercised in student government make a mockery of the democratic processes. Neither does the high school appear effective in finding any honest or real work with which to preoccupy the fast-maturing adolescent. The result today can be seen in the young adult who is convinced of his low status. He is a nobody, a nothing. He suffers from the lack of any utility function (except that of serving in the role of a perpetual scapegoat for the adult members of society who heap upon him all the debris of their own inadequacies). There is no more unimportant member of society than the adolescent. He is the outraged personality of the twentieth century, as indicated by the eloquent testimony in the mounting rebellion visible in the delinquency trends of any large city. Herein is frequently reflected the aggressive inferiority of modern youth. The nonfunctioning curriculum of the secondary school, coupled with compulsory school attendance, is rapidly turning the American public high school into an adolescent ghetto. Let us inspect the compulsory nature of this relationship between school and adolescent.

There are many captive students in American high schools. What proportion of its Negro pupils would the secondary schools lose if the compulsory school-attendance laws were revoked and if the attendance officers were taken off the job? In the educational mythology of compulsory secondary schooling, the public institutions have promised to educate every child of every parent in the strong middle-class tradition. For most pupils, as with Penrod, school has become "a place of confinement envenomed by mathematics," which we have recently replaced with a "new mathematics" curriculum and to which we have added a revised science program. Unfortunately these programs are not geared to all the individual differences that are visible through compulsory school attendance. The efforts made in improving and upgrading the math-science courses of study for the academically endowed and college-going student should be matched by equal effort and expenditure for the terminal high school student as well as for the potential dropout. Unfortunately, Dr. Conant's comprehensive high school is not comprehensive enough.

The tempo and rhythm of learning in the high schools is fast, brief, and staccato. The student studies by clock and calendar. Time concepts of Negro youngsters are not built on these two measures. Learning stops for frequent holiday and vacation periods. Entrance to school and withdrawal from school are based on birth certificates rather than on any criteria of ability, achievement, and readiness. Learning is always short timed and truncated. It operates in fifty-minute periods in which teacher and pupil study to beat the clock. All of this is alien to a studentship and a scholarship which is continuous and permeating and which must race in the long, arduous marathon rather than the fifty-minute dash in a five-period day. Much of the pseudointellectualism of our day can be traced to the "quickie" nature of the school's learning-teaching process.

Organizationally the high school program sorts out classes (not individuals) among teachers about every fifty minutes. The frequently shifted youngster belongs to no one. Even with a "home-room period," he suffers a feeling of rootlessness and impersonality. As a member of a class, he may achieve the status of a pupil, but he seldom calls attention to himself as a person except through misbehavior. Help may be extended to him, but it must be routed through the impersonal bureaucracy of the guidance department.

Secondary schools have shown a complete lack of imagination, of ingenuity, in developing programs that would ensure the establishment of strong and extended teacher-pupil and pupil-teacher relationships on which instruction and learning can be anchored. Attention should be given to the possibilities inherent in arranging programs in much longer time patterns by spending a half day or full day within each area of instruction, or even a week with the science teacher, followed by a full week each in the round of other teachers in other areas. High school programming will make learning and scholarship pervasive only when schooling itself is pervasive.

High school classes are very tightly grouped on the age-grade principle, with subdivisions according to interests in different curricula which reflect, in turn, educational and occupational levels of aspiration, resulting in strong social-class differentiation. Grouping tightly on the age-grade basis can affect behavior and misbehavior in several ways.

First, the grouping affects behavior by implying to both teachers and pupils an equality and homogeneity that actually does not exist and in consequence of which instruction is undifferentiated through the slavish use of the single text and the identical lesson assignment. This invites the problem of the bored learner at the upper levels and the frustrated learner within the lower ranges of ability and achievement. Only by individualizing instruction within the classroom can the great educational superstition be broken that all children of the same age who come to school can learn the same things at the same time at the same place and to the same degree. High school students taught under the American superstition of readiness and equality are bound to suffer the trauma of a bad hangover once they leave school and walk into the competitive climate in the world of work.

Second, grouping in tight age brackets tends to reinforce the already overly strong youth subcultures. The teen-ager notoriously would rather be wrong with his peers than right with his family or other adult authority. When this happens, as Margaret Mead has pointed out, American youth tend to surrender some moral autonomy for the comforts of the irresponsible crowd. This is the inherent nature of the delinquent act, particularly of the "group-intoxicated" and "socialized" types.

How much leeway is possible in grouping more broadly, but within the chronological age span of the secondary school, presents a real problem. Surely more could be done in the six-year secondary school by overlapping membership in some classes, such as music and art, and by adhering more closely to ability-achievement criteria in others, thereby breaking the solid age-grade-status grouping that now prevails. At the same time, the pressure to differentiate instruction for extremes will be lessened.

Contrary to some fears and even some evidence that preadolescents, adolescents, and postadolescents cannot be effectively grouped for instruction, careful observations of the social and emotional situations on the ski slope or in the swimming pool or on the stage (where instruction frequently is imparted to groups having very wide age ranges, but in accordance with a continuous-growth principle) will reveal many positive outcomes, particularly in terms of a reciprocal respect and a camaraderie rare even in closely knit pressure groups.

In connection with problems of homogeneity and grouping, two principles culled from the investigations of Riecken on the efficacy of work camps in changing attitudes are noteworthy. He reported that "attitudes could be more easily and successfully changed if a group rather than an isolated individual is the object of attempts to produce change." [12] He also has found that personality traits underwent the most positive changes when his subjects were introduced into totally different situations and when they were faced by radically different sets of relations from those to which they were habituated. Dr. Coles's intensive study of Negro and white youngsters in integrated schools in the South generally reaffirms similar positive changes, though not in every case.[13] There is powerful persuasion in the peer group, as many investigators have found. To shift one's values and to find oneself alienated or deviating from one's reference group can be hard; however, when a shift in values establishes a group standard, every pupil's new behavior will be reinforced by the class members. To organize classes in homogenized—if not homogeneous—units may lessen the opportunity for eliciting change. Implications can be drawn from these studies to strengthen open-enrollment programs and to answer questions concerning racial imbalance in predominantly Negro schools.

One implication, in view of the very strong hold that neighborhood segregation has on composition of enrollment in city schools, may be the necessity of forced mixing of children with varied backgrounds to provide positive racial encounters at an early age. In the event that this adaptation is made, it will be necessary to take into consideration other important variables, such as class status, which may prove to be more crucial than skin color. This may be one way, perhaps the only way, to raise the inferior status of schools that are found in low-income areas, as documented by Sexton in her big-city study.[14]

[12] Henry W. Riecken, *The Volunteer Work Camp: A Psychological Examination*, Reading, Massachusetts: Addison-Wesley Publishing Company, Inc., 1952, pp. 30–31.
[13] Robert Coles, *The Desegregation of Southern Schools: A Psychiatric Study*, New York: Anti-Defamation League of B'nai B'rith, and Atlanta, Georgia: Southern Regional Council, July 1963.
[14] Patricia Sexton, *Education and Income: Inequalities in Our Public Schools*, New York: The Viking Press, Inc., 1961.

Merely shifting youngsters from one school to another or redistricting in and of themselves may create problems, as well as providing the students with a rich opportunity to learn and value other students of dissimilar backgrounds. Social integration and lessons in democratic living will not accrue automatically and certainly not without careful prior planning. Much more can de done at the elementary school levels before racial and class-status ideologies have taken root, as Dr. Coles's study of younger Southern children in segregated schools bears out. But much more effort and skill will be required to work with older youth at the high school level. As Hollingshead reported of Elmtown, most interactions among students in school follow along social-class lines.

> By the time he reaches adolescence his personality is formed. Also, he has developed conceptions of (1) himself; (2) the social structure; (3) his place in it along with appropriate roles and statuses; (4) forms of behavior approved and disapproved; and (5) means of doing what he desires even though it involves the violation of laws and mores.[15]

At the secondary school level, a direct approach to the problem should be tried out in which the students themselves carry out self-studies of the impact of social-class differences on students (and perhaps on teachers). This could also be enlarged into a neighborhood study via such courses as problems of democracy, introduction to sociology, or psychology. High school pupils would thereby be encouraged to isolate and define problems, gather data, consider alternatives for action, and help to implement change.

Status in school is always linked to successful achievement in the classroom. For the adolescent, one source (often the only source) of teacher approval can be found in academic achievement via the report-card route. Unless the student shows a satisfactory level of attainment, he is not likely to find himself surrounded by smiling and approving adult faces.

School failure is frequently a concomitant and forerunner of deviant behavior. Studies of delinquents and nondelinquents[16] indicate a wide split between the educationally bankrupt and the educationally affluent. Delinquents frequently make a success of failure by using this means to thumb their noses at the school.

It is easy to understand how failure can be used to strike back at the teaching authority, or to demolish the school, by students whose neighborhood or peer-group value system is contrary to that of the school or of the dominant society. It may not be so easy to understand how the upper-middle-class child can use failure as a powerful weapon to cut down his parents. When school success becomes a paramount issue to the parent who draws selfishly his own brand of personal satisfaction from the achievement of his youngsters, academic failure can prove a subtle and satisfactory boomerang for any youngster. In fact, this

[15] A. B. Hollingshead, *Elmtown's Youth*, New York: John Wiley & Sons, Inc., 1949.
[16] William C. Kvaraceus, *Juvenile Delinquency and the School*, New York: Harcourt, Brace & World, Inc., 1945.
————. *The Community and the Delinquent*, New York: Harcourt, Brace & World, Inc., 1954.

is one of the few ways that many middle-class high school adolescents have of getting back at their predatory parents.

How to ensure success for the less academic or "nonacademic" pupil in the high school presents a difficult curriculum problem. Until this issue is met, students who must enter high school will run the risk of breaking their backs as they reach for unattainable goals. When satisfactions that can come only through achievement, success, and approval are not attainable, the youngsters may well resort to other means to achieve some measure of success. These means may frequently be the antisocial route of misbehavior.

The American school, if it is to diminish deviate behavior, must aim to develop inner behavioral controls that will make its graduates less dependent on the supervising, monitoring, and policing authority. Self-discipline as contrasted with external-control dependency has been the aim of the secondary school, but this aim can hardly be attained so long as the school culture continues to dominate with adult controls and to tell the student what to do, when to do it, how to do it, and whether it is right when it is done. Such heavy dependence upon forces of external and formal discipline tends to deepen the misunderstanding and resentment that exist between youth and adult and to intensify the hate and hostility now manifest in much of the deviate behavior in youth culture. Both the sociologist and the psychiatrist have independently come to the conclusion that the culture of formal and external controls, when it succeeds, frequently creates a reluctant and recalcitrant conformist living close to the letter of the law. When it fails, it creates "the outlaw," best exemplified by the overt, aggressive delinquent who is a member of an "outlaw gang" in the depths of the big city.

These and other cultural determinants found operating in most public secondary schools will continuously precipitate crises, tensions, and frustrations for the high school student. David Segel [17] has pointed out three kinds of behavior solutions that can follow on frustration in the high school: (1) regression, as exemplified by school leaving; (2) aggression, as seen in disorderly conduct, overt attack, and vandalism; (3) fixation, as found in the sitting out of the school activities, or "going through the motions."

Of all these behavior solutions to inimical school situations, perhaps the most wholesome or promising will be found in the overt-aggression pattern in which the youngster is doing something about it. He is putting up a fight. He is adjusting the best and usually the only way he knows how. He is calling our attention to himself and to his problem situation. He is not retreating, nor is he giving up, nor is he resorting to fantasy in solving his terrible problem. There is much that is positive—even wholesome—in the delinquency phenomenon. Needless to say, this is not well understood generally and can be readily misunderstood.

Knowledge of these cultural imperatives of behavior and misbehavior in

[17] David Segel, *Frustration in Adolescent Youth*, U.S. Office of Education Bulletin No. 1, 1951, p. 65.

school and classroom will enable the professional youth worker in school and community, together with the parent and the pupil, to plan cultural change. By changing the behavior of large masses of young people, the great American public school of the future may even be able to change and influence the culture of the community.

ROLE OF THE TEACHER
AS A PERSON AND AS A PROFESSIONAL WORKER

The most direct and effective way to strengthen the school as an ego-supporting institution is to improve the interpersonal relationships between teacher and students. It is the individual teacher who generally enjoys the most intimate and continuing relationship with the child outside the home and the family circle. Through the powerful instrument of this relationship, the teacher can do much to promote, via the normal educational processes, better mental health and educational growth. To achieve this, he must be a mature adult, committed to his responsibility of helping children and youth and presenting a positive image with which to identify. He must be aware of conscious and unconscious motivations (his own as well as those of the pupils) and be able to communicate with others. This is where those responsible for teacher preparation and in-service training of staff can make their most telling contribution: by seeking to improve and help teaching personalities as well as teacher competencies.

Every teacher faces the same basic problem. He must define and maintain his role as a mature professional adult. Teachers in the big-city school system usu-ally operate in a cumbersome bureaucracy. Surrounded by administrators, super-visors, and specialists, they often become uncertain of their own functions and the extent and direction of their own responsibility. Of particular significance is the study of the National Education Association [18] indicating that a substantially larger proportion of teachers in large school districts than teachers in small school districts felt that they lacked the rights and authority needed to maintain "effective control" over their pupils. This same study found that those teachers who felt that they had the necessary authority did have better-behaved pupils and fewer troublemakers in their classes.

It may well be that teachers in larger school districts, as compared with those in smaller districts, are less likely to have an important voice in determining the educational and disciplinary policies of their schools. Consideration should be given to including teachers of larger school units in any discussions related to policies and practices dealing with youngsters who offer learning problems and who are prone or vulnerable to social inadaptation.

At the same time, teachers constantly face the problem of resolving conflicts arising between their school-organization role and their teacher-helper role. The

[18] National Education Association, Research Division, "Teacher Opinion on Pupil Behavior 1955–56." *Research Bulletin*, April 1956, pp. 51–107.

organization commitment pulls in the direction of the enforcement and maintenance of standards of middle-class achievement, speech, dress, and behavior;
but the teacher-helper commitment demands the assistance of the young learner
in terms of his basic needs against the reality setting of his effective reference
group.

For example, in assisting the nonachiever or near-failure, the teacher-helper
provides the pupil with individual instruction and emotional support, but at the
end of the marking period the organization role may force the teacher to fail
the pupil in spite of the learning effort expended or the extenuating circumstances of the pupil's learning difficulties. Such a situation may lead to hostility
directed at the very pupil the teacher has been trying to help, but who also
precipitated the role conflict. In working with Negro youth in particular, the
teacher must be conscious of the problem he faces with this type of conflict.

Many teachers in big-city systems today indicate strong job dissatisfaction
and low self-concept, which often tend to reduce their frustration tolerance.
Watson has pointed up the lack of hero images in the education field. Answering
the question, "Why do we not have heroes in education?" he states:

> Somehow the idea is current that all educators and teachers are equal in competence.
> Therefore, none of them should be honored as exemplars, for this necessitates making
> choices among equals. Since some worthy person may not be honored, none should
> be. Or, when everyone is honored, none are distinguished. As a result, we have no
> figures which we hold before the youth or our graduate students saying, if you wish
> to succeed in education, be like these heroes.
>
> So to outsiders, educators appear as a spineless amorphous group lacking a clear
> image of its heroes.[19]

One almost hesitates to raise the question as to what youth from the other
subcultures really think of their teachers!

It is difficult to tell whether the figures on pupil misbehavior in big schools
and big districts reflect, in fact, a true difference in the incidence of social
inadaptation between big-city pupils and suburban pupils or whether they merely
reflect significant differences between irritability levels of city teachers who
work with great numbers of culturally deprived, including Negro, youngsters
and teachers employed in smaller schools and smaller communities who are
more frequently in contact with middle-class students. The fact is that many
teachers today seem to be fearful, anxious, or angry. This is especially manifest
in the teacher's relationship with the reluctant and recalcitrant learners in the
big cities. The frequent cry heard for sterner and harsher measures in dealing
with these pupils and for their removal from the regular classroom or exclusion
from school would indicate that too many educators are now more concerned
with the academic reputation of their school than with the welfare and well-
being of the nonachieving and nonconforming students.

[19] Fletcher G. Watson, "The Hero Image in Education," *Bulletin*, Harvard Graduate School
of Education Association, Fall 1962, p. 1. Reprinted from *Science Education*, December 1961.

Some teachers unconsciously fear their disturbed or disturbing pupils and resent their presence in the classroom. In relating to these children, the teacher may find forgotten fears of the past suddenly unlatched by a chance remark or episode. These unresolved threats and hidden anxieties can blind and deafen the teacher to classroom realities or can paralyze him temporarily. Sensing the precipitant of this recall process, the teacher may strike back at the pupil, using him as a symbol of the earlier offender. At times, the teacher may even try to work out or resolve his old problems through the problem behavior of his students. In a searching study of desegregation and its effects on Negro and white students, Dr. Coles has recently recommended greater emphasis on the teaching personality: "In desegregated schools teachers will be dealing with not only the problems of their children, but those of their own lives, their habits, and expectations. These teachers should not spare themselves careful self-examination." [20]

Nevertheless, there is also great strength to build on within the classroom teacher's commitment. Dr. Coles reports that he found in his interviews with teachers in Atlanta and New Orleans "a deep sense of professional integrity, of identity as teachers which transcended their private feelings about race." [21] None of this was lost on the students, white and Negro. This may constitute the pivotal resource around which the school agency can begin to build and improve in its service to Negro youngsters.

Teachers who work with many nonachieving and inadapted pupils are apt themselves to experience strong emotional difficulty. Someone must help them resolve the personal difficulties arising from work with these children. In the big school systems, aid can be provided through therapeutic counseling by psychiatrists, psychologists, and psychiatric social workers operating as mental health consultants. Help can come from a positive and understanding school administrator or supervisor who lends his ear to the troubled teacher. The principal of the school may even use his office as a way station in which the teacher can freely express his innermost anxieties and fears. To this end, consideration must be given to a much-needed shift in focus on the part of school-centered child-guidance clinics, whose effectiveness may be strengthened and broadened by their becoming more and more teacher-guidance clinics. The classroom is seldom without mental health hazards for the teacher. Unfortunately, most teachers have little direct or easy access to mental health aids.

In most classrooms, the cognitive aspect of life experience and the learning process are played up and the emotional aspects are played down. We understress the emotional life of the Negro pupil until his difficulties are so pronounced that this dimension can no longer be denied. The teacher generally does not

---

[20] Robert Coles, *The Desegregation of Southern Schools: A Psychiatric Study,* New York: Anti-Defamation League of B'nai B'rith, and Atlanta, Georgia: Southern Regional Council, July 1963, p. 24.

[21] Robert Coles, *The Desegregation of Southern Schools: A Psychiatric Study,* New York: Anti-Defamation League of B'nai B'rith, and Atlanta, Georgia: Southern Regional Council July 1963, p. 17.

trust emotions—his own or those of his pupils. Too often he only seeks to repress or deny them.

Teachers act in many classrooms today as though their Negro pupils were "clothes without bodies." In fact, the classroom is often used as a pacifier to calm down creative feelings, as though the school's aim were to produce dispassionate young adults. The result is often a boring ritual of learning and teaching.

The bigness of today's city schools and classrooms can breed anonymity, impersonality, and apathy. There is a growing threat of mechanization and isolation in many crowded classrooms today. In solving the problems of overcrowded classrooms and teacher shortages, innovations involving the more frequent use of self-teaching machines and devices have been widely recommended. There is the danger that this automated learning will reduce teacher-pupil interactions. Increased dependency on the TV screen, language tapes, teaching machines, movie and film projectors, and recordings should be justified not only in terms of learning increment but also in terms of the time saved for an increase rather than decrease of opportunities for more and deeper human relationships in the classroom. Otherwise teaching machines, robotlike human teaching as well as automation, can become a major threat to the adjustments of pupils who need the security and respect of a warm and reassuring human relationship in the big and impersonal world.

Teaching as a process involves planned interpersonal intervention aimed at changing ways in which other persons behave. The success of this process hangs in large measure on the extent to which pupils can establish a positive relationship and perhaps even identify with the teacher. "Who wants to be like you?" is a hard pay-off question that every teacher should pose for himself. A more uncomfortable question is, "Do I really want to stay with you?"

An effective relationship involving mutual trust and respect, with the acceptance of the reciprocal obligation reflected in the give-and-take of the learning-teaching process, will call for delicate classroom diplomacy between teachers and their Negro pupils. Differences in status, age, class, and skin color may interfere with the easy establishment of a good working relationship. We need to know more about the process of identification of Negro boys and girls. Teachers who are respected, accepted, and admired can become powerful objects of emulation. They can fill the need that exists in the paucity of good role models for both Negro boys and girls, but especially for boys. We do know that all youth are more impressed by what the teacher is and what he does than by what he says.

Baldwin testifies to the strong influence of a Negro principal in New York City. One can only speculate what the effect on Baldwin's own work might have been if the model had been a male Negro principal and if he had had more male Negro teachers.

At the time I was going to school in Harlem the only Negro school principal as far as I know in the entire history of New York was a Mrs. Ayer, and she liked me. In a way

I guess she proved to me that I didn't have to be entirely defined by my circumstances because you know that every Negro child knows what his circumstances are but he cannot articulate them, because he is born into a republic which assures him in as many ways as it knows how, and with great force, that he has a certain place and he can never rise above it. Mrs. Ayer was a living proof that I was not necessarily what the country said I was.[22]

The difficulties in identification—even the advisability of close identification of Negro youngsters with their teachers—represents a complex and only slightly researched classroom phenomenon. The early Greeks described adolescence as a period of trying on and taking off of different masks to find the mask of best fit. Switching masks frequently can annoy—even scare—parents and teachers. But the youngster must find his own identity, and it is true that keeping on the mentor's mask too long can inhibit or distort the best development of the growing child's personality. Adelson points out:

In adolescence especially they (identifications) sometimes seem to provide the means through which needed restructurings or crystallizations of personality take place. In some cases, the student can become himself only by first becoming someone else. He may find it difficult to acquire new and complex skills unless he protects himself psychically by borrowing, through identification, the teacher's power. Or he may use the identification as a mask, as a form of camouflage; while he pretends to himself and to others, that he is being a certain someone, achieving this or that identity, he is actually accomplishing the inner changes that will allow him to achieve an identity closer to his own talents and dispositions. In all of these uses the identification is shallow and temporary; it is used as a prop, a crutch, a smoke screen or a shield; once it has served its purpose it is dissolved. The identification serves as the means of achieving a new and necessary identity.[23]

Perhaps this is where the teacher-pupil relationship can be most supportive via the temporary role modeling to enable easier transition from one value system to another or from one subculture to another. Since the identity needs of Negro students vary from those of white students, as well as from other colored students within the Negro spectrum, it is not possible that any one teacher can hope to serve as an appropriate and attractive model for all the students in his class. It is important to have many teachers available in the parade of role models; it may even be necessary to import successful hero models from the Negro community in the form of resource personnel who may contribute to learning experiences of the pupils by discussing and describing their vocational and avocational skills, interests, and achievements, thus making learning smart, respectable, and obtainable. It is also necessary to recognize, as Adelson points out, the pluralism in teaching: "the many styles of influence, the many modes of connection that bind student and teacher to each other." [24] There is need to explore the typologies of relationships to Negro pupils in which various forms

[22] James Baldwin, "You've Done Everything You Can to Me . . . ," Conversation with Mr. Baldwin taped by WGBH-TV, Boston, Massachusetts.
[23] Joseph Adelson, "The Teacher as a Model," *The American Scholar*, Summer 1961, p. 389.
[24] Joseph Adelson, "The Teacher as a Model," *The American Scholar*, Summer 1961, p. 394.

of interaction can be studied in terms of personality development and achievement in school.

Insights concerning the adult leader's role in catalyzing desired adaptations within the subculture of adolescents which have direct implications for the teacher's role in developing self-direction and participation in community betterment come to us from studies carried out by the Center for Community and Field Service of New York University. Lukoff, Patterson, and Winick have reported:

> That emergence of an adolescent sub-culture characterized by self-directing community participation is not likely to occur without specific adult leadership which
>
> a. Gives supportive guidance; i.e., is responsive to adolescent problems, needs, and interests, both in terms of individuals and the group.
> b. Is positive and symbolic; i.e., in its behavior encourages identification with relevant values.
> c. Practices appropriate process manipulations; i.e., is sensitive and effective in both intervention and withdrawal tactics designed to maximize self-direction and community participation.[25]

The staff found that "where such an adult role was played subculture innovation developed; where it was not played . . . innovation either failed to occur or . . . (did not) last."[26]

Judging from the litany of repulsion as reflected in the school failure, disinterest, dislike, school vandalism, truancy, and dropout of Negro pupils, it may be even more urgent to study the strong powers of revulsion that are found in certain types of teachers. Perhaps as important as the "hero models" are the "antimodels" among the teachers who spawn discipline problems, distrust, and eventually defeat among the Negro students. The high incidence of the "transfer teacher," who flees from the classroom in the depressed areas of the inner city, provides grim evidence that many teachers would rather not be with the Negro student—to answer the question raised earlier.

Since there is no surplus of exemplary role models in home, neighborhood, and school for Negro youngsters, there is an urgent need to provide materials—including books, films, recordings, slides, etc.—that offer rich examples of Negro achievements and contributions in the United States and in other parts of the world. These should do more than reflect the Bunches, the Andersons, the Robinsons; they should tell the dramatic and heroic story of the middle-class and lower-middle-class Negroes whose station in life is nearer that of the majority of pupils, but who have made the upward move against familiar and difficult obstacles.

In a poignant biographical statement, Lena Horne comments on her own search for identity and cites the problem of the remoteness of the George Washington Carvers and the absence of any female images between the silent kitchen slavey and the streetwalker:

[25] Irving Lukoff, Franklin K. Patterson, and Charles Winick, "Is Society the Patient? Research and Action Implications," The Journal of Educational Sociology, October 1956, pp. 106–107.
[26] Irving Lukoff, Franklin K. Patterson, and Charles Winick, "Is Society the Patient? Research and Action Implications," The Journal of Educational Sociology, October 1956, p. 107.

I certainly never learned anything about my identity in school, because the only Negro mentioned in history books was George Washington Carver, and he was too pure and good to believe, though I did learn that other races had backgrounds they looked upon with pride. I kept trying to find some reason to feel the same way. Eventually, when "interested" people began to try and give me different "images" of myself, I came to the realization that nobody (and certainly not yet myself) seemed to understand the Negro woman who stood between the two conventionally accepted extremes: the "good," *quiet* colored woman who scrubbed and cooked and maybe made a respectable servant, and the whore....

So, by the time I was 16 and had returned to Brooklyn after spending seven years in the South, I may not have known who *I* was, but I had a pretty good idea of what white people were, and what *they* thought *we* were.[27]

Langston Hughes and Milton Melzer have given us a promising publication in *A Pictorial History of the Negro in America* that makes many little-known facts of the Negro contribution to medicine, science, industry, arts, and political science available to schools. The contributions of Negroes in the fight for freedom from the Revolutionary War to the present are featured. But this is only one example of a much-needed classroom aid; we need a library of such readers for every grade level.

What the teacher expects and does not expect of his Negro students and how he perceives them can serve to stimulate or to stunt the aspiration level and the development of Negro students. In recognition of the stereotypes of the Negro and the white-black (good-bad) thinking and projections that victimize these students, as elaborated by Dr. Grambs, safeguards must be set up to prevent premature foreclosure—conscious or unconscious—of what the culturally disadvantaged Negro can do or how far he can reach. Progress of the Negro student will be limited until all teachers free themselves in the classroom from the judgments, the assumptions, and the prejudices with which adults—even professionals—have for a long time approached the matter of estimating the nature of the individual Negro pupil.

Attention has been focused in recent years on the education of teachers who work with culturally deprived youngsters. Riessman has indicated the following traits and skills essential to the effective instructor:

The best type of teacher to win these children over to learning is a person of action who communicates in many ways and is not too dependent on words alone as a means of teaching. The leaders in the class and the rest of the children are likely to accept this type of person readily because he is close to the model after which they would like to pattern themselves....

The most successful teachers in terms of the culturally deprived children seem to combine the traditional concepts of structure, order, discipline, and strong external demands for achievement with the newer methods of down-to-earth learning by doing.[28]

Some consensus is visible within the Great Cities Projects suggesting that

[27] Lena Horne, "I Just Want To Be Myself," *Show*, September 1963, p. 62. [Reprinted by permission from *Show* September 1963 issue, copyright © 1963 by Hartford Publications, Inc.]

[28] Frank Riessman, *The Culturally Deprived Child*, New York: Harper & Row, Publishers, 1962, pp. 21–22.

teachers in the deprived areas do need special understandings, skills, and insights concerning the social matrix in which the Negro and white youngsters live and the kinds of special learning problems they present. There is also agreement that this preparation cannot be carried on by the teacher-education institutions working in isolation; rather, it calls for joint effort in recruiting, planning, training, placement, and in-service support and supervision between the city school systems and the colleges preparing classroom personnel.

Improvement in instruction will call for a reevaluation of the teacher-education curricula cutting across three major areas: (1) the substantive area—teachers must be well grounded in their major areas of instruction; (2) special methods—teachers must acquire special skills via a practicum tied to a methods-theory course or courses to bring the prospective teacher into close classroom contact with the culturally deprived youngster, his family, and his neighborhood; and (3) self—an awareness of himself as a person with reference to the dynamics of the teacher's own behavior, including his needs, job satisfactions, reactions to others, and their reactions to him. It is this last area that is most neglected in the preparation or improvement of teaching personalities and of teaching competencies. Experiences in the study of self can come through individual counseling in the advisory or supervisory situations, through group counseling sessions, through human relations training, and through psychiatric consultations.

This author questions whether pre-school programs can materially reduce the gap between disadvantaged and mainstream children. He suggests that many so-called disadvantaged youth are in reality not culturally deprived but hampered by poverty and weak self-concepts. A brief pre-school experience, he contends, can hardly reduce the effects of non-supportive family and social environments unless a full-scale revamping of the entire inner-city school system is undertaken.

Ivor Kraft

Are We Overselling the Pre-School Idea?

During the past year there has been a remarkable show of interest in nursery schools, especially for deprived, Negro children. In some ways this is gratifying, although it may result in overinvestment and forced faith in what is at best a very limited kind of educational innovation. It may also hatch another educational albatross to hang around our necks: tens of thousands of inferior custodial centers for small children.

Whether professional or lay people, most Americans believe that the first years of childhood are highly important in molding the well-adjusted personality, but this concern has never blinded us to what happens next. We have never settled for a "last chance" view of human nature.

For the good life beyond early childhood, schooling is essential in all advanced cultures, but no culture insists that three- four- or five-year-olds spend a structured part of the day in group outdoor play, indoor circle time, reading readiness, and so forth. Yet all cultures do seem to recognize that small children require freedom to play in benign surroundings and the more or less regular care of regularly available and responsible adults (usually the mother or a group of mother substitutes).

Group care of small children is often an enormous convenience to parents, and it can contribute a great deal to stable family life. Also, it makes all the difference in the world during emergencies. Nurseries fulfilled a vital role in Britain during the days of the blitz. During the Second World War we opened thousands of nurseries; while many of these centers were far from ideal, they made a great deal of difference for tens of thousands of American mothers who were working long hours in war industry.

Advocates of pre-schooling for "culturally deprived" children view it not as a baby-sitting service, but as a major compensatory device, a means of diminishing the inequalities of povery. Theoretically, this is an attractive approach. But there is sometimes a chasm between theory and practice.

To begin with, many of our so-called "culturally deprived" families are not culturally deprived. They are merely poor. They need more money, better housing, more dignified jobs, increased respect as human beings regardless of race or ethnic origin. These needs will not be met by pre-schooling.

To what extent will the pre-schooling be genuinely compensatory? What happens when fifteen or so homogeneously deprived children spend a few hours a day in the care of an ordinary or even untrained teacher, and return to the same old environment? Can we expect to transform them into little scholars when we do not even attempt this with more "advantaged" youngsters? Can we do it on the basis of perhaps twenty or thirty minutes of deliberately structured intellectual experiences? (We have to allow for dressing and undressing, juice time, rest time, toileting, etc.)

It would perhaps be a different story if we were talking about an eight- or ten-hour day, highly skilled teachers, much individual attention, close contact with parents, and if we kept the children in this careful setting for not three months but for three years. Such a program would require an expenditure of at least $2,000 per child per year, and not a bargain basement budget of $200 to $500 per child.

We can assume that the pre-schools will produce certain measurable improvements in conventional school readiness and a rise in I.Q. test scores. What will happen next, when these children reach the first grade?

That all depends on what takes place in the first grade. And the second grade—and so on throughout the ensuing school careers of those children who live in low-income and slum neighborhoods. No responsible child development specialist could possibly claim that a few months of good pre-schooling will set the child up for life. Indeed, it is highly unlikely that it will set him up for much beyond the first few weeks of the first grade.

Unless we close our eyes to the massive evidence that keeps pouring out of our inferior elementary schools in the inner-city systems across the nation, we can easily predict that even the finest pre-school experience for deprived and segregated children will wash out and disappear as these children pass through the grades. Their I.Q. test scores will fall. Many of them will become functional illiterates. Thirty per cent of them will be dropouts by the ninth grade.

Top-quality early childhood education has an important role to play in American life, but there are pitfalls in overselling the pre-school idea. We may deceive ourselves into thinking that pre-schools can seriously offset the severer familial effects of poverty, when they can never substitute for the broad range of healthful, normative home and family experiences of small children. Also, we may be deflecting attention from the really crucial sectors in educational reconstruction, the primary and secondary inner-city schools. It is here that massive expenditures and profound efforts at innovating are needed, from the first grade through the twelfth. In devoting overly optimistic attention to pre-schools we are perhaps behaving like pastry cooks hard at work on the icing without having bothered to bake the cake.

It may be that just as we have never found pre-schooling an essential to future educational success for typical middle-class youth, so we will not find it an essential to school achievement for non-middle-class youth, once we provide this youth with really satisfactory buildings, teachers, curricula, as well as the genuine promise of future success in life.

4 WORK

This article and the one following are U.S. government reports on out-of-school youth who were unemployed as of February 1963. Although new labor figures have continued to accumulate, these studies reflect current characteristics of unemployed youth including educational and family background, reasons for leaving school, and status in the labor force. The first study indicates that dropouts find fewer jobs and earn less money than high-school graduates.

Vera C. Perrella and Forrest A. Bogan

Out of School Youth — Part 1

Traditionally, entry into the full-time labor force follows upon leaving school, and youth and lack of work experience inevitably result in higher unemployment rates than for older, experienced workers. In addition to this age-old hurdle, today's young people are faced with the paradox of comparative prosperity overall and increasing difficulties for themselves in a labor market progressively and rapidly more selective under the impact of technological change. Jobs of the types which served as entering wedges for young workers are not increasing in proportion to the growing numbers competing for them.

Population and labor force projections indicate a sharpening of the problems of young people in the labor market. The decade of the sixties may be described as the decade of the young worker in terms of expected population and labor force developments. By 1970, it is estimated that the population 16 to 21 years old will number 22 million, almost half again as large as in 1960. Although the proportions in these ages who will be in school are expected to be higher, the number in the labor force is also expected to increase by 3½ million, constituting 28 percent of the total increase of 12.6 million in the labor force between 1960 and 1970.

To get information about the early work experience of youth, a sample survey of 16- to 21-year-old persons who were no longer in school and were not college graduates was made in February 1963.[1] The survey provides more extensive information about the socioeconomic characteristics of this group than was previously available on a nation-wide basis.

EDUCATIONAL ATTAINMENT

In February 1963, there were 6.7 million out-of-school persons 16 to 21 years old who were not college graduates. About 45 percent had dropped out before completing high school, 48 percent had completed high school, and 7 percent had completed 1 to 3 years of college. Three million did not have a high school diploma. One-fourth of these did not even reach high school, and one-half had dropped out in the second or third year of high school. The concentration of dropouts in the second and third year of high school seems to be largely the result of the normal coincidence of those school grades with the age of 16—in most States the minimum age at which students may stop going to school. Notwithstanding the usual legal age minimum, about a third of all dropouts had left school before reaching 16. Nonwhite students more often than whites had dropped out before they were 16 and before entering high school:

Percent of dropouts who—at time of dropout, were—	All dropouts	Nonwhite dropouts
Under 16 years of age	34.2	44.6
Under 15 years	12.8	21.5
15 years	21.4	23.2
Did not attend high school	22.9	30.7

A large proportion of dropouts were below the usual grade for their age at time of dropout:

[1] This and the following article are based primarily on information from supplementary questions in the February 1963 monthly survey of the labor force, conducted for the Bureau of Labor Statistics by the Bureau of the Census through its Current Population Survey. Data relate to persons 16 to 21 years of age who were no longer in school, were not college graduates, and were in the civilian noninstitutional population in the calendar week ending February 16, 1963. Members of the Armed Forces and inmates of institutions are excluded.

Since the estimates resulting from this survey are based on a sample, they may differ from the figures that would have been obtained from a complete census. The sampling variability may be relatively large in cases where the numbers are small. Because of the comparatively small size of the group covered in this survey, the number of sample cases that could be used was small. Consequently, numbers under 200,000 and percents based on them should be used with caution.

The findings of the survey may be compared with an earlier study on *School and Early Employment Experience of Youth, A Report on Seven Communities, 1952–57* (BLS Bulletin 1277, 1960).

Age at time of dropout	Usual grade[2]	Percent of dropouts below usual grade
15 to 18 years		42.4
15 years	2d or 1st year high school	26.8
16 years	3d or 2d year high school	47.1
17 years	4th or 3d year high school	38.2
18 years	4th year high school	71.0

REASONS FOR LEAVING SCHOOL

While it is possible that the relative importance of the various reasons leading to dropout would be different if reported by school authorities rather than by the dropouts themselves, the relevance of the dropouts' own report of what motivated them is indisputable, despite the coloration that subjective bias and the passage of time may have added.

Close to half the male dropouts attributed their leaving school to school-connected reasons (lack of interest in school, poor grades, difficulties with the school authorities) and about a fourth gave economic reasons (unemployment or inadequate income in the family). Half again as many white as nonwhite males gave school-connected reasons. About the same proportion of white and nonwhite males said they left school because of poor grades, and a higher proportion of nonwhite males than white left because of difficulties with the school authorities. However, the proportion of the white males who said they left because they were not interested in school was almost five times that of the nonwhite. There was no significant difference in the proportions of white and nonwhite males who gave economic reasons.

Among the female dropouts, the reasons most often given were marriage or pregnancy (40 percent) and school-connected factors (26 percent); the proportion who gave economic reasons was about half that of the males. About half the nonwhite girls left because of marriage or pregnancy, compared with 38 percent of the white girls.

Generally, then, for the males, school-connected rather than economic or other outside factors were the overriding consideration which led them to drop out of school, whatever other elements may have been weighed in making the decision. School-connected factors were also important among the females, though to a lesser extent.

FAMILY CHARACTERISTICS

The extent to which environmental factors influence the roles of both the student and the school is illustrated by a study of family characteristics, such as

[2] In this report, the two school grades with the largest numbers of students of a given age, as shown in the *Census of Population, 1960, Detailed Characteristics, U.S. Summary, PC(1)–1D,* U.S. Bureau of the Census, are considered the usual or normal grades for that age.

the money income of the student's family, the amount of schooling his parents had had, and their residence.

Income

Low levels of family income were highly associated with early school-leaving. For example, of the more recent dropouts who were unmarried and still living at home, 2 out of 5 were members of families with an annual income under $3,000; the income was less than $2,000 in more than half the families within that group. In contrast, of those who had completed at least 4 years of high school, only 1 out of 5 families had incomes under $3,000. The number of grades completed was also related to family income. Among youths in families with less than $3,000 income, the proportion who dropped out before reaching high school was almost double that of those who dropped out of high school. Farm residence may have had some influence here, since money income of farm families tends to be low, and relatively high proportions of farm dropouts leave school before reaching high school. Among both dropouts and graduates, greater proportions of nonwhite than white youths were in families with less than $3,000 income. Nonwhite graduates were four times as likely as white graduates, and even twice as likely as white dropouts, to be members of families in this low-income group.

Parents' Education

Another aspect of family background, the school attainment of parents, also plays a strong role in the student's school achievement. Among the young people for whom parents' schooling was reported, the great majority of dropouts were from families in which neither parent had completed high school. A high proportion—almost half—of the young people attained at least a high school diploma even though neither of their parents had graduated from high school, illustrating the increasing trend toward more education.

Residence

Historically, farm residents have left school earlier than nonfarm residents. Among this group of young people, too, those who were farm residents when they last attended school were somewhat more likely to be dropouts than those who were nonfarm residents. Moreover, the proportion of the farm males who dropped out of elementary school was about twice that of the nonfarm males; for girls from farm families, the proportion of elementary school dropouts was not quite double that of those from nonfarm families, as shown in the following tabulation:

MIGRATION

Since leaving school, about 4 out of 10 of the men and 6 out of 10 of the women who were farm residents when they last attended school had moved to

| Highest grade completed | Residence in last year of school | | | |
| | Farm | | Nonfarm | |
	Male	Female	Male	Female
Total (percent)	100.0	100.0	100.0	100.0
Less than 4 years of high school	54.5	48.5	50.7	40.3
8 years of elementary school, or less	34.6	19.8	16.4	11.8
1 to 3 years of high school	19.8	28.6	34.3	28.5
4 years of high school, or more	45.5	51.5	40.3	59.7

nonfarm areas. Among those with at least a high school diploma, the men were more likely to remain farm residents than the women, reflecting the lesser opportunity for jobs for women in farm areas. The continuing exodus of young people from farms has increased the supply of young people competing for jobs in non-agricultural industries, in addition to contributing to raising the median age of the farm population.

STATUS AFTER SCHOOL

The survey included a series of questions about labor force status, beginning with, "When you left school, did you have a job waiting for you?" Nearly 30 percent had a job waiting. Over 50 percent looked for a job after leaving school; a small proportion of the men, and about 1 in 4 of the women, did not look for work.

Among those who looked for work, a majority of both the graduates and dropouts found their first job, either full or part time, within 4 weeks after they started to look. About 13 percent had to look for 15 weeks or longer before finding a job, and about the same proportion had not yet found one as of February 1963 (some of these had undoubtedly started to look only a short time prior to the survey date). Dropouts were much more likely than graduates to have looked for work without finding any. The nonwhite graduates had the most difficulty in finding jobs. They were less likely than either white or non-white dropouts to have a job waiting when they left school, and—in contrast to the white graduates—it took them about as long to find work as it did the dropouts. This may reflect an unwillingness, at least initially, to settle for the less-skilled jobs more readily available to nonwhite workers.

Among the youths who had worked at some time since leaving school, fewer than one-tenth each of the men and the women had worked at part-time jobs only—a large majority of the men, and nearly half of the women, because they could not find full-time jobs.

In terms of the time which elapsed between leaving school and obtaining the first full-time job, graduates were better off than dropouts. One-half the high school graduates started to work on their first full-time job within a month after leaving school, compared with 40 percent of the dropouts. On the other hand, relatively twice as many dropouts as graduates did not start on their first full-time job for at least a year. The larger proportion of younger persons among the drop-outs may have some bearing here, since they may either have waited longer than the graduates before starting to look, or had to look longer because of their youth. A contributing factor may be that many jobs are not open to persons under 18 years of age. In addition, there is no way to tell how many of the youths, both graduates and dropouts, initially were not interested in working and therefore did not start looking for some time, or at first wanted only a part-time job and later decided to look for a full-time one.

Most of the young people obtained their first full-time jobs either by applying directly or through friends or relatives. Other methods such as referrals by schools, public or private employment offices, etc., accounted for about 15 per-cent of the dropouts' jobs and 30 percent of the graduates'. Graduates were more likely to apply directly than dropouts. Overall, larger proportions of white than nonwhite youths applied directly.

Occupations

About two-thirds of the men, both dropouts and graduates, found their first full-time jobs in blue-collar occupations. Male graduates were much more likely than dropouts to obtain white-collar jobs (22 percent and 8 percent, respectively). Dropouts were twice as likely as graduates to obtain work as farm laborers, reflecting to some extent the high proportion of dropouts that occur among farm youths.

There is no sharp evidence of the advantage of a high school diploma with re-spect to occupation groups of the jobs obtained by male graduates and drop-outs upon leaving school. The circumstances are somewhat different for women. In many occupations considered women's work (typing, stenography, clerical work, etc.), high school education has immediate, tangible relevancy. Among these 16- to 21-year-old women, 60 percent of the graduates were clerical work-ers in their first full-time jobs, a proportion about four times that of the dropouts. A majority of the latter were service workers (42 percent) and operatives (25 percent).

Earnings

The data on weekly earnings of two groups—graduates who had 4 years of high school or more, and dropouts—who were wage and salary workers in their first full-time jobs clearly buttress the advantage of a high school diploma. About two-fifths of the male graduates earned $60–$79 (their model group), compared with one-fifth of the dropouts. The proportion who earned $80 or more was also double that of the dropouts. About a fourth of the male dropouts—three times as many as graduates—earned less than $40.

Although women, on the average, earned less than men, the advantage of graduation was unmistakable. The proportion of graduates who earned less than $40 on their first full-time job was less than half that of the dropouts. Over half the graduates earned $50 or more on their first full-time job, compared with one-fifth of the dropouts. Forty percent of the female dropouts got their first full-time job in private household work or other service occupations, and almost all of these earned less than $40. The greater proportion of graduates in the higher earnings groups reflects to some extent the occupations they held.

Earnings differentials in the same occupation group further confirm the advantage the graduate has over the dropout. About half the male dropouts who were operatives earned less than $50 a week, compared with about a fourth of the graduates (chart 1). Among women clerical workers, relatively twice as many dropouts as graduates earned less than $50 a week.

CHART 1: Weekly Wage or Salary Earnings of Dropouts and High School Graduates on First Full-Time Job

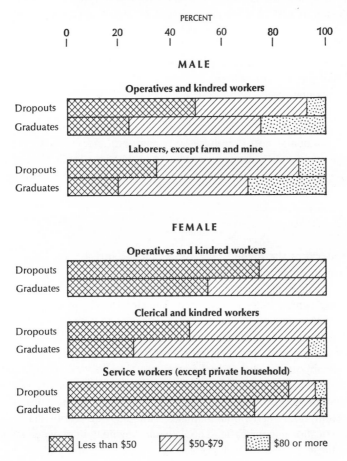

STATUS IN FEBRUARY 1963

Largely because many girls married and left the labor force, there was a reduction of about 13 percentage points (to 69 percent) in labor force participation
between the time of leaving school (varying, since they left school at different
times) and February 1963, the time of the survey. The decrease was greater among
the white than the nonwhite girls and among the dropouts than the graduates.

Most of the males who did not look for a job immediately after leaving school
had worked or looked for work since then. Among the women, the proportion
who had never worked and never looked remained high—close to one-fourth
of the dropouts and one-tenth of the graduates. Eighty-six percent of the
married women gave family responsibilities as the reason why they had never
looked for work. Among the single women, family responsibilities and taking
training were equally important—about 30 percent each.

Only 220,000 men (8 percent of the total) were not in the labor force in February 1963; about half of these were dropouts, and 1 out of 5 was nonwhite.
Almost two-thirds were taking job training, were waiting to join the Armed
Forces, or were ill or unable to work. A majority of the 220,000 had worked at
some time since leaving school. About 20 percent each had never looked for
work and had looked but without success.

Of all the women covered in the survey, 45 percent were not in the labor force
in February 1963. The proportion of dropouts who were not in the labor force
was two times that of the graduates. About 80 percent of those not in the labor
force—both graduates and dropouts—were married, and family responsibilities
bulked large among the reasons for not being in the labor force. However, about
1 in 6 of all the women not in the labor force was interested in working.

THE UNEMPLOYED

About 850,000 of these youths were unemployed in February 1963—18.6 percent of those in the labor force at that time. (The rate is not seasonally adjusted.)
There was considerable variation in the rate for different groups. Men had a
higher unemployment rate than women. The dropouts' rate of 27 percent was
twice that of the graduates'. The nonwhite rate was as high as that for all dropouts, largely because one-third of the nonwhite women graduates in the labor
force were unemployed. The male nonwhite graduates had improved their position considerably over what it had been right after leaving school, at least in
terms of having a job, since their unemployment rate in February was not significantly different from that of white male graduates. Farm males had lower
unemployment rates than nonfarm males. Among high school graduates who
had taken vocational courses in school, unemployment rates were appreciably
lower for those who also had postschool training, as apprentices, in special
schools, or elsewhere. For youths who had completed elementary school but

had dropped out of high school, training—whether taken in vocational courses in high school or subsequently—did not appear to have any significant effect on lowering unemployment rates.

Among unemployed males, unemployment of 15 weeks or more as of February 1963 was more common among dropouts (32 percent) than graduates (17 percent). On the other hand, there was no significant difference in the proportions for women graduates and women dropouts—about a fourth in each group had been unemployed 15 weeks or more. About one-third of the unemployed men and 40 percent of the unemployed women had never worked. Of the unemployed men who had worked at some time, three-fourths had been blue-collar workers, a larger proportion than among the employed. Among the women, two-fifths of the unemployed had been service workers on their last job, compared with one-fifth of the employed, as shown in the following tabulation:

	Men		Women	
	Experienced unemployed	Employed	Experienced unemployed	Employed
All occupations	100.0	100.0	100.0	100.0
White-collar workers	5.7	17.3	39.8	66.6
Blue-collar workers	76.0	64.7	19.3	13.6
Service workers	9.8	7.8	40.9	18.5
Farm workers	8.4	10.3	—	1.3

The young people who were unemployed were asked, "What is the lowest wage or salary you will accept?" and "If you were offered a job in another part of the country at this weekly wage or salary, would you take it?" Among the men, graduates, and dropouts showed the same willingness to move—3 out of 5. However, relatively three times as many graduates as dropouts attached conditions regarding the kind of work, living costs, and other considerations. Unemployed women were less willing to move, and this attitude was as strong for dropouts as for those with more schooling. Single women were somewhat more willing to move than married women. Men most often gave economic reasons for being unwilling to move (too expensive to move, wage or salary too low, etc.), as shown below:

Reason for unwillingness to move	Male	Female
Total	100.0	100.0
Home or family	30.4	44.3
Economic	52.1	36.1
Other	17.5	19.6

In February, roughly 3 out of 4 unemployed graduates and dropouts, men and women, were taking training, had definite plans to do so, or were interested in doing so:

	Men		Women	
	Dropouts	Graduates	Dropouts	Graduates
Total employed	100.0	100.0	100.0	100.0
With plans or interested	79.5	72.7	77.1	66.3
Taking training	3.3	5.6	—	4.6
Definite plans	9.5	25.2	14.0	15.4
Interested	66.8	42.0	63.1	46.3
Definitely	57.3	34.3	47.8	32.0
Maybe	9.5	7.7	15.3	14.3
Not interested in training	20.5	27.3	22.9	33.7

THE EMPLOYED

The total number employed in February 1963 was 3.8 million, almost equally divided between men and women. In addition to 350,000 men and women who had had 1 to 3 years of college, there were 1.8 million men and 1.7 million women who were either high school graduates or dropouts. Eighty-three percent of the men and 78 percent of the women were working full-time. Another 10 percent each of the men and the women usually worked full-time, although they worked part-time during the survey week.

In February 1963, approximately half the men worked in manufacturing industries and retail trade, with graduates more likely to be working in the better paying durable goods industries. Only 11 percent of the men worked in agriculture, and about 40 percent in service, construction, and the other industries. Among the women, proportionately more graduates than dropouts worked in service industries, including finance, but more dropouts worked in manufacturing and retail trade. Overall, for both graduates and dropouts these three industries accounted for more than 8 out of 10 of the jobs held by women.

In the job held in February 1963, as on the first full-time job they held after leaving school, most of the men were concentrated in blue-collar occupations; most of the women graduates were clerical and kindred workers, and the women dropouts were operatives and service workers.

Job-Changing

While many of the young people had changed jobs between their first full-time job and the job they held in February 1963, there were few overall changes in the proportions in the several broad occupation groups. There was some shifting from farm to nonfarm jobs among male dropouts. Fewer women graduates were in service (excluding private household) jobs, and more were in white-collar jobs. Among women dropouts, the proportion in service (excluding private household) occupations declined. The occupation groups of the longest held jobs for both men and women were much the same as for the first full-time and the current jobs.

About 1.7 million of these young people, at a minimum, had changed jobs at least once. It is likely that the volume of job changing was even greater, since this total excludes both those who never had a full-time job and those who may have held only part-time jobs before. Others who either were unemployed in February or had left the labor market are also excluded. Even this minimal figure represents about a third of the number who entered the labor force at the time of leaving school.

Earnings

Among those who had full-time jobs in February 1963, 20 percent of the male dropouts were earning less than $40, compared with 6 percent of the men who had at least a high school diploma; 71 percent of the latter were earning $60 or more, compared with 45 percent of the dropouts. Among women, 33 percent of the dropouts were earning less than $40 on full-time jobs, compared with 12 percent of the graduates. Substantially larger proportions of nonwhite than white workers had earnings in the low-income groups.

These earnings differentials between graduates and dropouts and between whites and nonwhites in the jobs held in February indicated a persistence of the contrast shown in their first jobs. However, both dropouts and graduates, men and women, showed improvement, as evidenced by the larger proportions who were earning over $50 a week at their current job (chart 2). Nonwhite men improved their earnings position, but nonwhite women did not; about 8 out of 10 were earning less than $50 a week on both the first and the February full-time jobs.

REVIEW OF FINDINGS

△ About 3 million, or half, of the young people 16 to 21 years old in February 1963 who were no longer in school and were not college graduates were school dropouts. Boys were somewhat more likely to have dropped out than girls.

△ Almost one-fourth of all the dropouts did not even reach high school, and half left school in the second or third year of high school. Among those who dropped out when 15 to 18 years old, 2 out of 5 were overage in grade.

△ About one-third of the dropouts had left school at 16—more than at any other age.

△ Close to half the boys and one-fourth of the girls said they dropped out of school because of school-connected reasons.

△ About one-fifth of the dropouts said they had to leave school because of economic reasons.

△ Two out of 5 of the dropouts who were still living at home were in families with incomes below $3,000.

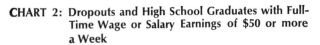

CHART 2: Dropouts and High School Graduates with Full-Time Wage or Salary Earnings of $50 or more a Week

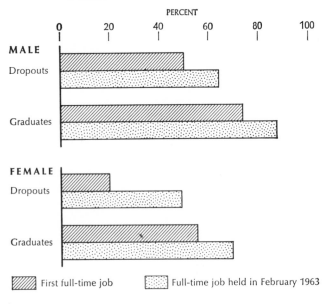

First full-time job   Full-time job held in February 1963

△ Half the high school graduates, but only one-fifth of the dropouts, had at least one parent who had graduated from high school.

△ More of the dropouts who lived on farms dropped out before going to high school, compared with nonfarm dropouts. A greater proportion of girls than of boys who were farm residents at the time of leaving school had since moved to nonfarm areas.

△ In February 1963, the unemployment rate for the dropouts was 27 percent— twice as high as for graduates.

△ Male dropouts were twice as likely as graduates to be out of work for long periods (15 weeks or more) before finding their first job.

△ Employed dropouts, on the average, earned less than employed graduates, even in the same occupation group.

△ Nonwhite youths had a more difficult time getting jobs than white youths, and earned less, on the average.

This is the second of two articles on unemployed youth issued by the Department of Labor in 1963. The studies reflect the kinds of data officially collected by this society about those of its youth who leave the school system. The following article points up a trend toward unemployability among disadvantaged youth in a society that appears increasingly to offer no work to the unskilled.

Thomas E. Swanstrom

Out of School Youth – Part 2

Education and training requirements for entry jobs have stiffened at a time when youth unemployment rates are on a high plateau. Youths entering the labor force for the first time are usually evaluated as prospective employees in terms of their education and training, since they have little or no work experience. Consequently, it is useful to examine the dropouts' and high school graduates' backgrounds as they relate to the problem of unemployment among young persons.

CURRICULUM

The purpose of a vocational or commercial program in high school is better to equip students who will look for jobs after they leave school. Only 30 percent of the youths who dropped out of high school followed such programs. It may be that the proportion with vocational or commercial programs would have been higher if more schools had offered these programs in the 9th and 10th grades—the highest grades attended by a majority of the high school dropouts included in the survey.

Among the young men who were high school graduates, about 38 percent had taken either of these programs, only a slightly higher proportion than for dropouts. But the differences in the proportions were more pronounced among the girls; 50 percent of the graduates had been enrolled in vocational or commercial programs, two-thirds again as high as for the dropouts. Since better educated and trained workers are more likely to be in the labor force, this variation may partially explain the higher post-school labor force participation rates of the female graduates. Probably a more important factor is the smaller proportion of graduates than dropouts who were married.

Even though most students do not follow a vocational or commercial program while in high school, almost 95 percent of the male graduates and about 70 percent of the dropouts completed at least one vocational or commercial course.

As shown in the following tabulation, nearly the same proportion of dropouts as graduates had completed the most commonly given vocational courses despite the shorter period of time that dropouts had been in school.

Proportions taking vocational or commercial courses

Male	Graduates	Dropouts	Female	Graduates	Dropouts
Typing	54	18	Typing	87	50
Machine Shop	37	28	Home Economics	73	76
Metal Working	34	27	Bookkeeping	52	21
Carpentry	32	29	Shorthand	51	15
Agriculture	29	18	Business Machines	36	5
Bookkeeping	21	6			

On the other hand, both the male and female graduates were much more likely than dropouts to have completed commercial courses, and this training doubtless gave the graduates an added advantage in finding clerical jobs; about 68 percent of the female graduates employed in February 1963 were employed in clerical jobs compared with only 20 percent of the female dropouts.

As part of their high school education, some students participate in a school-work program in which they attend school part-time and work part-time, while earning required school credit for their work. The outside work they do is directly related to the subject matter studied in school. These programs are given in comparatively few schools and primarily in the field of distributive (sales) and business education. Only 7 percent of the graduates and 3 percent of the dropouts reported enrollment in a school-work program.

EMPLOYMENT GUIDANCE

Since the end of World War II, a sharp rise in employment has occurred in those occupations which require high levels of training and skill. Since 1947, the proportion employed in white-collar occupations has increased sharply while that for the unskilled jobs has decreased; these trends are expected to continue during the remainder of this decade.

Yet only 4 out of 10 youths who had attended high school said they had received any guidance from a school official or from a State employment office about the kind of training they should have or the kind of work they should look for after leaving school;[1] a somewhat larger proportion of girls than boys had received such advice. Graduates were more likely than dropouts to have had guidance from their school or from the State employment service as shown below:

[1] Of course, some students may have received job guidance without recognizing it as such.

Source of job guidance	Both Sexes		Male		Female	
	Drop-outs	Grad-uates	Drop-outs	Grad-uates	Drop-outs	Grad-uates
Total	100.0	100.0	100.0	100.0	100.0	100.0
Received guidance	22.4	56.1	20.3	51.1	24.0	58.9
School only	17.1	37.8	14.4	34.6	19.2	39.6
Employment service only	4.2	4.9	5.1	4.8	3.6	5.0
School and employment service	1.0	13.4	.8	11.7	1.2	14.3
Did not receive guidance	77.6	43.9	79.7	48.9	76.0	41.1

Job guidance from the school or the employment service appeared to have had some beneficial results for the dropouts when they left school. Three out of ten of those who had received guidance had a job waiting when they left school, compared with about two out of ten of those who had not received job guidance. Job guidance did not benefit the graduates to a similar extent; about one-third had a job waiting whether they had obtained guidance or not.

TRAINING SINCE LEAVING SCHOOL

Youths were asked, "Since you left school, have you taken any training such as accounting, secretarial, electrician, laboratory technician, etc.?" It was found that high school graduates were much more likely than dropouts to have entered such training programs after leaving school—3 out of 10 graduates, but only 1 out of 10 dropouts. Girl graduates were more likely to have entered a training program than boys, as shown in the following tabulation:

	Proportions with training		
	Both Sexes	Male	Female
Dropouts	9.5	9.8	9.3
Graduates	29.0	23.8	31.8

Many of the boys took training as mechanics, repairmen, or clerical workers; girls chiefly studied to be secretaries, clerical workers, or beauticians.

The most common sources of instruction for post-school training programs for both dropouts and graduates were special schools, such as technical institutes, and secretarial or barber schools. Male dropouts and graduates had training in special schools in roughly the same proportions—slightly over one-third of each group with training. Female graduates, on the other hand, were about twice as likely as dropouts to have attended special schools—about three-fourths of the graduates with training compared with 40 percent of the dropouts. On-the-job training programs were the second most important source of training for both young men and women.

A high proportion of the youths who had taken post-school training found jobs using their new skills. About two-thirds of the females and half of the males who were no longer taking training used their training on a job. High school graduates were more successful than dropouts in obtaining jobs in their field of training, the ratios being 68 percent and 50 percent, respectively.

EMPLOYMENT WHILE IN SCHOOL

Many students work while they attend high school, some because of economic necessity and others to obtain extra spending money or for other reasons. Dropouts were much less likely than high school graduates to have worked while in school. Three out of five graduates had held a job as against one out of three dropouts. Of course, the graduates could be expected to have had more opportunity for employment since they were usually older at the time of leaving and probably had spent more time in school than the dropouts. The acquisition of a job may have enabled some youths to remain in high school until they graduated because it lessened the financial burden. This point is reinforced by the fact that one out of five dropouts reported they left school for economic reasons.

Male dropouts and graduates had worked in similar occupations while in school. One in four of each group had jobs as nonfarm laborers, while dropouts were somewhat more likely to take farm jobs than graduates. On the other hand, there were marked differences between the occupations at which female dropouts and graduates worked. A greater proportion of such dropouts worked as farm and as private household workers whereas the graduates were more likely to have worked at sales jobs while in school.

Both graduates and dropouts who held jobs while in school fared better in the job market after leaving school than those who did not. Among the dropouts, 30 percent of those who had worked during their school years had jobs waiting when they withdrew from school, compared with only 17 percent of those who did not work. Graduates who held a job while in school were almost three times as likely as those who did not work to have a job waiting upon graduation—44 percent and 17 percent, respectively. In a substantial number of cases, the jobs waiting for those who had worked while in school may have been the same ones held while in school.

MOBILITY

About 40 percent of the males and 60 percent of the females who had been farm residents in their last semester of elementary or high school had moved to nonfarm areas by February 1963. The farm to nonfarm shift was made by about the same proportions of dropouts and graduates.

About seven out of ten males who moved from a farm area after leaving school did so for economic reasons. Among young men who had moved from one farm residence to another or from one city or town to another, only four out of ten did so for economic reasons. Among young women, however, only a small group moved because of economic considerations; the majority reported the causes as marriage or that their husbands needed to move. There were no differences in the proportions of graduates and dropouts who moved for economic reasons.

Migrants were less likely to be unemployed than those who had not moved. Among nonfarm residents at the time of the survey, the unemployment rate for dropouts who had moved, 23 percent, was significantly lower than that for those who had not moved, 31 percent. Even among those who had completed at least four years of high school, the unemployment rate was twice as high for nonmovers as for movers—15 and 8 percent, respectively.

Girls, both graduates and dropouts, who had moved since their last year of school were much less likely than nonmovers to be in the labor force in February 1963. This tendency probably reflected the large proportion who moved because they had married or because their husbands had to move.

PROFILE OF THE UNEMPLOYED

Some 850,000 (18.6 percent) of the young people in the labor force were unemployed in February 1963, and dropouts were twice as likely as graduates to be looking for work. One-third of the unemployed men and 40 percent of the women had never worked. Unemployed persons who had worked at some time were asked why they had left their last job. About half of the boys and one-fourth of the girls said they had left for economic reasons—slack work, no more work available, or the firm had moved or gone out of business. Even though young workers have much difficulty in finding employment, one out of six quit their jobs to seek one where they could improve their status—to earn more money, work shorter hours, or better their chances for advancement, etc. The transitory nature of some of the jobs held by young women is illustrated by the high proportion (one-fourth) who left because their jobs were temporary. Nearly the same proportion of the girls had stopped working—at least temporarily—because of household responsibilities.

Many unemployed young people had to depend on members of their families for financial assistance since only a small minority received unemployment compensation. In February 1963, about half of all unemployed persons in the Nation were receiving unemployment benefits compared with only 14 percent of the unemployed out-of-school youth. Graduates were twice as likely as dropouts to be receiving unemployment benefits (19 and 9 percent, respectively). The prime reason for the wide variation in proportions may be that young workers, and especially dropouts, may not have worked long enough during the prior year to become eligible for benefits or may not have worked in industries or for employers covered by the unemployment insurance law.

In their search for work, both graduates and dorpouts most freqeuntly contacted their friends and relatives, employers other than those they had formerly worked for, and the State employment service. Male graduates tended to use more methods than dropouts, and they also applied to former employers and placed or answered advertisements to a more significant extent.

In response to the question, "What kind of work are you looking for?," 60 percent of the unemployed women graduates reported clerical jobs and approximately the same proportion of dropouts indicated service or operative jobs (chart 1). The percentages seeking these jobs were nearly the same as the actual proportion of jobs reported held by employed female graduates and dropouts. The job goals of the young men were not so well defined. About half of both the unemployed graduates and dropouts reported they would take "any kind" of job, thus suggesting they lacked specific skills.

Virtually all of the unemployed were looking for full-time jobs. In response to the question, "What is the lowest weekly wage or salary you will accept?,"

CHART 1: Types of Jobs Sought by Unemployed Dropouts and High School Graduates,[2] by Sex February 1963

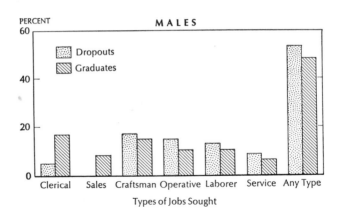

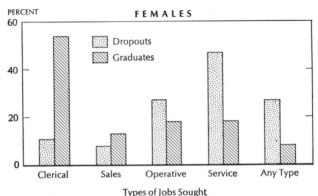

[2] Persons aged 16 to 21 who did not attend college

a greater proportion of the dropouts than graduates said they would be willing to work for less than $40 a week on a full-time job. Among the dropouts, one-fourth of the males and one-half of the females would accept that little money, significantly greater proportions than among the respective graduates (chart 2). The chart also shows that the minimum wage and salary desired was not un-realistic when compared with earnings of employed persons in the same age group and with comparable education.

CHART 2: Lowest Full-Time Earnings Unemployed Dropouts and High School Graduates[3] Would Accept Com-pared with Earnings of Employed Youths, by Sex, February 1963

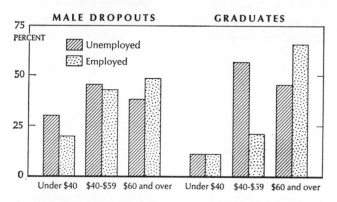

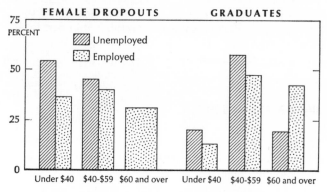

Actual or Acceptable Weekly Earnings

WORK EXPERIENCE IN 1962

Information was obtained on the extent of work experience and unemploy-ment during 1962 for those persons who had not attended college and who had dropped out or graduated from school prior to January 1963. While about equal

[3] Persons aged 16 to 21. Included among high school graduates were persons with some col-lege training

proportions (over 90 percent) of male dropouts and graduates had worked at some time during 1962, among the women, a much greater proportion of the graduates than dropouts had worked. Only half the female dropouts had worked, as compared with over eight out of ten graduates, primarily because a larger proportion of the dropouts were married and therefore had household responsibilities. Among dropouts who did work, two-thirds were employed for six months or less. Year-round employment at full-time jobs in 1962 was much more common among graduates even though a larger proportion of them had finished school during 1962 and therefore were not as likely as dropouts to have worked at such jobs all year.

Dropouts were more likely than graduates to have had unemployment during the course of a year. Among those in the labor force during the year, half the dropouts and about one-third of the graduates had been unemployed at one time or another in 1962. Greater proportions of males than females had at least one week of joblessness.

Among youths unemployed during the year were approximately a quarter of a million (60 percent of them dropouts) who had looked for work for at least one week but could not find any. Inability to find any work was particularly evident among female dropouts, with one out of four of the unemployed unable to find a job.

Of those who had worked at some time during the year but had also been unemployed, dropouts were twice as likely as graduates to have been jobless for a total of more than half a year. The percentages of dropouts with more than half a year of unemployment is especially striking since it was half again as large as the 15 percent of workers of all ages. The high proportion of dropouts with a substantial amount of unemployment may be attributed in part to the temporary nature of many of their jobs. Half of the dropouts had two or more periods of unemployment during 1962, compared with one-fourth of the graduates.

ACTIVITY SINCE LEAVING SCHOOL

In order to obtain a panoramic view of what the youth had done since leaving school, they were asked, "Looking back at the time since you last attended school, what were you doing most of the time?" Virtually all the young men—about nine out of ten—reported they had spent most of the time either working or looking for work. A somewhat higher proportion of graduates than dropouts had worked most of the time—79 percent and 72 percent, respectively. Dropouts were more likely to have worked at part-time jobs. A greater proportion of white graduates than dropouts worked most of the time, but among nonwhite males, there was virtually no difference in the proportions. About 17 percent of male dropouts had been unemployed most of the time since leaving school, compared with 11 percent of the graduates.

Of the 275,000 male graduates and dropouts who had been out of the labor force most of the time since leaving school, about 95,000 had been in the Armed Forces most of the time, 70,000 said they had been "doing nothing," and about 35,000 had taken job training. Dropouts were nearly three times as likely as graduates to have been "doing nothing." Virtually all of those who had spent their time in job training were graduates. The major activity was influenced to some extent both by the age of the youths and the length of time that had elapsed since leaving school, which was fairly recent for some.

A much larger proportion of the women (40 percent) than men had been out of the labor force most of the time since leaving school, primarily because of family responsibilities. Among the women, three out of five of the dropouts had not been in the labor force most of the time—a rate 2½ times that for graduates—reflecting mainly the greater proportion who were married. Relatively twice as many women graduates as dropouts had been working full-time most of the time, but the proportion of all the women who had worked part-time (9 percent) was about half that of the men. The lower percentage of women who had worked part-time most of the time since leaving school did not reflect the full extent to which they tend to be employed less than a whole week. Many of the women who had spent a major portion of their time out of the labor force probably had worked occasionally for a few hours a week.

The proportions of white and nonwhite women who had been in the labor force most of the time since leaving school were the same. However, about 23 percent of the nonwhite women had been unemployed most of the time compared with only 6 percent of the white. The greater prevalence of unemployment among nonwhite girls emphasizes the handicaps they have when they enter the work force. A higher proportion of them had failed to graduate from high school and a smaller percentage had taken post-school vocational or commercial training. When they left school, relatively fewer nonwhite girls had a job waiting, and among all the girls who looked for a job, it took nonwhite girls longer to find one. Also, nonwhite girls were much more likely than white girls to work in occupation groups which had higher unemployment rates than those in which white girls were concentrated. A majority of the employed nonwhite girls were working in private household and other service occupations and a relatively small proportion in clerical jobs; for white girls the situation was reversed.

"No," said Mr. Pinch, "No, I have been looking over the advertising sheet, thinking there might be something in it which would be likely to suit me. But, as I often think, the strange thing seems to be that nobody is suited. Here are all kinds of employers wanting all sorts of servants, and all sorts of servants wanting all kinds of employers, and they never seem to come together."

—CHARLES DICKENS, *Martin Chuzzlewit*

5 SOCIOPOLITICAL ACTION

The following account of the nationally-known Student Nonviolent Coordinating Committee suggests the enthusiasm which has characterized American youth's involvement in civil rights activities. The author's descriptions provide clues to the self-images of young people engaged in the movement that has spawned student leaders including Stokely Carmichael and H. Rap Brown.

Howard Zinn

The New Abolitionists

For the first time in our history a major social movement, shaking the nation to its bones, is being led by youngsters. This is not to deny the inspirational leadership of a handful of adults (Martin Luther King and James Farmer), the organizational direction by veterans in the struggle (Roy Wilkins and A. Philip Randolph), or the participation of hundreds of thousands of older people in the current Negro revolt. But that revolt, a long time marching out of the American past, its way suddenly lit up by the Supreme Court decision, and beginning to rumble in earnest when thousands of people took to the streets of Montgomery in the bus boycott, first flared into a national excitement with the sit-ins by college students that started the decade of the 1960's.

And since then, those same youngsters, hardened by countless jailings and beatings, now out of school and living in ramshackle headquarters all over the Deep South, have been striking the sparks, again and again, for that fire of change spreading through the South and searing the whole country.

These young rebels call themselves the Student Nonviolent Coordinating Committee, but they are more a movement than an organization, for no bureaucratized structure can contain their spirit, no printed program capture the fierce and elusive quality of their thinking. And while they have no famous leaders, very little money, no inner access to the seats of national authority, they are clearly the front line of the Negro assault on the moral comfort of white America.

To be with them, walking a picket line in the rain in Hattiesburg, Mississippi, or sleeping on a cot in a cramped "office" in Greenville, Mississippi; to watch them walk out of the stone jailhouse in Albany, Georgia; to see them jabbed by electric prod poles and flung into paddy wagons in Selma, Alabama, or link arms and sing at the close of a church meeting in the Delta—is to feel the presence of greatness. It is a greatness that comes from their relationship to history, and it does not diminish when they are discovered to be human: to make mistakes or feel fear, to act with envy, or hostility or even violence.

All Americans owe them a debt for—if nothing else—releasing the idealism locked so long inside a nation that has not recently tasted the drama of a social upheaval. And for making us look on the young people of the country with a new respect. Theirs was the silent generation until they spoke, the complacent generation until they marched and sang, the money-seeking generation until they renounced comfort and security to fight for justice in the dank and dangerous hamlets of the Black Belt.

Princeton philosopher Walter Kaufmann, writing in *The Faith of a Heretic,* called the young people born during World War II the "uncommitted genera-tion." He said: "What distinguishes them is that they are not committed to any cause." But this was written in 1960. And in that year, out of that same genera-tion which Kaufmann described, there emerged the first rebels of the decade. They came out of unexpected places: they were mostly black and therefore un-seen until they suddenly became the most visible people in America; they came out of Greensboro, North Carolina and Nashville, Tennessee and Rock Hill, South Carolina and Atlanta, Georgia. And they were committed. To the point of jail, which is a large commitment. And to the point of death, which hovers al-ways near a heretic in a police state and which turns to stare a Deep South Negro directly in the face at that moment when he utters that word so long taboo for Negroes in America, "No."

How do you measure commitment? Is it the willingness to take a day out of life and sacrifice it to history, to plunge for one morning or one afternoon into the unknown, to engage in one solitary act of defiance against all the arrayed power of established society? Then tens of thousands of young people, mostly black, some white, have committed themselves these past four years, by the simple act of joining a demonstration. Is commitment more than that—the will-ingness to wrench yourself out of your environment and begin anew, almost alone, in a social jungle which the most powerful forces in the nation have not dared to penetrate? Then the number is reduced to sixteen: those sixteen col-lege youngsters who, in the fall of 1961, decided to drop everything—school and family and approved ambition—and move into the Deep South to become the first guerrilla fighters of the Student Nonviolent Coordinating Committee.

By early 1964, the number was up to 150. In the most heated days of aboli-tionism before the Civil War, there were never that many dedicated people who turned their backs on ordinary pursuits and gave their lives wholly to the movement. There were William Lloyd Garrison and Wendell Philips and Theodore Weld and Frederick Douglass and Sojourner Truth and a handful of others, and there were hundreds of part-time abolitionists and thousands of followers. But for 150 youngsters today to turn on their pasts, to decide to live and work twenty-four hours a day in the most dangerous region of the United States, is cause for wonder. And wherever they have come from—the Negro colleges of the South, the Ivy League universities of the North, the small and medium colleges all over the country—they have left ripples of astonishment behind. This college generation as a whole is not committed, by any means. But it has been shaken.

These 150—who next year will be 250 or more, because the excitement grows daily on the college campuses—are the new abolitionists. It is not fanciful to invest them with a name that has the ring of history; we are always shy about recognizing the historic worth of events when they take place before our eyes, about recognizing heroes when they are still flesh and blood and not yet transfixed in marble. But there is no doubt about it: we have in this country today a movement which will take its place alongside that of the abolitionists, the Populists, the Progressives—and may outdo them all.

Their youth makes us hesitant to recognize their depth. But the great social upsurge of post-war America is the Negro revolt, and this revolt has gotten its most powerful impetus from young people, who gave it a new turn in 1960 and today, as anonymous as infantrymen everywhere, form the first rank in a nonviolent but ferocious war against the old order.

It would be easy to romanticize them, but they are too young, too vulnerable, too humanly frail to fit the stereotype of heroes. They don't match the storybook martyrs who face death with silent stoicism; the young fellows sometimes cry out when they are beaten; the girls may weep when abused in prison. Most often, however, they sing. This was true of the farmer and labor movements in this country, and of all the wars; but there has never been a singing movement like this one. Perhaps it is because most of them were brought up on the gospel songs and hymns of the Negro church in the South, perhaps also because they are young, probably most of all because what they are doing inspires song. They have created a new gospel music out of the old, made up of songs adapted or written in jail or on the picket line. Every battle station in the Deep South now has its Freedom Chorus, and the mass meetings there end with everyone standing, led by the youngsters of SNCC, linking arms, and singing "We shall Overcome."

The mood of these young people, which they convey to everyone around them in the midst of poverty, violence, terror, and centuries of bitter memories, is joy, confidence, the vision of victory: "We'll walk hand in hand...we are not afraid...." Occasionally there is sadness, as in "I Been 'Buked and I Been Scorned." But most often there is an exuberant defiance: "Ain't Gonna Let Chief Pritchett Turn Me Round...." They are happy warriors, a refreshing contrast to the revolutionaries of old. They smile and wave while being taken off in paddy wagons; they laugh and sing behind bars.

Yet they are the most serious social force in the nation today. They are not playing; it is no casual act of defiance, no irresponsible whim of adolescence, when young people of sixteen or twenty or twenty-five turn away from school, job, family, all the tokens of success in modern America, to take up new lives, hungry and hunted, in the hinterland of the Deep South. Jim Forman was a teacher in Chicago before he joined the SNCC, and an aspiring novelist; Bob Moses was a graduate of Harvard, teaching in New York; Charles Sherrod was a divinity school graduate in Virginia; Mendy Samstein, a graduate of Brandeis University, was on the faculty of a Negro college, working for his Ph.D. in history at the University of Chicago. Others found it easier—and harder—for they came right out of the Black Belt and, even though they tasted college, they had nowhere then to go but back towards danger and freedom: John Lewis, Sam Block, Willie Peacock, Lafayette Surney, MacArthur Cotton, Lawrence Guyot and too many more to name.

In his study *Young Man Luther,* the psychologist Erik Erikson ponders the "identity crisis" which young people face. "It occurs in that period of the life cycle when each youth must forge for himself some central perspective and direction, some working unity, out of the effective remnants of his childhood and the hopes of his anticipated adulthood; he must detect some meaningful resemblance between what he has come to see in himself and what his sharpened awareness tells him others judge and expect him to be." It would be hard to imagine a more startling contrast than that between the young Negro as the old South saw him (or rather half-saw him, blurred and not quite human) and the vision of himself he suddenly perceived in the glare of the 1960's.

The entire nation, caught suddenly in the intersection of two images where it always thought there was only one, has begun slowly to refocus its own vision. So that what started as an identity crisis for Negroes turned out to be an identity crisis for the nation. And we are still resolving it. It is one of the conditions of effective psychotherapy that the patient must begin to see himself as he really is, and the United States, now forced by the young Negro to see itself through *his* eyes (an ironic reversal, for the Negro was always compelled to see himself through the eyes of the white man), is coming closer to a realistic appraisal of its national personality.

All young people, in their late teens or early twenties, face this "identity crisis" which Erik Erikson describes. As Erikson points out: "Some young individuals will succumb to this crisis in all manner of neurotic, psychotic, or delinquent behavior; others will resolve it through participation in ideological movements passionately concerned with religion or politics, nature or art." We have seen the delinquent responses, or simply the responses of non-commitment, on the part of millions of young people of this generation who have not been able to find their way. Young Negroes were among these, were perhaps even the most delinquent, the most crisis-ridden of all. But today, by the handful, or the hundreds, or perhaps the thousands, they are making their way through this crisis with a firm grip on themselves, aided immeasurably by the fact that they are anchored to a great social movement.

We ought to note, however, that this "participation in ideological movements" today has a different quality than that of earlier American student movements—the radical movements of the thirties, for instance. The young people in the Student Nonviolent Coordinating Committee have not become followers of any dogma, have not pledged themselves to any rigid ideological system. Unswerving as they are in moving towards certain basic goals, they wheel freely in their thinking about society and how it needs to be changed. Erikson writes of a very few young people who, making their way through their identity crisis, "eventually come to contribute an original bit to an emerging style of life; the very danger which they have sensed has forced them to mobilize capacities to see and say, to dream and plan, to design and construct, in new ways." And this is true of those in the SNCC. They are radical, but not dogmatic; thoughtful, but not ideological. Their thinking is undisciplined; it is fresh, and it is new.

One must listen to Jane Stembridge speaking, a white girl from Virginia, part of that little band of black and white students who organized SNCC out of the turmoil of the 1960 sit-ins:

> ... finally it all boils down to human relationships. It has nothing to do finally with governments. It is the question of whether we ... whether *I* shall go on living in isolation or whether there shall be a *we*. The student movement is not a cause ... it is a collision between this one person and that one person. It is a *I am going to sit beside you*. ... Love alone is radical. Political statements are not; programs are not; even going to jail is not. ...

These new abolitionists are different from the earlier ones. The movement of the 1830's and 1840's was led by white New Englanders, bombarding the South and the nation with words. The present movement is planted firmly in the deepest furrows of the Deep South, and it consists mostly of Negroes who make their pleas to the nation more by physical acts of sacrifice than by verbal declamation. Their task is made easier by modern mass communication, for the nation, indeed the whole world, can see them, on the television screen or in newspaper photos—marching, praying, singing, *demonstrating* their message. The white people of America, to whom Negroes were always a dark, amorphous mass, are forced to see them for the first time sharply etched as individuals, their features—both physical and moral—stark, clear, and troubling.

But in one important way these young people are very much like the abolitionists of old: they have a healthy disrespect for respectability; they are not ashamed of being agitators and trouble-makers; they see it as the essence of democracy. In defense of William Lloyd Garrison, against the accusation that he was too harsh, a friend replied that the nation was in a sleep so deep "nothing but a rude and almost ruffian-like shake could rouse her." The same deliberate harshness lies behind the activities of James Forman, John Lewis, Bob Moses, and other leaders of SNCC. What Samuel May once said of Garrison and slavery might be said today of each of these people and segregation: "He will shake our nation to its center, but he will shake slavery out of it."

When SNCC leader Gloria Richardson in Cambridge, Maryland, refused, under a rain of criticism, to subject the issue of segregation to popular vote, one was reminded of the words of Wendell Phillips, explaining the apparent strange behavior of the abolitionists: "The reformer is careless of numbers, disregards popularity, and deals only with ideas, conscience, and common sense. . . . He neither expects, nor is overanxious for immediate success." Phillips contrasted the reformer with the politician, who "dwells in an everlasting now. . . ." In a similar mood, poet James Russell Lowell wrote: "The Reformer must expect comparative isolation, and he must be strong enough to bear it."

Yet the staff member of the Student Nonviolent Coordinating Committee can never be isolated as was the New England abolitionist of the 1830's, who was far from slave territory, and surrounded by whites unconcerned for the slave. The SNCC youngster is in the midst of his people, surrounded by them, protected by them. To be cut off, by harsh criticism of his "extremism," from Northern white intellectuals or from those in national political power is a minor blow, cushioned by a popularity based on the poor and the powerless, but perhaps even more comforting because of that.

Oddly enough—or perhaps naturally enough—the student movement has left the campuses where it began in those sit-ins of early 1960. The sit-in leaders have either graduated from or left college, and the fact that they call themselves the *Student* Nonviolent Coordinating Committee is primarily a reflection of their backgrounds, their youth, and perhaps their hope to return one day and bring a new dynamism to college education. Some go back to college after a year or two with the movement; others find a less formal but more genuine intellectual satisfaction in the movement. All live in a state of tension: there is the recognition that academic life is too far removed from the social struggle, alongside the frustration that exists for any intellectually aroused youngster separated from books and concentrated learning. At the same time, having exchanged college attire and the tree-lined campus for overalls and the dusty back roads of the rural South, they are getting the kind of education that no one else in the nation is getting.

There is another striking contrast to Garrison and Phillips, Lewis Tappon and Theodore Weld: these young people are not middle-class reformers who became somehow concerned about others. They come themselves from the ranks of the victims, not just because they are mostly Negroes, but because for the most part their fathers are janitors and laborers, their mothers maids and factory workers.

In late 1963 I checked the backgrounds of forty-one field workers for SNCC in Mississippi (roughly one-third of the total SNCC force in the Deep South). Thirty-five of them were Negro, and twenty-five of them came from the Deep South. Of the six white staff members two were from the Deep South. The white youngsters and most of the Northern Negroes came from middle-class homes; their fathers were ministers or teachers or civil service workers. All of the Southern Negroes, and some of the Northern Negroes (twenty-one out of thirty-five) came from homes where the mothers were maids or domestics, the fathers factory workers, truck drivers, farmers, bricklayers, carpenters. Twenty-nine (about three-fourths) of the total SNCC Mississippi staff were between fifteen and twenty-two years old. There were twelve between twenty-two and twenty-nine, and one person each in his thirties, forties, and fifties. Twenty-six, or about two-thirds, of the Mississippi SNCC staff were either college graduates or had some college education. Ten had finished high school or had some high school education and two had no more than part of an elementary school education. If one were to generalize roughly about the SNCC staff in the Deep South, one would say they are young, they are Negro, they come from the South, their families are poor and of the working class, but they have been to college. Northern middle-class whites and Negroes are a minority.

As of mid-1964, about 150 people worked full-time for SNCC, roughly 80 percent of them Negro. Of the whites, most were Northerners, but the few white Southerners played important roles (Jane Stembridge, the first office secretary in Atlanta; Bob Zellner and Sam Shirah, assigned to white college campuses; Sandra Hayden, in the Jackson, Mississippi, office). Of the Negro staff people, most were Southern born; more and more, young Negroes were being recruited out of Deep South towns to become SNCC field secretaries right there at home.

By 1963, the annual budget of SNCC was about $250,000, almost all of this coming from the contributions of individuals and organizations (churches, colleges, foundations). About one-fourth of this income was being used to pay the salaries of field secretaries, $10 a week for most of them, with a few married people in the Atlanta office receiving $50 or $60 a week. Most of the remaining income went to pay for field operations in Mississippi, southwest Georgia, and the other areas of concentration.

The two chief officers of SNCC are the Chairman (John Lewis) and the Executive Secretary (James Forman). One of the field secretaries in each major geographical area is known as a Project Director. An Executive Committee of twenty-one members, including two older "advisors," is the top policy-making body, and is elected at an annual conference in the spring.

Where do the 150 or so SNCC workers operate? Perhaps a dozen man the central office in Atlanta, a buzzing jumble of rooms above a tailor shop in the Negro section of Atlanta, not far from the Negro college campuses. Long-distance phone connections keep Jim Forman and John Lewis, the two top officers of SNCC, in day-to-day, sometimes hour-to-hour touch with crisis situations in those parts of the Deep South where SNCC maintains headquarters and "field secretaries" (as its staff members are called).

One of the two main areas of concentration is Mississippi, where SNCC's first penetration of the Deep South was made by Bob Moses and a few Negro youngsters from the Delta. A half-dozen spots in Mississippi have had varying degrees of attention: Greenwood, Hattiesburg, Jackson, Liberty, Greenville, Clarksdale. The other major focus of activity is southwest Georgia, where Charles Sherrod, a divinity school student from Virginia, came in the fall of 1961 and stayed to become a legend. Albany has been the center there, and, radiating from it, SNCC workers have moved into the terror-ridden towns of the old Cotton Kingdom: Americus, Dawson, Camilla, Sasser. Outside of Mississippi and southwest Georgia, SNCC groups function in Selma, Alabama; Danville, Virginia; Cambridge, Maryland; Pine Bluff, Arkansas; and other places; they register voters, distribute food and clothing, lead demonstrations, conduct classes, vitalize long-dormant communities.

To visit SNCC field headquarters in these rural outposts of the Deep South is like visiting a combat station in wartime. Living conditions are crude. Sometimes there is a "Freedom House," an old frame dwelling with cots and blankets for the field secretaries and whoever else is staying over for the night. At other times, field people stay in homes in the Negro community. It may take weeks or months to dispel the initial fear on the part of local Negroes now aware of impending change and trouble. Negro women in town often become mothers to the SNCC youngsters far from home and family; they put them up, make meals for them, tend them when they are sick, go out on the line with them in demonstrations. One thinks of Mrs. Boynton in Selma, Mrs. Woods in Hattiesburg, and Mrs. Daniels in Dawson. (Sheriff Jim Clark in Selma, hoping to arrest SNCC leader Prathia Hall, went straight to the home of Mrs. Boynton to find her.)

Over every one of these headquarters in the field, whether a "Freedom House" rented by SNCC, or a home or office donated by a local supporter, there hangs the constant threat of violence. The first SNCC headquarters in Selma was burned down; in Greenwood, two SNCC workers found themselves under siege by a mob of armed men and had to make their way over rooftops to safety; in Danville, police simply marched into the SNCC office and arrested everyone in sight.

"These are beautiful people down here," Sandra Hayden wrote to me from Mississippi shortly after she arrived there to work for SNCC. She was speaking about the Negroes of the Delta, aroused to take their first step out of the past—but she was not speaking of color or of that ordered set of physical characteristics which American society has charactertized as "beauty." She was speaking of the souls of black folk—and of white folk too. She was speaking of a beauty of spirit, of a courage beyond comprehension, which pervades the ranks of the new abolitionists in the Deep South. It is expressed in Sandra Hayden herself, tall, blonde, slender, a Texas girl who moved from the University of Texas into the student movement; it is expressed in the rugged, black, smiling face of Chuck McDew, peering through the bars of Baton Rouge jail; or the tawny, delicate features of Peggy Day in Terrell County; or the agonized, shining eyes of Mrs. Fannie Hamer, a middle-aged woman thrown off her land in Ruleville, Mississippi, who has gone to work for SNCC.

Those who join the SNCC staff agree to work for subsistence wages; this usually means $10.00 a week ($9.64 after deductions), and often weeks going by with no checks coming from Atlanta. It may mean knocking on doors for food, scrounging around for a pair of shoes, riding a mule along a country road because the car donated by some sympathizer has broken down. A typical SNCC automobile has always just run out of gas, and the driver has no money left to buy more. "You know it's like they're in another world," a college girl said after visiting SNCC headquarters in Greenwood, Mississippi.

These are young radicals; the word "revolution" occurs again and again in their speech. Yet they have no party, no ideology, no creed. They have no clear idea of a blueprint for a future society. But they do know clearly that the values of present American society—and this goes beyond racism to class distinction, to commercialism, to profit-seeking, to the setting of religious or national barriers against human contact—are not for them.

They are prepared to use revolutionary means against the old order. They believe in civil disobedience. They are reluctant to rely completely on the niceties of negotiation and conciliation, distrustful of those who hold political and economic power. They have a tremendous respect for the potency of the demonstration, an eagerness to move out of the political maze of normal parliamentary procedure and to confront policy-makers directly with a power beyond orthodox politics—the power of people in the streets and on the picket line.

They are nonviolent in that they suffer beatings with folded arms and will not strike back. There have been one or two rare exceptions of discipline being broken, yet this must be laid against hundreds of instances of astounding self-control in the face of unspeakable brutality.

Next to the phrase "nonviolence," however, what you hear most often among SNCC workers is "direct action." They believe, without inflicting violence, and while opening themselves to attack, in confronting a community boldly with the sounds and sights of protest. When it is argued that this will inevitably bring trouble, even violence, the answer is likely to be that given by James Bevel, who in his activity with the Southern Christian Leadership Conference works closely with SNCC in Alabama and Mississippi: "Maybe the Devil has got to come out of these people before we will have peace. . . ."

They have no closed vision of the ideal community. They are fed up with what has been; they are open to anything new and are willing to start from scratch. Erik Erikson talks about young rebels with a "rock-bottom" attitude, who "want to be reborn in identity and to have another chance at becoming once-born, but this time on their own terms." Nineteen-year-old SNCC verteran Cordell Reagan, brown-skinned, slender, explains himself this way:

It's not hard to interpret what our parents mean by a better world. You know, go to school, son, and get a good education. And what do you do with this? You get a degree, you move out into some little community housing project, you get married, five kids and two cars, and you don't care what's happening. . . . So I think when we talk about growing up in a better world, a new world, we mean changing the world to a different place.

Is it any wonder that Cordell Reagan and so many other SNCC workers have been put in jail again and again by Deep-South sheriffs for "contributing to the delinquency of minors"?

A young white student, explaining why he wanted to join SNCC, wrote about his new-found view of life:

> I have never felt so intense, alive, such a sense of well-being which is not to be confused with the illusion of "happiness" equated to "having fun." I have chosen to be outside of society after having been very much inside. I intend to fight that society which lied to and smothered me for so long, and continues to do so to vast numbers of people.... My plans are unstructured in regards to anything but the immediate future. I believe in freedom, and must take the jump; I must take the chance of action.

The nation has suddenly become aware that the initiative today is in the hands of these 150 young people who have moved into the Deep South to transform it. Everyone waits on their next action: the local police, the state officials, the national government, the mass media of the country, Negroes and whites sitting at their radios and television sets across the land. Meanwhile, these people are living, hour by hour, the very ideals which this country has often thought about, but not yet managed to practice: they are courageous, though afraid; they live and work together in a brotherhood of black and white. Southerner and Northerner, Jew and Christian and agnostic, the likes of which this country has not yet seen. They are creating new definitions of success, of happiness, of democracy.

It is just possible that the momentum created by their enormous energy—now directed against racial separation—may surge, before it can be contained, against other barriers which keep people apart in the world: poverty, and nationalism, and all tyranny over the minds and bodies of men. If so, the United States may truly be on the verge of a revolution—nonviolent, but sweeping in its consequences—and led by those who, perhaps, are most dependable in a revolution: the young.

Some indication of the problems besetting disadvantaged groups and the possibilities which exist for effective action to abate them is given in the following documents. They suggest that traditional avenues for reform are no longer viable, while new federal efforts to assist disadvantaged groups do not appear to be making contact with them. They illustrate how what might have become a model for participatory democracy became instead a conflict between people and bureaucracy.

Five Documents from Greenville, Mississippi

Poverty and the Federal Government

1. NOW IS THE TIME FOR SOMETHING ELSE

On January 28 a four day Poor Peoples conference sponsored by the Freedom Democratic Party, the Mississippi Freedom Labor Union and the Delta Ministry was held at the Mt. Beulah campus near Edwards, Mississippi.

Over 700 poor people, mainly from the Delta, discussed the problems they faced—a Jim Crow State Welfare Department, mass evictions from plantations, lack of jobs, and a standstill on the poverty programs. One lady said:

I'm tired of going to Washington. I've been there three times and don't see nothing come of it. They don't want to talk to poor folk, they just want to talk to people they select.

Another member of the conference complained:

When they want to know about people in Mississippi they ask [Senators] Eastland or Stennis. They don't represent us because they and the other whites made sure we never got a chance to choose our representatives.

A man said:

The poverty program don't speak to us. Poor Negro folk ran a good program this summer—even Shriver said so. But Stennis doesn't want us to have nothing. Five months now the Office of Economic Opportunity promised us money for our Headstart, and nothing's happened. OEO's more interested in listening to Stennis than to poor peoples.

On Sunday the conference drafted a list of demands, including commodity and job-training programs administered by poor people, federal lands for housing, income for poor people, and the reopening of the Headstart schools with control by poor people.

One woman commented:

> We been taking our problems through all the channels of the government for the last three years and ain't got nothing, now it's time to do something else.

On Sunday night, January 30, the Conference decided to leave their shacks and move to the abandoned Air Force Base near Greenville. There are 13 acres of empty housing facilities. The news of two elderly Negroes freezing to death in their Delta shacks emphasized the need for the action. An elderly Negro man summed it all up:

> We need to go there and set us up one of those refugee camps, 'cause that's what we are. And being right by that air strip the government can fly in surplus commodities right to our door and we can give 'em out without them expensive middle men. They say the buildings don't have heat or lights or running water. Well, just as long as it don't leak it'll still be a damn sight better than the shack I been living in.

2. EVENTS AT THE AIR BASE

Monday, January 31

About forty poor Negroes drive to the Greenville Air Force Base, where they occupy an abandoned barracks building. A sign is hung outside the door reading "This is our home—please knock before entering."

7:00 a.m.: Lt. Colonel Andrews enters the barracks and orders them to leave. "You are trespassing on government property," he says. He is presented with the group's official statement of demands and replies "My only concern is with this building." He locks all the doors to seal off the occupants, stumbles into a group of people, and accuses a white volunteer of kicking him in the shins.

9:00 a.m.: Local law officials leave the scene, claiming they have no jurisdiction on property under federal control. Police Chief W. C. Burnley, asked if he is pulling his men out replies, "You're damn right." A local official says, "It is a case of breaking and entering on what may be city property on what might be a federal reservation in what we know is Washington County, Mississippi."

11:00 a.m.: Fifteen more people arrive, including a large family from a Sunflower County plantation. Coal stoves, food, mattresses and blankets are brought in.

12:00 noon: Air base officials stop traffic through the gate but people and supplies continue to come over and through the surrounding fence.

1:00 p.m.: An administrative assistant from the Civil Rights Commission calls the Delta Ministry office demanding to know why the people occupied the base. He is told of the general condition of poor people in the Delta and that two Negroes froze to death in their Washington County home last week. He says,

"We can't deal with the general condition, give me some specific facts." He says there is no excuse for breaking the law. He is told that if he has anything to say he must speak to those in the barracks.

2:00 p.m.: A three-man council is elected to represent the occupants. The afternoon is spent holding meetings. Committees are elected to keep barracks clean, prepare food and tend the stoves.

7:30 p.m.: A spaghetti dinner is served. About ten more people join the group.

12:00 midnight: More supplies arrive through the fence. Occupants bedded down for the night with a few people appointed to keep watch on the stoves. Reports come that police under the command of Maj. Gen. R. W. Puryear are arriving at the base.

Tuesday, February 1

7:00 a.m.: Group arises and clean-up committees roll up mattresses and blankets. A meeting is called to discuss plans for the day.

11:15 a.m.: Major General Puryear and 150 air police march in and assemble outside barracks. The General tells the group that he has a message from the Justice and Agriculture Departments telling them to inform the departments of their grievances and they will try to help. He says the group has twenty minutes to abandon the barracks. Occupants discuss the offer and vote to reject it, stating that Washington has been informed of their grievances for the last three years.

11:30 a.m.: The one hundred and fifty air police break windows spattering glass over the people and open the doors of the barracks. People are dragged roughly from the building. A lady from Hattiesburg collapses while being hauled away and is taken to a Negro doctor in Greenville at the insistence of her friends. One man says "four of them approached me and said 'let's get that son-of-a-bitch.' They threw me out, tearing my clothes." A few moments later an elderly Negro lady is arrested on alleged profanity charges.

12:00 noon: All the people expelled from the base begin an eight mile walk back to town through the mud alongside the highway.

3. "WHY WE ARE HERE"

We are here because we are hungry and cold and we have no jobs or land. We don't want charity. We are willing to work for ourselves if given a chance. We need help to get started now.

We are at the Greenville Air Force Base because it is federal property and there are dozens of empty houses and buildings. We need those houses and the land.

We demand food. We are here because we are hungry. Our children can't be taught in school because they are hungry. They can't even get food in school because they have to buy it and don't have money.

We demand jobs. Many of us have been thrown off the plantations where we worked for nothing all our lives. We don't want charity. We demand our right to jobs, so that we can do something with our lives and build us a future.

We demand job training. We demand that people be trained for things that they want to do and that they be paid while they are being trained.

We demand income. We demand that poor people be given an income. But until we get an income for our families we want commodities which are fit to eat. The commodities we get now are old and full of bugs and weevils. We want fresh vegetables, fruit and meat. We want to decide what foods we want to eat.

The federal government tells us to go directly to the state and county for help but when we go there they don't know what we are talking about.

We demand land. There are thousands of acres here that the government owns. We are supposed to be part of that government. We want the clear land and the unclear land and we'll clear the unclear land ourselves.

We want "Operation Help" to be stopped. We don't want the Mississippi county boards of supervisors to have another chance to decide whether poor people should get food. We don't recognize these county boards because they don't recognize us. We want the Office of Economic Opportunity and the U.S. Department of Agriculture to hire poor people we say represent us. We the poor people want to distribute the food.

We demand that Operation Headstart schools be started now. We demand that the Office of Economic Opportunity give us the money which they promised us last September so that our children can be taught in the headstart schools.

We are ready now to ask of President Johnson: "Whose side are you on—the poor people's or the millionaires'?"

4. FACT SHEET

△ Median income of Negroes in the Delta: $456 a year (U.S. Department of Agriculture report, November 1964).

△ Of 26,000 tractor drivers living with their families on Delta plantations, *6,500 will be jobless by Spring* (Ralph Alewine, Mississippi Employment Security Commission, November 18, 1965).

△ Eight counties of Mississippi have no commodities distribution at all. Thirty-nine counties give them only to people on welfare. *Only 13* of the 82 counties give surplus commodities to all poor people.

△ On November 24 the state got $1.5 million dollars in anti-poverty funds to distribute $24 million worth of surplus commodities in a special six-months program. None of this food has been distributed. Many people have been told by county welfare officials that they never heard of the program, called Operation HELP.

△ The chances of a Negro baby's dying in its first year in Mississippi are more than twice those of a white baby's—and higher than that of a white baby in 1913 (U.S. Census, 1960).

△ Over 90 per cent of the Negro, rural homes in Mississippi have no flush toilets, no bathtub and no shower. Only one-third are in sound condition (1960 census).

△ The standard pay for tractor drivers in the Delta is $6 a day and for cotton choppers is $3 a day—sunrise to sunset. Plantation families have no income during the six months between growing seasons; owners often make advances against the coming year's wages.

△ A family of five without a breadwinner (or whose breadwinner is unemployed) must live on $627 a year in general assistance (about $12 a week). The federal government says a family of five making less than $4,000 is living in poverty.

△ Less than one-half per cent of Negro children in the state go to school with white children. Fifteen Mississippi school districts have no desegregation at all.

△ In the Delta, over half the males over 25 years old have less than a sixth-grade education. Mississippi does not at present have a compulsory school attendance law.

△ Greenville Air Force Base, formally a jet training facility, has not been in use by the air force in more than a year. Its residential area includes 30 apartments and covers 13 acres. (A recent local news story says the housing area will be deeded to the state.)

5. "WE HAVE NO GOVERNMENT"

This is an edited transcript of a press conference held in the Greenville office of the Delta Ministry, Tuesday evening, February 1. The participants were: Mr. Isaac Foster of Tribbett, a leader in last spring's strike of plantation workers; Mrs. Ida Mae Lawrence of Rosedale, chairman of the Mississippi Freedom Labor Union local; and Rev. Arthur Thomas of Greenville, director of the Delta Ministry of the National Council of Churches.

Mr. Foster: The people are going to set up Tent City out at Tribbett and work on getting poor people to come and build a new city. Because of the fact that we was refused by the federal government and evicted, it's important that we start planning our own government.

Mrs. Blackwell: I feel that the federal government have proven that it don't care about poor people. Everything that we have asked for through these years has been handed down on paper. It's never been a reality.

We the poor people of Mississippi is tired. We're tired of it so we're going to build for ourselves, because we don't have a government that represents us.

Mrs. Lawrence: See, you can only accept poor peoples by being poor and really know what being poor is like. And all this stuff about poverty programs and federal funds, that's out for poor peoples.

We were looked upon as just a civil-rights demonstration. But really we were there demanding and waiting and asking that these things be brought there to fill some desperate needs. And we was asking that the poor peoples be accepted as they stood. And instead of getting what we was asking, we got the whole air force troopers in on us. To me, that's our government.

Mr. Foster: Was.

Mrs. Lawrence: Yeah, was. Now, we're our own government—government by poor people. Where do we go from here? To brighter days on our own. And we know we'll reach that goal. But in their world, that's something that doesn't exist.

Reporter: About the poor peoples government. Would this be an idea for a lot of people to come and live around Tribbett or somewhere in particular? Would this be a larger tent city?

Mr. Foster: I know and you know that the tents are not going to stand forever. But I wouldn't be surprised if it wouldn't start that way.

Reporter: Does this mean that you would not consider yourself bound by the restraints, the actions of county, state or federal law enforcement officers?

Mr. Foster: From nothing we must start building a new country, with our own laws, our own enforcement. No part of the system has any authority or control over us. Our goal is leading away from depending on the system for anything. And I would like to say that every poor person that will come is welcome.

Reporter: Does this mean that you won't sit down and talk to the Attorney General or other government representatives about your grievances?

Mr. Foster: If they would like to talk, we'll be willing to talk. But they didn't want to talk. They sent some Mississippian chief or sergeant or something. He said give me the names of people who need relocation and I'll see what can be done about it. How can we leave the base when peoples don't have a house to stay in?

Mr. Foster: The only reason that Colonel Jones could give for eviction was that the building that we was in didn't have running water and didn't have any type of fire protection. And see I know that the federal government can't tell me that was the reason we was put out, because all over Mississippi houses don't have running water or fire protection.

Rev. Thomas: It was cruel and inhuman of Orville Freeman and Nicholas Katzenbach to send the kind of message to us at the air base they sent today. They said nothing to us that hasn't been said for months and years. We were tired of waiting around for these people to live up to their words.

Reporter: Mr. Thomas, could you go a little more into Operation HELP?

Rev. Thomas: Over a year ago the Delta Ministry, in cooperation with the National Students Association, pointed out the need for a commodity program for Mississippi poor people. And we gave as an example of what local people could do, what was happening in Forrest County, where the people had set up their own distribution system for contributed food and clothing. It works very well.

We offered to make Forrest County a trial case for food distribution if the Department would release the commodities to us.

Instead, the Department of Agriculture notified the State Department of Welfare that volunteer groups were willing and able to distribute commodities in Forrest County. In the face of that kind of possibility, the county Board of Supervisors voted for the first time in years and years to participate in a commodity program. Immediately, the Department of Agriculture found it necessary to send an investigator in there to investigate charges of discrimination in that program.

We then made the same offer in regard to Madison County. Again Washington called the state welfare people, who notified the County Board of Supervisors. They came up with a Food Stamp program. Of course poor people can't afford to be in a food stamp program because it costs money and they don't have any income.

We then offered to set up distribution in any county that didn't have a program. In the face of this possibility the state Welfare Department came up with the proposal called Operation HELP—and keep in mind this was in August. All over the state people had gone without food through the winter while the Welfare Department and the Agriculture Department played politics with each other.

Under this plan, the Welfare Department will get 24 million dollars worth of surplus commodities from the Department of Agriculture and 1.6 million dollars from the Office of Economic Opportunity to distribute the food to 500,000 people for six months.

In view of the criticisms of the program—which is based on the untenable assumption that welfare agencies and county boards of supervisors will act in a nondiscriminatory manner—OEO put certain conditions on the grant: one, that a bi-racial committee supervise the program and, two, that hiring and distribution be done on a non-discriminatory basis.

Our information has it that no such committee has been set up, although the proposal was submitted in August and granted in November. Dr. Aaron Henry, head of the state NAACP was asked to nominate the Negroes for the committee. Why weren't poor people asked to nominate people? In regard to the second condition, the food was supposed to be ready for distribution by January 23. When that day came we could not find one poor person employed in the program and no food being given out. And now it's February.

Mrs. Lawrence: I'd like to add to that. To live, we got to go out and chop cotton for $3 a day, maybe two or three days a week. At the end of cotton picking, we gets the same for picking the scrap the machines leave. Then in November when they start qualifying you for the commodities, they say you got to find out how many people you worked for and get them to sign for you as being poor. If they don't feel like signing, like maybe they don't like you for civil-rights activities, you don't get commodities. But you still poor, whether the white boss says so or not.

Mrs. Blackwell: See, if you belong to any civil-rights group or participate, they tell you you can't get a job with the poverty program, because that's political and you know, you can't have that. And that's what's happening with the poverty program: it's political—that's the reason it's not doing anything for the poor.

Reporter: Mr. Thomas, why do you think the federal government is afraid to let poor Negroes go ahead and run the program?

Rev. Thomas: I could try to avoid that question and say that it is their problem. These people have the problem of not being fed. I will not avoid it and say nobody is unaware of the power of Congressman Whitten in the House Subcommittee on Agriculture. Nobody is unaware of the critical power of John Stennis in the Senate and its Finance Appropriations Committee. And those are the kinds of people who are supposed to represent the poor people in Congress.

Reporter: Are you saying that the people who run the poverty program are kowtowing to the white power structure from here?

Rev. Thomas: That's what I'm saying. The poverty program and the Department of Agriculture.

I'd like to add one footnote. OEO says it's introducing an experimental program for food distribution. Well, I don't think these people ought to be experimented on. They're hungry now. They need food now. And there's no reason why food could not have been airlifted in to those people.

Also, poor people in this state last year organized themselves into a Headstart program through the Child Development Group of Mississippi. Shriver and others said it was one of the best Headstarts anywhere in the country. In September they were told they would be funded in October; in October the money was coming in November; in November the money was coming in December and so on each month. Over 1100 local Mississippi poor people who have been promised money have been cheated by OEO.

Mrs. Lawrence: You know, we ain't dumb, even if we are poor. We need jobs. We need food. We need houses. But even with the poverty program we ain't got nothin' but needs. That's why we was pulled off that building that wasn't being used for anything. We is ignored by the government. The thing about poverty upset them, but the thing about poor people don't. So there's no way out but to begin your own beginning, whatever way you can. So far as I'm concerned, that's all I got to say about the past. We're beginning a new future.

DISCUSSION TOPICS

1. What are critical differences between mainstream and disadvantaged adolescent peer groups? Is one more supportive of positive identity formation than the other? In what ways does the notion of masculinity affect the peer relationships of disadvantaged boys? Is the adolescent peer group a fruitful locus for integration efforts?

2. How does the usual value-set of the public school affect the self concept of disadvantaged youth? Is the oft-remarked conflict between the goals of the school and the personal goals of disadvantaged adolescents inherent in the nature of any formal educational process, or can adjustments in curricula, teacher-training, and school organization relieve this conflict? Does the school have a responsibility to help develop a firm self concept in disadvantaged youth? If so, how might it carry this out?

3. Discuss reasons for the persistently high unemployment rate among Negro males between the ages of 16 and 21. Should young people born and raised in impoverished areas such as Appalachia and Michigan's upper peninsula be encouraged to leave the

area? What are the possible effects of federally financed programs like Upward Bound and Job Training Corps centers on the work picture among disadvantaged youth?

4. Discuss the role of youth in the pattern of summer rioting that has developed in recent years. From the standpoint of adolescent development, what are the crucial differences between a riot such as that in Watts, a riot at a summer resort, and a University demonstration? What might be the relationship of the current decline in gang-fighting and the accompanying rise in dope addiction and crime in urban ghettos to the actions of adolescents today? Is it possible to find positive channels for the hostility and violence of an urban riot?

5. What are the relative merits of programs which emphasize ethnic consciousness and those stressing integration and assimilation, for the development of disadvantaged youth?

IV PROJECTION FOR ADULTHOOD

In conclusion, we consider ways in which adulthood tomorrow will be different from adulthood today or yesterday. Youth now on the threshold of adult life must face not only all the traditional problems inherent in the assumption of adult roles but problems unique to this era as well: an extended society in which the emotional well-being of every individual is the concern of society at large, the collapse of man's faith in the future, the impersonality inherent in modern mass culture, and the unparalleled destructive power of a technology that for the first time in history can bring about universal death. In addition to an examination of one of these problems, each article in this part projects means by which it may be possible to control and utilize the new forces.

Social change leading to a continually expanding public sector is about to transform traditional modes of mental health care, according to psychologist Freeman. We are at a crossroads, he suggests, beyond which the vast majority of mental health activity will be bound up with federal programs directed at curing social ills, especially among lower socioeconomic groups. Just as the massive social improvement programs of this decade have attempted to reshape the economic and cultural environment of individuals, so future large-scale mental health efforts may result in comprehensive plans for reaching out to poorly adjusted individuals through multipurpose public centers.

Closely allied to the emotional health of the next generation of adults and their children is the fullness of their spiritual life. If contemporary man believes that God is dead—and it appears to the theologian whose sermon appears here that this is so—what can fill the spiritual void thus created? At one time, it might have been possible to replace discarded deistic concepts with a belief in man's ability to dominate nature and assist her in yielding an earthly paradise. But this faith was itself shattered by the nuclear explosion at Hiroshima, with the result that twentieth-century man is echoing the elemental question of primitive man: whether we live in a world ruled by beneficence or by an indifferent or even malevolent force. For youth coming of age today, Mead suggests, the most viable faith may well be a faith in man himself: man as a social being, needing the support of other men.

Among the most provocative descriptions of the new world into which today's youth will emerge are those of Marshall McLuhan, who has postulated that the new technology has already created a generation whose life-style is alien to that of their parents. With the demise of the mechanized technology of the industrial age, he contends, a new electronic technology has ushered in an electrically configured world which must be viewed in radically new ways. The study of configurations or integral patterns, as opposed to the collection of information characteristic of the mechanistic era, will be man's task in such a world. Today's youth, already sensitive to forces that must help shape its future identity, has replaced the old virtue of objectivity with a new virtue, depth involvement.

McLuhan has drawn a critical distinction between the concept of being totally involved, or *cool,* and being fragmented, or *square.* In his *Understanding Media,* he relates a favorite joke of contemporary college students: "What is purple and hums?" The answer: "An electric grape." "Why does it hum?" "It doesn't know the words."

"Humor," according to McLuhan, "is presumably not 'cool' when it inclines us to laugh *at* something instead of getting us empathetically involved *in* something." Adolescents tell us that they appreciate any situation that permits involvement, allowing them to be "in" it. They consider as a cool teacher, for example, any teacher who permits a maximum of depth involvement on students' parts. The square teacher, in contrast, restricts involvement to only a small aspect of what is possible. The student who wishes to comply with the square teacher must focus from a small fragment of his total being on, say, the writing of a grammatically correct sentence.

Today's youth, the TV generation, is rediscovering texture, movement, color, light, and sound, all of which require the employment of little-used senses which television, the new-wave films, and other new cool media serve to massage and enliven. Lack of structure tends to accompany depth involvement as adolescents practice it in new dance forms, the blurring of sexual distinctions in dress and hairstyles, and cool low-structural jazz or electronic music. The shift from the dehumanized man of the industrial era to the involved, more human man of the electronic age is coming about. It can be summed up in the words of a University of Massachusetts student who said recently that participation, for her generation, is not a means but an end. One result is the widening gap between youth and the adult world. Nor will it suffice for adults to explain away this gap as the inevitable conflict between generations; today's young people are growing up differently.

The extent of technology's influence on social, psychological, economic and industrial change has barely begun to manifest itself, according to the writers of "The Triple Revolution," the final article in our collection. Cybernetics has the potential to systematize man's activities to an extent that few have so far envisioned. The necessity for men to "do" something for eight hours a day may be removed, with all the advantages and problems that would entail. For one thing, the question of income and distribution of wealth comes into play as soon as jobs cease to be integral to the economic scheme of things. The further question, how such a society can be administered, and to what extent the public sector will dominate individual activity, looms large in this article.

Today's adolescents will be the first generation to encounter on a massive scale the dichotomies and contradictions of a society in such rapid transition. The dimensions of the new society are still in question, but there can be no doubt that today's adolescents will be carving out new cultural patterns.

1 EMOTIONAL ISSUES

This article examines ways in which mental health care may be vastly altered and extended as this country becomes increasingly concerned with the socialization and adjustment of all its citizens. The author suggests that present large-scale federal efforts in the health and welfare fields carry important implications for future mental health care. In particular, he cites current trends in group treatment and multi-purpose centers.

Howard E. Freeman

Social Change
and the Organization
of Mental Health Care

Innovation and modification in medical care practices at least in the western world supposedly are based on science and rationality.[1] Scientific thought, we are told, evolves slowly. Even apparently marked changes are the results of previous converging tendencies, and "great discoveries" usually are natural steps in a long-term process.[2] Perhaps the development of preventive and treatment practices in some areas is consistent with these observations, but such practices do not characterize program development in the mental health field. Apparently the treatment of mental illness within the known history of man has been dominated by social, political and ideological factors. Mental health programs are

[1] C. P. Loomis, *Social Systems*, Princeton, New Jersey: D. Van Nostrand Company, Inc., 1960, p. 298.
[2] E. G. Boring, *History, Psychology, and Science: Selected Papers*, New York: John Wiley and Sons, Inc., 1963, p. 64.

rooted more in moral and legislative elements than in medical and scientific ones.[3]

It is tempting to dwell on the reasons underlying the limited "internal" strength of the mental health field. But comments on its unscientific qualities, on the limited agreement about its boundaries, and on its ambiguous, interstitial place between the medical and social sciences are unnecessary. The field is most conspicuous as the object of criticism and as the subject of harsh popular and scholarly reviews.

The pace and flow of program modification are to be noted, however. Views on the needs and length of hospitalization; notions on the function of community health centers; opinions on the treatment roles of psychologists, social workers and other nonmedically trained persons, and ideas on the substance of preventive programs have changed radically.[4] To some extent these changes are a consequence of research efforts, but to a much larger degree, they are a matter of extrascientific influence. Without disputing the appropriateness of these changes, it is fair to observe that the structure of the mental health field is unstable. The rate of reorientation has been so rapid and the shift so extreme that the reintegrating and institutionalization that usually occur after a period of sharp modification have not yet taken place.[5]

Undoubtedly mental health treatment programs will continue in their own right, and there is considerable energy being expended in order to implement the Joint Commission's recommendations.[6] But the field also is an attractive entry point for the "great society" efforts of today. Given the current volatile state of the mental health field and its historic responsiveness to political and social processes, marked and dramatic philosophical and program shifts may be predicted.

In the past several decades the social and political forces have intervened both directly and indirectly in mental health practices and efforts. But the current round of change is likely to come largely secondhand from ideological and program modifications in other areas through the convergence of a set of "forces" on the mental health field. In public health there is a renewed interest in the treatment of existing disease conditions in comparison with incipient ones. Thus there is considerable restructuring of organizational arrangements for health programs and of the roles of the consortium of practitioners engaged in community health activities.[7] In the field of welfare there is marked dissatisfaction

[3] G. Rosen, "The Mentally Ill and the Community in Western and Central Europe During the Late Middle Ages and the Renaissance," *Journal of History of Medicine and Allied Sciences,* 1964, 19, p. 388.
[4] R. H. Felix, "Community Appraisal of Mental Health Centers," *American Journal of Public Health,* 1964, 54, pp. 1964–69. And S. F. Yolles, "Community Appraisal of Mental Health Practices," *American Journal of Public Health,* 1964, 54, pp. 1970–76.
[5] B. Berelson and G. A. Steiner, *Human Behavior: An Inventory of Scientific Findings,* New York: Harcourt, Brace & World, Inc., 1964, p. 616.
[6] M. S. Schwartz and C. G. Schwartz, *Social Approaches to Mental Patient Care,* New York: Columbia University Press, 1964.
[7] J. D. Stoeckle and I. K. Zola, "Views, Problems, and Potentialities of the Clinic," *Medicine,* 1964, 43, pp. 413–422.

with the existing definitions of agency boundaries, client populations and the concept of individualized treatment. These attitudes are reflected in an increased emphasis on a sociological rather than a psychiatric frame of reference in the academic training of professional social workers as well as the inclusion and increased respect for "indigenous participation" in community efforts.[8] Finally, in the social sciences there is increased concern with the problems of program evaluation and with the roles of social scientists in the development of health and welfare policy. Both at a local and federal level views and program ideas of social scientists have been widely implemented.[9]

The current posture of public health, the present stance of social welfare and the shifts in interest among social scientists have at least to some extent resulted in changes in policy at a political level although undoubtedly there is a to-and-fro process with these groups being responsive to current political policy as well as influential in it. Nothwithstanding the direction of influence, it is rather evident that a set of principles for action has evolved that in many ways is discontinuous with the current mental health programming. Although in the writing of certain social psychiatrists one may find pronouncements similar to those that underlie the "great society" efforts and the activities of the Office of Economic Opportunity, certainly much of antipoverty programming does not square with current activities in the mental health field. At a general level in the new scheme of things health in itself is looked upon as a means, *not* as an end, of program efforts. The objective of the "great society" program is to modify the social order in ways that minimize discriminatory and exclusion practices associated with ethnic and cultural variables and with intergenerational competency.

The acceptable slogans of the day are "stamp out the lower class," *not* "reduce intrapsychiatric problems" and "cut down on anomie," *not* "resolve oedipal conflict." Health, including mental health, certainly is important for the unemployed person who is mentally or physically ill, needs medical care, cannot make use of job training and educational opportunities and consequently fails to participate fully in the "great society." But the restoration of health is not the end in itself or looked upon as a gain unless it leads to economic and social advancement.

Likewise, the criteria of success are not individual characteristics but communal ones. Self-satisfaction of persons and their performance in ways consistent with personal value commitments are, of course, recognized as important, but only because it is assumed that these must be realized in order to provide the proper motivational outlook and level of aspirations so as to participate as fully as possible in the economic and social life of the community. The hobo, for example, no matter how "happy" and "well adjusted" he is, has no place in the

---

[8] M. Rein, "The Social Service Crisis," *Trans-Action*, January-February 1964.
[9] H. E. Freeman, "Conceptual Approaches to Assessing Impacts of Large-Scale Intervention Programs," Proceedings of the Social Statistics Section, the American Statistical Association, Chicago, Illinois, 1964, pp. 192–198.

scheme of things.[10] Some may argue, of course, that these viewpoints are not inconsistent with current mental health activities and particularly with community programs, but I would question whether or not this is indeed the case.

Almost without exception mental health programs and the vast majority of community clinics begin with the supposition that their clients are "special" cases. This position is perhaps most clear in treatment programs for formerly hospitalized patients. Thus they concentrate on the treatment of emotional disorders and emphasize the remission of symptoms of psychiatric illness. It seems rather clear, however, that many of the problems of work behavior among those in psychiatric treatment are not illness-connected but stem from the complexities and strains inherent in the development of an occupational career itself. One may well argue that the treatment of the work problems of the patient as part of his illness is likely to reinforce his notion that he cannot take his place as a worker just like "anybody else" and to suggest to him additional justification of his occupational failure. To quote a forthcoming report [subsequently published] by Simmons:

> The problems of matching whatever skills and experience he may have to a job or helping to acquire such skills and knowledge are sufficiently complex and difficult and not likely to be resolved by focusing attention and effort on his illness.[11]

The differences between the current organization of mental health programs and the "war on poverty" are apparent in the various program components recommended for inclusion in local community efforts. Among components held important is the development of a one-door principle of entry for service. That is, there should be a single agency without criteria for eligibility in which the patient is seen for the maintenance and treatment of *all* of his illness. How consistent is this position with the current development of separate community mental health clinics and the planning of separate community centers for the treatment of the retarded? Second, it is recommended that indigenous persons within the lower-income population collaborate with professionals in the provision of treatment and that subprofessionals and technical aids be recruited from among the ranks of the poor. Given the strain toward professionalization, to what extent can the typical mental health program move in this direction? A third activity that is advocated is aggressive case-finding. It is held that the health professions must reach out and bring service to clients who do not ordinarily seek it. It is held that the social realities of being poor must be understood by the health professional and accounted for by the provision of transportation, adoption of clinic hours and the ways in which drugs and directions for

[10] Some of the material here is taken from an address by Sanford Kravitz of the Office of Economic Opportunity, presented at the annual meeting of the New Jersey Public Health Association, November, 1964. I have taken great liberty, however, with some of his material, and he is in no way to be held responsible for the statements in this paper.

[11] O. G. Simmons, in collaboration with H. M. Hughes, *Work and Mental Illness*, New York: John Wiley and Sons, Inc., 1965, Chapter 10.

care are provided. The difficulties of therapy with lower-class individuals and the differential use of treatment by socioeconomic groups are well known from several studies of psychiatric practice.[12] But in what ways are revisions now taking place?

There are, of course, a number of attempts being made to develop programs consistent with these principles, many hopefully with mechanisms for evaluation. These attempts are part of various community activity projects and demonstration grants by the Office of Economic Opportunity and the President's Committee on Youth Crime. In Boston, for example, as part of a new multiservice center the plan is for mental health activities to function alongside programs of legal services, occupational training and so on. The mental health activities in such multiservice centers are looked upon as a horizontal component—important but no more important than other social service programs. Several experiments on the use of indigenous community members as case aids now are being implemented in various parts of the country, and the special problems of mental health education with lower socioeconomic groups are being given serious consideration.[13]

Thus, I do not wish to imply that the field of mental health is entirely unresponsive to the new demands. But the shifts in orientation required are marked ones—radical departures from the program emphasis of the last decade or two, in which most of the energy and resources went into the development of autonomous mental health treatment centers and the building of a separate identity for the field of mental health. The issue at hand is whether or not the field of mental health has the robustness and flexibility to accommodate and modify its stance in terms of the broad objectives of the new society programs.

One reaction may be a shift or perhaps more accurately a return to a categorical disease orientation by mental health practitioners. Such an orientation is not inconsistent with the view held by some in the field at present. Further recruitment of persons to a categorical disease orientation is a possibility. But I doubt that this shift will typify the changes that take place in the field. The emphasis in the socialization of the current generation of practitioners in interpersonal processes, the extensive financial support for the new programs and the social values of persons in the field militate against a categorical disease view becoming the dominant orientation of the field.

Rather, I suggest a reorganization of the field is most likely—one that results in sharply modified roles for the different mental health professions and for the style of work in the field. For example, the psychiatrist's role is likely to be greatly modified. My prediction is that he will operate mostly in a technical level and deal with the control of symptomatic expressions of illness, with the determination of the physical basis of behavioral inadequacies and with the referral of such cases to other medical specialists.

[12] A. B. Hollingshead and F. C. Redlich, Social Class and Mental Illness, New York: John Wiley and Sons, Inc., 1958.
[13] F. Riessman, "New Approaches to Mental Health Treatment of Labor and Low-Income Groups," Written for the National Institute for Labor Education, Mental Health Programs, New York, February, 1964.

One reason why I suggest a marked change in the role behavior of the various professional groups is the differential speed and potential for modification of practice principles. The duration of training and academic requirements of the psychiatrist (and only to a somewhat lesser extent of the clinical psychologist) are held rigid by accreditation demands. Thus these groups are least likely to take the new emphasis into account in education programs. It is already the case that a few social work schools and certain educational counseling programs have specialized curriculums to deal with the low-income client. Such shifts in educational programs are easier to implement within the "less established" professional groups.

The psychiatrist is likely, however, in order to bolster his position in the new scheme of things to encourage the care of community members whose problems are consistent with his medical orientation. Thus the formerly hospitalized patient is likely to find the doors of the new "multipurpose" center open to him. There also is a greater likelihood of treatment within such community centers being offered the psychotic, with consequences for the programs of the mental hospitals and the autonomous mental health center.

The increased emphasis on work and educational performance undoubtedly will change the composition of most mental health teams, and the various groups of professionals will find that their levels of influence and prestige shift. Some of the groups now in a "marginal status" with respect to their degree of professionalization will take advantage of the opportunity to further advance their identity, to establish more formal criteria of professional accreditation and eligibility and to secure for themselves a more permanent and stable place within the structure of the mental health field. Intense conflict because of overlapping domains of activity and severe problems because of competition related to proprietary responsibility for clients are to be expected.

I could continue to speculate on the possible situational and role changes. The extent, duration and degree of influence on the field of indigenous community members, whose participation is now being encouraged, are questions that one could discuss at length. Changes that may occur in criteria of therapeutic success could be considered in great detail. The provision of future services for the "middle-class" patient who now receives so much attention is an issue that could be thoroughly examined.

There are other changes in the provision of psychiatric treatment by no means unrelated to the impact of the "great society" program that also need to be taken into account. For example, there is an acceleration of union activity in the provision of mental health services; a noteworthy market is the newly negotiated contract of the United Auto Workers.[14] The treatment of mental illness on an ambulatory basis within group practices as well as the massive programs being promulgated under the poverty program raise additional questions on the

[14] L. A. Falk, "Current Patterns of Health Care: Mental Health Services in Collective Bargaining and Prepaid Group Practice," Paper read at the American Orthopsychiatric Annual Meeting, March, 1965.

structure of mental health programs. The role relationships of mental health practitioners vis-a-vis other medical personnel; the provision of care in differentiated, bureaucratic treatment settings, and the reallocation of personnel in the light of the demands and needs of new population groups are issues that require immediate consideration.

Clearly, however, neither the previous changes in the mental health field nor the knowledge of the social sciences of innovation and change provides the basis for a prediction of the future of the field. It is possible to argue convincingly that the speculations offered in this paper are not likely to characterize the shifts that take place. But one thing is certain: shifts will occur.

Admittedly, it is somewhat out of style to end a paper with a call for research. But there is an unparalleled opportunity to examine experimentally and longitudinally changes in structural and organizational elements in the mental health field, ideological commitments, role relationships and performance of mental health practitioners, and patient outcome in psychiatric and social terms. Considering the intense interest in the impact of organizational variables and values on patients and practitioners in the mental health field and the limited information on the dynamics of change in a field historically most sensitive to political and social forces, it is to be hoped that some of us will take advantage of a unique chance to add to our scanty knowledge of the dynamics of social change.

This contemporary sermon addresses itself to modern man's spiritual emptiness. Dr. Mead examines some historical shifts in religious thinking beginning with the weakening of traditional religious concepts and extending through a subsequent belief in progress and man's ability to control nature. He concludes with a suggestion of the primacy of man in a social context.

Sidney E. Mead

The Lost Dimension and the Age of Longing

It is good now and then to try to take our bearings as we sail through or drift with the oceanic currents of the universe. For, as Abraham Lincoln said, "If we could first know where we are and whither we are tending, we could better judge what to do and how to do it."

But to know where we are and whither tending religiously is not easy. Even a modicum of confidence that we are following a charted course to some destination other than dusty death, rests upon an unstable foundation of knowledge, faith, and desire. Therefore, in speaking of where I think many of us are today, all I can hope to do is sketch an impressionistic mood-picture concocted of some sound history, of hunches, and sheer feeling.

In sketching such a picture I am quite aware that we today as unique individuals and heirs of all the diversity provided by the attics of the ages, live mentally and spiritually in different worlds. My impression of our present religious state may not be yours. So be it. I have no desire to make converts—and trust you have none either.

But where are we? Max Weber once characterized the movement of history during the past several centuries as "the progressive disenchantment of the world." More recently a historian characterized the history of the past two centuries as the story "of ultimate solutions gone sour." Both leave the impression that there has been a linear movement along a chronological line from "faith" to "doubt." The impression is wrong. History is not that simple, except to the simple-minded.

I have a friend—a professor and historian who has published many volumes on the history of Christianity from his point of view. To me he appears to live in a stable belief-world, in which the Scriptures provide a source of certain knowledge about man's past, present, and future, and a definite set of standards for judging the meaning of events and the values to be sought. He lives in a world different from the one I inhabit. But, he lives, and he is productive, and he seems to be as contented as the lot of man permits. He "believes" in the traditional sense.

On the other end of the spectrum I know, and you know (perhaps from personal experience), people who live in what has been called "the existential vacuum." Such people, being human, are not guided by instincts. And their drift with the intellectual gulf stream of western civilization has carried them far away from traditional religious beliefs. Of such a person an eminent psychiatrist has said, "No instinct tells him what he has to do, and no tradition tells him what he ought to do; soon he will not know what he wants to do. More and more he will be governed by what others want (and tell) him to do." This describes the "lonely crowd" of David Riesman's "other-directed people." These extremes of belief and unbelief are contemporary. The two poles do not represent a chronological movement as is often supposed.

But by and large we intellectuals are toward the "belief-vacuum" end of the continuum. Perhaps most vocal are those for whom an exhibitionist lack of belief is the hallmark of sophistication. So they pluck the strings of their rebellion against the "faith of our fathers" and chant their cleverness in ferreting out the absurdities of religion. It is better than they should be thus than apathetic.

But for others the kill has been made—the enemy slain. For them the old religious orthodoxy is dead, and to them it seems silly to continue to beat a corpse. As the lust of the hunt and the battle has cooled, reflectively they examine the dead face of religious belief and it "seems no longer that of an enemy." Perhaps their mood is close to that of Archy—Don Marquis' famous cockroach—as he saw the moth fly into the flame and become "a small unsightly cinder": "i wish/there was something i wanted/as badly as he wanted to fry himself."

It is the mood of those who would like to believe, but have discovered that they cannot believe—at least on the terms commonly offered them. They realize now that "believing" is not something one can by taking thought turn on or off. It is not a matter of simple choice but something that flows to one through subtle channels that Christians knew as "grace."

"So I won't believe" some say. But it is not as simple as that either. For apparently if one is to live at all it is not optional whether he will believe in *something* or not. "Where there is no vision the people perish," wrote the ancient author of Proverbs. And two psychiatrists who watched their fellow prisoners live and die in the concentration camps have said about the same thing respecting individuals. Wrote one, "the vast majority of the thousands of prisoners who died at Buchenwald each year died soon. They simply died of exhaustion, both physical and psychological, due to a loss of desire to live." To this the other adds, "The prisoner who had lost faith in the future—his future—was doomed. With his loss of belief in the future, he also lost his spiritual hold; he let himself decline and became subject to mental and physical decay."

But—believe what? The difficulty many people have with much of orthodoxy is the seeming insistence of its representatives that "you must believe *this,* and you must believe it *this way.*" It is for this reason that people in churches are often afraid to express their doubts, and sometimes feel guilty for having them. It was encouraging to note in recent news that there was a conference of Protestant, Roman Catholic, and Jewish laymen who began their discussion of "The Relevance of Faith in Modern Man" with a frank recognition that doubt of the beliefs and practices of his church often betokens the dawn of the member's real faith in God.

I am speaking to those people for whom traditional orthodoxy, as they have known it, is dead, and who know that for them it is dead. At most, with Matthew Arnold on *Dover Beach,* they hear "Its melancholy, long, withdrawing roar." They poignantly stare at the dead face of the old religious belief and sense within themselves a lost dimension—a vacuum to be filled, a longing.

A longing for what? Perhaps few would say it as I say it—they are longing for a "church" almost, not quite, in the traditional sense.

We Americans are the heirs of all the ages, of every land, of every people. But most of the basic motifs of our culture were launched on that "sea of faith" that "was once, too, at the full. . . ." It has been said that a culture is the tangible form of religious belief—and the religion of our culture is—or was—the Christian religion.

For centuries—say from the fourth to the eighteenth—the great majority of our Western ancestors lived and moved and had their being in the context of the Christian drama. It was a wonderful myth of the life of Everyman, and of Mankind.

The story of creation, redemption, and judgment enabled the average man to understand universal experience—"and it consoled him . . . to realize that his own life, however barren and limited . . . was but a concrete exemplification of the experience which God had decreed for all the generations of men." He was, like Emerson, held down to his place by the weight of the universe. He knew that at the end there would be a day of reckoning when infallible judgment, cutting through the moral and spiritual ambiguities known to man, would separate the evil from the good and allot to each its just reward. Then the great judge would stoop from above and wipe the tears from the tired eyes of the humblest person when he put earth's burdens down. He knew what human life was, for He was once born of a woman—"O little town of Bethlehem"—lived as a man among **men**—"was crucified, dead, and buried." But "the third day he rose from the dead"—and that is why the great hallelujah chorus reverberates down through the ages.

Sadly it must be said that somewhere along the line, for many people, the curtain went down on that drama—and neither curtain nor God have risen again. Friedrich Nietzsche's madman still rushes about in our marketplaces crying, "I seek God! . . . Where is God gone? I mean to tell you! We have killed him,—you and I! . . . God is dead!"

"God is dead!"—the line has become so common that even timid clergymen now use it in an attempt to be "honest to God." Meanwhile an increasing number of people who believe well enough that *that* God is dead, say it with the sad observation expressed by one of Arthur Koestler's characters—"Each time a god dies there is trouble in history. . . ."

But why did our God die? Did we kill him? If we did I think it was unintentional deicide committed while we thought we were but obeying His command to go forth and gain dominion over all other created things.

So we may point to that vast, vague area in our history that we call "the rise of science." Concurrently men of faith began to realize that as they marched to fulfill this promise their universe was changing into an immense machine that ran with inexorable precision and without concern for man. The subtle alchemy of human experience was changing God the father of the Lord Jesus Christ with whom we were fellow heirs into an engineer-mechanic who had designed and built the machine, but now was about as remote as those semimythical monsters who in the flat Olympus of Detroit design our automobiles.

A chill settled over the Christian world as God seemed to be fading away like Alice's Cheshire cat, leaving among a residue of the intellectually invincible a disembodied and sentimental grin. "It was," as Carl Becker put it, "as if a rumor—had at least become too insistent to be longer disregarded: the rumor that God, having departed secretly in the night, was about to cross the frontiers of the known world and leave mankind in the lurch."

For many this meant what Bertrand Russell suggested: "that man is the product of causes which had no prevision of the end they were achieving; that his origin, his growth, his hopes and fears, his loves and his beliefs, are but the outcome of accidental collocations of atoms; . . . that the whole temple of man's achievement must inevitably be buried beneath the debris of a universe in ruins. . . ."

For the first time in Christendom people were confronted with the question: "Were they living in a world ruled by a beneficent mind, or in a world ruled by an indifferent force?" But what really shocked them was that when they finally became self-consciously aware of the question, they had already accepted the latter answer. One of their spokesmen toward the end of the nineteenth century exclaimed that "he could not agree . . . that the 'new faith' constituted a desirable substitute for 'the waning splendour of the old.' " There is, he continued, an "appalling contrast between the hallowed glory of that creed which once was mine, and the lonely mystery of existence as now I find it. . . ." Such men *felt* "the lost dimension."

What was the "new faith" of which this scientist spoke? It was faith in man. But this is no simple matter.

It has been persuasively argued that as the eighteenth century philosophers dismantled the celestial heaven they rebuilt it on earth of earthly materials. Rejecting salvation mediated through the one who was "truly man and truly God" they postulated salvation through the efforts of successive generations of men. Living on in posterity took the place of an immortality in heaven as a sustaining belief. Robespierre, one of the leaders of the French revolution, addressed a prayer to the new-model god: "O posterity, sweet and tender hope of humanity, thou are not a stranger to us; it is for thee that we brave all the blows of tyranny; it is thy happiness which is the price of our painful struggles; often discouraged by the obstacles that surround us, we feel the need of thy consolations; it is to thee that we confide the task of completing our labors, and the destiny of all unborn generations! . . . Make haste, O posterity, to bring to pass the hour of equality, of justice, of happiness." Thereafter down through the nineteenth century—indeed, down to the present for many people—the hope for one's future and hence the significance of one's life was found in identification with a movement that was likely to endure in history. So Abraham Lincoln at Gettysburg said, "the world will little note nor long remember what we say here, but it can never forget what they did here."

Men holding this belief could be as naively rapturous about the bright future of man on earth as ever the writer of the book of Revelation was about the New Jerusalem where death would have no dominion and where there would be no night. Listen to Winwood Reade, writing in 1872: "The beautiful legend will come true; . . . Earth, which is now a purgatory, will be made a paradise, . . . by the efforts of man himself. . . . Hunger and starvation will then be unknown. . . . Governments will be conducted with the quietude and regularity of club committees. The interest which is now felt in politics will be transferred to science. . . . Poetry and the fine arts will take that place in the heart which religion now holds. . . . Not only will Man subdue the forces of evil that are without; he will also subdue those that are within. . . . A time will come when Science will transform (men's bodies). . . . Disease will be extirpated; the causes of decay will be removed; immortality will be invented . . . (and) Man then will be perfect; . . . he will therefore be what the vulgar worship as a god."

That, also, was a beautiful faith—a faith by which thousands of enlightened people lived and did great deeds, creating an era when even "wise men hoped" and believed in progress. But it must sadly be said that god—incarnate in mankind and consequently immortal only as posterity is immortal—that god also died in 1945 when a pigmy bomb left a mushroom-shaped cloud over a Japanese city. What men like Winwood Reade hailed as the god who would transform men's lives and institutions and invent immortality for all, had shown another face. The potential producer of all good was now seen as the potential producer of universal death—by flame and radiation, or slow starvation because of overpopulation, or sheer pollution of the earth's surface.

Slowly it seems to be dawning upon those people who placed their faith and found meaning for their lives in progress through posterity that there may be no "everafter" for mankind to live happily in. There may be no future. Posterity, worshiped as a god, may be even more vulnerable than the old Christian God because we can kill him as easily as we can "overkill" mankind.

There are, then, two aspects of the "lost dimension"—the loss of the ability to believe in the traditional Christian sense, and the loss of ability to assure ourselves that a posterity is a sure thing. For many people god the latter is just as dead as god the former.

It is because the faith in man's future which the eighteenth century taught us to substitute for faith in the Christian God has also collapsed that this becomes *The Age of Longing*—the title of Arthur Koestler's novel of 1951.

Longing for what? Longing for faith, for belief, for a meaning to one's life, and the work one does, for the ability to see something more than a "tale told by an idiot, signifying nothing" in the daily chores one has to do in order to live.

Of course this does not strike everyone at the same time or in the same way. Remember my friend who lives, and lives well, in the old Christian world. And I, as you, know technical intellectuals who still live, apparently quite happily, in the world of Winwood Reade. Others seem to be gifted with the capacity to earn enough in our affluent society to keep up with all the Joneses, all without any apparent concern about the family gods. Of course sometimes we eventually learn that as they gravitated toward the couch, or into an expensive slumber room, they had been living lives of "quiet desperation"—as Henry David Thoreau thought was the fate of most of his friends in staid old Concord.

The people of Koestler's novel are these "dispossessed of faith; the physically or spiritually homeless." The burden of their anguish is, "LET ME BELIEVE IN SOMETHING."

What I have given is the description of a mood—not universal of course, but widely prevalent among sensitive people. These people cannot give themselves either to faith in the traditional sense, or to the rich spontaneous faith in man and progress. Therefore it is not to be supposed, as some preachers seem to suppose today, that ridiculing and undermining the belief in man will restore the old kind of faith in God. But, on the other hand, neither can it be supposed—as other preachers appear to do—that undermining faith in the Christian God where it still exists, and ridiculing traditional Christian beliefs and practices will restore the lost faith in man's future. A plague on both these houses!

The people I have in mind seek religious faith—whether they would call it that or not does not matter. Their mood, to repeat, is akin to that of Emerson's soldier after the battle who realizes that the life he had to take cannot ever be recalled—that an enemy once dead is no longer an enemy—that the space he, or it, occupied may now be a fearful vacuum. It is to these people that a church ought to speak—must speak if it is to be more than a congenial company of irrelevant people. What is to be said?

At this point, having tied the religious situation into a desperately complex and hard knot, I wish that like some hardy true-believers I could pronounce it "Gordian" and cut it apart with one deft stroke of the "Sword of the Spirit," the Word of God. But already, it seems to me, too many preachers who do not even understand the question these people of the age of longing are asking, are blithely telling them that "Jesus is the answer."

I cannot be that definite. I can only make a suggestion through the use of figures. There is the figure of "the god behind the gods." The tribes of men forget that human life is a pilgrimage and make comfortable camps beside lakes and pools of truth from which they drink the water of life that sustains them in their particularity. But, Thoreau once said, when a tribe's lake or pool of truth dries up—as all lakes and pools must do—then they must "gird up their loins once more, and continue their pilgrimage toward its fountainhead." Some, of course, will resist moving on and prefer to become fossilized in the drying mud of the old pool. But those who do move toward the living stream might well take as their slogan, "God is dead—God alone is immortal!"

Then there is the figure of the church. And if the church be these people on their pilgrimage toward the fountainhead of life, then the essence of that church is to be found in the congenial relationship between these good companions. For God, 'tis said, is love. And to find other people who are congenial company on the pilgrimage, is to know the presence of that elemental love that is the creative ground of all human *being*.

So I can summarize what I have tried to say in words taken from J. Robert Oppenheimer: ". . . this, as I see it, is the condition of man; and in this condition we can help, because we can love one another."

I hope you can see what he meant, and I mean.

2 TECHNOLOGICAL CHANGE

If Mead has spoken of a lost dimension in man, Marshall McLuhan might be said to have identified a new dimension in contemporary life. Stressing those aspects of today's technologically charged universe that are global and organically unified rather than linear or framgentary, he conjures up a vastly altered world in which communication is instantaneous and interdependence total. In such an expanded social sphere, he prophesies, men will need radically new perceptions and information.

Marshall McLuhan

Automation:
Learning a Living

A newspaper headline recently read, "Little Red Schoolhouse Dies When Good Road Built." One-room schools, with all subjects being taught to all grades at the same time, simply dissolve when better transportation permits specialized space and specialized teaching. At the extreme of speeded-up movement, however, specialism of space and subject disappears once more. With automation, it is not only jobs that disappear, and complex roles that reappear. Centuries of specialist stress in pedagogy and in the arrangement of data now end with the instantaneous retrieval of information made possible by electricity. Automation is information and it not only ends jobs in the world of work, it ends subjects in the world of learning. It does not end the world of learning. The future of work consists of learning a living in the automation age. This is a familiar pattern in electric technology in general. It ends the old dichotomies between culture and technology, between art and commerce, and between work and leisure. Whereas in the mechanical age of fragmentation leisure had been the absence of work, or mere idleness, the reverse is true in the electric age. As the age of information demands the simultaneous use of all our faculties, we discover that we are most at leisure when we are most intensely involved, very much as with the artists in all ages.

In terms of the industrial age, it can be pointed out that the difference between the previous mechanical age and the new electric age appears in the different kinds of inventories. Since electricity, inventories are made up not so much of goods in storage as of materials in continuous process of transformation at spatially removed sites. For electricity not only gives primacy to *process*, whether in making or in learning, but it makes independent the source of energy from the location of the process. In entertainment media, we speak of this fact as "mass media" because the source of the program and the process of experiencing it are independent in space, yet simultaneous in time. In industry this basic fact causes the scientific revolution that is called "automation" or "cybernation."

In education the conventional division of the curriculum into subjects is already as outdated as the medieval trivium and quadrivium after the Renaissance. Any subject taken in depth at once relates to other subjects. Arithmetic in grade three or nine, when taught in terms of number theory, symbolic logic, and cultural history, ceases to be mere practice in problems. Continued in their present patterns of fragmented unrelation, our school curricula will insure a citizenry unable to understand the cybernated world in which they live.

Most scientists are quite aware that since we have acquired some knowledge of electricity it is not possible to speak of atoms as pieces of matter. Again, as more is known about electrical "discharges" and energy, there is less and less tendency to speak of electricity as a thing that "flows" like water through a wire, or is "contained" in a battery. Rather, the tendency is to speak of electricity as painters speak of space; namely, that it is a variable condition that involves the special positions of two or more bodies. There is no longer any tendency to speak of electricity as "contained" in anything. Painters have long known that objects are not contained in space, but that they generate their own spaces. It was the dawning awareness of this in the mathematical world a century ago that enabled Lewis Carroll, the Oxford mathematician, to contrive *Alice in Wonderland,* in which times and spaces are neither uniform nor continuous, as they had seemed to be since the arrival of Renaissance perspective. As for the speed of light, that is merely the speed of total causality.

It is a principal aspect of the electric age that it establishes a global network that has much of the character of our central nervous system. Our central nervous system is not merely an electric network, but it constitutes a single unified field of experience. As biologists point out, the brain is the interacting place where all kinds of impressions and experiences can be exchanged and translated, enabling us to *react to the world as a whole.* Naturally, when electric technology comes into play, the utmost variety and extent of operations in industry and society quickly assume a unified posture. Yet this organic unity of interprocess that electromagnetism inspires in the most diverse and specialized areas and organs of action is quite the opposite of organization in a mechanized society. Mechanization of any process is achieved by fragmentation, beginning with the mechanization of writing by movable types, which has been called the "monofracture of manufacture."

The electric telegraph, when crossed with typography, created the strange new form of the modern newspaper. Any page of the telegraph press is a surrealistic mosaic of bits of "human interest" in vivid interaction. Such was the art form of Chaplin and the early silent movies. Here, too, an extreme speed-up of mechanization, an assembly line of still shots on celluloid, led to a strange reversal. The movie mechanism, aided by the electric light, created the illusion of organic form and movement as much as a fixed position had created the illusion of perspective on a flat surface five hundred years before.

The same thing happens less superficially when the electric principle crosses the mechanical lines of industrial organization. Automation retains only as much of the mechanical character as the motorcar kept of the forms of the horse and the carriage. Yet people discuss automation as if we had not passed the oat barrier, and as if the horse-vote at the next poll would sweep away the automation regime.

Automation is not an extension of the mechanical principles of fragmentation and separation of operations. It is rather the invasion of the mechanical world by the instantaneous character of electricity. That is why those involved in automation insist that it is a way of thinking, as much as it is a way of doing. Instant synchronization of numerous operations has ended the old mechanical pattern of setting up operations in lineal sequence. The assembly line has gone the way of the stag line. Nor is it just the lineal and sequential aspect of mechanical analysis that has been erased by the electric speed-up and exact synchronizing of information that is automation.

Automation or cybernation deals with all the units and components of the industrial and marketing process exactly as radio or TV combine the individuals in the audience into new interprocess. The new kind of interrelation in both industry and entertainment is the result of the electric instant speed. Our new electric technology now extends the instant processing of knowledge by interrelation that has long occurred within our central nervous system. It is that same speed that constitutes "organic unity" and ends the mechanical age that had gone into high gear with Gutenberg. Automation brings in real "mass production," not in terms of size, but of an instant inclusive embrace. Such is also the character of "mass media." They are an indication, not of the size of their audiences, but of the fact that everybody becomes involved in them at the same time. Thus commodity industries under automation share the same structural character of the entertainment industries in the degree that both approximate the condition of instant information. Automation affects not just production, but every phase of consumption and marketing; for the consumer becomes producer in the automation circuit, quite as much as the reader of the mosaic telegraph press makes his own news, or just is *his* own news.

But there is a component in the automation story that is as basic as tactility to the TV image. It is the fact that, in any automatic machine, or galaxy of machines and functions, the generation and transmission of power is quite separate from the work operation that uses the power. The same is true in all servomechanist structures that involve feedback. The source of energy is separate from the process of translation of information, or the applying of knowledge. This is obvious in the telegraph, where the energy and channel are quite independent of whether written code is French or German. The same separation of power and process obtains in automated industry, or in "cybernation." The electric energy can be applied indifferently and quickly to many kinds of tasks.

Such was never the case in the mechanical systems. The power and the work done were always in direct relation, whether it was hand and hammer, water and wheel, horse and cart, or steam and piston. Electricity brought a strange elasticity in this matter, much as light itself illuminates a total field and does not dictate what shall be done. The same light can make possible a multiplicity of tasks, just as with electric power. Light is a nonspecialist kind of energy or power that is identical with information and knowledge. Such is also the relation of electricity to automation, since both energy and information can be applied in a great variety of ways.

Grasp of this fact is indispensable to the understanding of the electronic age, and of automation in particular. Energy and production now tend to fuse with information and learning. Marketing and consumption tend to become one with learning, enlightenment, and the intake of information. This is all part of the electric *implosion* that now follows or succeeds the centuries of *explosion* and increasing specialism. The electronic age is literally one of illumination. Just as light is at once energy and information, so electric automation unites production, consumption, and learning in an inextricable process. For this reason, teachers are already the largest employee group in the U.S. economy, and may well become the *only* group.

The very same process of automation that causes a withdrawal of the present work force from industry causes learning itself to become the principal kind of production and consumption. Hence the folly of alarm about unemployment. Paid learning is already becoming both the dominant employment and source of new wealth in our society. This is the new *role* for men in society, whereas the older mechanistic idea of "jobs," or fragmented tasks and specialist slots for "workers," becomes meaningless under automation.

It has often been said by engineers that, as information levels rise, almost any sort of material can be adapted to any sort of use. This principle is the key to the understanding of electric automation. In the case of electricity, as energy for production becomes independent of the work operation, there is not only the speed that makes for total and organic interplay, but there is, also, the fact that electricity is sheer information that, in actual practice, illuminates all it touches. Any process that approaches instant interrelation of a total field tends to raise itself to the level of conscious awareness, so that computers seem to "think." In fact, they are highly specialized at present, and quite lacking in the full process of interrelation that makes for consciousness. Obviously, they can be made to simulate the process of consciousness, just as our electric global networks now begin to simulate the condition of our central nervous system. But a conscious computer would still be one that was an extension of our consciousness, as a telescope is an extension of our eyes, or as a ventriloquist's dummy is an extension of the ventriloquist.

Automation certainly assumes the servomechanism and the computer. That is to say, it assumes electricity as store and expediter of information. These traits of store, or "memory," and accelerator are the basic features of any medium of communication whatever. In the case of electricity, it is not corporeal substance that is stored or moved, but perception and information. As for technological acceleration, it now approaches the speed of light. All nonelectric media had merely hastened things a bit. The wheel, the road, the ship, the airplane, and even the space rocket are utterly lacking in the character of instant movement. Is it strange, then, that electricity should confer on all previous human organization a completely new character? The very toil of man now becomes a kind of enlightenment. As unfallen Adam in the Garden of Eden was appointed the task of the contemplation and naming of creatures, so with automation. We have now only to name and program a process or a product in order for it to be accomplished. Is it not rather like the case of Al Capp's Schmoos? One had only to look at a Schmoo and think longingly of pork chops or caviar, and the Schmoo ecstatically transformed itself into the object of desire. Automation brings us into the world of the Schmoo. The custom-built supplants the mass-produced.

Let us, as the Chinese say, move our chairs closer to the fire and see what we are saying. The electric changes associated with automation have nothing to do with ideologies or social programs. If they had, they could be delayed or controlled. Instead, the technological extension of our central nervous system that we call the electric media began more than a century ago, subliminally. Subliminal have been the effects. Subliminal they remain. At no period in human culture have men understood the psychic mechanisms involved in invention and technology. Today it is the instant speed of electric information that, for the first time, permits easy recognition of the patterns and the formal contours of change and development. The entire world, past and present, now reveals itself to us like a growing plant in an enormously accelerated movie. Electric speed is synonymous with light and with the understanding of causes. So, with the use of electricity in previously mechanized situations, men easily discover causal connections and patterns that were quite unobservable at the slower rates of mechanical change. If we play backward the long development of literacy and printing and their effects on social experience and organization, we can easily see how these forms brought about that high degree of social uniformity and homogeneity of society that is indispensable for mechanical industry. Play them backward, and we get just that shock of unfamiliarity in the familiar that is necessary for the understanding of the life of forms. Electricity compels us to play our mechanical development backward, for it reverses much of that development. Mechanization depends on the breaking up of processes into homogenized but unrelated bits. Electricity unifies these fragments once more because its speed of operation requires a high degree of interdependence among all phases of any operation. It is this electric speed-up and interdependence that has ended the assembly line in industry.

This same need for organic interrelation, brought in by the electric speed of synchronization, now requires us to perform, industry-by-industry, and country-by-country, exactly the same organic interrelating that was first effected in the individual automated unit. Electric speed requires organic structuring of the global economy quite as much as early mechanization by print and by road led to the acceptance of national unity. Let us not forget that nationalism was a mighty invention and revolution that, in the Renaissance, wiped out many of the local regions and loyalties. It was a revolution achieved almost entirely by the speed-up of information by means of uniform movable types. Nationalism cut across most of the traditional power and cultural groupings that had slowly grown up in various regions. Multinationalisms had long deprived Europe of its economic unity. The Common Market came to it only with the Second War. War is accelerated social change, as an explosion is an accelerated chemical reaction and movement of matter. With electric speeds governing industry and social life, explosion in the sense of crash development becomes normal. On the other hand, the old-fashioned kind of "war" becomes as impracticable as playing hopscotch with bulldozers. Organic interdependence means that disruption of any part of the organism can prove fatal to the whole. Every industry has had to "rethink through" (the awkwardness of this phrase betrays the painfulness of the process), function by function, its place in the economy. But automation forces not only industry and town planners, but government and even education, to come into some relation to social facts.

The various military branches have had to come into line with automation very quickly. The unwieldy mechanical forms of military organization have gone. Small teams of experts have replaced the citizen armies of yesterday even faster than they have taken over the reorganization of industry. Uniformly trained and homogenized citizenry, so long in preparation and so necessary to a mechanized society, is becoming quite a burden and problem to an automated society, for automation and electricity require depth approaches in all fields and at all times. Hence the sudden rejection of standardized goods and scenery and living and education in America since the Second War. It is a switch imposed by electric technology in general, and by the TV image in particular.

Automation was first felt and seen on a large scale in the chemical industries of gas, coal, oil, and metallic ores. The large changes in these operations made possible by electric energy have now, by means of the computer, begun to invade every kind of white-collar and management area. Many people, in consequence, have begun to look on the whole of society as a single unified machine for creating wealth. Such has been the normal outlook of the stockbroker, manipulating shares and information with the cooperation of the electric media of press, radio, telephone, and teletype. But the peculiar and abstract manipulation of information as a means of creating wealth is no longer a monopoly of the stockbroker. It is now shared by every engineer and by the entire communications industries. With electricity as energizer and synchronizer, all aspects of production, consumption, and organization become incidental to communications. The very idea of communication as interplay is inherent in the electrical, which combines both energy and information in its intensive manifold.

Anybody who begins to examine the patterns of automation finds that perfecting the individual machine by making it automatic involves "feedback." That means introducing an information loop or circuit, where before there had been merely a one-way flow or mechanical sequence. Feedback is the end of the lineality that came into the Western world with the alphabet and the continuous forms of Euclidean space. Feedback or dialogue between the mechanism and its environment brings a further weaving of individual machines into a galaxy of such machines throughout the entire plant. There follows a still further weaving of individual plants and factories into the entire industrial matrix of materials and services of a culture. Naturally, this last stage encounters the entire world of policy, since to deal with the whole industrial complex as an organic system affects employment, security, education, and politics, demanding full understanding in advance of coming structural change. There is no room for witless assumptions and subliminal factors in such electrical and instant organizations.

As artists began a century ago to construct their works backward, *starting with the effect,* so now with industry and planning. In general, electric speed-up requires complete knowledge of ultimate effects. Mechanical speed-ups, however radical in their reshaping of personal and social life, still were allowed to happen sequentially. Men could, for the most part, get through a normal life span on the basis of a single set of skills. That is not at all the case with electric speed-up. The acquiring of new basic knowledge and skill by senior executives in middle age is one of the most common needs and harrowing facts of electric technology. The senior executives, or "big wheels," as they are archaically and ironically designated, are among the hardest pressed and most persistently harassed groups in human history. Electricity has not only demanded ever deeper knowledge and faster interplay, but has made the harmonizing of production schedules as rigorous as that demanded of the members of a large symphony orchestra. And the satisfactions are just as few for the big executives as for the symphonists, since a player in a big orchestra can hear nothing of the music that reaches the audience. He gets only noise.

The result of electric speed-up in industry at large is the creation of intense sensitivity to the interrelation and interprocess of the whole, so as to call for ever-new types of organization and talent. Viewed from the old perspectives of the machine age, this electric network of plants and processes seems brittle and tight. In fact, it is not mechanical, and it does begin to develop the sensitivity and pliability of the human organism. But it also demands the same varied nutriment and nursing as the animal organism.

With the instant and complex interprocesses of the organic form, automated industry also acquires the power of adaptability to multiple uses. A machine set up for the automatic production of electric bulbs represents a combination of processes that were previously managed by several machines. With a single attendant, it can run as continuously as a tree in its intake and output. But, unlike the tree, it has a built-in system of jigs and fixtures that can be shifted to cause the machine to turn out a whole range of products from radio tubes and glass tumblers to Christmas-tree ornaments. Although an automated plant is almost like a tree in respect to the continuous intake and output, it is a tree that can change from oak to maple to walnut as required. It is part of the automation or electric logic that specialism is no longer limited to just one specialty. The automatic machine may work in a specialist way, but it is not limited to one line. As with our hands and fingers that are capable of many tasks, the automatic unit incorporates a power of adaptation that was quite lacking in the pre-electric and mechanical stage of technology. As *anything* becomes more complex, it becomes less specialized. Man is more complex and less specialized than a dinosaur. The older mechanical operations were designed to be more efficient as they became larger and more specialized. The electric and automated unit, however, is quite otherwise. A new automatic machine for making automobile tailpipes is about the size of two or three office desks. The computer control panel is the size of a lectern. It has in it no dies, no fixtures, no settings of any kind, but rather certain general-purpose things like grippers, benders, and advancers. On this machine, starting with lengths of ordinary pipe, it is possible to make eighty different kinds of tailpipe in succession, as rapidly, as easily, and as cheaply as it is to make eighty of the same kind. And the characteristic of electric automation is all in this direction of return to the general-purpose handicraft flexibility that our own hands possess. The programming can now include endless changes of program. It is the electric feedback, or dialogue pattern, of the automatic and computer-programmed "machine" that marks it off from the older mechanical principle of one-way movement.

This computer offers a model that has the characteristics shared by all automation. From the point of intake of materials to the output of the finished product, the operations tend to be independently, as well as interdependently, automatic. The synchronized concert of operations is under the control of gauges and instruments that can be varied from the control-panel boards that are themselves electronic. The material of intake is relatively uniform in shape, size, and chemical properties, as likewise the material of the output. But the processing under these conditions permits use of the highest level of capacity for any needed period. It is, as compared with the older machines, the difference between an oboe in an orchestra and the same tone on an electronic music instrument. With the electronic music instrument, any tone can be made available in any intensity and for any length of time. Note that the older symphony orchestra was, by comparison, a machine of separate instruments that *gave the effect of organic unity*. With the electronic instrument, one *starts* with organic unity as an immediate fact of perfect synchronization. This makes the attempt to create the effect of organic unity quite pointless. Electronic music must seek other goals.

Such is also the harsh logic of industrial automation. All that we had previously achieved mechanically by great exertion and coordination can now be done electrically without effort. Hence the specter of joblessness and propertylessness in the electric age. Wealth and work become information factors, and totally new structures are needed to run a business or relate it to social needs and markets. With the electric technology, the new kinds of instant interdependence and interprocess that take over production also enter the market and social organizations. For this reason, markets and education designed to cope with the products of servile toil and mechanical production are no longer adequate. Our education has long ago acquired the fragmentary and piecemeal character of mechanism. It is now under increasing pressure to acquire the depth and inter-relation that are indispensable in the all-at-once world of electric organization.

Paradoxically, automation makes liberal education mandatory. The electric age of servomechanisms suddenly releases men from the mechanical and specialist servitude of the preceding machine age. As the machine and the motorcar released the horse and projected it onto the plane of entertainment, so does automation with men. We are suddenly threatened with a liberation that taxes our inner resources of self-employment and imaginative participation in society. This would seem to be a fate that calls men to the role of artist in society. It has the effect of making most people realize how much they had come to depend on the fragmentalized and repetitive routines of the mechanical era. Thousands of years ago man, the nomadic food-gatherer, had taken up positional, or relatively sedentary, tasks. He began to specialize. The development of writing and printing were major stages of that process. They were supremely specialist in separating the roles of knowledge from the roles of action, even though at times it could appear that "the pen is mightier than the sword." But with electricity and automation, the technology of fragmented processes suddenly fused with the human dialogue and the need for over-all consideration of human unity. Men are suddenly nomadic gatherers of knowledge, nomadic as never before, informed as never before, free from fragmentary specialism as never before—but also involved in the total social process as never before; since with electricity we extend our central nervous system globally, instantly interrelating every human experience. Long accustomed to such a state in stock-market news or front-page sensations, we can grasp the meaning of this new dimension more readily when it is pointed out that it is possible to "fly" unbuilt airplanes on computers. The specifications of a plane can be programmed and the plane tested under a variety of extreme conditions before it has left the drafting board. So with new products and new organizations of many kinds. We can now, by computer, deal with complex social needs with the same architectural certainty that we previously attempted in private housing. Industry as a whole has become the unit of reckoning, and so with society, politics, and education as wholes.

Electric means of storing and moving information with speed and precision make the largest units quite as manageable as small ones. Thus the automation of a plant or of an entire industry offers a small model of the changes that must occur in society from the same electric technology. Total interdependence is the starting fact. Nevertheless, the range of choice in design, stress, and goal within that total field of electromagnetic interprocess is very much greater than it ever could have been under mechanization.

Since electric energy is independent in the place or kind of work-operation, it creates patterns of decentralism and diversity in the work to be done. This is a logic that appears plainly enough in the difference between firelight and electric light, for example. Persons grouped around a fire or candle for warmth or light are less able to pursue independent thoughts, or even tasks, than people supplied with electric light. In the same way, the social and educational patterns latent in automation are those of self-employment and artistic autonomy. Panic about automation as a threat of uniformity on a world scale is the projection into the future of mechanical standardization and specialism, which are now past.

Affects of the ongoing cybernetic revolution on industry in particular and society in general are analyzed in this article, which offers recommendations for planning and managing the vast social change that lies ahead. The authors suggest that totally new and enlarged production capabilities are about to render contemporary social and economic systems obsolete.

The Ad Hoc Committee on the Triple Revolution, W. H. Ferry, et al.

The Triple Revolution

This statement is written in the recognition that mankind is at a historic conjuncture which demands a fundamental reexamination of existing values and institutions. At this time three separate and mutually reinforcing revolutions are taking place:

The Cybernation Revolution

A new era of production has begun. Its principles of organization are as different from those of the industrial era as those of the industrial era were different from the agricultural. The cybernation revolution has been brought about by the combination of the computer and the automated self-regulating machine. This results in a system of almost unlimited productive capacity which requires progressively less human labor. Cybernation is already reorganizing the economic and social system to meet its own needs.

The Weaponry Revolution

New forms of weaponry have been developed which cannot win wars but which can obliterate civilization. We are recognizing only now that the great weapons have eliminated war as a method for resolving international conflicts. The ever-present threat of total destruction is tempered by the knowledge of the final futility of war. The need of a "warless world" is generally recognized, though achieving it will be a long and frustrating process.

The Human Rights Revolution

A universal demand for full human rights is now clearly evident. It continues to be demonstrated in the civil rights movement within the United States. But this is only the local manifestation of a worldwide movement toward the establishment of social and political regimes in which every individual will feel valued and none will feel rejected on account of his race.

We are particularly concerned in this statement with the first of these revolutionary phenomena. This is not because we underestimate the significance of the other two. On the contrary, we affirm that it is the simultaneous occurrence and interaction of all three developments which make evident the necessity for radical alterations in attitude and policy. The adoption of just policies for coping with cybernation and for extending rights to all Americans is indispensable to the creation of an atmosphere in the U.S. in which the supreme issue, peace, can be reasonably debated and resolved.

The Negro claims, as a matter of simple justice, his full share in America's economic and social life. He sees adequate employment opportunities as a chief means of attaining this goal: The March on Washington demanded freedom *and* jobs. The Negro's claim to a job is not being met. Negroes are the hardest-hit of the many groups being exiled from the economy by cybernation. Negro unemployment rates cannot be expected to drop substantially. Promises of jobs are a cruel and dangerous hoax on hundreds of thousands of Negroes and whites alike who are especially vulnerable to cybernation because of age or inadequate education.

The demand of the civil rights movement cannot be fulfilled within the present context of society. The Negro is trying to enter a social community and a tradition of work-and-income which are in the process of vanishing even for the hitherto privileged white worker. Jobs are disappearing under the impact of highly efficient, progressively less costly machines.

The U.S. operates on the thesis, set out in the Employment Act of 1964, that every person will be able to obtain a job if he wishes to do so and that this job will provide him with resources adequate to live and maintain a family decently. Thus jobholding is the general mechanism through which economic resources are distributed. Those without work have access only to a minimal income, hardly sufficient to provide the necessities of life, and enabling those receiving it to function as only "minimum consumers." As a result, the goods and services which are needed by these crippled consumers, and which they would buy if they could, are not produced. This, in turn deprives other workers of jobs, thus reducing their incomes and consumption.

Present excessive levels of unemployment would be multiplied several times if military and space expenditures did not continue to absorb 10% of the gross national product (i.e., the total goods and services produced). Some 6 to 8 million people are employed as a direct result of purchases for space and military activities. At least an equal number hold their jobs as an indirect result of military and space expenditures. In recent years, the military and space budgets have absorbed a rising proportion of national production and formed a strong support for the economy.

However, these expenditures are coming in for more and more criticism, at least partially in recognition of the fact that nuclear weapons have eliminated war as an acceptable method for resolving international conflicts. Early in 1964 President Johnson ordered a curtailment of certain military expenditures. Defense Secretary McNamara is closing shipyards, airfields, and Army bases, and Congress is pressing the National Space Administration to economize. The future of those strong props to the economy is not as clear today as it was even a year ago.

HOW THE CYBERNATION REVOLUTION SHAPES UP

Cybernation is manifesting the characteristics of a revolution in production. These include the development of radically different techniques and the subsequent appearance of novel principles of the organization of production; a basic reordering of man's relationship to his environment; and a dramatic increase in total available and potential energy.

The major difference between the agricultural, industrial and cybernation revolutions is the speed at which they developed. The agricultural revolution began several thousand years ago in the Middle East. Centuries passed in the shift from a subsistence base of hunting and foodgathering to settled agriculture.

In contrast, it has been less than 200 years since the emergence of the industrial revolution, and direct and accurate knowledge of the new productive techniques has reached most of mankind. This swift dissemination of information is generally held to be the main factor leading to widespread industrialization.

While the major aspects of the cybernation revolution are for the moment restricted to the U.S., its effects are observable almost at once throughout the industrial world and large parts of the non-industrial world. Observation is rapidly followed by analysis and criticism. The problems posed by the cybernation revolution are part of a new era in the history of all mankind but they are first being faced by the people of the U.S. The way Americans cope with cybernation will influence the course of this phenomenon everywhere. This country is the stage on which the machines-and-man drama will first be played for the world to witness.

The fundamental problem posed by the cybernation revolution in the U.S. is that it invalidates the general mechanism so far employed to undergird people's rights as consumers. Up to this time economic resources have been distributed on the basis of contributions to production, with machines and men competing for employment on somewhat equal terms. In the developing cybernated system, potentially unlimited output can be achieved by systems of machines which will require little cooperation from human beings. As machines take over production from men, they absorb an increasing proportion of resources while the men who are displaced become dependent on minimal and unrelated government measures—unemployment insurance, social security, welfare payments.

These measures are less and less able to disguise a historic paradox: That a substantial proportion of the population is subsisting on minimal income, often below the poverty line, at a time when sufficient productive potential is available to supply the needs of everyone in the U.S.

INDUSTRIAL SYSTEM FAILS
TO PROVIDE FOR ABOLITION OF POVERTY

The existence of this paradox is denied or ignored by conventional economic analysis. The general economic approach argues that potential demand, which if filled would raise the number of jobs and provide incomes to those holding them, is underestimated. Most contemporary economic analysis states that all of the available labor force and industrial capacity is required to meet the needs of consumers and industry and to provide adequate public services: Schools, parks, roads, homes, decent cities, and clean water and air. It is further argued that demand could be increased, by a variety of standard techniques, to any desired extent by providing money and machines to improve the conditions of the billions of impoverished people elsewhere in the world, who need food and shelter, clothes and machinery and everything else the industrial nations take for granted.

There is no question that cybernation does increase the potential for the provision of funds to neglected public sectors. Nor is there any question that cybernation would make possible the abolition of poverty at home and abroad. But the industrial system does not possess any adequate mechanisms to permit these potentials to become realities. The industrial system was designed to produce an everincreasing quantity of goods as efficiently as possible, and it was assumed that the distribution of the power to purchase these goods would occur almost automatically. The continuance of the income-through-jobs link as the only major mechanism for distributing effective demand—for granting the right to consume—now acts as the main brake on the almost unlimited capacity of a cybernated productive system.

Recent administrations have proposed measures aimed at achieving a better distribution of resources, and at reducing unemployment and underemployment. A few of these proposals have been enacted. More often they have failed to secure congressional support. In every case, many members of Congress have criticized the proposed measures as departing from traditional principles for the allocation of resources and the encouragement of production. Abetted by budget-balancing economists and interest groups they have argued for the maintenance of an economic machine based on ideas of scarcity to deal with the facts of abundance produced by cybernation. This time-consuming criticism has slowed the workings of Congress and has thrown out of focus for that body the inter-related effects of the triple revolution.

An adequate distribution of the potential abundance of goods and services will be achieved only when it is understood that the major economic problem is not how to increase production but how to distribute the abundance that is the great potential of cybernation. There is an urgent need for a fundamental change in the mechanisms employed to insure consumer rights.

FACTS AND FIGURES OF THE CYBERNATION REVOLUTION

No responsible observer would attempt to describe the exact pace or the full sweep of a phenomenon that is developing with the speed of cybernation. Some aspects of this revolution, however, are already clear:

The rate of productivity increase has risen with the onset of cybernation.

An industrial economic system postulated on scarcity has been unable to distribute the abundant goods and services produced by a cybernated system or potential in it.

Surplus capacity and unemployment have thus co-existed at excessive levels over the last six years.

The underlying cause of excessive unemployment is the fact that the capability of machines is rising more rapidly than the capacity of many human beings to keep pace.

A permanent impoverished and jobless class is established in the midst of potential abundance.

Evidence for these statements follows:

(1) The increased efficiency of machine systems is shown in the more rapid increase in productivity per man-hour since 1960, a year that marks the first visible upsurge of the cybernation revolution. In 1961, 1962 and 1963,

productivity per man-hour rose at an average pace above 3.5%—a rate well above both the historical average and the postwar rate.

Companies are finding cybernation more and more attractive. Even at the present early stage of cybernation, costs have already been lowered to a point where the price of a durable machine may be as little as one-third of the current annual wage-cost of the worker it replaces. A more rapid rise in the rate of productivity increase per man-hour can be expected from now on.

(2) In recent years it has proved to increase demand fast enough to bring about the full use of either men or plant capacities. The task of developing sufficient additional demand promises to become more difficult each year. A $30 billion annual increase in gross national product is now required to prevent unemployment rates from rising. An additional $40 to $60 billion increase would be required to bring unemployment rates down to an acceptable level.

(3) The official rate of unemployment has remained at or above 5.5% during the Sixties. The unemployment rate for teenagers has been rising steadily and now stands around 15%. The unemployment rate for Negro teenagers stands about 30%. The unemployment rate for teenagers in minority ghettos sometimes exceeds 50%. Unemployment rates for Negroes are regularly more than twice those for whites, whatever their occupation, educational level, age or sex. The unemployment position for other racial minorities is similarly unfavorable. Unemployment rates in depressed areas often exceed 50%.

UNEMPLOYMENT IS FAR WORSE THAN FIGURES INDICATE

These official figures seriously underestimate the true extent of unemployment. The statistics take no notice of underemployment or featherbedding. Besides the 5.5% of the labor force who are officially designated as unemployed, nearly 4% of the labor force sought full-time work in 1962 but could find only part-time jobs. In addition, methods of calculating unemployment rates—a person is counted as unemployed only if he has actively sought a job recently—ignore the fact that many men and women who would like to find jobs have not looked for them because they know there are no employment opportunities.

Underestimates for this reason are pervasive among groups whose unemployment rates are high—the young, the old, and racial minorities. Many people in the depressed agricultural, mining and industrial areas, who by official definition hold jobs but who are actually grossly underemployed, would move if there were prospects of finding work elsewhere. It is reasonable to estimate that over 8,000,000 people are not working who would like to have jobs today as compared with the 4,000,000 shown in the official statistics.

Even more serious is the fact that the number of people who have voluntarily removed themselves from the labor force is not constant but increases continuously. These people have decided to stop looking for employment and seem to have accepted the fact that they will never hold jobs again. This decision is largely irreversible, in economic and also in social and psychological terms. The older worker calls himself "retired"; he cannot accept work without affecting his social security status. The worker in his prime years is forced onto relief: In most states the requirements for becoming a relief recipient bring about such fundamental alterations in an individual's situation that a reversal of the process is always difficult and often totally infeasible. Teenagers, especially "drop-outs" and Negroes, are coming to realize that there is no place for them in the labor force but at the same time they are given no realistic alternative. These people and their dependents make up a large part of the "poverty" sector of the American population.

Statistical evidence of these trends appears in the decline in the proportion of people claiming to be in the labor force—the so-called labor force participation rate. The recent apparent stabilization of the unemployment rate around 5.5% is therefore misleading: It is a reflection of the discouragement and defeat of people who cannot find employment and have withdrawn from the market rather than a measure of the economy's success in creating jobs for those who want to work.

(4) An efficiently functioning industrial system is assumed to provide the great majority of new jobs through the expansion of the private enterprise sector. But well over half of the new jobs created during 1957–1962 were in the public sector—predominantly in teaching. Job creation in the private sector has now almost entirely ceased except in services; of the 4,300,000 jobs created in this period, only about 200,000 were provided by private industry through its own efforts. Many authorities anticipate that the application of cybernation to certain service industries, which is only just beginning, will be particularly effective. if this is the case, no significant job creation will take place in the private sector in coming years.

(5) Cybernation raises the level of the skills of the machine. Secretary of Labor Wirtz has recently stated that the machines being produced today have, on the average, skills equivalent to a high school diploma. If a human being is to compete with such machines, therefore, he must at least possess a high school diploma. The Department of Labor estimates, however, that on the basis of present trends, as many as 30% of all students will be high school drop-outs in this decade.

(6) A permanently depressed class is developing in the U.S. Some 38,000,000 Americans, almost one-fifth of the nation, still live in poverty. The percentage of total income received by the poorest 20% of the population was 4.9% in 1944 and 4.7% in 1963.

Secretary Wirtz recently summarized these trends. "The confluence of surging population and driving technology is splitting the American labor force into tens of millions of 'have's' and millions of 'have-nots.' In our economy of 69,000,000 jobs, those with wanted skills enjoy opportunity and earning power. But the others face a new and stark problem—exclusion on a permanent basis, both as producers and consumers, from economic life. This division of people threatens to create a human slag heap. We cannot tolerate the development of a separate nation of the poor, the unskilled, the jobless, living within another nation of the well-off, the trained and the employed."

NEW CONSENSUS NEEDED

The stubbornness and novelty of the situation that is conveyed by these statistics is now generally accepted. Ironically, it continues to be assumed that it is possible to devise measures which will reduce unemployment to a minimum and thus preserve the over-all viability of the present productive system. Some authorities have gone so far as to suggest that the pace of technological change should be slowed down "so as to allow the industrial productive system time to adapt."

We believe, on the contrary, that the industrial productive system is no longer viable. We assert that the only way to turn technological change to the benefit of the individual and the service of the general welfare is to accept the process and to utilize it rationally and humanely. The new science of political economy will be built on the encouragement and planned expansion of cybernation. The issues raised by cybernation are particularly amenable to intelligent policy-making: Cybernation itself provides the resources and tools that are needed to ensure minimum hardship during the transition process.

But major changes must be made in our attitudes and institutions in the fore-seeable future. Today Americans are being swept along by three simultaneous revolutions while assuming they have them under control. In the absence of real understanding of any of these phenomena, especially of technology, we may be allowing an efficient and dehumanized community to emerge by default. Gaining control of our future requires the conscious formation of the society we wish to have. Cybernation at last forces us to answer the historic questions: What is man's role when he is not dependent upon his own activities for the material basis of his life? What should be the basis for distributing individual access to national resources? Are there other proper claims on goods and services besides a job?

Because of cybernation, society no longer needs to impose repetitive and meaningless (because unnecessary) toil upon the individual. Society can now set the citizen free to make his own choice of occupation and vocation from a wide range of activities not now fostered by our value system and our accepted modes of "work." But in the absence of such a new consensus about cybernation, the nation cannot begin to take advantage of all that it promises for human betterment.

PROPOSAL FOR ACTION

As a first step to a new consensus it is essential to recognize that the traditional link between jobs and incomes is being broken. The economy of abundance can sustain all citizens in comfort and economic security whether or not they engage in what is commonly reckoned as work. Wealth produced by machines rather than by men is still wealth. We urge, therefore, that society, through its appropriate legal and governmental institutions, undertake an unqualified commitment to provide every individual and every family with an adequate income as a matter of right.

This undertaking we consider to be essential to the emerging economic, social and political order in this country. We regard it as the only policy by which the quarter of the nation now dispossessed and soon-to-be dispossessed by lack of employment can be brought within the abundant society. The unqualified right to an income would take the place of the patchwork of welfare measures—from unemployment insurance to relief—designed to ensure that no citizen or resident of the U.S. actually starves.

We do not pretend to visualize all of the consequences of this change in our values. It is clear, however, that the distribution of abundance in a cybernated society must be based on criteria strikingly different from those of an economic system based on scarcity. In retrospect, the establishment of the right to an income will prove to have been only the first step in the reconstruction of the value system of our society brought on by the triple revolution.

The present system encourages activities which can lead to private profit and neglects those activities which can enhance the wealth and the quality of life of our society. Consequently, national policy has hitherto been aimed far more at the welfare of the productive process than at the welfare of people. The era of cybernation can reverse this emphasis. With public policy and research concentrated on people rather than processes we believe that many creative activities and interests commonly thought of as non-economic will absorb the time and the commitment of many of those no longer needed to produce goods and services.

Society as a whole must encourage new modes of constructive, rewarding and ennobling activity. Principal among these are activities such as teaching and learning that relate people to people rather than people to things. Education has never been primarily conducted for profit in our society; it represents the first and most obvious activity inviting the expansion of the public sector to meet the needs of this period of transition.

We are not able to predict the long-run patterns of human activity and commitment in a nation when fewer and fewer people are involved in production of goods and services, nor are we able to forecast the over-all patterns of income distribution that will replace those of the past full employment system. However, these are not speculative and fanciful matters to be contemplated at leisure for a society that may come into existence in three or four generations. The outlines of the future press sharply into the present. The problems of joblessness, inadequate incomes, and frustrated lives confront us now; the American Negro, in his rebellion, asserts the demands—and the rights—of all the disadvantaged. The Negro's is the most insistent voice today, but behind him stand the millions of impoverished who are beginning to understand that cybernation, properly understood and used, is the road out of want and toward a decent life.

THE TRANSITION[1]

We recognize that the drastic alternations in circumstances and in our way of life ushered in by cybernation and the economy of abundance will not be completed overnight. Left to the ordinary forces of the market such change, however, will involve physical and psychological misery and perhaps political chaos. Such misery is already clearly evident among the unemployed, among relief clients into the third generation and more and more among the young and the old for whom society appears to hold no promise of dignified or even stable lives. We must develop programs for this transition designed to give hope to the dispossessed and those cast out by the economic system, and to provide a basis for the rallying of people to bring about those changes in political and social institutions which are essential to the age of technology.

The program here suggested is not intended to be inclusive but rather to indicate its necessary scope. We propose:

(1) A massive program to build up our educational system, designed especially with the needs of the chronically undereducated in mind. We estimate that tens of thousands of employment opportunities in such areas as teaching and research and development, particularly for younger people, may be thus created. Federal programs looking to the training of an additional 100,000 teachers annually are needed.

(2) Massive public works. The need is to develop and put into effect programs of public works to construct dams, reservoirs, ports, water and air pollution facilities, community recreation facilities. We estimate that for each $1 billion per year spent on public works 150,000 to 200,000 jobs would be created. $2 billion or more a year should be spent in this way, preferably as matching funds aimed at the relief of economically distressed or dislocated areas.

(3) A massive program of low-cost housing, to be built both publicly and privately, and aimed at a rate of 700,000–1,000,000 units a year.

[1] This view of the transitional period is not shared by all the signers. Robert Theobald and James Boggs hold that the two major principles of the transitional period will be (1) that machines rather than men will take up new conventional work openings and (2) that the activity of men will be directed to new forms of "work" and "leisure." Therefore, in their opinion, the specific proposals outlined in this section are more suitable for meeting the problems of the scarcity-economic system than for advancing through the period of transition into the period of abundance.

(4) Development and financing of rapid transit systems, urban and interurban; and other programs to cope with the spreading problems of the great metropolitan centers.

(5) A public power system built on the abundance of coal in distressed areas, designed for low-cost power to heavy industrial and residential sections.

(6) Rehabilitation of obsolete military bases for community or educational use.

(7) A major revision of our tax structure aimed at redistributing income as well as apportioning the costs of the transition period equitably. To this end an expansion of the use of excess profits tax would be important. Subsidies and tax credit plans are required to ease the human suffering involved in the transition of many industries from man power to machine power.

(8) The trade unions can play an important and significant role in this period in a number of ways:

a. Use of collective bargaining to negotiate not only for people at work but also for those thrown out of work by technological change.

b. Bargaining for perquisites such as housing, recreational facilities, and similar programs as they have negotiated health and welfare programs.

c. Obtaining a voice in the investment of the unions' huge pension and welfare funds, and insisting on investment policies which have as their major criteria the social use and function of the enterprise in which the investment is made.

d. Organization of the unemployed so that these voiceless people may once more be given a voice in their own economic destinies, and strengthening of the campaigns to organize white-collar and professional workers.

(9) The use of the licensing power of government to regulate the speed and direction of cybernation to minimize hardship; and the use of minimum wage power as well as taxing powers to provide the incentives for moving as rapidly as possible toward the goals indicated by this paper.

These suggestions are in no way intended to be complete or definitively formulated. They contemplate expenditures of several billions more each year than are now being spent for socially rewarding enterprises, and a larger role for the government in the economy than it has now or has been given except in times of crisis. In our opinion, this is a time of crisis, the crisis of a triple revolution. Public philosophy for the transition must rest on the conviction that our economic, social and political institutions exist for the use of man and that man does not exist to maintain a particular economic system. This philosophy centers on an understanding that governments are instituted among men for the purpose of making possible life, liberty and the pursuit of happiness and that government should be a creative and positive instrument toward these ends.

CHANGE MUST BE MANAGED

The historic discovery of the post-World War II years is that the economic destiny of the nation can be managed. Since the debate over the Employment Act of 1946 it has been increasingly understood that the federal government bears primary responsibility for the economic and social well-being of the country. The essence of management is planning. The democratic requirement is planning by public bodies for the general welfare. Planning by private bodies such as corporations for their own welfare does not automatically result in additions to the general welfare, as the impact of cybernation on jobs has already made clear.

The hardships imposed by sudden changes in technology have been acknowledged by Congress in proposals for dealing with the long and short-run "dislocations," in legislation for depressed and "impacted" areas, retraining of workers replaced by machines, and the like. The measures so far proposed have not been "transitional" in conception. Perhaps for this reason they have had little effect on the situations they were designed to alleviate. But the primary weakness of this legislation is not ineffectiveness but incoherence. In no way can these disconnected measures be seen as a plan for remedying deep ailments but only, so to speak, as the superficial treatment of surface wounds.

Planning agencies should constitute the network through which pass the stated needs of the people at every level of society, gradually building into a national inventory of human requirements, arrived at by democratic debate of elected representatives.

The primary tasks of the appropriate planning institutions should be:

To collect the data necessary to appaise the effects, social and economic, of cybernation at different rates of innovation.

To recommend ways, by public and private initiative, of encouraging and stimulating cybernation.

To work toward optimal allocations of human and natural resources in meeting the requirements of society.

To develop ways to smooth the transition from a society in which the norm is full employment within an economic system based on scarcity, to one in which the norm will be either non-employment, in the traditional sense of productive work, or employment on the great variety of socially valuable but "non-productive" tasks made possible by an economy of abundance; to bring about the conditions in which men and women no longer needed to produce goods and services may find their way to a variety of self-fulfilling and socially useful occupations.

To work out alternatives to defense and related spending that will commend themselves to citizens, entrepreneurs and workers as a more reasonable use of common resources.

To integrate domestic and international planning. The technological revolution has related virtually every major domestic problem to a world problem.

The vast inequities between the industrialized and the underdeveloped countries cannot long be sustained.

The aim throughout will be the conscious and rational direction of economic life by planning institutions under democratic control.

In this changed framework the new planning institutions will operate at every level of government—local, regional and federal—and will be organized to elicit democratic participation in all their proceedings. These bodies will be the means for giving direction and content to the growing demand for improvement in all departments of public life. The planning institutions will show the way to turn the growing protest against ugly cities, polluted air and water, an inadequate educational system, disappearing recreational and material resources, low levels of medical care, and the haphazard economic development into an integrated effort to raise the level of general welfare.

We are encouraged by the record of the planning institutions both of the Common Market and of several European nations and believe that this country can benefit from studying their weaknesses and strengths.

A principal result of planning will be to step up investment in the public sector. Greater investment in this area is advocated because it is overdue, because the needs in this sector comprise a substantial part of the content of the general welfare, and because they can be readily afforded by an abundant society. Given the knowledge that we are now in a period of transition it would be deceptive, in our opinion, to present such activities as likely to produce full employment. The efficiencies of cybernation should be as much sought in the public as in the private sector, and a chief focus of planning would be one means of bringing this about. A central assumption of planning institutions would be the central assumption of this statement, that the nation is moving into a society in which production of goods and services is not the only or perhaps the chief means of distributing income.

THE DEMOCRATIZATION OF CHANGE

The revolution in weaponry gives some dim promise that mankind may finally eliminate institutionalized force as the method of settling international conflict and find for it political and moral equivalents leading to a better world. The Negro revolution signals the ultimate admission of this group to the American community on equal social, political and economic terms. The cybernation revolution proffers an existence qualitatively richer in democratic as well as material values. A social order in which men make the decisions that shape their lives becomes more possible now than ever before; the unshackling of men from the bonds of unfulfilling labor frees them to become citizens, to make themselves and to make their own history.

But these enhanced promises by no means constitute a guarantee. Illuminating and making more possible the "democratic vistas" is one thing; reaching them is quite another, for a vision of democratic life is made real not by technological change but by men consciously moving toward that ideal and creating institutions that will realize and nourish the vision in living form.

Democracy, as we use the term, means a community of men and women who are able to understand, express and determine their lives as dignified human beings. Democracy can only be rooted in a political and economic order in which wealth is distributed by and for people, and used for the widest social benefit. With the emergence of the era of abundance we have the economic base for a true democracy of participation, in which men no longer need to feel themselves prisoners of social forces and decisions beyond their control or comprehension.

DISCUSSION TOPICS

1. Cybernation is said to have broken the link between jobs and income. Discuss, in light of this revolutionary development, the kind of future youth may face.

2. The Committee on the Triple Revolution has outlined several ways in which to turn the consequences of the new technology to advantage. Design the kind of society that would result if the Committee's recommendations were put into practice.

3. What is Mead's "lost dimension" in Western theology? Discuss the immediate and long-range implications, both secular and theological, of man's current spiritual state.

4. What is the potential impact of automation on adolescent development? Suggest ways in which the use of the computer might encourage individuality and diversity, as well as ways in which it might destroy them.

5. Is it possible that the public issues of the next decade can be resolved in such a way as to make the growing-up process smoother and less discontinuous?

6. Has the emergence of what McLuhan calls the "electric age" made individuality irrelevant? Why or why not?

The Contributors

Yitzhak Bakal is a psychiatric social worker. He is Director of Counseling for the Upward Bound project at the University of Massachusetts.

Bruno Bettelheim, Vienna-born psychologist who worked under Freud, is presently Professor of Educational Psychology at the University of Chicago and Principal of the Orthogenic School for disturbed children operated by the University. He has published a number of books in child psychology, among them *Love Is Not Enough, The Treatment of Emotionally Disturbed Children, Truants From Life, The Informed Heart,* and *The Empty Fortress.*

H. Kirk Dansereau is Professor of Sociology at Pennsylvania State University. An industrial sociologist, he is concerned with the social impact of industrial developments.

Kingsley Davis, currently a sociologist at the University of California at Berkeley, was one of the earliest social scientists to address himself to the conflict between adolescent development and societal demands.

S. N. Eisenstadt is Professor of Sociology at Hebrew University in Jerusalem. He is interested in problems of youth and youth culture and has contributed a major book on this subject, *From Generation to Generation.*

Erik H. Erikson, who is Professor of Human Development and lecturer on psychiatry at Harvard University, has studied the individual's personal-social development at several stages from childhood to middle age. His publications include *Childhood and Society, Young Man Luther, Insight and Responsibility,* and *Identity and the Life Cycle.*

Dana L. Farnsworth, M.D., is Professor of Hygiene and Director of University Health Services at Harvard University. A former Dean of Students at M.I.T. and a Diplomate of the American Board of Psychiatry and Neurology, Dr. Farnsworth has had a lifelong concern for the problems of college students. His major publications in this field include *Mental Health in College and University* and *Psychiatry, Education, and the Young.*

W. H. Ferry, major spokesman for The Ad Hoc Committee on The Triple Revolution, is Vice-President of The Center for the Study of Democratic Institutions at Santa Barbara, California.

Howard E. Freeman is Professor of Social Research and Director of the Research Center at the Florence Heller Graduate School for Advanced Studies in Social Welfare, at Brandeis University.

Anna Freud, daughter of the founder of psychoanalysis, Sigmund Freud, is Director of the Hampstead Child-Therapy Clinic in England. Her book, *The Ego and the Mechanisms* *of Defense,* is a classic study of adolescence from the psychoanalytic vnewpoint.

Edgar Z. Friedenberg, who is Professor of Education at the University of California at Davis, has been called one of education's "romantic critics." Interested primarily in the secondary schools and their students, he has written *The Vanishing Adolescent* and *The Dignity of Youth and Other Atavisms.*

Rochelle Gatlin was graduated summa cum laude from San Francisco State College in the spring of 1965. Mrs. Gatlin is now a graduate student in American Civilization at the University of Pennsylvania.

Paul Goodman is a social critic and author who has taught at the University of Chicago, New York University, and Black Mountain College. His 1956 social critique, *Growing Up Absurd,* is considered to have provided an ideological rationale for student unrest such as that which has broken out on the Berkeley campus of the University of California in recent years.

Harold E. Jones, a psychologist currently at the University of California, is best known for his longitudinal studies of physical development and social behavior. Much of his work relating to adolescence is contained in his *Development in Adolescence: Approaches to the Study of the Individual.*

Ivor Kraft, a distinguished educator, is with the Division of Research of the Children's Bureau, in the Welfare Administration of the U.S. Department of Health, Education, and Welfare.

William C. Kvaraceus is currently Director of Youth Studies at The Lincoln Filene Center for Citizenship and Public Affairs in Boston, and Professor of Education at Tufts University. His major interest is in the problems of the inadapted pupil in the large city school. His books in this area include *Juvenile Delinquency and the School* and *The Community and the Delinquent.*

Sandor Lorand, M.D., is Clinical Professor of Psychiatry in the Psychoanalytic Division of Education at the State University of New York at Brooklyn. A practicing psychoanalyst, he is interested in the treatment of emotionally disturbed adolescents.

William Madaus is a guidance counselor at a Worcester, Massachusetts, junior high school. During the Summer of 1966 he served as a group counselor in the University of Massachusetts' Upward Bound project.

Marshall McLuhan has been called the "oracle of the electronic age," for his writings on the effects of technology on modern man in *The Gutenberg Galaxy: The Making of Typographic Man, Understanding Media: The Extensions of Man,* and *The Medium is the Massage.* Formerly Director of the Center for Culture and Technology at the University of Toronto, he is currently Albert Schweitzer Professor of the Humanities at Fordham University.

Sidney E. Mead is Professor of Religion at the State University of Iowa. He is ordained in the Unitarian Church. His publications concerning the future of religion include *The Church in the Modern West* (with A. H. Nichols) and *The Lively Experiment.*

Walter B. Miller is a Cultural Anthropologist who is currently Director of Research for the Delinquency Control Project at Boston University. Many of his publications explore the social status determinants of behavior.

Frank Musgrove is a British sociologist and cultural anthropologist currently teaching at Leeds University. He brings a cross-cultural outlook to the question of the effects of historical and sociological processes upon the youth of a culture.

Vera C. Perrella and **Forrest A. Bogan** are members of the Division of Population and Labor Force Studies of the Bureau of Labor Statistics in Washington.

Lee Rainwater is Professor of Sociology and Anthropology at Washington University in St. Louis and Research Associate in the University's Social Science Institute. Among his major works are *And the Poor Get Children* and *Family Design*.

Thomas E. Swanstrom is a member of the Division of Population and Labor Force Studies of the Bureau of Labor Statistics in Washington.

Kermit T. Wiltse is Associate Professor in the School of Social Welfare at the University of California at Berkeley. His interests include the administration of public welfare services.

Howard Zinn, Professor of History and Social Science at Spelman College, Atlanta, Georgia, is one of the few American social scientists to involve himself actively and intellectually in the Civil Rights Movement.

The Editors

Alvin E. Winder, author and coauthor of pieces in this collection, is Associate Professor of Education and Guidance at the University of Massachusetts. A clinical psychologist, he is Chief Consultant for the University's Upward Bound project with disadvantaged adolescents.

David L. Angus, Assistant Professor of Education at the University of Michigan, is an educational sociologist. Growing out of his interest in the school's effect on human development, his current work deals with the education of inner city youth.

Glossary

acting out	Manifesting the purposive behavior appropriate to a former situation in a new situation that symbolically represents it
ambiance	The surrounding or pervading atmosphere; the environment
anomaly	Deviation from the norm
anomie	That condition in an individual in which normative standards of conduct and belief are weak or lacking, usually characterized by disorientation, anxiety, and isolation
anorexia nervosa	Also called apepsia hysteria—the chief symptoms of which are inability to eat, weight loss, and amenorrhea, usually accompanied by depression; occurs typically in females between the ages of twelve and twenty-one
apocalyptic	Pertaining to a prophetic revelation
archetype	An original pattern, of which all things of the same type are copies; a highly typical example
autonomy	Guidance or control by oneself of one's own actions; used in discussions of the ethical bearings of behavior, in opposition to the rigid stimulus-response view, or as opposed to determination
castration	Loss of the male genital organs. *Castration anxiety* is the mental state associated with the fear of castration. *Castration complex* is a reaction to intimidation stemming from the fear of castration or the restraint of early infantile sexual activity.
cataclysmic	Marked by overwhelming upheaval and demolition
cathexis	Investment of libidinal energy in a person, object, or idea
cognitive	Pertaining to the processes involved in learning by means of the intellect
compensatory education	An educational program, usually involving extensive guidance, designed to make up for the poor academic environment of the culturally deprived
convergent thinking	According to Getzels and Jackson, a process representing intellectual acquisitiveness and conformity; contrasted with divergent thinking, a process of intellectual inventiveness and innovation

correlation coefficient A number indicating the strength of the tendency of two or more variables to vary concomitantly. Perfect correspondence between the two is expressed by +1.00, perfect inverse correspondence by −1.00, and complete lack of correspondence by 0.00.

cybernetics The scientific study of messages and regulatory or control mechanisms, especially those involving feedback, in machines, persons, social groups, or institutions

defense mechanism An unconscious device or adjustment by which ideas become divested of their affects or emotional coefficients

delayed adolescence Experiencing, at an age beyond that usually marking the onset of adolescence, the feelings and fantasies appropriate to adolescence

dialectics Any systematic reasoning, exposition, or argument that juxtaposes opposed or contradictory ideas, usually seeking to resolve their conflict

drive Any intraorganic activity or condition that supplies stimulation for a particular type of behavior; used as a general term to include instinctive and other impulses or motive forces prompting an animal to direct activity towards an end

dynamic psychology A systematic interpretation of mental phenomena regarded as a succession of causes and effects, with emphasis upon internal drives and motives

ego In Sigmund Freud's theory, one of three divisions of the personality; that conscious part of the personality which mediates both the inner instinctive impulses of the id and the externally learned conscience directives of the superego (cf. *id, superego*)

ego ideal . A part of the ego related to but distinguished from the superego, representing the sum of positive identifications with loving, reassuring parents or parent substitutes including society and God, giving rise to desired standards of goodness and excellence; distinguished from the dictates of the superego, which incorporates the punitive, stern, forbidding aspect of the parent

endemic Native to or characteristic of a particular people or region

epiphyses Those parts of the bone that ossify separately; usually the ends

ethnic Pertaining to groups of people believed to be biologically related, or to any important continuing group or division of mankind

etiology The investigation of the causes or significant antecedents of a given phenomenon; in a broader sense, the study of causal relations

gemeinschaften In the language of sociology, small, organic, closely-knit communities, in contrast to *gesellschaften,* the large, impersonal atomistic communities with which they are frequently replaced

id In Sigmund Freud's view of the personality, that unconscious part which provides the organism's basic undifferentiated energy or drives, from which libido is derived (cf. *ego, super-ego, libido, drive*)

identification   An unconscious mental process expressing itself in the form of an emotional tie with another person, a group, or situation, in which the subject behaves and feels as if he were the person with whom he feels this tie

in loco parentis   Standing in or taking the place of one's parents

infancy   An arbitrary division of the human life-span made, like adolescence, on the basis of chronological age; usually defined as the period from birth to one year

inner city   The central section of a city, usually the oldest and first part to be settled, commonly by a new wave of immigrants who later moved on; presently a common site of Negro ghettos

libido   Emotional or psychic energy derived from primitive biological urges, usually directed toward the satisfaction of a basic need in the organism

marginal   Characterized by the incomplete incorporation of habits and values from two divergent cultures

milieu   The immediate environment, physical, social, or both, sometimes including also the internal state of the organism

model   That which is to be copied, especially an ideal or perfect form

narcissism   A synonym for self-love; the persistence of an early stage of psychosexual development, in which the sexual or love object remains the self

norm   A pattern, standard or representative value for a group type; the mean, median or model score of the subjects employed in standardizing a given test or measure

object   That portion of the environment related to the individual in a psychological experience; whatever is present in the mind during a cognitive experience

oedipal   Deriving from the Oedipus complex, the desire, usually unconscious, of a son to possess his mother and be hostile to or destroy his father

orthopsychiatry   That branch of preventive psychiatry which applies preventive treatment in cases of incipient mental and behavioral disorders in the young

paradigm   A model, pattern, or example exhibiting all the variable forms of something: e.g., a pattern showing all the grammatical forms of a word

parameter   Any constant that defines the curve of the equation for some psychological function (e.g., learning, growth). A parameter may be rational (based on a particular theory) or empirical (a generalization of actual data), but even when empirical the parameter is a property of a hypothetical infinite population or set of causes and hence is always an estimate.

pathology   Something abnormal; the anatomic and physiologic deviations from the normal that constitute disease or characterize a particular disease; deviation from propriety or from an assumed normal state

peer group The group with which a child or adolescent associates on terms of approximate equality, usually strongly heterogeneous since the equality is only approximate

personality The distinguishing qualities of an individual taken as a unit, especially those that distinguish him in social relations

positive transference The development of an emotional attitude on the part of a patient towards an analyst, in the form of an affectionate reaction

pregenital phase The organization of the sexual life of the child during the early infantile period, in which the genital zone has not yet assumed a dominating role

primary identification Accepting as one's own the purposes and values of another person or group; merging or submerging one's own purposes and values with others'. According to psychoanalysis, the primary identification is with parents and is the basis of the superego.

projective test A type of mental test aiming at determining personality traits through the completion of sentences, interpretation of inkblots and the like, or interpretation of pictures and the making of designs

psychedelic Of or denoting a mental state of great calm and intensely pleasurable perception derived through the senses

psychiatric Of or relating to that branch of medicine dealing with mental, emotional and behavioral disorders

psychoanalysis A method of looking into personality developed by Freud, based on the theory that abnormal mental reactions are caused by unawareness of conflicts present in the unconscious mind

radical Extreme; disposed to make basic changes in existing views, habits, conditions, or institutions

reaction formation The establishment of a trait or a regular pattern of behavior that is directly opposed to a strong unconscious trend; also the pattern itself, as in the development of aggressive behavior as a means of repressing or denying fear, or great sympathy as a means of repressing sadistic impulses

reference group Any group with which a person identifies and/or compares himself to such an extent that he tends to adopt its standards, attitudes, and behaviors as his own. Such reference groups may or may not correspond to actual membership groups.

repression Reversion to an earlier mental or behavioral level

ressentiment Resentment

rites de passage Ritual actions accompanying the passage of an individual from one social status to another in the course of his life; e.g., in nonliterate cultures, a young man fasting in the desert prior to tribal ceremonies marking his entry into the adult group

sadomasochistic	Loosely, love of being cruel; the compulsive tendency to act aggressively and destructively towards another person
situational	Dealing with the sum total of internal and external stimuli that act upon an organism within a given time interval
superego	In Sigmund Freud's theory, that part of the personality which aids in character formation by internalizing the rules of society as perceived through the actions and admonitions of parents and others. A major portion of the mind, the superego is only partly conscious (cf. *ego, id*).
symbiotic	Characterized as living or existing together, although dissimilar, in a mutually beneficial relationship
syndrome	Denoting the aggregate symptoms of a disease, i.e., a symptom complex
synergistic	Relating to cooperative action between discrete agencies such that the total effect is greater than the sum of the two effects taken independently
therapeutic	Of or relating to the treatment of disease or disorders by remedial agents or methods (*therapy*)
totalistic	Totalitarian
transference	The redirection of feelings and desires, especially those unconsciously retained from childhood, towards a new object, as towards a psychoanalyst conducting therapy
wanderschaft	As used in this text, a search through travel, as in youth being "on the road"

Index

Adolescence
  as second infancy, 5–6
  as upset, 14–17
  Negro school experience, 217, 226, 228, 230–232, 236–237
  normality in, 22–23
  physical changes during, 5–12
  search for meaning during, 102–110, 114–117, 159–161
  therapeutic treatment in, 24–33
  see also Parent-adolescent conflict, Therapy with adolescents, Youth
Adulthood, entry into
  in African tribes, 140–142, 144–147, 150–152
  in American Indians, 140, 144–145, 152
  in Polynesian tribes, 147–149
  see also Parent-adolescent conflict
African tribal structure, 140–142, 144–147, 150–155
Aggression
  among Negro adolescents, 226, 228, 232
  handled by peers in Upward Bound project, 211
  of "high creatives" in high school, 92–95
Aid to Dependent Children
  see Social deprivation
Alienation, 206–207, 211–212, 214
  of college students, 115–117
Athletics, 125–126
Authority
  culturally deprived teen-agers' attitudes towards, 206–207, 209–211, 213
  parental, 73–76
Automation
  see Cybernation

Bakal, Yitzhak, 204–215
Berkeley demonstrations, 158–161
Bettelheim, Bruno, 114–117
Bogan, Forrest A., 243–254

Cicourel, Aaron, 111–113

Civil rights
  for Negroes, 168, 177–181
  SNCC, 264–273
College
  high school preparation for, 111–113
  lack of meaning in, 159, 161
Communication
  adolescent speechlessness, 105–106
  lack of, in colleges, 108–109
  lack of original, 102–110
  presumed consensus in America, 109
Counseling
  see High-school counseling
Creativity, 92–101
Cybernation
  affect on the Negro, 309–310
  and democracy, 320–321
  and education, 307
  definition of, 301, 303, 308–309
  effects of, 302–308
  electric, 299–308
  problems of, 310–313
  solutions to, 315–318

Dansereau, H. Kirk, 118–126
Dating, 172–173
Davis, Kingsley, 69–79
Delinquency, 217–219, 227–229, 238
  hostile, 232–234
  school, 219
  sources of, 225
  see also Lower class
Deprivation
  cultural, 217–218
  social, 240–242
Dropouts, 91–92, 117, 122
  and apathy, 235
  and Negro teen-agers, 216, 218–219, 225, 227, 232–233
  "Out-of-school Youth," 243–254, 255–263
  reasons for, 245
  unemployment rate of, 250–251
  see also Education, Out-of-school youth

Dylan, Bob, 86–89

Education
    compensatory, 204, 214–215
    fostering conformity, 80–101, 151
    future of, 114–117
    pre-school, 241
    see also School
Eisenstadt, S. N., 53–64
Employment
    and teen-agers, 118–126
    low status of youth in, 121–122
    mobility in, 123
    out-of-school youth, 253–254, 255–263
    reasons for, 119–120
    see also Jobs, Negroes, Unemployment,
        Work
Erikson, Erik H., 33–52, 159

Family, 70, 245–246
Farnsworth, Dana L., 80–85
Ferry, W. H., 308–321
Freeman, Howard E., 286–292
Freud, Anna, 13–24, 221
Freud, Sigmund, 40, 44–47, 159
Friedenberg, Edgar Z., xiii–xv, 90–101, 111–113

Gangs
    see Lower class
Gatlin, Rochelle, 156–158
Goodman, Paul, 102–110, 127–137

High-school counseling
    and search for talent, 112–113
    for future out-of-school youth, 256–257
    power of counselors, 111–113
    with Negro students, 218, 221, 235, 240
Hostility
    see Aggression

Idealism
    among SNCC workers, 264–269, 271–273
    youthful, vs. adult realism, 71–73
Immigrants, acculturation of, 152
Income
    see Money
Indian, American
    acculturation of, 140, 145–146, 152
    status of youth, 145–146

Jobs
    attitudes of youth towards, 136–137
    discrimination against teen-agers in, 120–
        122
    frustrations of job selection, 127–137
    lack of worthwhile, 134–135
    placement of youth in, 133
    plight of uneducated in, 135–136
    types of, for teen-agers, 121
    see also Employment, Negroes,
        Unemployment, Work

Jones, Harold E., 4–12

Kitsuse, John I., 111–113
Kraft, Ivor, 240–242
Kvaraceus, William C., 216–240

Lorand, Sandor, 24–33
Lower class
    delinquency in, 189–190
    focal points of, 190–197
    groups and grouping, 198–203
    relation to academic achievement, 201–210

Mad Magazine, 159–160
Madaus, William, 204–215
Marriage
    among Polynesians, 148
    among slum Negroes, 167, 172–174
    as a sign of adult status, 142–143, 145,
        150–151
    see also Negroes
McLuhan, Marshall, xv, 299–308
Mead, Sidney E., 292–298
Mental health
    and the "great society" program, 287–290
    and social forces, 286–287
    future, 290–292
Miller, Walter, 189–204
Money
    as individual property among slum Negroes,
        167
    as used by teen-agers, 46
    as used in Polynesian tribes, 148
    income of out-of-school youth, 253–254
    see also Employment, Jobs, Negroes,
        Unemployment
Musgrove, Frank, 138–156

Negroes
    autonomy of, in ghetto, 167
    children, 170–176, 217, 224–225, 228, 230–231
    compared to whites, 169, 174–177
    dating, 172–173
    in SNCC, 264–273
    marriage, 167, 172–174
    matrifocal character, 199
    mothers, boyfriends of, 172
    out-of-school youth, 244, 246–248, 250,
        253–254
    relations with whites, 167–168, 193–194, 204,
        224, 227, 231, 264–273
    solutions of ghetto problems, 220–223
    strategies for living, 176–177, 220–223
    see also Kvaraceus, William C.

Out-of-school youth, 243–263
    activity since leaving school, 247–250, 257–
        258, 262–263
    educational attainment of, 243–245, 255–256,
        258

employment, 252–254
family characteristics, 245–246
mobility, 258–259
unemployment, 252–254, 260–261, 263
see also Dropouts

Parent-adolescent conflict, 106–107, 108
and socialization, 70–73
causes of, 69–79
physiological differences, 71
psychosocial differences, 71–73
recognized in Upward Bound Project, 13–14
sociological differences, 73–78
Peer groups
among Negro adolescents, 175–176
among Upward Bound students, 209–211, 213, 214
Perrella, Vera C., 243–254
Physical changes in adolescence
see Adolescence
Polynesian tribal structure, 147–149
Popularity, 125–126
Poverty
and the federal government, 274–281
future end of, 117
in Mississippi, 274–281
see also Social deprivation
Pregnancy among adolescents, 172
Pre-school education
see Education, Social deprivation

Rainwater, Lee, 166–181
Religion
lack of influence of, 104
modern dilemma of, 98, 292

School
as a solution for ghetto problems, 179–181
"brainwashing" in, 102–104
elementary, and Negro youth, 230, 240
employment while in, 258
fostering conformity, 151–166
future of, 114–117
goals of, 90–92
in Africa, 142
in ghetto, 177
social environment in, 90–101
see also High-school counseling, Education, Negroes
Sex
among adolescents, 108
among slum Negroes, 172–174
and college student morality, 80–85
as cause of family tension, 77–78
behavior in Upward Bound project, 212
roles, 20–24
Social adjustment, 124–126
in Upward Bound project, 204–215
of early-maturing boys, 11
of early-maturing girls, 8–10

of late-maturing boys, 11
of late-maturing girls, 10–11
Social change
and parent-adolescent conflict, 70–79
and youth, 138–156
brought about by returning African tribesmen, 155–156
brought about by SNCC, 264–273
Social deprivation
and pseudo-depression syndrome, 184–187
in Aid to Dependent Children families, 182–184
in Upward Bound project, 204–215
increase of public aid for, 187–188
treatment of, 187
see also Education
Socialization, deceleration of, 70–71
Student Nonviolent Coordinating Committee (SNCC), 264–273
Swanstrom, Thomas E., 255–263

Therapy with adolescents, 24–33
Tolkien, J. R. R., 86–89

Unemployment, 243–254, 260, 261, 263
see also Employment, Jobs, Negroes, Work
Upward Bound, at University of Massachusetts, 204–215

Wiltse, Kermit T., 181–188
Winder, Alvin E., 86–89, 158–161, 204–215
Work
and social change among African and Polynesian tribesmen, 144, 147–149, 152–153, 155
and teen-agers, 118–126
attitudes towards, 123, 126
values, 123–124
see also Jobs, Employment, Negroes, Unemployment

Youth
and identity, 35–40, 42–46, 49–52, 86–89
and liberalism, 157–158
and search for values, 34–35, 41–42, 50, 51
and social reform, 157
cultural definition of, 53–56, 57
culture, 57–58
in modern society, 58–64, 72–74, 106–108
in primitive societies, 54, 55, 56, 58
integration with adults, 140, 147–149
physical development of, 40–42
segregation of, 140, 144–147, 149–151
social organization of, 55–57
status and social change, 138–156
see also Adolescence, Parent-adolescent conflict, Out-of-school youth, Negroes

Zinn, Howard, 264–273